T0367235

LOEB CLASSICAL LIBRARY

FOUNDED BY JAMES LOEB 1911

EDITED BY

JEFFREY HENDERSON

SENECA

VI

LCL 77

SENECA

EPISTLES

93–124

WITH AN ENGLISH TRANSLATION BY

RICHARD M. GUMMERE

HARVARD UNIVERSITY PRESS

CAMBRIDGE, MASSACHUSETTS

LONDON, ENGLAND

First published 1925

LOEB CLASSICAL LIBRARY® is a registered trademark
of the President and Fellows of Harvard College

ISBN 978-0-674-99086-9

*Printed on acid-free paper and bound by
The Maple-Vail Book Manufacturing Group*

CONTENTS

CONTENTS

CONTENTS

THE EPISTLES OF SENECA

L. ANNAEI SENECAE AD LUCILIUM EPISTULAE

XCIII.

Seneca Lvcilio svo salvtem

1   In epistula, qua de morte Metronactis philosophi
querebaris tamquam et potuisset diutius vivere et
debuisset, aequitatem tuam desideravi, quae tibi in
omni persona, in omni negotio superest, in una re
deest, in qua omnibus.   Multos inveni aequos adversus homines, adversus deos neminem.   Obiurgamus
cotidie fatum: " quare ille in medio cursu raptus
est?   Quare ille non rapitur?   Quare senectutem et
sĭbi et aliis gravem extendit ? "

2   Utrum, obsecro te, aequius iudicas te naturae an
tibi parere naturam?   Quid autem interest, quam
cito exeas, unde utique exeundum est ?   Non ut diu
vivamus curandum est, sed ut satis ; nam ut diu
vivas, fato opus est, ut satis, animo.   Longa est vita,

ᵃ A philosopher of Naples, mentioned as giving lectures
there : cf. Ep. lxxvi. 4.
  ᵇ i.e., " adequately," equivalent to ὡς δεῖ.

2

THE EPISTLES OF SENECA

XCIII. ON THE QUALITY, AS CONTRASTED WITH THE LENGTH, OF LIFE

WHILE reading the letter in which you were lamenting the death of the philosopher Metronax *a* as if he might have, and indeed ought to have, lived longer, I missed the spirit of fairness which abounds in all your discussions concerning men and things, but is lacking when you approach one single subject, —as is indeed the case with us all. In other words, I have noticed many who deal fairly with their fellow-men, but none who deals fairly with the gods. We rail every day at Fate, saying : " Why has A. been carried off in the very middle of his career ? Why is not B. carried off instead ? Why should he prolong his old age, which is a burden to himself as well as to others ? "

But tell me, pray, do you consider it fairer that you should obey Nature, or that Nature should obey you ? And what difference does it make how soon you depart from a place which you must depart from sooner or later ? We should strive, not to live long, but to live rightly *b* ; for to achieve long life you have need of Fate only, but for right living you

3

si plena est; impletur autem, cum animus sibi bonum
3 suum reddidit et ad se potestatem sui transtulit. Quid
illum octoginta anni iuvant per inertiam exacti? Non
vixit iste, sed in vita moratus est, nec sero mortuus
est, sed diu. Octoginta annis vixit. Interest, mortem
4 eius ex quo die numeres. At ille obiit viridis. Sed
officia boni civis, boni amici, boni filii executus est;
in nulla parte cessavit. Licet aetas eius inperfecta
sit, vita perfecta est. Octoginta annis vixit. Immo
octoginta annis fuit, nisi forte sic vixisse eum dicis,
quomodo dicuntur arbores vivere.

Obsecro te, Lucili, hoc agamus, ut quemadmodum
pretiosa rerum sic vita nostra non multum pateat,
sed multum pendeat. Actu illam metiamur, non
tempore. Vis scire, quid inter hunc intersit vegetum
contemptoremque fortunae functum omnibus vitae
humanae stipendiis atque in summum bonum eius
evectum, et illum, cui multi anni transmissi sunt?
Alter post mortem quoque est, alter ante mortem
periit.
5 Laudemus itaque et in numero felicium reponamus
eum, cui quantulumcumque temporis contigit, bene
conlocatum est. Vidit enim veram lucem. Non fuit

---

[a] For a complete definition of the Supreme Good *cf.*
Ep. lxxi. 4 ff.
[b] *i.e.*, the Metronax mentioned above.
[c] For the same phrase see *Ep.* lxvi. 30 and footnote.
[d] *Cf. Ep.* lx. 4 *mortem suam antecesserunt.*

4

need the soul. A life is really long if it is a full life ; but fulness is not attained until the soul has rendered to itself its proper Good,[a] that is, until it has assumed control over itself. What benefit does this older man derive from the eighty years he has spent in idleness ? A person like him has not lived ; he has merely tarried awhile in life. Nor has he died late in life ; he has simply been a long time dying. He has lived eighty years, has he ? That depends upon the date from which you reckon his death ! Your other friend,[b] however, departed in the bloom of his manhood. But he had fulfilled all the duties of a good citizen, a good friend, a good son ; in no respect had he fallen short. His age may have been incomplete, but his life was complete. The other man has lived eighty years, has he ? Nay, he has existed eighty years, unless perchance you mean by " he has lived " what we mean when we say that a tree " lives."

Pray, let us see to it, my dear Lucilius, that our lives, like jewels of great price, be noteworthy not because of their width but because of their weight.[c] Let us measure them by their performance, not by their duration. Would you know wherein lies the difference between this hardy man who, despising Fortune, has served through every campaign of life and has attained to life's Supreme Good, and that other person over whose head many years have passed ? The former exists even after his death ; the latter has died even before he was dead.[d]

We should therefore praise, and number in the company of the blest, that man who has invested well the portion of time, however little, that has been allotted to him ; for such a one has seen the true light. He has not been one of the common herd.

5

unus e multis. Et vixit et viguit. Aliquando sereno usus est, aliquando, ut solet, validi sideris fulgor per nubila emicuit. Quid quaeris quamdiu vixerit? Vivit; ad posteros usque transiluit et se in memoriam dedit.

6 Nec ideo mihi plures annos accedere recusaverim, nihil tamen mihi ad beatam vitam defuisse dicam, si spatium eius inciditur. Non enim ad eum diem me aptavi, quem ultimum mihi spes avida promiserat, sed nullum non tamquam ultimum aspexi. Quid me interrogas, quando natus sim, an inter iuniores adhuc

7 censear? Habeo meum. Quemadmodum in minore corporis habitu potest homo esse perfectus, sic et in minore temporis modo potest vita esse perfecta. Aetas inter externa est. Quamdiu sim, alienum est; quamdiu ero,[1] ut sim, meum est. Hoc a me exige, ne velut per tenebras aevum ignobile emetiar, ut agam vitam, non ut praetervehar.

8 Quaeris quod sit amplissimum vitae spatium? Usque ad sapientiam vivere. Qui ad illam pervenit, attigit non longissimum finem, sed maximum. Ille vero glorietur audacter et dis agat gratias interque eos sibi, et rerum naturae inputet, quod fuit. Merito enim inputabit; meliorem illi vitam reddidit quam

---

[1] *ero* Buecheler; *vero* BA.

---

 i.e., the Sun.
 As in the original *comitia centuriata*, men between the ages of seventeen and forty-six.
 As riches, health, etc.

He has not only lived, but flourished. Sometimes he enjoyed fair skies ; sometimes, as often happens, it was only through the clouds that there flashed to him the radiance of the mighty star.[a] Why do you ask : " How long did he live ? " He still lives ! At one bound he has passed over into posterity and has consigned himself to the guardianship of memory.

And yet I would not on that account decline for myself a few additional years ; although, if my life's space be shortened, I shall not say that I have lacked aught that is essential to a happy life. For I have not planned to live up to the very last day that my greedy hopes had promised me ; nay, I have looked upon every day as if it were my last. Why ask the date of my birth, or whether I am still enrolled on the register of the younger men ? [b] What I have is my own. Just as one of small stature can be a perfect man, so a life of small compass can be a perfect life. Age ranks among the external things.[c] How long I am to exist is not mine to decide, but how long I shall go on existing in my present way is in my own control. This is the only thing you have the right to require of me,—that I shall cease to measure out an inglorious age as it were in darkness, and devote myself to living instead of being carried along past life.

And what, you ask, is the fullest span of life ? It is living until you possess wisdom. He who has attained wisdom has reached, not the furthermost, but the most important, goal. Such a one may indeed exult boldly and give thanks to the gods— aye, and to himself also—and he may count himself Nature's creditor for having lived. He will indeed have the right to do so, for he has paid her back a better life than he has received. He has set up the

accepit. Exemplar boni viri posuit, qualis quantusque esset ostendit. Si quid adiecisset, fuisset simile praeterito.

9 Et tamen quo usque vivimus? Omnium rerum cognitione fruiti sumus. Scimus a quibus principiis[1] natura se adtollat, quemadmodum ordinet mundum, per quas annum vices revocet, quemadmodum omnia, quae usquam erant, cluserit et se ipsam finem sui fecerit. Scimus sidera impetu suo vadere, praeter terram nihil stare, cetera continua velocitate decurrere. Scimus quemadmodum solem luna praetereat, quare tardior velociorem post se relinquat, quomodo lumen accipiat aut perdat, quae causa inducat noctem, quae reducat diem. Illuc eundum est, ubi ista

10 propius aspicias. "Nec hac spe," inquit sapiens ille, "fortius exeo, quod patere mihi ad deos meos iter iudico. Merui quidem admitti et iam inter illos fui animumque illo meum misi et ad me illi suum miserant. Sed tolli me de medio puta et post mortem nihil ex homine restare; aeque magnum animum habeo, etiam si nusquam transiturus excedo."

11 "Non tam multis vixit annis quam potuit." Et paucorum versuum liber est et quidem laudandus atque utilis; annales Tanusii[2] scis quam ponderosi

---

[1] *principiis* Lipsius; *principalis* BA.
[2] *an(n)ale est anusii* BA; corr. edd.

---

[a] *i.e.*, Nature herself is eternal.
[b] See, however, Seneca, *N.Q.* vii. 2. 3 *sciamus utrum mundus terra stante circumeat an mundo stante terra vertatur.* For such doubts and discoveries *cf.* Arnold, *Roman Stoicism*, pp. 178 f.
[c] See Index of Proper Names.

pattern of a good man, showing the quality and the greatness of a good man. Had another year been added, it would merely have been like the past.

And yet how long are we to keep living? We have had the joy of learning the truth about the universe. We know from what beginnings Nature arises; how she orders the course of the heavens; by what successive changes she summons back the year; how she has brought to an end all things that ever have been, and has established herself as the only end of her own being.[a] We know that the stars move by their own motion, and that nothing except the earth stands still, while all the other bodies run on with uninterrupted swiftness.[b] We know how the moon outstrips the sun; why it is that the slower leaves the swifter behind; in what manner she receives her light, or loses it again; what brings on the night, and what brings back the day. To that place you must go where you are to have a closer view of all these things. "And yet," says the wise man, "I do not depart more valiantly because of this hope—because I judge the path lies clear before me to my own gods. I have indeed earned admission to their presence, and in fact have already been in their company; I have sent my soul to them as they had previously sent theirs to me. But suppose that I am utterly annihilated, and that after death nothing mortal remains; I have no less courage, even if, when I depart, my course leads—nowhere."

"But," you say, "he has not lived as many years as he might have lived." There are books which contain very few lines, admirable and useful in spite of their size; and there are also the *Annals of Tanusius*,[c]—you know how bulky the book is, and

sint et quid vocentur. Hoc est vita quorumdam
12 longa, et quod Tanusii sequitur annales. Numquid
feliciorem iudicas eum, qui summo die muneris,
quam eum, qui medio occiditur ? Numquid aliquem
tam stulte cupidum esse vitae putas, ut iugulari in
spoliario quam in harena malit ? Non maiore spatio
alter alterum praecedimus. Mors per omnes it ; qui
occidit, consequitur occisum. Minimum est, de quo
sollicitissime agitur. Quid autem ad rem pertinet,
quam diu vites, quod evitare non possis ? VALE.

XCIV.

SENECA LVCILIO SVO SALVTEM

1   Eam partem philosophiae, quae dat propria cuique
personae praecepta nec in universum conponit
hominem, sed marito suadet quomodo se gerat
adversus uxorem, patri quomodo educet liberos,
domino quomodo servos regat, quidam solam rece-
perunt, ceteras quasi extra utilitatem nostram va-
gantes reliquerunt, tamquam quis posset de parte
suadere nisi qui summam prius totius vitae complexus
est.
2   Sed Ariston Stoicus contrario hanc partem levem
existimat et quae non descendat in pectus usque

---

^a For technical terms in *Epp.* xciv. and xcv. see
Appendix A.
^b See Cicero, *De off.* i. 3. 7 ff. for a full discussion of
principles and duties. As one would expect, the Romans
were more interested in practical precepts than were the
Greeks.
^c Frag. 358 von Arnim.

what men say of it. This is the case with the long life of certain persons,—a state which resembles the *Annals of Tanusius*! Do you regard as more fortunate the fighter who is slain on the last day of the games than one who goes to his death in the middle of the festivities? Do you believe that anyone is so foolishly covetous of life that he would rather have his throat cut in the dressing-room than in the amphitheatre? It is by no longer an interval than this that we precede one another. Death visits each and all; the slayer soon follows the slain. It is an insignificant trifle, after all, that people discuss with so much concern. And anyhow, what does it matter for how long a time you avoid that which you cannot escape? Farewell.

XCIV. ON THE VALUE OF ADVICE [a]

That department of philosophy which supplies precepts [b] appropriate to the individual case, instead of framing them for mankind at large—which, for instance, advises how a husband should conduct himself towards his wife, or how a father should bring up his children, or how a master should rule his slaves—-this department of philosophy, I say, is accepted by some as the only significant part, while the other departments are rejected on the ground that they stray beyond the sphere of practical needs—as if any man could give advice concerning a portion of life without having first gained a knowledge of the sum of life as a whole!

But Aristo the Stoic, on the contrary, believes [c] the above-mentioned department to be of slight import: he holds that it does not sink into the mind,

11

anilia[1] habentem praecepta, plurimum ait proficere
ipsa decreta philosophiae constitutionemque summi
boni. Quam qui bene intellexit ac didicit, quid in
3 quaque re faciendum sit sibi ipse praecipit.[2] Quemadmodum qui iaculari discit, destinatum locum captat
et manum format ad derigenda quae mittet, cum
hanc vim ex disciplina et exercitatione percepit,
quocumque vult illa utitur, didicit enim non hoc aut
illud ferire, sed quodcumque voluerit : sic qui se ad
totam vitam instruxit, non desiderat particulatim
admoneri, doctus in totum, non enim quomodo cum
uxore aut cum filio viveret, sed quomodo bene
viveret. In hoc est et quomodo cum uxore ac
liberis vivat.

4 Cleanthes utilem quidem iudicat et hanc partem,
sed inbecillam nisi ab universo fluit, nisi decreta ipsa
philosophiae et capita cognovit. In duas ergo quaestiones locus iste dividitur : utrum utilis an inutilis sit,
et an solus virum bonum possit efficere, id est utrum
supervacuus sit an omnes faciat supervacuos.

5 Qui hanc partem videri volunt supervacuam, hoc
aiunt : "Si quid oculis oppositum moratur aciem,
removendum est. Illo quidem obiecto operam perdit[3]

---

[1] *anilia* Buecheler ; *anilla* B ; *anillam* or *atillam* A.
[2] *praecipit* later MSS. ; *praecepit* BA.
[3] *perdit* Buecheler and others ; *perdidit* BA.

having in it nothing but old wives' precepts, and that the greatest benefit is derived from the actual dogmas of philosophy and from the definition of the Supreme Good. When a man has gained a complete understanding of this definition and has thoroughly learned it, he can frame for himself a precept directing what is to be done in a given case. Just as the student of javelin-throwing keeps aiming at a fixed target and thus trains the hand to give direction to the missile, and when, by instruction and practice, he has gained the desired ability, he can then employ it against any target he wishes (having learned to strike not any random object, but precisely the object at which he has aimed),—so he who has equipped himself for the whole of life does not need to be advised concerning each separate item, because he is now trained to meet his problem as a whole; for he knows not merely how he should live with his wife or his son, but how he should live aright. In this knowledge there is also included the proper way of living with wife and children.

Cleanthes holds that this department of wisdom is indeed useful, but that it is a feeble thing unless it is derived from general principles — that is, unless it is based upon a knowledge of the actual dogmas of philosophy and its main headings. This subject is therefore twofold, leading to two separate lines of inquiry: first, Is it useful or useless? and, second, Can it of itself produce a good man?—in other words, Is it superfluous, or does it render all other departments superfluous?

Those who urge the view that this department is superfluous argue as follows: " If an object that is held in front of the eyes interferes with the vision, it must be removed. For just as long as it is in the

13

qui praecipit : sic ambulabis, illo manum porriges.
Eodem modo ubi aliqua res occaecat animum et ad
officiorum dispiciendum ordinem inpedit, nihil agit
qui praecipit : sic vives cum patre, sic cum uxore.
Nihil enim proficient praecepta, quamdiu menti error
offusus est ; si ille discutitur, apparebit, quid cuique
debeatur officio. Alioqui doces illum,[1] quid sano
6 faciendum sit, non efficis sanum. Pauperi ut agat
divitem monstras ; hoc quomodo manente paupertate fieri potest ? Ostendis esurienti quid tamquam
satur faciat ; fixam potius medullis famem detrahe.

" Idem tibi de omnibus vitiis dico : ipsa removenda
sunt, non praecipiendum quod fieri illis manentibus
non potest. Nisi opiniones falsas, quibus laboramus,
expuleris, nec avarus, quomodo pecunia utendum sit,
exaudiet, nec timidus, quomodo periculosa contem-
7 nat. Efficias oportet, ut sciat pecuniam nec bonum
nec malum esse ; ostendas illi miserrimos divites.
Efficias, ut quicquid publice expavimus, sciat non
esse tam timendum quam fama circumfert, nec
dolere [2] nec mori ; saepe in morte, quam pati lex est,
magnum esse solacium, quod ad neminem redit ; in

[1] *illum* cod. Rhedig.[2]; *illo* BA.
[2] von Arnim removed *quemquam* after *dolere.*

ᵃ In other words, that it is one of the " external " things,
media, indifferentia.

14

way, it is a waste of time to offer such precepts as these : ' Walk thus and so ; extend your hand in that direction.' Similarly, when something blinds a man's soul and hinders it from seeing a line of duty clearly, there is no use in advising him : ' Live thus and so with your father, thus and so with your wife.' For precepts will be of no avail while the mind is clouded with error ; only when the cloud is dispersed will it be clear what one's duty is in each case. Otherwise, you will merely be showing the sick man what he ought to do if he were well, instead of making him well. Suppose you are trying to reveal to the poor man the art of ' acting rich ' ; how can the thing be accomplished as long as his poverty is unaltered ? You are trying to make clear to a starveling in what manner he is to act the part of one with a well-filled stomach ; the first requisite, however, is to relieve him of the hunger that grips his vitals.

" The same thing, I assure you, holds good of all faults ; the faults themselves must be removed, and precepts should not be given which cannot possibly be carried out while the faults remain. Unless you drive out the false opinions under which we suffer, the miser will never receive instruction as to the proper use of his money, nor the coward regarding the way to scorn danger. You must make the miser know that money is neither a good nor an evil ; [a] show him men of wealth who are miserable to the last degree. You must make the coward know that the things which generally frighten us out of our wits are less to be feared than rumour advertises them to be, whether the object of fear be suffering or death ; that when death comes—fixed by law for us all to suffer—it is often a great solace to reflect that it can never come again ; that in the midst of suffering

15

dolore pro remedio futuram obstinationem animi,
qui levius sibi facit, quicquid contumaciter passus
est. Optimam doloris esse naturam, quod non
potest nec qui extenditur magnus esse nec qui est
magnus extendi ; omnia fortiter excipienda, quae
nobis mundi necessitas imperat.

8   " His decretis cum illum in conspectum suae condicionis adduxeris et cognoverit beatam esse vitam
non quae secundum voluptatem [1] est, sed secundum
naturam, cum virtutem unicum bonum hominis
adamaverit, turpitudinem solum malum fugerit, reliqua omnia, divitias, honores, bonam valitudinem,
vires, imperia, scierit esse mediam partem nec bonis
adnumerandam nec malis, monitorem non desiderabit [2] ad singula, qui dicat : sic incede, sic cena.
Hoc viro hoc feminae, hoc marito hoc caelibi con-
9 venit. Ista enim qui diligentissime monent, ipsi
facere non possunt. Haec paedagogus puero, haec
avia nepoti praecipit, et irascendum non esse magister
iracundissimus disputat. Si ludum litterarium in-
traveris, scies ista, quae ingenti supercilio philosophi
iactant, in puerili esse praescripto.

10   "Utrum deinde manifesta an dubia praecipies ? Non
desiderant manifesta monitorem, praecipienti dubia
non creditur ; supervacuum est ergo praecipere. Id

---

[1] *voluptatem* later MSS. ; *voluntatem* BA.
[2] *desiderabit* later MSS. ; *desideravit* BA.

---

[a] Compare, among similar passages, *Ep.* xxiv. 14 *levis
es, si ferre possum, brevis es, si ferre non possum.*

16

resoluteness of soul will be as good as a cure, for the soul renders lighter any burden that it endures with stubborn defiance. Remember that pain has this most excellent quality : if prolonged it cannot be severe, and if severe it cannot be prolonged; [a] and that we should bravely accept whatever commands the inevitable laws of the universe lay upon us.

"When by means of such doctrines you have brought the erring man to a sense of his own condition, when he has learned that the happy life is not that which conforms to pleasure, but that which conforms to Nature, when he has fallen deeply in love with virtue as man's sole good and has avoided baseness as man's sole evil, and when he knows that all other things—riches, office, health, strength, dominion—fall in between and are not to be reckoned either among goods or among evils, then he will not need a monitor for every separate action, to say to him : ' Walk thus and so ; eat thus and so. This is the conduct proper for a man and that for a woman ; this for a married man and that for a bachelor.' Indeed, the persons who take the greatest pains to proffer such advice are themselves unable to put it into practice. It is thus that the pedagogue advises the boy, and the grandmother her grandson ; it is the hottest-tempered school-master who contends that one should never lose one's temper. Go into any elementary school, and you will learn that just such pronouncements, emanating from high-browed philosophers, are to be found in the lesson-book for boys !

"Shall you then offer precepts that are clear, or precepts that are doubtful ? Those which are clear need no counsellor, and doubtful precepts gain no credence ; so the giving of precepts is superfluous.

17

adeo sic disce. Si id mones, quod obscurum est et ambi-
guum, probationibus adiuvandum erit. Si probaturus
es, illa per quae probas plus valent satisque per se sunt.
11 Sic amico utere, sic cive, sic socio. Quare? Quia
iustum est. Omnia ista mihi de iustitia locus tradit.
Illic invenio aequitatem per se expetendam, nec metu
nos ad illam cogi nec mercede conduci, non esse
iustum, cui quidquam in hac virtute placet praeter
ipsam. Hoc cum persuasi mihi et perbibi,[1] quid ista
praecepta proficiunt, quae eruditum docent? Praecepta dare scienti supervacuum est, nescienti parum.
Audire enim debet non tantum, quid sibi prae-
12 cipiatur, sed etiam quare. Utrum, inquam, veras
opiniones habenti de bonis malisque sunt necessaria
an non habenti? Qui non habet, nihil a te adiu-
vabitur; aures eius contraria monitionibus tuis fama
possedit. Qui habet exactum iudicium de fugiendis
petendisque, scit, quid[2] sibi faciendum sit, etiam te
tacente. Tota ergo pars ista philosophiae sum-
moveri potest.

13 "Duo sunt, propter quae delinquimus: aut inest
animo pravis opinionibus malitia contracta aut, etiam
si non est falsis occupatus, ad falsa proclivis est et

[1] perbibi later MSS.; perhibi BA.
[2] scit quid later MSS.; scit BA.

18

Indeed you should study the problem in this way : if you are counselling someone on a matter which is of doubtful clearness and doubtful meaning, you must supplement your precepts by proofs ; and if you must resort to proofs, your means of proof are more effective and more satisfactory in themselves. ' It is thus that you must treat your friend, thus your fellow-citizen, thus your associate.' And why ? ' Because it is just.' Yet I can find all that material included under the head of Justice. I find there that fair play is desirable in itself, that we are not forced into it by fear nor hired to that end for pay, and that no man is just who is attracted by anything in this virtue other than the virtue itself. After convincing myself of this view and thoroughly absorbing it, what good can I obtain from such precepts, which only teach one who is already trained ? To one who knows, it is superfluous to give precepts ; to one who does not know, it is insufficient. For he must be told, not only what he is being instructed to do, but also why. I repeat, are such precepts useful to him who has correct ideas about good and evil, or to one who has them not ? The latter will receive no benefit from you ; for some idea that clashes with your counsel has already monopolized his attention. He who has made a careful decision as to what should be sought and what should be avoided knows what he ought to do, without a single word from you. Therefore, that whole department of philosophy may be abolished.

" There are two reasons why we go astray : either there is in the soul an evil quality which has been brought about by wrong opinions, or, even if not possessed by false ideas, the soul is prone to false-hood and rapidly corrupted by some outward appear-

cito specie quo non oportet trahente corrumpitur.
Itaque debemus aut percurare mentem aegram et
vitiis liberare, aut vacantem [1] quidem, sed ad peiora
pronam praeoccupare. Utrumque decreta philosophiae faciunt; ergo tale praecipiendi genus nil
14 agit. Praeterea si praecepta singulis damus, incon-
prehensibile opus est. Alia enim dare debemus
faeneranti, alia colenti agrum, alia negotianti, alia
regum amicitias sequenti, alia pares, alia inferiores
15 amaturo. In matrimonio praecipies, quomodo vivat
cum uxore aliquis, quam virginem duxit, quomodo
cum ea, quae alicuius ante matrimonium experta est,
quemadmodum cum locuplete, quemadmodum cum
indotata. An non putas aliquid esse discriminis inter
sterilem et fecundam, inter provectiorem et puellam,
inter matrem et novercam? Omnes species conplecti
non possumus, atqui singulae propria exigunt; leges
autem philosophiae breves sunt et omnia alligant.
16 Adice nunc, quod sapientiae praecepta finita debent
esse et certa: si qua finiri non possunt, extra sapientiam sunt; sapientia rerum terminos novit.

" Ergo ista praeceptiva pars summovenda est, quia
quod paucis promittit, praestare omnibus non potest;
17 sapientia autem omnes tenet. Inter insaniam pub-

[1] *vacantem* later MSS.; *vagantem* BA.

ance which attracts it in the wrong direction. For this reason it is our duty either to treat carefully the diseased mind and free it from faults, or to take possession of the mind when it is still unoccupied and yet inclined to what is evil. Both these results can be attained by the main doctrines of philosophy; therefore the giving of such precepts is of no use. Besides, if we give forth precepts to each individual, the task is stupendous. For one class of advice should be given to the financier, another to the farmer, another to the business man, another to one who cultivates the good graces of royalty, another to him who will seek the friendship of his equals, another to him who will court those of lower rank. In the case of marriage, you will advise one person how he should conduct himself with a wife who before her marriage was a maiden, and another how he should behave with a woman who had previously been wedded to another ; how the husband of a rich woman should act, or another man with a dowerless spouse. Or do you not think that there is some difference between a barren woman and one who bears children, between one advanced in years and a mere girl, between a mother and a step-mother ? We cannot include all the types, and yet each type requires separate treatment ; but the laws of philosophy are concise and are binding in all cases. Moreover, the precepts of wisdom should be definite and certain : when things cannot be defined, they are outside the sphere of wisdom ; for wisdom knows the proper limits of things.

" We should therefore do away with this department of precepts, because it cannot afford to all what it promises only to a few ; wisdom, however, embraces all. Between the insanity of people in general and

licam et hanc, quae medicis traditur, nihil interest
nisi quod haec morbo laborat, illa opinionibus falsis.
Altera causas furoris traxit ex valitudine, altera
animi mala valitudo est. Si quis furioso praecepta
det, quomodo loqui debeat, quomodo procedere,
quomodo in publico se gerere, quomodo in privato,
erit ipso, quem monebit, insanior. Ei bilis[1] nigra
curanda est et ipsa furoris causa removenda. Idem
in hoc alio animi furore faciendum est. Ipse discuti
debet; alioqui abibunt in vanum monentium verba."

18 Haec ab Aristone dicuntur; cui respondebimus ad
singula. Primum adversus illud, quod ait, si quid
obstat oculo et inpedit visum, debere removeri.
Fateor huic non esse opus praeceptis ad videndum,
sed remedio, quo purgetur acies et officientem sibi
moram effugiat. Natura enim videmus, cui usum sui
reddit qui removet[2] obstantia. Quid autem cuique
19 debeatur officio, natura non docet. Deinde cuius
curata suffusio est, is non protinus cum visum
recepit, aliis quoque potest reddere; malitia liberatus
et liberat. Non opus est exhortatione, ne consilio
quidem, ut colorum proprietates oculus intellegat, a
nigro album etiam nullo monente distinguet. Multis

[a] For the same figure, in the same connexion, see *Ep.*
lxviii. 8 *in pectore ipso collectio et vomica est.*
[b] By means of hellebore, Lat. *veratrum*, the favourite
cathartic of the ancients.

the insanity which is subject to medical treatment, there is no difference, except that the latter is suffering from disease and the former from false opinions.[a] In the one case, the symptoms of madness may be traced to ill-health ; the other is the ill-health of the mind. If one should offer precepts to a madman—how he ought to speak, how he ought to walk, how he ought to conduct himself in public and in private, he would be more of a lunatic than the person whom he was advising. What is really necessary is to treat the black bile [b] and remove the essential cause of the madness. And this is what should also be done in the other case—that of the mind diseased. The madness itself must be shaken off; otherwise, your words of advice will vanish into thin air."

This is what Aristo says ; and I shall answer his arguments one by one. First, in opposition to what he says about one's obligation to remove that which blocks the eye and hinders the vision. I admit that such a person does not need precepts in order to see, but that he needs treatment for the curing of his eyesight and the getting rid of the hindrance that handicaps him. For it is Nature that gives us our eyesight ; and he who removes obstacles restores to Nature her proper function. But Nature does not teach us our duty in every case. Again, if a man's cataract is cured, he cannot, immediately after his recovery, give back their eyesight to other men also ; but when we are freed from evil we can free others also. There is no need of encouragement, or even of counsel, for the eye to be able to distinguish different colours ; black and white can be differentiated without prompting from another.

23

contra praeceptis eget animus, ut videat, quid agendum sit in vita ; quamquam oculis quoque aegros
20 medicus non tantum curat sed etiam monet. "Non
est," inquit, "quod protinus inbecillam aciem com-
mittas inprobo lumini ; a tenebris primum ad um-
brosa procede, deinde plus aude et paulatim claram
lucem pati adsuesce. Non est quod post cibum
studeas, non est quod plenis oculis ac tumentibus
imperes ; adflatum et vim frigoris in os occurrentis
evita " ; alia eiusmodi, quae non minus quam medica-
menta proficiunt. Adicit remediis medicina consilium.
21   " Error," inquit, " est causa peccandi. Hunc nobis
praecepta non detrahunt nec expugnant opiniones
de bonis ac malis falsas." Concedo per se efficacia
praecepta non esse ad evertendam pravam animi
persuasionem ; sed non ideo nihil ne¹ aliis quidem
adiecta proficiunt. Primum memoriam renovant ;
deinde quae in universo confusius videbantur, in
partes divisa diligentius considerantur. Aut isto²
modo licet et consolationes dicas supervacuas et
exhortationes ; atqui non sunt supervacuae, ergo ne
monitiones quidem.
22   " Stultum est," inquit, " praecipere aegro, quid
facere tamquam sanus debeat, cum restituenda
sanitas sit, sine qua inrita sunt praecepta." Quid,

¹ *nihil ne* added by Buecheler.
² *aut isto* Buecheler ; *aut in isto* BA.

ᵃ This is in harmony with the idea of Socrates; sin is a
lack of knowledge regarding what is true and what is false.
ᵇ *i.e.,* Aristo and others.

The mind, on the other hand, needs many precepts in order to see what it should do in life ; although in eye-treatment also the physician not only accomplishes the cure, but gives advice into the bargain. He says : " There is no reason why you should at once expose your weak vision to a dangerous glare ; begin with darkness, and then go into half-lights, and finally be more bold, accustoming yourself gradually to the bright light of day. There is no reason why you should study immediately after eating; there is no reason why you should impose hard tasks upon your eyes when they are swollen and inflamed ; avoid winds and strong blasts of cold air that blow into your face,"—and other suggestions of the same sort, which are just as valuable as drugs themselves. The physician's art supplements remedies by advice.

" But," comes the reply, " error is the source of sin ;[a] precepts do not remove error, nor do they rout our false opinions on the subject of Good and Evil." I admit that precepts alone are not effective in overthrowing the mind's mistaken beliefs ; but they do not on that account fail to be of service when they accompany other measures also. In the first place, they refresh the memory ; in the second place, when sorted into their proper classes, the matters which showed themselves in a jumbled mass when considered as a whole, can be considered in this way with greater care. According to our opponents'[b] theory, you might even say that consolation and exhortation were superfluous. Yet they are not superfluous ; neither, therefore, is counsel.

" But it is folly," they retort, " to prescribe what a sick man ought to do, just as if he were well, when you should really restore his health ; for without health precepts are not worth a jot." But have not

THE EPISTLES OF SENECA

quod habent aegri quaedam sanique communia, de
quibus admonendi sunt? Tamquam ne avide cibos
adpetant, ut lassitudinem vitent. Habent quaedam
23 praecepta communia pauper et dives. "Sana,"[1]
inquit, "avaritiam, et nihil habebis quod admoneas
aut pauperem aut divitem, si cupiditas utriusque
consedit.[2]" Quid, quod aliud est non concupiscere
pecuniam, aliud uti pecunia scire? Cuius avari
modum ignorant, etiam non avari usum. "Tolle,"
inquit, "errores; supervacua praecepta sunt."
Falsum est. Puta enim avaritiam relaxatam, puta
adstrictam esse luxuriam, temeritati frenos iniectos,
ignaviae subditum calcar; etiam remotis vitiis quid
et quemadmodum debeamus facere, discendum est.
24 "Nihil," inquit, "efficient monitiones admotae
gravibus vitiis." Ne medicina quidem morbos in-
sanabiles vincit, tamen adhibetur aliis in remedium,
aliis in levamentum. Ne ipsa quidem universae
philosophiae vis, licet totas in hoc vires suas advocet,
duram iam et veterem animis extrahet pestem. Sed
25 non ideo nihil sanat, quia non omnia. "Quid prodest,"
inquit, "aperta monstrare?" Plurimum; interdum
enim scimus nec adtendimus. Non docet admonitio,

---

[1] *sana* later MSS.; *saniat* BA.
[2] *consedit* Schweighaeuser; *considet* BA.

sick men and sound men something in common, concerning which they need continual advice? For example, not to grasp greedily after food, and to avoid getting over-tired. Poor and rich have certain precepts which fit them both. " Cure their greed, then," people say, " and you will not need to lecture either the poor or the rich, provided that in the case of each of them the craving has subsided." But is it not one thing to be free from lust for money, and another thing to know how to use this money? Misers do not know the proper limits in money matters, but even those who are not misers fail to comprehend its use. Then comes the reply : " Do away with error, and your precepts become unnecessary." That is wrong ; for suppose that avarice is slackened, that luxury is confined, that rashness is reined in, and that laziness is pricked by the spur ; even after vices are removed, we must continue to learn what we ought to do, and how we ought to do it.

" Nothing," it is said, " will be accomplished by applying advice to the more serious faults." No ; and not even medicine can master incurable diseases ; it is nevertheless used in some cases as a remedy, in others as a relief. Not even the power of universal philosophy, though it summon all its strength for the purpose, will remove from the soul what is now a stubborn and chronic disease. But Wisdom, merely because she cannot cure everything, is not incapable of making cures. People say : " What good does it do to point out the obvious ? " A great deal of good ; for we sometimes know facts without paying attention to them. Advice is not teaching ; it merely engages the attention and rouses us, and

sed advertit, sed excitat, sed memoriam continet nec
patitur elabi. Pleraque ante oculos posita transimus.
Admonere genus adhortandi est. Saepe animus
etiam aperta dissimulat; ingerenda est itaque illi
notitia rerum notissimarum. Illa hoc loco in Va-
tinium Calvi repetenda sententia est : " factum esse
26 ambitum scitis, et hoc vos scire omnes sciunt." Scis
amicitias sancte colendas esse, sed non facis. Scis
inprobum esse, qui ab uxore pudicitiam exigit, ipse
alienarum corruptor uxorum ; scis ut illi nil cum
adultero, sic [1] tibi nil esse debere cum paelice, et non
facis. Itaque subinde ad memoriam reducendus es ;
non enim reposita illa esse oportet, sed in promptu.
Quaecumque salutaria sunt, saepe agitari debent,
saepe versari, ut non tantum nota sint nobis, sed
etiam parata. Adice nunc, quod aperta quoque
apertiora fieri solent.
27 " Si dubia sunt," inquit, " quae praecipis, probationes adicere debebis ; ergo illae, non praecepta
proficient." Quid, quod etiam sine probationibus
ipsa monentis auctoritas prodest ? Sic quomodo
iurisconsultorum valent responsa, etiam si ratio non
redditur. Praeterea ipsa, quae praecipiuntur, per se
multum habent ponderis, utique si aut carmini
intexta sunt aut prosa oratione in sententiam

[1] *sic* later MSS. ; *sit* BA.

---

[a] *monitio* includes *consolatio, dissuasio, obiurgatio,
laudatio,* and *hortatio.* Cf. § 39 of this letter.
[b] Quoted also by Quintilian, vi. 1. 13. Between the
years 58 and 54 b.c. Calvus, a friend of the poet Catullus,
in three famous speeches prosecuted Vatinius, one of the
creatures of Caesar who had illegally obtained office.

concentrates the memory, and keeps it from losing grip. We miss much that is set before our very eyes. Advice is, in fact, a sort of exhortation.[a] The mind often tries not to notice even that which lies before our eyes; we must therefore force upon it the knowledge of things that are perfectly well known. One might repeat here the saying of Calvus about Vatinius:[b] "You all know that bribery has been going on, and everyone knows that you know it." You know that friendship should be scrupulously honoured, and yet you do not hold it in honour. You know that a man does wrong in requiring chastity of his wife while he himself is intriguing with the wives of other men; you know that, as your wife should have no dealings with a lover, neither should you yourself with a mistress; and yet you do not act accordingly. Hence, you must be continually brought to remember these facts; for they should not be in storage, but ready for use. And whatever is wholesome should be often discussed and often brought before the mind, so that it may be not only familiar to us, but also ready to hand. And remember, too, that in this way what is clear often becomes clearer.

"But if," comes the answer. "your precepts are not obvious, you will be bound to add proofs; hence the proofs, and not the precepts, will be helpful." But cannot the influence of the monitor avail even without proofs? It is like the opinions of a legal expert, which hold good even though the reasons for them are not delivered. Moreover, the precepts which are given are of great weight in themselves, whether they be woven into the fabric of song, or condensed into prose proverbs, like the famous *Wisdom of*

29

coartata, sicut illa Catoniana : " emas non quod
opus est, sed quod necesse est ; quod non opus est,
asse carum est," qualia sunt illa aut reddita oraculo
28 aut similia : " tempori parce," " te nosce." Numquid rationem exiges, cum tibi aliquis hos dixerit
versus ?

> Iniuriarum remedium est oblivio.
> Audentes fortuna iuvat, piger ipse sibi opstat.

Advocatum ista non quaerunt ; adfectus ipsos tangunt et natura vim suam exercente proficiunt.
29 Omnium honestarum rerum semina animi gerunt,
quae admonitione excitantur, non aliter quam scin-
tilla flatu levi adiuta ignem suum explicat. Erigitur
virtus, cum tacta est et inpulsa. Praeterea quaedam
sunt quidem in animo, sed parum prompta, quae
incipiunt in expedito esse, cum dicta sunt. Quaedam
diversis locis iacent sparsa, quae contrahere inexer-
citata mens non potest. Itaque in unum conferenda
sunt et iungenda, ut plus valeant animumque magis
30 adlevent. Aut si praecepta nihil adiuvant, omnis
institutio tollenda est, ipsa natura contenti esse
debemus.

Hoc qui dicunt, non vident alium esse ingenii
mobilis et erecti, alium tardi et hebetis, utique
alium alio ingeniosiorem. Ingenii vis praeceptis
alitur et crescit novasque persuasiones adicit innatis
31 et depravata corrigit. " Si quis," inquit, " non habet

---

a Catonis Reliq. p. 79 Iordan.
b From Publilius Syrus—Frag. 250 Ribbeck.
c A verse made up from Vergil, *Aen.* x. 284, and an
unknown author. *d i.e.,* who would abolish precepts.

Cato [a] : " Buy not what you need, but what you must have. That which you do not need, is dear even at a farthing." Or those oracular or oracular-like replies, such as " Be thrifty with time !" " Know thyself !" Shall you need to be told the meaning when someone repeats to you lines like these :

Forgetting trouble is the way to cure it. [b]

Fortune favours the brave ; but the coward is foiled by his faint heart. [c]

Such maxims need no special pleader ; they go straight to our emotions, and help us simply because Nature is exercising her proper function. The soul carries within itself the seed of everything that is honourable, and this seed is stirred to growth by advice, as a spark that is fanned by a gentle breeze develops its natural fire. Virtue is aroused by a touch, a shock. Moreover, there are certain things which, though in the mind, yet are not ready to hand but begin to function easily as soon as they are put into words. Certain things lie scattered about in various places, and it is impossible for the unpractised mind to arrange them in order. Therefore, we should bring them into unity, and join them, so that they may be more powerful and more of an uplift to the soul. Or, if precepts do not avail at all, then every method of instruction should be abolished, and we should be content with Nature alone.

Those who maintain this view [d] do not understand that one man is lively and alert of wit, another sluggish and dull, while certainly some men have more intelligence than others. The strength of the wit is nourished and kept growing by precepts ; it adds new points of view to those which are inborn and corrects depraved ideas. " But suppose,"

31

recta decreta, quid illum admonitiones iuvabunt
vitiosis obligatum ? " Hoc scilicet, ut illis liberetur ;
non enim extincta in illo indoles naturalis est, sed
obscurata et oppressa. Sic quoque temptat resurgere
et contra prava nititur, nancta vero praesidium et
adiuta praeceptis evalescit, si tamen illam diutina
pestis non infecit nec enecuit ; hanc enim ne disciplina quidem philosophiae toto inpetu suo conisa
restituet. Quid enim interest inter decreta philosophiae et praecepta, nisi quod illa generalia praecepta sunt, haec specialia ? Utraque res praecipit,
sed altera in totum, particulatim altera.

32 " Si quis," inquit, " recta habet et honesta decreta,
hic ex supervacuo monetur." Minime ; nam hic
quoque doctus quidem est facere quae debet, sed
haec non satis perspicit. Non enim tantum adfectibus inpedimur, quo minus probanda faciamus, sed
inperitia inveniendi quid quaeque res exigat. Habemus interdum compositum animum, sed residem et
inexercitatum ad inveniendam[1] officiorum viam,
33 quam admonitio demonstrat. " Expelle," inquit,
" falsas opiniones de bonis et malis, in locum autem
earum veras repone, et nihil habebit admonitio, quod
agat." Ordinatur sine dubio ista ratione animus,

[1] *ad inveniendam* later MSS. ; *adveniendam* BA.

people retort, " that a man is not the possessor of sound dogmas, how can advice help him when he is chained down by vicious dogmas ? " In this, assuredly, that he is freed therefrom ; for his natural disposition has not been crushed, but over-shadowed and kept down. Even so it goes on endeavouring to rise again, struggling against the influences that make for evil ; but when it wins support and receives the aid of precepts, it grows stronger, provided only that the chronic trouble has not corrupted or annihilated the natural man. For in such a case, not even the training that comes from philosophy, striving with all its might, will make restoration. What difference, indeed, is there between the dogmas of philosophy and precepts, unless it be this—that the former are general and the latter special ? Both deal with advice—the one through the universal, the other through the particular.

Some say : " If one is familiar with upright and honourable dogmas, it will be superfluous to advise him." By no means ; for this person has indeed learned to do things which he ought to do ; but he does not see with sufficient clearness what these things are. For we are hindered from accomplishing praiseworthy deeds not only by our emotions, but also by want of practice in discovering the demands of a particular situation. Our minds are often under good control, and yet at the same time are inactive and untrained in finding the path of duty,—and advice makes this clear. Again, it is written : " Cast out all false opinions concerning Good and Evil, but replace them with true opinions ; then advice will have no function to perform." Order in the soul can doubtless be established in this way ; but these are not the

sed non ista tantum. Nam quamvis argumentis
collectum sit, quae bona malaque sint, nihilominus
habent praecepta partes suas. Et prudentia et
iustitia officiis constat, officia praeceptis disponuntur.

34 Praeterea [1] ipsum de malis bonisque iudicium con-
firmatur officiorum exsecutione, ad quam praecepta
perducunt. Utraque enim inter se consentiunt ; nec
illa possunt praecedere, ut non haec sequantur. Et
haec ordinem sequuntur suum ; unde apparet illa
praecedere.

35 "Infinita," inquit, "praecepta sunt." Falsum est.
Nam de maximis ac necessariis rebus non sunt
infinita. Tenues autem differentias habent, quas
exigunt tempora, loca, personae, sed his quoque
36 dantur praecepta generalia. "Nemo," inquit, " praeceptis curat insaniam ; ergo ne malitiam quidem."
Dissimile est. Nam si insaniam sustuleris, sanitas
redit, at [2] si falsas opiniones exclusimus, non statim
sequitur dispectus rerum agendarum. Ut sequatur,
tamen admonitio conroborabit rectam de bonis
malisque sententiam. Illud quoque falsum est, nihil
apud insanos proficere praecepta. Nam quemadmodum sola non prosunt, sic curationem adiuvant.
Et denuntiatio et castigatio insanos coercuit. De illis
nunc insanis loquor, quibus mens mota est, non
erepta.

37 "Leges," inquit, "ut faciamus, quod oportet, non
efficiunt, et quid aliud sunt quam minis mixta praecepta ? " Primum omnium ob hoc illae non per-
suadent, quia minantur, at haec non cogunt, sed

[1] *praeterea* later MSS. ; *praeter* BA.
[2] *redit, at* Buecheler ; *redita est* BA.

---

[a] A further answer to the objection in § 17 above, where
all madness is held curable by physical treatment.

only ways. For although we may infer by proofs just what Good and Evil are, nevertheless precepts have their proper rôle. Prudence and justice consist of certain duties; and duties are set in order by precepts. Moreover, judgment as to Good and Evil is itself strengthened by following up our duties, and precepts conduct us to this end. For both are in accord with each other; nor can precepts take the lead unless the duties follow. They observe their natural order; hence precepts clearly come first.

" Precepts," it is said, " are numberless." Wrong again! For they are not numberless so far as concerns important and essential things. Of course there are slight distinctions, due to the time, or the place, or the person; but even in these cases, precepts are given which have a general application. " No one, however," it is said, " cures madness by precepts, and therefore not wickedness either." There is a distinction; for if you rid a man of insanity, he becomes sane again, but if we have removed false opinions, insight into practical conduct does not at once follow. Even though it follows, counsel will none the less confirm one's right opinion concerning Good and Evil. And it is also wrong to believe that precepts are of no use to madmen. For though, by themselves, they are of no avail, yet they are a help towards the cure.[a] Both scolding and chastening rein in a lunatic. Note that I here refer to lunatics whose wits are disturbed but not hopelessly gone.

" Still," it is objected, " laws do not always make us do what we ought to do; and what else are laws than precepts mingled with threats?" Now first of all, the laws do not persuade just because they threaten; precepts, however, instead of coercing,

35

THE EPISTLES OF SENECA

exorant. Deinde leges a scelere deterrent, praecepta in officium adhortantur. His adice quod[1] leges quoque proficiunt ad bonos mores, utique si
38 non tantum imperant, sed docent. In hac re dissentio a Posidonio, qui " inprobo," inquit, " quod[2] Platonis legibus adiecta principia sunt. Legem enim brevem esse oportet, quo facilius ab imperitis teneatur. Velut emissa divinitus vox sit; iubeat, non disputet. Nihil videtur mihi frigidius, nihil ineptius quam lex cum prologo. Mone,[3] dic, quid me velis fecisse; non disco, sed pareo." Proficiunt vero[4]; itaque malis moribus uti videbis civitates usas malis legibus. " At non apud omnis proficiunt."
39 Ne philosophia quidem; nec ideo inutilis et formandis animis inefficax est. Quid autem? Philosophia non vitae lex est? Sed putemus non proficere leges; non ideo sequitur, ut ne monitiones quidem proficiant. Aut sic et consolationes nega proficere dissuasionesque et adhortationes et obiurgationes et laudationes. Omnia ista monitionum genera sunt. Per ista ad perfectum animi statum pervenitur.
40 Nulla res magis animis honesta induit dubiosque et in pravum inclinabiles revocat ad rectum quam bonorum virorum conversatio. Paulatim enim descendit in pectora, et vim praeceptorum obtinet frequenter aspici, frequenter audiri.

[1] *quod* later MSS.; *quo* BA.
[2] *qui inprobo inquit quod* Rossbach; *qui pro (eo) quod* BA.
[3] *cum prologo. mone* Erasmus; *cum prolegomene* BA.
[4] *proficiunt vero* Schweighaeuser; *proficiuntur* BA.

[a] See, for example, the Fifth Book, which opens with the preliminary remarks of the Athenian Stranger (pp. 726-34 St.).
[b] A frequent thought in Seneca, *cf. Ep.* xxv. 6, lii. 8, etc.

correct men by pleading. Again, laws frighten one out of communicating crime, while precepts urge a man on to his duty. Besides, the laws also are of assistance towards good conduct, at any rate if they instruct as well as command. On this point I disagree with Posidonius, who says : " I do not think that Plato's *Laws* should have the preambles[a] added to them. For a law should be brief, in order that the uninitiated may grasp it all the more easily. It should be a voice, as it were, sent down from heaven ; it should command, not discuss. Nothing seems to me more dull or more foolish than a law with a preamble. Warn me, tell me what you wish me to do ; I am not learning but obeying." But laws framed in this way are helpful ; hence you will notice that a state with defective laws will have defective morals. " But," it is said, " they are not of avail in every case." Well, neither is philosophy ; and yet philosophy is not on that account ineffectual and useless in the training of the soul. Furthermore, is not philosophy the Law of Life ? Grant, if we will, that the laws do not avail ; it does not necessarily follow that advice also should not avail. On this ground, you ought to say that consolation does not avail, and warning, and exhortation, and scolding, and praising ; since they are all varieties of advice. It is by such methods that we arrive at a perfect condition of mind. Nothing is more successful in bringing honourable influences to bear upon the mind, or in straightening out the wavering spirit that is prone to evil, than association with good men.[b] For the frequent seeing, the frequent hearing of them little by little sinks into the heart and acquires the force of precepts.

Occursus mehercules ipse sapientium iuvat, et est aliquid. quod ex magno viro vel tacente [1] proficias.

41 Nec tibi facile dixerim quemadmodum prosit, sicut illud intellego [2] profuisse. "Minuta quaedam," ut ait Phaedon, "animalia cum mordent non sentiuntur; adeo tenuis illis et fallens in periculum vis est. Tumor indicat morsum et in ipso tumore nullum vulnus apparet. Idem tibi in conversatione virorum sapientium eveniet: non deprehendes, quemadmodum aut quando tibi prosit, profuisse deprendes."

42 Quorsus, inquis, hoc pertinet? Aeque praecepta bona, si saepe tecum sint, profutura quam bona exempla. Pythagoras ait alium animum fieri intrantibus templum deorumque simulacra ex vicino cernentibus et alicuius oraculi opperientibus vocem.

43 Quis autem negabit [3] feriri quibusdam praeceptis efficaciter etiam inperitissimos? Velut his brevissimis vocibus, sed multum habentibus ponderis:

> Nil nimis.
> Avarus animus nullo satiatur lucro.
> Ab alio exspectes, alteri quod feceris.

Haec cum ictu quodam audimus, nec ulli licet dubitare aut interrogare "quare?"; adeo etiam

44 sine ratione ipsa veritas ducit. Si reverentia frenat animos ac vitia compescit, cur non et admonitio idem possit? Si inponit pudorem castigatio, cur admonitio non faciat, etiam si nudis praeceptis utitur? Illa vero efficacior est et altius penetrat, quae

---

[1] *tacente* later MSS.; *iacente* BA.
[2] *intellego* Schweighaeuser; *intellegam* MSS.
[3] *negabit* Buecheler and Windhaus; *negavit* BA.

---

[a] Presumably Phaedo the friend of Plato and pupil of Socrates, author of dialogues resembling those of Plato.

[b] Com. incert., Frag. 81 Ribbeck, and Pub. Syrus, Frag. 2 Ribbeck.

EPISTLE XCIV.

We are indeed uplifted merely by meeting wise men ; and one can be helped by a great man even when he is silent. I could not easily tell you how it helps us, though I am certain of the fact that I have received help in that way. Phaedo [a] says : " Certain tiny animals do not leave any pain when they sting us ; so subtle is their power, so deceptive for purposes of harm. The bite is disclosed by a swelling, and even in the swelling there is no visible wound." That will also be your experience when dealing with wise men : you will not discover how or when the benefit comes to you, but you will discover that you have received it. " What is the point of this remark ? " you ask. It is, that good precepts, often welcomed within you, will benefit you just as much as good examples. Pythagoras declares that our souls experience a change when we enter a temple and behold the images of the gods face to face, and await the utterances of an oracle. Moreover, who can deny that even the most inexperienced are effectively struck by the force of certain precepts ? For example, by such brief but weighty saws as : " Nothing in excess," " The greedy mind is satisfied by no gains," " You must expect to be treated by others as you yourself have treated them." [b] We receive a sort of shock when we hear such sayings ; no one ever thinks of doubting them or of asking : " Why ? " So strongly, indeed, does mere truth, unaccompanied by reason, attract us. If reverence reins in the soul and checks vice, why cannot counsel do the same ? Also, if rebuke gives one a sense of shame, why has not counsel the same power, even though it does use bare precepts ? The counsel which assists suggestion by reason—which adds the motive

adiuvat ratione quod praecipit, quae adicit, quare quidque faciendum sit et quis facientem oboedientemque praeceptis fructus exspectet. Si imperio proficitur, et admonitione; atqui[1] proficitur imperio; ergo et admonitione.

45 In duas partes virtus dividitur, in contemplationem veri et actionem. Contemplationem institutio tradit, actionem admonitio. Virtutem et exercet et ostendit recta actio. Acturo autem si prodest qui suadet, et qui monet proderit. Ergo si recta actio virtuti necessaria est, rectas autem actiones admonitio
46 demonstrat, et admonitio necessaria est. Duae res plurimum roboris animo dant, fides veri et fiducia; utramque[2] admonitio facit. Nam et creditur illi et, cum creditum est, magnos animus spiritus concipit ac fiducia impletur. Ergo admonitio non est supervacua.

M. Agrippa, vir ingentis animi, qui solus ex iis, quos civilia bella claros potentesque fecerunt, felix in publicum fuit, dicere solebat multum se huic debere sententiae: " Nam concordia parvae res crescunt, discordia maximae dilabuntur." Hac se
47 aibat et fratrem et amicum optimum factum. Si eiusmodi sententiae familiariter in animum receptae formant eum, cur non haec pars philosophiae, quae talibus sententiis constat, idem possit? Pars virtutis disciplina constat, pars exercitatione; et discas oportet et quod didicisti agendo confirmes. Quod si est, non tantum scita sapientiae prosunt, sed etiam

---

[1] *atqui* Erasmus; *atque* B; *aeque* A.
[2] *utramque* Pincianus (from an old MS.); *utraque* BA.

---

[a] *i.e.*, belief.
[b] From Sallust, *Jugurtha*, x. 6.

for doing a given thing and the reward which awaits one who carries out and obeys such precepts—is more effective and settles deeper in the heart. If commands are helpful, so is advice. But one is helped by commands; therefore one is helped also by advice.

Virtue is divided into two parts—into contemplation of truth, and conduct. Training teaches contemplation, and admonition teaches conduct. And right conduct both practises and reveals virtue. But if, when a man is about to act, he is helped by advice, he is also helped by admonition. Therefore, if right conduct is necessary to virtue, and if, moreover, admonition makes clear right conduct, then admonition also is an indispensable thing. There are two strong supports to the soul—trust[a] in the truth and confidence; both are the result of admonition. For men believe it, and when belief is established, the soul receives great inspiration and is filled with confidence. Therefore, admonition is not superfluous.

Marcus Agrippa, a great-souled man, the only person among those whom the civil wars raised to fame and power whose prosperity helped the state, used to say that he was greatly indebted to the proverb "Harmony makes small things grow; lack of harmony makes great things decay."[b] He held that he himself became the best of brothers and the best of friends by virtue of this saying. And if proverbs of such a kind, when welcomed intimately into the soul, can mould this very soul, why cannot the department of philosophy which consists of such proverbs possess equal influence? Virtue depends partly upon training and partly upon practice; you must learn first, and then strengthen your learning by action. If this be true, not only do the doctrines

41

praecepta, quae adfectus nostros velut edicto coercent et ablegant.

48 " Philosophia," inquit, " dividitur in haec, scientiam et habitum animi. Nam qui didicit et facienda ac vitanda percepit, nondum sapiens est, nisi in ea, quae didicit, animus eius transfiguratus est. Tertia ista pars praecipiendi ex utroque est, et ex decretis et ex habitu. Itaque supervacua est ad implendam

49 virtutem, cui duo illa sufficiunt." Isto ergo modo et consolatio supervacua est, nam haec quoque ex utroque est, et adhortatio et suasio et ipsa argumentatio. Nam et haec ab habitu animi compositi validique proficiscitur. Sed quamvis ista ex optimo habitu animi veniant, optimus animi habitus ex his

50 est ; et facit illa et ex illis ipse fit. Deinde istud, quod dicis, iam perfecti viri est ac summam consecuti felicitatis humanae. Ad haec autem tarde pervenitur ; interim etiam inperfecto sed proficienti demonstranda est in rebus agendis via. Hanc forsitan etiam sine admonitione dabit sibi ipsa sapientia, quae iam eo perduxit animum, ut moveri nequeat nisi in rectum. Inbecillioribus quidem ingeniis necessarium est aliquem praeire : hoc vitabis, hoc

51 facies. Praeterea si expectat tempus, quo per se sciat quid optimum factu sit, interim errabit et

---

ᵃ Cf. Ep. xciv. 12 *exactum iudicium de fugiendis petendisque.*
ᵇ The last stage of knowledge—complete assent—according to the Stoic view, which went beyond the mere sensation-theory of Epicurus.

42

of wisdom help us, but the precepts also, which check and banish our emotions by a sort of official decree.

It is said : " Philosophy is divided into knowledge and state of mind. For one who has learned and understood what he should do and avoid,[a] is not a wise man until his mind is metamorphosed into the shape of that which he has learned. This third department—that of precept—is compounded from both the others, from dogmas of philosophy and state of mind. Hence it is superfluous as far as the perfecting of virtue is concerned ; the other two parts are enough for the purpose." On that basis, therefore, even consolation would be superfluous, since this also is a combination of the other two, as likewise are exhortation, persuasion, and even proof [b] itself. For proof also originates from a well-ordered and firm mental attitude. But, although these things result from a sound state of mind, yet the sound state of mind also results from them ; it is both creative of them and resultant from them. Furthermore, that which you mention is the mark of an already perfect man, of one who has attained the height of human happiness. But the approach to these qualities is slow, and in the meantime, in practical matters, the path should be pointed out for the benefit of one who is still short of perfection, but is making progress. Wisdom by her own agency may perhaps show herself this path without the help of admonition ; for she has brought the soul to a stage where it can be impelled only in the right direction. Weaker characters, however, need someone to precede them, to say : " Avoid this," or " Do that." Moreover, if one awaits the time when one can know of oneself what the best line of action is, one will sometimes go astray and by going astray will be

43

errando inpedietur, quo minus ad illud perveniat,
quo possit se esse contentus. Regi ergo debet, dum
incipit posse se regere. Pueri ad praescriptum
discunt. Digiti illorum tenentur et aliena manu
per litterarum simulacra ducuntur, deinde imitari
iubentur proposita[1] et ad illa reformare chiro-
graphum. Sic animus noster dum eruditur ad prae-
52 scriptum, iuvatur.[2] Haec sunt, per quae probatur
hanc philosophiae partem supervacuam non esse.

Quaeritur deinde, an ad faciendum sapientem sola
sufficiat. Huic quaestioni suum diem dabimus; interim omissis argumentis nonne apparet opus esse
nobis aliquo advocato, qui contra populi praecepta
53 praecipiat? Nulla ad aures nostras vox inpune
perfertur; nocent qui optant, nocent qui execrantur.
Nam et horum inprecatio falsos nobis metus inserit
et illorum amor male docet bene optando. Mittit
enim nos ad longinqua bona et incerta et errantia,
54 cum possimus felicitatem domo promere. Non licet,
inquam, ire recta via. Trahunt in pravum parentes,
trahunt servi. Nemo errat uni sibi, sed dementiam
spargit in proximos accipitque invicem. Et ideo in
singulis vitia populorum sunt, quia illa populus dedit.
Dum facit quisque peiorem, factus est; didicit deteriora, deinde[3] docuit, effectaque est ingens illa

---

[1] *proposita* later MSS.; *praeposita* BA.
[2] *iuvatur* later MSS.; *iuvat* A; *vivat* B.
[3] *deinde* later MSS.; *dein* BA.

---

[a] In this whole discussion Seneca is a much sounder
Stoic than Aristo and the opposition. The next letter
(*Ep.* xcv.) develops still further the preceptive function of
philosophy—through προκοπή (progress) to μεταβολή (con-
version).

hindered from arriving at the point where it is possible to be content with oneself. The soul should accordingly be guided at the very moment when it is becoming able to guide itself.[a] Boys study according to direction. Their fingers are held and guided by others so that they may follow the outlines of the letters; next, they are ordered to imitate a copy and base thereon a style of penmanship. Similarly, the mind is helped if it is taught according to direction. Such facts as these prove that this department of philosophy is not superfluous.

The question next arises whether this part alone is sufficient to make men wise. The problem shall be treated at the proper time; but at present, omitting all arguments, is it not clear that we need someone whom we may call upon as our preceptor in opposition to the precepts of men in general? There is no word which reaches our ears without doing us harm; we are injured both by good wishes and by curses. The angry prayers of our enemies instil false fears in us; and the affection of our friends spoils us through their kindly wishes. For this affection sets us a-groping after goods that are far away, unsure, and wavering, when we really might open the store of happiness at home. We are not allowed, I maintain, to travel a straight road. Our parents and our slaves draw us into wrong. Nobody confines his mistakes to himself; people sprinkle folly among their neighbours, and receive it from them in turn. For this reason, in an individual, you find the vices of nations, because the nation has given them to the individual. Each man, in corrupting others, corrupts himself; he imbibes, and then imparts, badness;— the result is a vast mass of wickedness, because the

nequitia congesto in unum quod cuique pessimum
scitur.

55 Sit ergo aliquis custos et aurem subinde pervellat
abigatque rumores et reclamet populis laudantibus.
Erras enim, si existimas nobiscum vitia nasci ; super-
venerunt, ingesta sunt. Itaque monitionibus crebris
56 opiniones, quae nos circumsonant, repellantur. Nulli
nos vitio natura conciliat ; illa [1] integros ac liberos
genuit. Nihil quo avaritiam nostram inritaret, posuit
in aperto. Pedibus aurum argentumque subiecit
calcandumque ac premendum dedit quidquid est
propter quod calcamur ac premimur. Illa vultus
nostros erexit ad caelum et quidquid magnificum
mirumque fecerat, videri a suspicientibus voluit.
Ortus occasusque et properantis mundi volubilem
cursum, interdiu terrena aperientem, nocte caelestia,
tardos siderum incessus si conpares toti, citatissimos
autem si cogites, quanta spatia numquam intermissa
velocitate circumeant, defectus solis ac lunae invicem
obstantium, alia deinceps digna miratu, sive per
ordinem subeunt sive subitis causis mota prosiliunt,
ut nocturnos [2] ignium tractus et sine ullo ictu sonitu-
que fulgores caeli patescentis columnasque ac trabes
et varia simulacra flammarum. Haec supra nos itura
57 disposuit ; aurum quidem et argentum et propter ista
numquam pacem agens ferrum, quasi male nobis

---

[1] *illa* later MSS. ; *nulla* BA.
[2] *nocturnos* Buccheler ; *nocturni* BA.

---

[a] This theme is carefully elaborated in *Ep.* vii., " On
Crowds " : " There is no person who does not make some
vice attractive to us, or stamp it upon us, or taint us unconsciously therewith " (§ 2).
[b] These are fully discussed in Seneca's *Naturales
Quaestiones*, a work almost contemporary with the Letters.

worst in every separate person is concentrated in one mass.[a]

We should, therefore, have a guardian, as it were, to pluck us continually by the ear and dispel rumours and protest against popular enthusiasms. For you are mistaken if you suppose that our faults are inborn in us; they have come from without, have been heaped upon us. Hence, by receiving frequent admonitions, we can reject the opinions which din about our ears. Nature does not ally us with any vice; she produced us in health and freedom. She put before our eyes no object which might stir in us the itch of greed. She placed gold and silver beneath our feet, and bade those feet stamp down and crush everything that causes us to be stamped down and crushed. Nature elevated our gaze towards the sky and willed that we should look upward to behold her glorious and wonderful works. She gave us the rising and the setting sun, the whirling course of the on-rushing world which discloses the things of earth by day and the heavenly bodies by night, the movements of the stars, which are slow if you compare them with the universe, but most rapid if you reflect on the size of the orbits which they describe with unslackened speed; she showed us the successive eclipses of sun and moon, and other phenomena, wonderful because they occur regularly or because, through sudden causes, they leap into view—such as nightly trails of fire, or flashes in the open heavens unaccompanied by stroke or sound of thunder, or columns and beams and the various phenomena of flames.[b] She ordained that all these bodies should proceed above our heads; but gold and silver, with the iron which, because of the gold and silver, never brings peace, she has hidden away, as if they

47

committerentur, abscondit. Nos in lucem, propter quae pugnaremus, extulimus ; nos et causas periculorum nostrorum et instrumenta disiecto terrarum pondere eruimus ; nos fortunae mala nostra tradidimus nec erubescimus summa apud nos haberi, quae 58 fuerant ima terrarum. Vis scire, quam falsus oculos tuos deceperit fulgor ? Nihil est istis, quamdiu mersa et involuta caeno suo iacent, foedius, nihil obscurius, quidni ? Quae per longissimorum cuniculorum tenebras extrahuntur. Nihil est illis, dum fiunt et a faece sua separantur, informius. Denique ipsos opifices intuere, per quorum manus sterile terrae genus et infernum perpurgatur ; videbis quanta 59 fuligine oblinantur. Atqui ista magis inquinant animos quam corpora, et in possessore eorum quam in artifice plus sordium est.

Necessarium itaque admoneri est,[1] habere aliquem advocatum bonae mentis et in tanto [2] fremitu tumultuque falsorum unam denique audire vocem. Quae erit illa vox ? Ea scilicet, quae tibi tantis clamoribus ambitionis exsurdato salubria insusurret 60 verba, quae dicat : non est quod invideas istis, quos magnos felicesque populus vocat, non est quod tibi compositae mentis habitum et sanitatem plausus excutiat, non est quod tibi tranquillitatis tuae fastidium faciat ille sub illis fascibus purpura cultus, non

---

[1] *est* Buecheler ; *et* BA.
[2] *et in tanto* Schweighaeuser ; *etantanto* BA.

---

[a] Both literally and figuratively,—the sheen of the metal and the glitter of the false idea.
[b] *i.e.*, the bundle of rods and axes, carried by the attendants of a Roman magistrate.

were dangerous things to trust to our keeping. It is we ourselves that have dragged them into the light of day to the end that we might fight over them; it is we ourselves who, tearing away the superincumbent earth, have dug out the causes and tools of our own destruction; it is we ourselves who have attributed our own misdeeds to Fortune, and do not blush to regard as the loftiest objects those which once lay in the depths of earth. Do you wish to know how false is the gleam *a* that has deceived your eyes? There is really nothing fouler or more involved in darkness than these things of earth, sunk and covered for so long a time in the mud where they belong. Of course they are foul; they have been hauled out through a long and murky mine-shaft. There is nothing uglier than these metals during the process of refinement and separation from the ore. Furthermore, watch the very workmen who must handle and sift the barren grade of dirt, the sort which comes from the bottom; see how soot-besmeared they are! And yet the stuff they handle soils the soul more than the body, and there is more foulness in the owner than in the workman.

It is therefore indispensable that we be admonished, that we have some advocate with upright mind, and, amid all the uproar and jangle of falsehood, hear one voice only. But what voice shall this be? Surely a voice which, amid all the tumult of self-seeking, shall whisper wholesome words into the deafened ear, saying: " You need not be envious of those whom the people call great and fortunate; applause need not disturb your composed attitude and your sanity of mind; you need not become disgusted with your calm spirit because you see a great man, clothed in purple, protected by the well-known symbols of authority; *b* you need not judge the

49

est quod feliciorem eum iudices cui summovetur,
quam te quem[1] lictor semita deicit. Si vis exercere
tibi utile, nulli autem grave imperium, summove
61 vitia. Multi inveniuntur qui ignem inferant urbibus,
qui inexpugnabilia saeculis et per aliquot aetates
tuta prosternant, qui aequum arcibus aggerem
attollant et muros in miram altitudinem eductos
arietibus ac machinis quassent. Multi sunt qui ante
se agant agmina et tergis hostium[2] graves instent et
ad mare magnum perfusi caede gentium veniant; sed
hi quoque, ut vincerent hostem, cupiditate victi sunt.
Nemo illis venientibus restitit, sed nec ipsi ambitioni
crudelitatique restiterant; tunc, cum agere alios visi
62 sunt, agebantur. Agebat infelicem Alexandrum
furor aliena vastandi et ad ignota mittebat. An tu
putas sanum, qui a Graeciae primum cladibus, in qua
eruditus est, incipit? Qui quod cuique optimum est,
eripit, Lacedaemona servire iubet, Athenas tacere?
Non contentus tot civitatium strage, quas aut vicerat
Philippus aut emerat, alias alio loco proicit et toto
orbe arma circumfert, nec subsistit usquam lassa
crudelitas immanium ferarum modo, quae plus quam
63 exigit fames mordent. Iam in unum regnum multa

---

[1] *quem* later MSS.; om. BA.
[2] later MSS. omit *et* (BA) after *hostium*.

---

[a] A name usually applied to the eastern end of the
Mediterranean.
[b] Especially Thebes in 335 B.C., which he sacked. Athens
and Sparta were treated with more consideration.

magistrate for whom the road is cleared to be any happier than yourself, whom his officer pushes from the road. If you would wield a command that is profitable to yourself, and injurious to nobody, clear your own faults out of the way. There are many who set fire to cities, who storm garrisons that have remained impregnable for generations and safe for numerous ages, who raise mounds as high as the walls they are besieging, who with battering-rams and engines shatter towers that have been reared to a wondrous height. There are many who can send their columns ahead and press destructively upon the rear of the foe, who can reach the Great Sea *a* dripping with the blood of nations ; but even these men, before they could conquer their foe, were conquered by their own greed. No one withstood their attack ; but they themselves could not withstand desire for power and the impulse to cruelty ; at the time when they seemed to be hounding others, they were themselves being hounded. Alexander was hounded into misfortune and dispatched to unknown countries by a mad desire to lay waste other men's territory. Do you believe that the man was in his senses who could begin by devastating Greece, the land where he received his education ? One who snatched away the dearest guerdon of each nation, bidding Spartans be slaves, and Athenians hold their tongues ? Not content with the ruin of all the states which Philip had either conquered or bribed into bondage,*b* he overthrew various commonwealths in various places and carried his weapons all over the world ; his cruelty was tired, but it never ceased—like a wild beast that tears to pieces more than its hunger demands. Already he has joined many kingdoms into one

regna coniecit; iam Graeci Persaeque eundem
timent; iam etiam a Dareo liberae nationes iugum
accipiunt: it tamen ultra oceanum solemque, in-
dignatur ab Herculis Liberique vestigiis victoriam
flectere, ipsi naturae vim parat. Non ille ire vult,
sed non potest stare, non aliter quam in praeceps
deiecta pondera, quibus eundi finis est iacuisse.

64 Ne Gnaeo quidem Pompeio externa bella ac
domestica virtus aut ratio suadebat, sed insanus
amor magnitudinis falsae. Modo in Hispaniam et
Sertoriana arma, modo ad colligandos [1] piratas ac
65 maria pacanda vadebat. Hae praetexebantur causae
ad continuandam potentiam. Quid illum in Africam,
quid in septentrionem, quid in Mithridaten et
Armeniam et omnis Asiae angulos traxit? Infinita
scilicet cupido crescendi, cum sibi uni parum magnus
videretur. Quid C. Caesarem in sua fata pariter ac
publica inmisit? Gloria et ambitio et nullus supra
66 ceteros eminendi modus. Unum ante se ferre
non potuit, cum res publica supra se duos ferret.
Quid, tu C. Marium semel consulem—unum enim
consulatum accepit, ceteros rapuit—cum Teutonos
Cimbrosque concideret, cum Iugurtham per Africae deserta sequeretur, tot pericula putas adpetisse
virtutis instinctu? Marius exercitus, Marium ambitio
ducebat.

[1] *colligandos* Madvig; *colligendos* BA.

[a] *i.e.*, the Hyrcanians, and other tribes attacked during
and after 330 B.C.
[b] Heracles in his various forms hails all the way from
Tyre to the Atlantic Ocean; Dionysus from India through
Lydia, Thrace, and the Eastern Mediterranean to Greece.
[c] 76 B.C.　　　[d] 67 B.C.
[e] Beginning with the passage of the Manilian Law of
66 B.C.
[f] 107 B.C. (also 104, 103, 102, 101, 100, and 86).

kingdom ; already Greeks and Persians fear the same lord ; already nations Darius had left free submit to the yoke :[a] yet he passes beyond the Ocean and the Sun, deeming it shame that he should shift his course of victory from the paths which Hercules and Bacchus had trod ;[b] he threatens violence to Nature herself. He does not wish to go ; but he cannot stay ; he is like a weight that falls headlong, its course ending only when it lies motionless.

It was not virtue or reason which persuaded Gnaeus Pompeius to take part in foreign and civil warfare ; it was his mad craving for unreal glory. Now he attacked Spain and the faction of Sertorius ;[c] now he fared forth to enchain the pirates and subdue the seas.[d] These were merely excuses and pretexts for extending his power. What drew him into Africa, into the North, against Mithridates, into Armenia and all the corners of Asia ?[e] Assuredly it was his boundless desire to grow bigger ; for only in his own eyes was he not great enough. And what impelled Gaius Caesar to the combined ruin of himself and of the state ? Renown, self-seeking, and the setting no limit to pre-eminence over all other men. He could not allow a single person to outrank him, although the state allowed two men to stand at its head. Do you think that Gaius Marius, who was once consul[f] (he received this office on one occasion, and stole it on all the others) courted all his perils by the inspiration of virtue when he was slaughtering the Teutons and the Cimbri, and pursuing Jugurtha through the wilds of Africa ?[g] Marius commanded armies, ambition Marius.

[f] 102 and 101 B.C. at Aquae Sextiae and Vercellae ; the Jugurthine war lasted from 109 to 106 B.C.

67 Isti cum omnia concuterent, concutiebantur turbinum more, qui rapta convolvunt, sed ipsi ante volvuntur et ob hoc maiore impetu incurrunt, quia nullum illis sui regimen est ideoque cum multis fuerunt malo, pestiferam illam vim, qua plerisque nocuerunt, ipsi quoque sentiunt. Non est quod credas quemquam fieri aliena infelicitate felicem.

68 Omnia ista exempla, quae oculis atque auribus nostris ingeruntur, retexenda sunt et plenum malis sermonibus pectus exhauriendum. Inducenda in occupatum locum virtus, quae mendacia et contra verum placentia exstirpet, quae nos a populo, cui nimis credimus, separet ac sinceris opinionibus reddat. Hoc est enim sapientia, in naturam converti et eo restitui,

69 unde publicus error expulerit. Magna pars sanitatis est hortatores insaniae reliquisse et ex isto coitu invicem noxio procul abisse.

Hoc ut esse verum scias, aspice, quanto aliter unusquisque populo vivat, aliter sibi. Non est per se magistra innocentiae solitudo nec frugalitatem docent rura, sed ubi testis ac spectator abscessit, vitia subsidunt, quorum monstrari et conspici fructus

70 est. Quis eam, quam nulli ostenderet, induit purpuram? Quis posuit secretam in auro dapem? Quis sub alicuius arboris rusticae proiectus umbra luxu-

---

[a] *i.e.*, as Pompeius, Caesar, Marius.

EPISTLE XCIV.

When such men as these^a were disturbing the
world, they were themselves disturbed—like cyclones
that whirl together what they have seized, but
which are first whirled themselves and can for this
reason rush on with all the greater force, having no
control over themselves ; hence, after causing such
destruction to others, they feel in their own body
the ruinous force which has enabled them to cause
havoc to many. You need never believe that a
man can become happy through the unhappiness of
another. We must unravel all such cases^a as are
forced before our eyes and crammed into our ears ;
we must clear out our hearts, for they are full
of evil talk. Virtue must be conducted into the
place these have seized,—a kind of virtue which may
root out falsehood and doctrines which contravene
the truth, or may sunder us from the throng, in
which we put too great trust, and may restore us
to the possession of sound opinions. For this is
wisdom—a return to Nature and a restoration to the
condition from which man's errors have driven us. It
is a great part of health to have forsaken the coun-
sellors of madness and to have fled far from a
companionship that is mutually baneful.

That you may know the truth of my remark, see
how different is each individual's life before the
public from that of his inner self. A quiet life does
not of itself give lessons in upright conduct; the
countryside does not of itself teach plain living ;
no, but when witnesses and onlookers are removed,
faults which ripen in publicity and display sink into
the background. Who puts on the purple robe for
the sake of flaunting it in no man's eyes ? Who uses
gold plate when he dines alone ? Who, as he flings
himself down beneath the shadow of some rustic tree,

THE EPISTLES OF SENECA

riae suae pompam solus explicuit ?   Nemo oculis suis
lautus est, ne paucorum quidem aut familiarium,
sed apparatum vitiorum suorum pro modo turbae
71 spectantis expandit. Ita est : inritamentum est
omnium, in quae insanimus, admirator et conscius.
Ne concupiscamus efficies, si ne ostendamus effeceris.
Ambitio et luxuria et inpotentia scaenam desiderant ;
sanabis ista, si absconderis.

72   Itaque si in medio urbium fremitu conlocati sumus,
stet ad latus monitor et contra laudatores ingentium
patrimoniorum laudet parvo divitem et usu opes
metientem.   Contra illos, qui gratiam ac potentiam
attollunt, otium ipse suspiciat traditum litteris et
73 animum ab externis ad sua reversum.   Ostendat ex
constitutione vulgi beatos in illo invidioso fastigio suo
trementes et adtonitos longeque aliam de se opinionem habentes quam ab aliis habetur.   Nam quae
aliis excelsa videntur, ipsis praerupta sunt.   Itaque
exanimantur et trepidant, quotiens despexerunt in
illud magnitudinis suae praeceps.   Cogitant enim
74 varios casus et in sublimi maxime lubricos.   Tunc
adpetita formidant et quae illos graves aliis reddit,
gravior ipsis felicitas incubat.   Tunc laudant otium
lene et sui iuris, odio est fulgor et fuga a rebus
adhuc stantibus quaeritur. Tunc demum videas
philosophantis metu [1] et aegrae fortunae sana con-

[1] *metu* Muretus ; *metus* BA.

56

displays in solitude the splendour of his luxury? No one makes himself elegant only for his own beholding, or even for the admiration of a few friends or relatives. Rather does he spread out his well-appointed vices in proportion to the size of the admiring crowd. It is so: claqueurs and witnesses are irritants of all our mad foibles. You can make us cease to crave, if you only make us cease to display. Ambition, luxury, and waywardness need a stage to act upon; you will cure all those ills if you seek retirement.

Therefore, if our dwelling is situated amid the din of a city, there should be an adviser standing near us. When men praise great incomes, he should praise the person who can be rich with a slender estate and measures his wealth by the use he makes of it. In the face of those who glorify influence and power, he should of his own volition recommend a leisure devoted to study, and a soul which has left the external and found itself. He should point out persons, happy in the popular estimation, who totter on their envied heights of power, who are dismayed and hold a far different opinion of themselves from what others hold of them. That which others think elevated, is to them a sheer precipice. Hence they are frightened and in a flutter whenever they look down the abrupt steep of their greatness. For they reflect that there are various ways of falling and that the topmost point is the most slippery. Then they fear that for which they strove, and the good fortune which made them weighty in the eyes of others weighs more heavily upon themselves. Then they praise easy leisure and independence; they hate the glamour and try to escape while their fortunes are still unimpaired. Then at last you may see them studying philosophy amid their fear, and

silia. Nam quasi ista inter se contraria sint, bona
fortuna et mens bona, ita melius in malis sapimus ;
secunda rectum auferunt. VALE.

XCV.

SENECA LVCILIO SVO SALVTEM

1 Petis a me, ut id, quod in diem suum dixeram
debere differri, repraesentem et scribam tibi, an haec
pars philosophiae, quam Graeci paraeneticen vocant,
nos praeceptivam dicimus, satis sit ad consummandam[1] sapientiam. Scio te in bonam partem
accepturum si negavero. Eo magis promitto et verbum publicum perire non patior : " postea noli
2 rogare, quod inpetrare nolueris." Interdum enim
enixe petimus id, quod recusaremus, si quis offerret.
Haec sive levitas est sive vernilitas, punienda est
annuendi[2] facilitate. Multa videri volumus velle,
sed nolumus. Recitator historiam ingentem attulit
minutissime scriptam, artissime plicatam, et magna
parte perlecta " desinam," inquit, " si vultis.[3] "
Adclamatur " recita, recita " ab iis, qui illum om-

---

[1] *consummandam* later MSS. ; *consum(m)endam* BA.
[2] *annuendi* Windhaus and Buecheler ; *mutendi* BA.
[3] *si vultis* later MSS. ; *si multis* B ; *simultis* A.

---

[a] Literally, to pay money on the spot or perform a task
without delay.
[b] *i.e.*, the department of " advice by precepts," discussed
in the preceding letter from another angle. The Greek
term is nearest to the Latin sub-division *hortatio*.
[c] *i.e.*, the pertness of a home-bred slave (*verna*).

hunting sound advice when their fortunes go awry. For these two things are, as it were, at opposite poles—good fortune and good sense ; that is why we are wiser when in the midst of adversity. It is prosperity that takes away righteousness. Farewell.

XCV. ON THE USEFULNESS OF BASIC PRINCIPLES

You keep asking me to explain without postponement [a] a topic which I once remarked should be put off until the proper time, and to inform you by letter whether this department of philosophy which the Greeks call *paraenetic*,[b] and we Romans call the " preceptorial," is enough to give us perfect wisdom. Now I know that you will take it in good part if I refuse to do so. But I accept your request all the more willingly, and refuse to let the common saying lose its point :

> Don't ask for what you'll wish you hadn't got.

For sometimes we seek with effort that which we should decline if offered voluntarily. Call that fickleness or call it pettishness,[c]—we must punish the habit by ready compliance. There are many things that we would have men think that we wish, but that we really do not wish. A lecturer sometimes brings upon the platform a huge work of research, written in the tiniest hand and very closely folded ; after reading off a large portion, he says : " I shall stop, if you wish ; " and a shout arises : " Read on, read on ! " from the lips of those who are anxious for the speaker to hold

59

mutescere illic cupiunt. Saepe aliud volumus, aliud
optamus et verum ne dis quidem dicimus, sed di aut
3 non exaudiunt aut miserentur. Ego me omissa
misericordia vindicabo et tibi ingentem epistulam
inpingam, quam tu si invitus leges, dicito: "ego
mihi hoc contraxi" teque inter illos numera, quos
uxor magno ducta ambitu torquet, inter illos, quos
divitiae per summum adquisitae sudorem male
habent, inter illos, quos honores nulla non arte
atque opera petiti discruciant, et ceteros malorum
suorum compotes.

4 Sed ut omisso principio rem ipsam adgrediar,
"beata," inquiunt, "vita constat ex actionibus rectis;
ad actiones rectas praecepta perducunt; ergo ad
beatam vitam praecepta sufficiunt." Non semper
ad actiones rectas praecepta perducunt, sed cum
obsequens ingenium est; aliquando frustra admoven-
5 tur, si animum opiniones obsident pravae. Deinde
etiam si recte faciunt, nesciunt facere se recte. Non
potest enim quisquam nisi ab initio formatus et tota
ratione compositus omnes exequi numeros, ut sciat,
quando oporteat et in quantum et cum quo et
quemadmodum et quare. Non potest toto animo honesta[1] conari, ne constanter quidem aut libenter,
sed respiciet, sed haesitabit.

6 "Si honesta," inquit, "actio ex praeceptis venit,
ad beatam vitam praecepta abunde sunt; atqui est[2]

---

[1] *animo honesta* Hense; *animo ad honesta* later MSS.;
animoteonesta BA.
[2] *atqui est* Pincianus; *atque* BA.

60

his peace then and there. We often want one thing and pray for another, not telling the truth even to the gods, while the gods either do not hearken, or else take pity on us. But I shall without pity avenge myself and shall load a huge letter upon your shoulders; for your part, if you read it with reluctance, you may say: "I brought this burden upon myself," and may class yourself among those men whose too ambitious wives drive them frantic, or those whom riches harass, earned by extreme sweat of the brow, or those who are tortured with the titles which they have sought by every sort of device and toil, and all others who are responsible for their own misfortunes.

But I must stop this preamble and approach the problem under consideration. Men say: "The happy life consists in upright conduct; precepts guide one to upright conduct; therefore precepts are sufficient for attaining the happy life." But they do not always guide us to upright conduct; this occurs only when the will is receptive; and sometimes they are applied in vain, when wrong opinions obsess the soul. Furthermore, a man may act rightly without knowing that he is acting rightly. For nobody, except he be trained from the start and equipped with complete reason, can develop to perfect proportions, understanding when he should do certain things, and to what extent, and in whose company, and how, and why. Without such training a man cannot strive with all his heart after that which is honourable, or even with steadiness or gladness, but will ever be looking back and wavering.

It is also said: "If honourable conduct results from precepts, then precepts are amply sufficient for the happy life; but the first of these statements is

61

illud, ergo et hoc." His respondebimus actiones
honestas et praeceptis fieri, non tantum praeceptis.
7 " Si aliae," inquit, " artes contentae sunt praeceptis,
contenta erit et sapientia, nam et haec ars vitae est.
Atqui gubernatorem facit ille, qui praecipit : sic
move gubernaculum, sic vela summitte, sic secundo
vento utere, sic adverso resiste, sic dubium com-
munemque tibi vindica. Alios quoque artifices praecepta conformant[1] ; ergo in hoc idem poterunt
8 artifice vivendi." Omnes istae artes circa instrumenta vitae occupatae sunt, non circa totam vitam.
Itaque multa illas inhibent extrinsecus et inpediunt,
spes, cupiditas, timor. At haec, quae artem vitae
professa est, nulla re, quo minus se exerceat, vetari
potest ; discutit enim inpedimenta et traicit[2] obstantia. Vis scire, quam dissimilis sit aliarum artium
condicio et huius ? In illis excusatius est voluntate
peccare quam casu, in hac maxima culpa est sponte
9 delinquere. Quod dico, tale est. Grammaticus non
erubescet soloecismo, si sciens fecit, erubescet, si
nesciens ; medicus si deficere aegrum non intellegit,
quantum ad artem, magis peccat quam si se intellegere dissimulat. At in hac arte vivendi turpior
volentium culpa est.

Adice nunc, quod artes quoque pleraeque, immo
ex omnibus liberalissimae habent decreta sua, non

---

[1] *conformant* Hermes and Gertz ; *confirmant* BA.
[2] *traicit* Bartsch ; *tractat* BA.

---

[a] The argument here is similar to *Ep.* lxxxviii. 20 *hae
. . . artes ad instrumenta vitae plurimum conferunt, tamen
ad virtutem non pertinent.*
[b] *i.e.,* philosophy.

EPISTLE XCV.

true ; therefore the second is true also." We shall
reply to these words that honourable conduct is, to
be sure, brought about by precepts, but not by
precepts alone. " Then," comes the reply, " if the
other arts are content with precepts, wisdom will
also be content therewith ; for wisdom itself is an
art of living. And yet the pilot is made by precepts
which tell him thus and so to turn the tiller, set his
sails, make use of a fair wind, tack, make the best
of shifting and variable breezes,—all in the proper
manner. Other craftsmen also are drilled by
precepts ; hence precepts will be able to accomplish
the same result in the case of our craftsman in the
art of living." Now all these arts are concerned
with the tools of life, but not with life as a whole.[a]
Hence there is much to clog these arts from without
and to complicate them—such as hope, greed, fear.
But that art[b] which professes to teach the art of
life cannot be forbidden by any circumstance from
exercising its functions ; for it shakes off complica-
tions and pierces through obstacles. Would you like
to know how unlike its status is to the other arts ?
In the case of the latter, it is more pardonable to err
voluntarily rather than by accident ; but in the case
of wisdom the worst fault is to commit sin wilfully.
I mean something like this : A scholar will blush for
shame, not if he makes a grammatical blunder intentionally, but if he makes it unintentionally ; if a
physician does not recognize that his patient is
failing, he is a much poorer practitioner than if he
recognizes the fact and conceals his knowledge. But
in this art of living a voluntary mistake is the more
shameful.

Furthermore, many arts, aye and the most liberal
of them all, have their special doctrines, and not mere

63

THE EPISTLES OF SENECA

tantum praecepta, sicut medicina. Itaque alia est
Hippocratis secta, alia Asclepiadis, alia Themisonis.
10 Praeterea nulla ars contemplativa sine decretis suis
est, quae Graeci vocant dogmata, nobis vel decreta
licet appellare vel scita vel placita, quae et in geo-
metria et in astronomia invenies. Philosophia autem
et contemplativa est et activa ; spectat simul agitque.
Erras enim, si tibi illam putas tantum terrestres
operas[1] promittere ; altius spirat. Totum, inquit,
mundum scrutor nec me intra contubernium mortale
contineo suadere vobis ac dissuadere contenta.
Magna me vocant supraque vos posita :

11   Nam tibi de summa caeli ratione deumque
        Disserere incipiam et rerum primordia pandam :
        Unde omnis natura creet res, auctet alatque,
        Quoque eadem rursus [2] natura perempta resolvat,

ut ait Lucretius. Sequitur ergo ut, cum contem-
12 plativa sit, habeat decreta sua. Quid ? Quod facienda quoque nemo rite obibit nisi is, cui ratio erit
tradita, qua in quaque re omnes officiorum numeros
exequi possit, quos non servabit, qui in rem praesentem[3] praecepta acceperit, non in omnem.[4] In-
becilla sunt per se et, ut ita dicam, sine radice, quae
partibus dantur. Decreta sunt, quae muniant, quae
securitatem nostram tranquillitatemque tueantur,
quae totam vitam totamque rerum naturam simul

        [1] *operas* later MSS. ; *opera* BA.
        [2] *quove eadem rursum* Lucr.
        [3] *in rem praesentem* Hermes ; *in rem* BA.
        [4] *omnem* later MSS. ; *omne* BA.

        [a] Hippocrates belonged to the " Clinical " School ;
        Asclepiades and his pupil Themison to the " Methodical."
        See Index of Proper Names.
        [b] "Axioms" and "postulates."
        [c] i. 54 ff.

precepts of advice—the medical profession, for
example. There are the different schools of Hippo-
crates, of Asclepiades, of Themison.[a] And besides,
no art that concerns itself with theories can exist
without its own doctrines; the Greeks call them
dogmas, while we Romans may use the term
" doctrines," or " tenets," or " adopted principles," [b]
—such as you will find in geometry or astronomy.
But philosophy is both theoretic and practical; it
contemplates and at the same time acts. You
are indeed mistaken if you think that philosophy
offers you nothing but worldly assistance; her aspira-
tions are loftier than that. She cries: " I investigate
the whole universe, nor am I content, keeping myself
within a mortal dwelling, to give you favourable
or unfavourable advice. Great matters invite and
such as are set far above you. In the words of
Lucretius: [c]

> To thee shall I reveal the ways of heaven
> And of the gods, spreading before thine eyes
> The atoms,—whence all things are brought to birth,
> Increased, and fostered by creative power,
> And eke their end when Nature casts them off.

Philosophy, therefore, being theoretic, must have
her doctrines. And why? Because no man can
duly perform right actions except one who has been
entrusted with reason, which will enable him, in all
cases, to fulfil all the categories of duty. These
categories he cannot observe unless he receives precepts for every occasion, and not for the present
alone. Precepts by themselves are weak and, so to
speak, rootless if they be assigned to the parts and
not to the whole. It is the doctrines which will
strengthen and support us in peace and calm, which
will include simultaneously the whole of life and the

65

contineant. Hoc interest inter decreta philosophiae et praecepta, quod inter elementa et membra ; haec ex illis dependent, illa et horum causae sunt et omnium.

13 " Antiqua," inquit, " sapientia nihil aliud quam facienda ac vitanda praecepit, et tunc longe meliores erant viri. Postquam docti prodierunt, boni desunt. Simplex enim illa et aperta virtus in obscuram et sollertem scientiam versa est docemurque disputare,

14 non vivere." Fuit sine dubio, ut dicitis, vetus illa sapientia cum maxime nascens rudis non minus quam ceterae artes, quarum in processu subtilitas crevit. Sed ne opus quidem adhuc erat remediis diligentibus. Nondum in tantum nequitia surrexerat nec tam late se sparserat. Poterant vitiis simplicibus obstare remedia simplicia ; nunc necesse est tanto operosiora esse munimenta, quanto vehementiora sunt, quibus

15 petimur. Medicina quondam paucarum fuit scientia herbarum, quibus sisteretur fluens sanguis, vulnera coirent ; paulatim deinde in hanc pervenit tam multi- plicem varietatem. Nec est mirum tunc illam minus negotii habuisse firmis adhuc solidisque corporibus et facili cibo nec per artem voluptatemque corrupto, qui postquam coepit non ad tollendam, sed ad inritandam famem quaeri et inventae sunt mille conditurae, quibus aviditas excitaretur, quae desiderantibus ali-

16 menta erant, onera sunt plenis. Inde pallor et nervorum vino madentium tremor et miserabilior ex cruditatibus quam ex fame macies. Inde incerti

---

ᵃ Whether *elementa* and *membra* mean " letters and clauses " or " matter and forms of matter " is difficult to say.

ᵇ *i.e.*, before the advent of any theoretical philosophy.

universe in its completeness. There is the same difference between philosophical doctrines and precepts as there is between elements and members [a]; the latter depend upon the former, while the former are the source both of the latter and of all things.

People say : " The old-style wisdom advised only what one should do and avoid ; [b] and yet the men of former days were better men by far. When savants have appeared, sages have become rare. For that frank, simple virtue has changed into hidden and crafty knowledge ; we are taught how to debate, not how to live." Of course, as you say, the old-fashioned wisdom, especially in its beginnings, was crude ; but so were the other arts, in which dexterity developed with progress. Nor indeed in those days was there yet any need for carefully-planned cures. Wickedness had not yet reached such a high point, or scattered itself so broadcast. Plain vices could be treated by plain cures ; now, however, we need defences erected with all the greater care, because of the stronger powers by which we are attacked. Medicine once consisted of the knowledge of a few simples, to stop the flow of blood, or to heal wounds ; then by degrees it reached its present stage of complicated variety. No wonder that in early days medicine had less to do ! Men's bodies were still sound and strong ; their food was light and not spoiled by art and luxury, whereas when they began to seek dishes not for the sake of removing, but of rousing, the appetite, and devised countless sauces to whet their gluttony,—then what before was nourishment to a hungry man became a burden to the full stomach. Thence come paleness, and a trembling of wine-sodden muscles, and a repulsive thinness, due rather to indigestion than to hunger. Thence weak tottering

THE EPISTLES OF SENECA

labantium[1] pedes et semper qualis in ipsa ebrietate
titubatio. Inde in totam cutem umor admissus dis-
tentusque venter, dum male adsuescit plus capere
quam poterat. Inde suffusio luridae bilis et decolor
vultus tabesque in se putrescentium et retorridi digiti
articulis obrigescentibus nervorumque sine sensu
iacentium torpor aut palpitatio[2] sine intermissione
17 vibrantium. Quid capitis vertigines dicam? Quid
oculorum auriumque tormenta et cerebri exaestuan-
tis verminationes et omnia, per quae exoneramur,
internis ulceribus adfecta? Innumerabilia praeterea
febrium genera, aliarum impetu saevientium, aliarum
tenui peste repentium, aliarum cum horrore et multa
18 membrorum quassatione venientium? Quid alios
referam innumerabiles morbos, supplicia luxuriae?

Immunes erant ab istis malis, qui nondum se
deliciis solverant, qui sibi imperabant, sibi mini-
strabant. Corpora opere ac vero labore durabant aut
cursu defatigati aut venatu aut tellure[3] versanda.[4]
Excipiebat illos cibus, qui nisi esurientibus placere
non posset. Itaque nihil opus erat tam magna
medicorum supellectile nec tot ferramentis atque
pyxidibus. Simplex erat ex causa simplici valitudo;
19 multos morbos multa fericula fecerunt. Vide, quantum rerum per unam gulam transiturarum permisceat
luxuria, terrarum marisque vastatrix. Necesse est
itaque inter se tam diversa dissideant et hausta male[5]

---

[1] *labantium* later MSS.; *labentium* BA.
[2] Muretus removed *corporum* after *palpitatio*: Buecheler
suggested *praecordiorum*, and Windhaus *cordum*.
[3] *tellure* later MSS.; *tollere* BA.
[4] *versanda* Windhaus; *versantia* BA.
[5] Gertz added another *male* to the text.

---

[a] *verminatio*, defined by Festus as *cum corpus quodam
minuto motu quasi a vermibus scindatur.*

steps, and a reeling gait just like that of drunkenness. Thence dropsy, spreading under the entire skin, and the belly growing to a paunch through an ill habit of taking more than it can hold. Thence yellow jaundice, discoloured countenances, and bodies that rot inwardly, and fingers that grow knotty when the joints stiffen, and muscles that are numbed and without power of feeling, and palpitation of the heart with its ceaseless pounding. Why need I mention dizziness? Or speak of pain in the eye and in the ear, itching and aching [a] in the fevered brain, and internal ulcers throughout the digestive system? Besides these, there are countless kinds of fever, some acute in their malignity, others creeping upon us with subtle damage, and still others which approach us with chills and severe ague. Why should I mention the other innumerable diseases, the tortures that result from high living?

Men used to be free from such ills, because they had not yet slackened their strength by indulgence, because they had control over themselves, and supplied their own needs.[b] They toughened their bodies by work and real toil, tiring themselves out by running or hunting or tilling the earth. They were refreshed by food in which only a hungry man could take pleasure. Hence, there was no need for all our mighty medical paraphernalia, for so many instruments and pill-boxes. For plain reasons they enjoyed plain health; it took elaborate courses to produce elaborate diseases. Mark the number of things —all to pass down a single throat—that luxury mixes together, after ravaging land and sea. So many different dishes must surely disagree; they are

[b] For this sort of Golden Age reminiscence see *Ep.* xc. 5 ff. (vol. ii. p. 397) and note.

male digerantur aliis alio nitentibus. Nec mirum, quod inconstans variusque ex discordi cibo morbus est et illa ex contrariis naturae partibus in eundem compulsa redundant. Inde tam multo[1] aegrotamus
20 genere quam vivimus. Maximus ille medicorum et huius scientiae conditor feminis nec capillos defluere dixit nec pedes laborare; atqui et capillis destituuntur et pedibus aegrae sunt. Non mutata feminarum natura, sed victa est; nam cum virorum licentiam aequaverint, corporum quoque virilium
21 incommoda aequarunt. Non minus pervigilant, non minus potant, et oleo et mero viros provocant; aeque invitis ingesta visceribus per os reddunt et vinum omne vomitu remetiuntur; aeque nivem rodunt, solacium stomachi aestuantis. Libidine vero ne maribus quidem cedunt, pati natae, di illas deaeque male perdant! Adeo perversum commentae genus inpudicitiae viros ineunt. Quid ergo mirandum est maximum medicorum ac naturae peritissimum in mendacio prendi, cum tot feminae podagricae calvaeque sint? Beneficium sexus sui vitiis perdiderunt et, quia feminam exuerant, damnatae sunt morbis virilibus.

22 Antiqui medici nesciebant dare cibum saepius et

---

[1] *multo* Haupt; *nullo* BA.

bolted with difficulty and are digested with difficulty, each jostling against the other. And no wonder, that diseases which result from ill-assorted food are variable and manifold; there must be an overflow when so many unnatural combinations are jumbled together. Hence there are as many ways of being ill as there are of living. The illustrious founder of the guild and profession of medicine *a* remarked that women never lost their hair or suffered from pain in the feet; and yet nowadays they run short of hair and are afflicted with gout. This does not mean that woman's physique has changed, but that it has been conquered; in rivalling male indulgences, they have also rivalled the ills to which men are heirs. They keep just as late hours, and drink just as much liquor; they challenge men in wrestling and carousing; they are no less given to vomiting from distended stomachs and to thus discharging all their wine again; nor are they behind the men in gnawing ice, as a relief to their fevered digestions. And they even match the men in their passions, although they were created to feel love passively (may the gods and goddesses confound them!). They devise the most impossible varieties of unchastity, and in the company of men they play the part of men. What wonder, then, that we can trip up the statement of the greatest and most skilled physician, when so many women are gouty and bald! Because of their vices, women have ceased to deserve the privileges of their sex; they have put off their womanly nature and are therefore condemned to suffer the diseases of men.

Physicians of old time knew nothing about prescribing frequent nourishment and propping the

71

vino fulcire venas cadentes, nesciebant sanguinem
mittere et diutinam aegrotationem balneo sudoribus-
que laxare, nesciebant crurum vinculo brachiorum-
que latentem vim et in medio sedentem ad
extrema revocare. Non erat necesse circumspicere
multa auxiliorum genera, cum essent periculorum
23 paucissima. Nunc vero quam longe processerunt
mala valitudinis! Has usuras voluptatium pendimus
ultra modum fasque concupitarum. Innumerabiles
esse morbos non miraberis: cocos numera. Cessat
omne studium et liberalia professi sine ulla frequentia
desertis angulis praesident. In rhetorum ac philosophorum scholis solitudo est; at quam celebres
culinae sunt, quanta circa nepotum focos iuventus
24 premitur! Transeo puerorum infelicium greges, quos
post transacta convivia aliae cubiculi contumeliae
exspectant. Transeo agmina exoletorum per nationes
coloresque discripta, ut eadem omnibus levitas sit,
eadem primae mensura lanuginis, eadem species
capillorum, ne quis, cui rectior est coma, crispulis
misceatur. Transeo pistorum turbam, transeo minis-
tratorum, per quos signo dato ad inferendam cenam
discurritur. Di boni, quantum hominum unus venter
exercet! Quid? Tu illos boletos, voluptarium venenum, nihil occulti operis iudicas facere, etiam si
25 praesentanei non fuerunt? Quid? Tu illam aesti-
vam nivem non putas callum iocineribus obducere?

ᵃ Mushrooms, as in the case of the Emperor Claudius,
were a frequent aid to secret murder.

feeble pulse with wine; they did not understand the practice of blood-letting and of easing chronic complaints with sweat-baths; they did not understand how, by bandaging ankles and arms, to recall to the outward parts the hidden strength which had taken refuge in the centre. They were not compelled to seek many varieties of relief, because the varieties of suffering were very few in number. Nowadays, however, to what a stage have the evils of ill-health advanced! This is the interest which we pay on pleasures which we have coveted beyond what is reasonable and right. You need not wonder that diseases are beyond counting: count the cooks! All intellectual interests are in abeyance; those who follow culture lecture to empty rooms, in out-of-the-way places. The halls of the professor and the philosopher are deserted; but what a crowd there is in the cafés! How many young fellows besiege the kitchens of their gluttonous friends! I shall not mention the troops of luckless boys who must put up with other shameful treatment after the banquet is over. I shall not mention the troops of catamites, rated according to nation and colour, who must all have the same smooth skin, and the same amount of youthful down on their cheeks, and the same way of dressing their hair, so that no boy with straight locks may get among the curly-heads. Nor shall I mention the medley of bakers, and the numbers of waiters who at a given signal scurry to carry in the courses. Ye gods! How many men are kept busy to humour a single belly! What? Do you imagine that those mushrooms, the epicure's poison, work no evil results in secret,[a] even though they have had no immediate effect? What? Do you suppose that your summer snow does not harden

Quid? Illa ostrea, inertissimam carnem caeno sagina-
tam, nihil existimas limosae gravitatis inferre?
Quid? Illud sociorum garum, pretiosam malorum
piscium saniem, non credis urere salsa tabe praecordia?
Quid? Illa purulenta et quae tantum non ex ipso
igne in os transferuntur, iudicas sine noxa in ipsis
visceribus extingui? Quam foedi itaque pestilentes-
que ructus sunt, quantum fastidium sui exhalan-
tibus crapulam veterem! Scias putrescere sumpta,
non concoqui.

26 Memini fuisse quondam in sermone nobilem
patinam, in quam quicquid apud lautos solet diem
ducere, properans in damnum suum popina con-
gesserat; veneriae spondylique et ostrea eatenus
circumcisa, qua eduntur, intervenientibus distingue-
bantur echinis. Totam dissecti structique[1] sine ullis
27 ossibus mulli constraverant. Piget esse iam singula;
coguntur in unum sapores. In cena fit, quod fieri
debebat[2] in ventre. Expecto iam, ut manducata
ponantur. Quantulo autem hoc minus est, testas
excerpere atque ossa et dentium opera cocum fungi?

"Gravest luxuriari per singula; omnia semel et
in eundem saporem versa ponantur. Quare ego ad
unam rem manum porrigam? Plura veniant simul,

---

[1] *dissecti structique* Buecheler; *destructique* BA.
[2] *debebat* Gertz; *debet saturo* BA.

a The finest variety of *garum* was made from Spanish
mackerel-roe.

the tissue of the liver? What? Do you suppose
that those oysters, a sluggish food fattened on slime,
do not weigh one down with mud-begotten heaviness?
What? Do you not think that the so-called "Sauce
from the Provinces," a the costly extract of poisonous
fish, burns up the stomach with its salted putrefaction?
What? Do you judge that the corrupted dishes
which a man swallows almost burning from the
kitchen fire, are quenched in the digestive system
without doing harm? How repulsive, then, and
how unhealthy are their belchings, and how disgusted
men are with themselves when they breathe forth
the fumes of yesterday's debauch! You may be
sure that their food is not being digested, but is
rotting.

I remember once hearing gossip about a notorious
dish into which everything over which epicures love
to dally had been heaped together by a cookshop
that was fast rushing into bankruptcy; there were
two kinds of mussels, and oysters trimmed round at
the line where they are edible, set off at intervals
by sea-urchins; the whole was flanked by mullets
cut up and served without the bones. In these
days we are ashamed of separate foods; people mix
many flavours into one. The dinner table does work
which the stomach ought to do. I look forward
next to food being served masticated! And how
little we are from it already when we pick out shells
and bones and the cook performs the office of the
teeth!

They say: "It is too much trouble to take our
luxuries one by one; let us have everything served
at the same time and blended into the same flavour.
Why should I help myself to a single dish? Let us
have many coming to the table at once; the dainties of

multorum ferculorum ornamenta coeant et cohaere-
28 ant.   Sciant protinus hi, qui iactationem ex istis peti
et gloriam aiebant, non ostendi ista, sed conscientiae
dari.   Pariter sint, quae disponi solent, uno iure
perfusa.   Nihil intersit : ostrea, echini, spondyli,
mulli perturbati concoctique ponantur."   Non esset
29 confusior vomentium cibus.   Quomodo ista perplexa
sunt, sic ex istis non singulares morbi nascuntur, sed
inexplicabiles, diversi, multiformes, adversus quos et
medicina armare se coepit multis generibus, multis
observationibus.

Idem tibi de philosophia dico.   Fuit aliquando sim-
plicior inter minora peccantes et levi quoque cura
remediabiles ; adversus tantam morum eversionem
omnia conanda sunt.   Et utinam sic denique lues
30 ista vindicetur !   Non privatim solum, sed publice
furimus.   Homicidia compescimus et singulas caedes ;
quid bella et occisarum gentium gloriosum scelus ?
Non avaritia, non crudelitas modum novit.   Et ista
quamdiu furtim et a singulis fiunt, minus noxia
minusque monstruosa sunt ;   ex senatus consultis
plebisque scitis saeva exercentur et publice iubentur
31 vetata privatim.   Quae clam commissa capite luerent,
tum quia paludati fecere, laudamus.   Non pudet [1]
homines, mitissimum genus, gaudere sanguine alterno

---

[1] *pudet* later MSS. ; *putet* BA.

various courses should be combined and confounded. Those who used to declare that this was done for display and notoriety should understand that it is not done for show, but that it is an oblation to our sense of duty! Let us have at one time, drenched in the same sauce, the dishes that are usually served separately. Let there be no difference: let oysters, sea-urchins, shell-fish, and mullets be mixed together and cooked in the same dish." No vomited food could be jumbled up more helter-skelter. And as the food itself is complicated, so the resulting diseases are complex, unaccountable, manifold, variegated; medicine has begun to campaign against them in many ways and by many rules of treatment.

Now I declare to you that the same statement applies to philosophy. It was once more simple because men's sins were on a smaller scale, and could be cured with but slight trouble; in the face, however, of all this moral topsy-turvy men must leave no remedy untried. And would that this pest might so at last be overcome! We are mad, not only individually, but nationally. We check manslaughter and isolated murders; but what of war and the much-vaunted crime of slaughtering whole peoples? There are no limits to our greed, none to our cruelty. And as long as such crimes are committed by stealth and by individuals, they are less harmful and less portentous; but cruelties are practised in accordance with acts of senate and popular assembly, and the public is bidden to do that which is forbidden to the individual. Deeds that would be punished by loss of life when committed in secret, are praised by us because uniformed generals have carried them out. Man, naturally the gentlest class of being, is not ashamed to revel in the blood of others, to wage

77

et bella gerere gerendaque liberis tradere, cum inter
32 se etiam mutis ac feris pax sit. Adversus tam potentem explicitumque late furorem operosior philosophia facta est et tantum sibi virium sumpsit,
quantum iis, adversus quae parabatur, accesserat.

Expeditum erat obiurgare indulgentes mero et
petentes delicatiorem cibum; non erat animus ad
frugalitatem magna vi reducendus, a qua paullum
discesserat :

33   Nunc manibus rapidis opus est, nunc arte magistra.

Voluptas ex omni quaeritur. Nullum intra se manet
vitium; in avaritiam luxuria praeceps est. Honesti
oblivio invasit. Nihil turpest, cuius placet pretium.
Homo, sacra res homini, iam per lusum ac iocum
occiditur et quem erudiri ad inferenda accipiendaque
vulnera nefas erat, is iam nudus inermisque producitur satisque spectaculi ex homine mors est.

34   In hac ergo morum perversitate desideratur solito
vehementius aliquid, quod mala inveterata discutiat ;
decretis agendum est, ut revellatur penitus falsorum
recepta persuasio. His si adiunxerimus praecepta,
consolationes, adhortationes, poterunt valere ; per
35 se inefficaces sunt. Si volumus habere obligatos et
malis, quibus iam tenentur, avellere, discant, quid
malum, quid bonum sit. Sciant omnia praeter virtu-

ᵃ Vergil, *Aen.* viii. 442.

war, and to entrust the waging of war to his sons, when even dumb beasts and wild beasts keep the peace with one another. Against this overmastering and widespread madness philosophy has become a matter of greater effort, and has taken on strength in proportion to the strength which is gained by the opposition forces.

It used to be easy to scold men who were slaves to drink and who sought out more luxurious food ; it did not require a mighty effort to bring the spirit back to the simplicity from which it had departed only slightly. But now

> One needs the rapid hand, the master-craft.[a]

Men seek pleasure from every source. No vice remains within its limits ; luxury is precipitated into greed. We are overwhelmed with forgetfulness of that which is honourable. Nothing that has an attractive value, is base. Man, an object of reverence in the eyes of man, is now slaughtered for jest and sport ; and those whom it used to be unholy to train for the purpose of inflicting and enduring wounds, are thrust forth exposed and defenceless ; and it is a satisfying spectacle to see a man made a corpse.

Amid this upset condition of morals, something stronger than usual is needed,—something which will shake off these chronic ills ; in order to root out a deep-seated belief in wrong ideas, conduct must be regulated by doctrines. It is only when we add precepts, consolation, and encouragement to these, that they can prevail ; by themselves they are ineffective. If we would hold men firmly bound and tear them away from the ills which clutch them fast, they must learn what is evil and what is good. They must know

79

tem mutare nomen, modo mala fieri, modo bona.
Quemadmodum primum militiae vinculum est religio
et signorum amor et deserendi nefas, tunc deinde
facile cetera exiguntur mandanturque iusiurandum
adactis, ita in iis, quos velis ad beatam vitam perducere : prima fundamenta iacienda sunt et insinu-
anda virtus. Huius quadam superstitione teneantur ;
hanc ament ; cum hac vivere velint, sine hac nolint.

36 " Quid ergo ? Non quidam sine institutione subtili
evaserunt probi magnosque profectus adsecuti sunt,
dum nudis tantum praeceptis obsecuntur ? " Fateor,
sed felix illis ingenium fuit et salutaria in transitu
rapuit. Nam ut di inmortales nullam didicere virtutem cum omni editi et pars naturae eorum est bonos
esse, ita quidam ex hominibus egregiam sortiti
indolem in ea, quae tradi solent, perveniunt sine
longo magisterio et honesta complexi sunt, cum
primum audiere ; unde ista tam rapacia virtutis
ingenia vel ex se fertilia. Illis autem[1] hebetibus et
optusis aut mala consuetudine obsessis diu robigo
37 animorum effricanda est. Ceterum, ut illos in bonum
pronos citius educit ad summa, et hos inbecilliores
adiuvabit malisque opinionibus extrahet, qui illis
philosophiae placita tradiderit ; quae quam sint

---

[1] *illis autem* cod. Harl. ; *et illis aut* BA.

[a] *Cf. Ep.* xxxvii. 2 *uri, vinciri, ferroque necari* and note.
[b] *i.e.*, not reinforced by general dogmas.

that everything except virtue changes its name and becomes now good and now bad. Just as the soldier's primary bond of union is his oath of allegiance and his love for the flag, and a horror of desertion, and just as, after this stage, other duties can easily be demanded of him, and trusts given to him when once the oath *a* has been administered ; so it is with those whom you would bring to the happy life : the first foundations must be laid, and virtue worked into these men. Let them be held by a sort of superstitious worship of virtue ; let them love her ; let them desire to live with her, and refuse to live without her.

" But what, then," people say, " have not certain persons won their way to excellence without complicated training ? Have they not made great progress by obeying bare precepts alone *b* ? " Very true ; but their temperaments were propitious, and they snatched salvation as it were by the way. For just as the immortal gods did not learn virtue— having been born with virtue complete, and containing in their nature the essence of goodness — even so certain men are fitted with unusual qualities and reach without a long apprenticeship that which is ordinarily a matter of teaching, welcoming honourable things as soon as they hear them. Hence come the choice minds which seize quickly upon virtue, or else produce it from within themselves. But your dull, sluggish fellow, who is hampered by his evil habits, must have this soul-rust incessantly rubbed off. Now, as the former sort, who are inclined towards the good, can be raised to the heights more quickly : so the weaker spirits will be assisted and freed from their evil opinions if we entrust to them the accepted principles of philosophy ; and you may understand how

necessaria, sic licet [1] videas. Quaedam insident nobis, quae nos ad alia pigros, ad alia temerarios faciunt. Nec haec audacia reprimi potest nec illa inertia suscitari, nisi causae eorum eximuntur, falsa admiratio et falsa formido. Haec nos quamdiu possident, dicas licet : " Hoc patri praestare debes, hoc liberis, hoc amicis, hoc hospitibus ; " temptantem avaritia retinebit. Sciet pro patria pugnandum esse, dissuadebit timor ; sciet pro amicis desudandum esse ad extremum usque sudorem,[2] sed deliciae vetabunt ; sciet in uxore gravissimum esse genus iniuriae paelicem, sed illum libido in contraria inpinget.[3]

38 Nihil ergo proderit dare praecepta, nisi prius amoveris obstatura praeceptis, non magis quam proderit arma in conspectu posuisse propiusque admovisse, nisi usurae manus expediuntur. Ut ad praecepta, quae damus, possit animus ire, solvendus

39 est. Putemus aliquem facere, quod oportet ; non faciet adsidue, non faciet aequaliter : nesciet enim, quare faciat. Aliqua vel casu vel exercitatione exibunt recta, sed non erit in manu regula, ad quam exigantur, cui credat recta esse, quae fecit. Non promittet se talem in perpetuum, qui bonus casu [4]

40 est. Deinde praestabunt tibi fortasse praecepta ut

---

[1] *sic licet* Haase ; *scilicet* BA.

[2] We retain *usque sudorem*, the reading of A, in spite of the objections of Gruter and others.

[3] *impinget* Erasmus ; *inpingit* BA.

[4] *casu* later MSS. ; *casus* BA.

essential these principles are in the following way. Certain things sink into us, rendering us sluggish in some ways, and hasty in others. These two qualities, the one of recklessness and the other of sloth, cannot be respectively checked or roused unless we remove their causes, which are mistaken admiration and mistaken fear. As long as we are obsessed by such feelings, you may say to us : " You owe this duty to your father, this to your children, this to your friends, this to your guests " ; but greed will always hold us back, no matter how we try. A man may know that he should fight for his country, but fear will dissuade him. A man may know that he should sweat forth his last drop of energy on behalf of his friends, but luxury will forbid. A man may know that keeping a mistress is the worst kind of insult to his wife, but lust will drive him in the opposite direction. It will therefore be of no avail to give precepts unless you first remove the conditions that are likely to stand in the way of precepts ; it will do no more good than to place weapons by your side and bring yourself near the foe without having your hands free to use those weapons. The soul, in order to deal with the precepts which we offer, must first be set free. Suppose that a man is acting as he should ; he cannot keep it up continuously or consistently, since he will not know the reason for so acting. Some of his conduct will result rightly because of luck or practice ; but there will be in his hand no rule by which he may regulate his acts, and which he may trust to tell him whether that which he has done is right. One who is good through mere chance will not give promise of retaining such a character for ever. Furthermore, precepts will perhaps help you to do what should be done ; but

THE EPISTLES OF SENECA

quod oportet faciat, non praestabunt ut quemadmodum oportet ; si hoc non praestant, ad virtutem non perducunt. Faciet quod oportet monitus, concedo ; sed id parum est, quoniam quidem non in facto laus
41 est, sed in eo, quemadmodum fiat. Quid est cena sumptuosa flagitiosius et equestrem censum consumente ? Quid tam dignum censoria nota, si quis, ut isti ganeones loquuntur, sibi hoc et genio suo praestet ? Et deciens[1] tamen sestertio aditiales cenae frugalissimis viris constiterunt. Eadem res, si gulae datur, turpis est; si honori, reprensionem effugit. Non enim luxuria, sed inpensa sollemnis est.
42 Mullum ingentis formae—quare autem non pondus adicio et aliquorum gulam inrito ? quattuor pondo et selibram fuisse aiebant—Tiberius Caesar missum sibi cum in macellum deferri et veniri iussisset : " amici," inquit, " omnia me fallunt, nisi istum mullum aut Apicius emerit aut P. Octavius." Ultra spem illi coniectura processit : liciti sunt, vicit Octavius et ingentem consecutus est inter suos gloriam, cum quinque sestertiis emisset piscem, quem Caesar vendiderat, ne Apicius quidem emerat. Numerare tantum Octavio fuit turpe, non illi,[2] qui emerat, ut Tiberio mitteret, quamquam illum quoque reprenderim ; admiratus est rem, qua putavit Caesarem dignum.

[1] *deciens* Hermes ; *docens* BA.
[2] *non illi* Pincianus ; *nam ille* BA.

---

[a] The *nota* was the mark of disgrace which the censor registered when he struck a man's name off the list of senators or knights.
[b] The *genius* was properly a man's *alter ego* or " better self " : every man had his *genius*. For the colloquial use compare the " indulge genio " of the Roman poets.
[c] See Index of Proper Names.

they will not help you to do it in the proper way;
and if they do not help you to this end, they do not
conduct you to virtue. I grant you that, if warned,
a man will do what he should ; but that is not enough,
since the credit lies, not in the actual deed, but in
the way it is done. What is more shameful than a
costly meal which eats away the income even of a
knight ? Or what so worthy of the censor's condemnation [a] as to be always indulging oneself and
one's " inner man," [b] if I may speak as the gluttons
do ? And yet often has an inaugural dinner cost
the most careful man a cool million ! The very sum
that is called disgraceful if spent on the appetite,
is beyond reproach if spent for official purposes!
For it is not luxury but an expenditure sanctioned
by custom.

A mullet of monstrous size was presented to the
Emperor Tiberius. They say it weighed four and
one half pounds (and why should I not tickle the
palates of certain epicures by mentioning its
weight ?). Tiberius ordered it to be sent to the
fish-market and put up for sale, remarking : " I
shall be taken entirely by surprise, my friends, if
either Apicius [c] or P. Octavius [c] does not buy that
mullet." The guess came true beyond his expectation : the two men bid, and Octavius won, thereby
acquiring a great reputation among his intimates
because he had bought for five thousand sesterces
a fish which the Emperor had sold, and which even
Apicius did not succeed in buying. To pay such a
price was disgraceful for Octavius, but not for the
individual who purchased the fish in order to present
it to Tiberius,—though I should be inclined to blame
the latter as well ; but at any rate he admired a
gift of which he thought Caesar worthy.

43   Amico aliquis aegro adsidet : probamus. At hoc hereditatis causa facit : vultur est, cadaver expectat. Eadem aut turpia sunt aut honesta ; refert, quare aut quemadmodum fiant. Omnia autem honesta fient, si honesto nos addixerimus idque unum in rebus humanis bonum iudicaverimus quaeque ex eo sunt ;
44 cetera in diem bona sunt. Ergo infigi debet persuasio ad totam pertinens vitam : hoc est, quod decretum voco. Qualis haec persuasio fuerit, talia erunt, quae agentur, quae cogitabuntur. Qualia autem haec fuerint, talis vita erit. In particulas suasisse totum
45 ordinanti parum est. M. Brutus in eo libro, quem περὶ καθήκοντος inscripsit, dat multa praecepta et parentibus et liberis et fratribus ; haec nemo faciet quemadmodum debet, nisi habuerit quo referat.[1] Proponamus oportet finem summi boni, ad quem nitamur, ad quem omne factum nostrum dictumque respiciat ; veluti navigantibus ad aliquod sidus
46 derigendus est cursus. Vita sine proposito vaga est : quod si utique proponendum est, incipiunt necessaria esse decreta. Illud, ut puto, concedes, nihil esse turpius dubio et incerto ac timide [2] pedem referente. Hoc in omnibus rebus accidet nobis, nisi [3] eximuntur, quae reprendunt [4] animos et detinent et periclitari conarique [5] totos vetant.
47   Quomodo sint di colendi, solet praecipi. Accendere aliquem lucernas sabbatis prohibeamus, quoniam

----

[1] *referat* Muretus ; *perferat* BA.
[2] *ac timide* Bartsch ; *actimido* BA.
[3] *nisi* later MSS. ; om. BA.
[4] *reprendunt* later MSS. ; *reppendunt* BA.
[5] *periclitari conarique* Hense ; *et preconarique* BA.

----

[a] A frequent vice under the Empire, nicknamed *captatio*.
[b] Περὶ καθήκοντος,—a subject handled by Panaetius, and by Cicero (*De Officiis*).

EPISTLE XCV.

When people sit by the bedsides of their sick friends, we honour their motives. But when people do this for the purpose of attaining a legacy,[a] they are like vultures waiting for carrion. The same act may be either shameful or honourable : the purpose and the manner make all the difference. Now each of our acts will be honourable if we declare allegiance to honour and judge honour and its results to be the only good that can fall to man's lot ; for other things are only temporarily good. I think, then, that there should be deeply implanted a firm belief which will apply to life as a whole : this is what I call a " doctrine." And as this belief is, so will be our acts and our thoughts. As our acts and our thoughts are, so will our lives be. It is not enough, when a man is arranging his existence as a whole, to give him advice about details. Marcus Brutus, in the book which he has entitled *Concerning Duty,*[b] gives many precepts to parents, children, and brothers; but no one will do his duty as he ought, unless he has some principle to which he may refer his conduct. We must set before our eyes the goal of the Supreme Good, towards which we may strive, and to which all our acts and words may have reference—just as sailors must guide their course according to a certain star. Life without ideals is erratic : as soon as an ideal is to be set up, doctrines begin to be necessary. I am sure you will admit that there is nothing more shameful than uncertain and wavering conduct, than the habit of timorous retreat. This will be our experience in all cases unless we remove that which checks the spirit and clogs it, and keeps it from making an attempt and trying with all its might.

Precepts are commonly given as to how the gods should be worshipped. But let us forbid lamps to

87

nec lumine di egent et ne homines quidem delec-
tantur fuligine. Vetemus salutationibus matutinis
fungi et foribus adsidere templorum; humana ambitio istis officiis capitur, deum colit qui novit. Vetemus lintea et strigiles Iovi ferre et speculum tenere
Iunoni; non quaerit ministros deus. Quidni? Ipse
humano generi ministrat, ubique et omnibus praesto
est. Audiat licet, quem modum servare in sacrificiis
debeat, quam procul resilire a molestis superstitioni-
bus, numquam satis profectum erit, nisi qualem debet
deum mente conceperit, omnia habentem, omnia
tribuentem, beneficum [1] gratis. Quae causa est dis
49 bene faciendi? Natura. Errat, si quis illos putat
nocere nolle; non possunt. Nec accipere iniuriam
queunt nec facere; laedere etenim laedique coniunc-
tum est. Summa illa ac pulcherrima omnium natura
quos periculo exemit, ne periculosos quidem fecit.

50   Primus est deorum cultus deos credere; deinde
reddere illis maiestatem suam, reddere bonitatem,
sine qua nulla maiestas est. Scire illos esse, qui
praesident mundo, qui universa vi sua temperant,
qui humani generis tutelam gerunt interdum incuriosi [2] singulorum. Hi nec dant malum nec habent;
ceterum castigant quosdam et coercent et inrogant

---

[1] *beneficum* cod. Velz., also Windhaus and Madvig;
beneficium BA.
[2] *incuriosi* Madvig; *curiosi* BA.

---

[a] *i.e.*, the significant features of athletics and adornment
for men and women respectively.

be lighted on the Sabbath, since the gods do not
need light, neither do men take pleasure in soot.
Let us forbid men to offer morning salutation and
to throng the doors of temples ; mortal ambitions
are attracted by such ceremonies, but God is
worshipped by those who truly know Him   Let us
forbid bringing towels and flesh-scrapers to Jupiter,
and proffering mirrors to Juno ; [a] for God seeks no
servants. Of course not ; he himself does service to
mankind, everywhere and to all he is at hand to
help. Although a man hear what limit he should
observe in sacrifice, and how far he should recoil
from burdensome superstitions, he will never make
sufficient progress until he has conceived a right idea
of God,—regarding Him as one who possesses all
things, and allots all things, and bestows them without
price. And what reason have the gods for doing
deeds of kindness ? It is their nature. One who
thinks that they are unwilling to do harm, is wrong ;
they *cannot* do harm. They cannot receive or inflict
injury ; for doing harm is in the same category as
suffering harm. The universal nature, all-glorious
and all-beautiful, has rendered incapable of inflicting
ill those whom it has removed from the danger of
ill.

The first way to worship the gods is to believe in
the gods ; the next to acknowledge their majesty,
to acknowledge their goodness without which there
is no majesty. Also, to know that they are supreme
commanders in the universe, controlling all things
by their power and acting as guardians of the human
race, even though they are sometimes unmindful of
the individual. They neither give nor have evil ; but
they do chasten and restrain certain persons, and
impose penalties, and sometimes punish by bestowing

89

poenas et aliquando specie boni puniunt. Vis deos propitiare ? Bonus esto. Satis illos coluit, quisquis imitatus est.

51 Ecce altera quaestio, quomodo hominibus sit utendum. Quid agimus ? Quae damus praecepta ? Ut parcamus sanguini humano ? Quantulum est ei non nocere, cui debeas prodesse ! Magna scilicet laus est, si homo mansuetus homini est. Praecipiemus, ut naufrago manum porrigat, erranti viam monstret, cum esuriente panem suum dividat ? Quando omnia, quae praestanda ac vitanda sunt, dicam, cum possim breviter hanc illi formulam humani

52 officii tradere : omne hoc, quod vides, quo divina atque humana conclusa sunt, unum est ; membra sumus corporis magni. Natura nos cognatos edidit, cum ex isdem et in eadem gigneret. Haec nobis amorem indidit mutuum et sociabiles fecit. Illa aequum iustumque composuit ; ex illius constitutione miserius est nocere quam laedi. Ex illius im-

53 perio paratae sint iuvandis manus. Ille versus et in pectore et in ore sit :

Homo sum, humani nihil a me alienum puto.

Habeamus in commune ; nati sumus. Societas nostra lapidum fornicationi simillima est, quae casura, nisi in vicem obstarent, hoc ipso sustinetur.

54 Post deos hominesque dispiciamus, quomodo rebus

---

* Terence, *Heautontimorumenos*, 77.

that which seems good outwardly. Would you win over the gods? Then be a good man. Whoever imitates them, is worshipping them sufficiently.

Then comes the second problem,—how to deal with men. What is our purpose? What precepts do we offer? Should we bid them refrain from bloodshed? What a little thing it is not to harm one whom you ought to help! It is indeed worthy of great praise, when man treats man with kindness! Shall we advise stretching forth the hand to the shipwrecked sailor, or pointing out the way to the wanderer, or sharing a crust with the starving? Yes, if I can only tell you first everything which ought to be afforded or withheld; meantime, I can lay down for mankind a rule, in short compass, for our duties in human relationships: all that you behold, that which comprises both god and man, is one—we are the parts of one great body. Nature produced us related to one another, since she created us from the same source and to the same end. She engendered in us mutual affection, and made us prone to friendships. She established fairness and justice; according to her ruling, it is more wretched to commit than to suffer injury. Through her orders, let our hands be ready for all that needs to be helped. Let this verse be in your heart and on your lips:

> I am a man; and nothing in man's lot
> Do I deem foreign to me.[a]

Let us possess things in common; for birth is ours in common. Our relations with one another are like a stone arch, which would collapse if the stones did not mutually support each other, and which is upheld in this very way.

Next, after considering gods and men, let us see

sit utendum. In supervacuum praecepta iactavimus, nisi illud praecesserit, qualem de quacumque re habere debeamus opinionem, de paupertate de divitiis, de gloria de ignominia, de patria de exilio. Aestimemus singula fama remota et quaeramus, quid sint, non quid vocentur.

55 Ad virtutes transeamus. Praecipiet aliquis, ut prudentiam magni aestimemus, ut fortitudinem complectamur, iustitiam, si fieri potest, propius etiam quam ceteras nobis adplicemus. Sed nil aget, si ignoramus, quid sit virtus, una sit an plures, separatae aut innexae, an qui unam habet et ceteras habeat,

56 quo inter se differant. Non est necesse fabro de fabrica quaerere, quod eius initium, quis usus sit, non magis quam pantomimo de arte saltandi ; omnes istae artes si se sciunt,[1] nihil deest ; non enim ad totam pertinent vitam. Virtus et aliorum scientia est et sui ; discendum de ipsa est, ut ipsa discatur.

57 Actio recta non erit, nisi recta fuerit voluntas, ab hac enim est actio. Rursus voluntas non erit recta, nisi habitus animi rectus fuerit, ab hoc enim est voluntas. Habitus porro animi non erit in optimo, nisi totius vitae leges perceperit et quid de quoque iudicandum sit, exegerit, nisi res ad verum redegerit. Non contingit tranquillitas nisi inmutabile certumque iudi-

---

[1] *istae artes si se sciunt* Haupt ; *ista certa esse sciunt* BA.

how we should make use of things. It is useless for us to have mouthed out precepts, unless we begin by reflecting what opinion we ought to hold concerning everything—concerning poverty, riches, renown, disgrace, citizenship, exile. Let us banish rumour and set a value upon each thing, asking what it is and not what it is called.

Now let us turn to a consideration of the virtues. Some persons will advise us to rate prudence very high, to cherish bravery, and to cleave more closely, if possible, to justice than to all other qualities. But this will do us no good if we do not know what virtue is, whether it is simple or compound, whether it is one or more than one, whether its parts are separate or interwoven with one another; whether he who has one virtue possesses the other virtues also; and just what are the distinctions between them. The carpenter does not need to inquire about his art in the light of its origin or of its function, any more than a pantomime need inquire about the art of dancing; if these arts understand themselves, nothing is lacking, for they do not refer to life as a whole. But virtue means the knowledge of other things besides herself: if we would learn virtue we must learn all about virtue. Conduct will not be right unless the will to act is right; for this is the source of conduct. Nor, again, can the will be right without a right attitude of mind; for this is the source of the will. Furthermore, such an attitude of mind will not be found even in the best of men unless he has learned the laws of life as a whole and has worked out a proper judgment about everything, and unless he has reduced facts to a standard of truth. Peace of mind is enjoyed only by those who have attained a fixed and unchanging

cium adeptis ; ceteri decidunt subinde et reponuntur
et inter missa adpetitaque alternis fluctuantur.
58 Causa his [1] quae iactationis est? Quod nihil liquet
incertissimo regimine utentibus, fama. Si vis eadem
semper velle, vera oportet velis. Ad verum sine
decretis non pervenitur ; continent vitam. Bona et
mala, honesta et turpia, iusta et iniusta, pia et impia,
virtutes ususque virtutum, rerum commodarum
possessio, existimatio ac dignitas,[2] valitudo, vires,
forma, sagacitas [3] sensuum ; haec omnia aestima-
torem desiderant. Scire liceat, quanti quidque in
59 censum deferendum sit. Falleris enim et pluris
quaedam quam sunt putas, adeoque falleris, ut,
quae maximi inter nos habentur, divitiae, gratia,
potentia, sestertio nummo aestimanda sint.

Hoc nescies, nisi constitutionem ipsam, qua ista
inter se aestimantur, inspexeris. Quemadmodum
folia per se virere non possunt, ramum desiderant,
cui inhaereant, ex quo trahant sucum ; sic ista
praecepta, si sola sunt, marcent ; infigi volunt sectae.
60 Praeterea non intellegunt hi, qui decreta tollunt, eo
ipso confirmari illa, quo tolluntur. Quid enim dicunt?
Praeceptis vitam satis explicari, supervacua esse
decreta sapientiae, id est dogmata. Atqui hoc

---

[1] *causa his* Gertz ; *causarisque* BA.
[2] *dignitas* later MSS. ; *dignitatis* BA.
[3] *sagacitas* later MSS. ; *sagittas* or *sanitas* BA.

---

a Cf. Ep. xciv. 12 and note.

standard of judgment; the rest of mankind continually ebb and flow in their decisions, floating in a condition where they alternately reject things and seek them And what is the reason for this tossing to and fro ? It is because nothing is clear to them, because they make use of a most unsure criterion—rumour. If you would always desire the same things,[a] you must desire the truth. But one cannot attain the truth without doctrines ; for doctrines embrace the whole of life. Things good and evil, honourable and disgraceful, just and unjust, dutiful and undutiful, the virtues and their practice, the possession of comforts, worth and respect, health, strength, beauty, keenness of the senses—all these qualities call for one who is able to appraise them. One should be allowed to know at what value every object is to be rated on the list ; for sometimes you are deceived and believe that certain things are worth more than their real value ; in fact, so badly are you deceived that you will find you should value at a mere pennyworth those things which we men regard as worth most of all—for example, riches, influence, and power.

You will never understand this unless you have investigated the actual standard by which such conditions are relatively rated. As leaves cannot flourish by their own efforts, but need a branch to which they may cling and from which they may draw sap, so your precepts, when taken alone, wither away ; they must be grafted upon a school of philosophy. Moreover, those who do away with doctrines do not understand that these doctrines are proved by the very arguments through which they seem to disprove them. For what are these men saying ? They are saying that precepts are sufficient to develop life, and that the doctrines of wisdom (in other words, dogmas) are

THE EPISTLES OF SENECA

ipsum, quod dicunt, decretum est tam me hercules [1]
quam si nunc ego dicerem recedendum a praeceptis
velut supervacuis, utendum esse decretis, in haec
sola studium conferendum ; hoc ipso, quo negarem
61 curanda esse praecepta, praeciperem. Quaedam ad-
monitionem in philosophia desiderant, quaedam
probationem et quidem multam,[2] quia involuta sunt
vixque summa diligentia ac summa subtilitate ape-
riuntur. Si probationes necessariae sunt, et decreta,
quae veritatem argumentis colligunt. Quaedam
aperta sunt, quaedam obscura : aperta, quae sensu
conprehenduntur, quae memoria ; obscura, quae
extra haec sunt.

Ratio autem non impletur manifestis ; maior eius
pars pulchriorque in occultis est. Occulta probationem exigunt, probatio non sine decretis est ;
62 necessaria ergo decreta sunt. Quae res communem
sensum facit, eadem perfectum, certa rerum [3] persuasio ; sine qua si omnia in animo natant, necessaria
sunt decreta, quae dant animis inflexibile iudicium.
63 Denique cum monemus aliquem, ut amicum eodem
habeat loco, quo se, ut ex inimico cogitet fieri
posse amicum, in illo amorem incitet, in hoc odium
moderetur, adicimus : " iustum est et honestum."
Iustum autem honestumque decretorum nostrorum
continet ratio ; ergo haec necessaria est, sine qua
64 nec illa sunt. Sed utrumque iungamus. Namque

---

[1] *tam me hercules* cod. Velz. ; *tam hercules* BA.
[2] *multam* Madvig ; *multa* BA.
[3] *certa rerum* Schweighaeuser ; *certarum* and *certum* BA.

---

[a] *i.e.*, progressing from a φαντασία in general to a φαντασία
καταληπτική.
[b] Seneca characteristically ignores the unpleasant half of
the proverb : φιλεῖν ὡς μισήσων καὶ μισεῖν ὡς φιλήσων.

superfluous. And yet this very utterance of theirs is a doctrine,—just as if I should now remark that one must dispense with precepts on the ground that they are superfluous, that one must make use of doctrines, and that our studies should be directed solely towards this end ; thus, by my very statement that precepts should not be taken seriously, I should be uttering a precept. There are certain matters in philosophy which need admonition ; there are others which need proof, and a great deal of proof, too, because they are complicated and can scarcely be made clear with the greatest care and the greatest dialectic skill. If proofs are necessary, so are doctrines ; for doctrines deduce the truth by reasoning. Some matters are clear, and others are vague : those which the senses and the memory can embrace are clear ; those which are outside their scope are vague.

But reason is not satisfied by obvious facts ; its higher and nobler function is to deal with hidden things. Hidden things need proof ; proof cannot come without doctrines ; therefore, doctrines are necessary. That which leads to a general agreement, and likewise to a perfect one,[a] is an assured belief in certain facts ; but if, lacking this assurance, all things are adrift in our minds, then doctrines are indispensable ; for they give to our minds the means of unswerving decision. Furthermore, when we advise a man to regard his friends as highly as himself, to reflect that an enemy may become a friend,[b] to stimulate love in the friend, and to check hatred in the enemy, we add : "This is just and honourable." Now the just and honourable element in our doctrines is embraced by reason ; hence reason is necessary ; for without it the doctrines cannot exist, either. But let us unite the two. For indeed branches are useless

97

et sine radice inutiles rami sunt et ipsae radices iis, quae genuere, adiuvantur. Quantum utilitatis manus habeant, nescire nulli licet, aperte iuvant ; cor illud, quo manus vivunt, ex quo impetum sumunt, quo moventur, latet. Idem dicere de praeceptis possum : aperta sunt, decreta vero sapientiae in abdito. Sicut sanctiora sacrorum tantum initiati sciunt, ita in philosophia arcana illa admissis receptisque in sacra ostenduntur ; at praecepta et alia eiusmodi profanis quoque nota sunt.

65   Posidonius non tantum praeceptionem, nihil enim nos hoc verbo uti prohibet, sed etiam suasionem et consolationem et exhortationem necessariam iudicat. His adicit causarum inquisitionem, aetiologian quam quare nos dicere non audeamus, cum grammatici, custodes Latini sermonis, suo iure ita appellent, non video. Ait utilem futuram et descriptionem cuiusque virtutis ; hanc Posidonius ethologian vocat, quidam characterismon appellant, signa cuiusque virtutis ac vitii et notas reddentem, quibus inter se similia

66 discriminentur. Haec res eandem vim [1] habet quam praecipere. Nam qui praecipit, dicit : " illa facies, si voles temperans esse." Qui describit, ait : " temperans est, qui illa facit, qui illis abstinet." Quaeris, quid intersit ? Alter praecepta virtutis dat, alter exemplar. Descriptiones has et, ut publicanorum

---

[1] *eandem vim* cod. Velz. ; *eam demum* BA.

---

a *e.g.*, in the mysteries of Eleusis, etc.
b For these terms see Spengel, *Rhet. Graec.*, *passim*. Quintilian i. 9. 3 says *ethologia personis continetur* ; and Cicero, *De Orat.* iii. 205, in a list of figures with which the orator should be familiar, includes *characterismos*, or *descriptio*.

without their roots, and the roots themselves are strengthened by the growths which they have produced. Everyone can understand how useful the hands are; they obviously help us. But the heart, the source of the hands' growth and power and motion, is hidden. And I can say the same thing about precepts: they are manifest, while the doctrines of wisdom are concealed. And as only the initiated [a] know the more hallowed portion of the rites, so in philosophy the hidden truths are revealed only to those who are members and have been admitted to the sacred rites. But precepts and other such matters are familiar even to the uninitiated.

Posidonius holds that not only precept-giving (there is nothing to prevent my using this word), but even persuasion, consolation, and encouragement, are necessary. To these he adds *the investigation of causes* (but I fail to see why I should not dare to call it *aetiology*, since the scholars who mount guard over the Latin language thus use the term as having the right to do so). He remarks that it will also be useful to illustrate each particular virtue; this science Posidonius calls *ethology*, while others call it *characterization*.[b] It gives the signs and marks which belong to each virtue and vice, so that by them distinction may be drawn between like things. Its function is the same as that of precept. For he who utters precepts says: "If you would have self-control, act thus and so!" He who illustrates, says: "The man who acts thus and so, and refrains from certain other things, possesses self-control." If you ask what the difference here is, I say that the one gives the precepts of virtue, the other its embodiment. These illustrations, or, to use a commercial

99

utar verbo, iconismos [1] ex usu esse confiteor ; pro-
67 ponamus laudanda, invenietur imitator. Putas utile
dari tibi argumenta, per quae intellegas nobilem
equum, ne fallaris empturus, ne operam perdas in
ignavo ? Quanto hoc utilius est, excellentis animi
notas nosse, quas ex alio in se transferre permittitur.

68 Continuo pecoris generosi pullus in arvis
 Altius ingreditur et mollia crura reponit ;
 Primus et ire viam et fluvios temptare minantis
 Audet et ignoto sese committere ponti,
 Nec vanos horret strepitus. Illi ardua cervix
 Argutumque caput, brevis alvus obesaque terga,
 Luxuriatque toris animosum pectus. . . .
 . . . Tum, si qua sonum procul arma dederunt,
 Stare loco nescit, micat auribus et tremit artus
 Conlectumque premens volvit sub naribus ignem.

69 Dum aliud agit, Vergilius noster descripsit virum
fortem ; ego certe non aliam imaginem magno viro
dederim. Si mihi M. Cato exprimendus sit,[2] inter
fragores bellorum civilium inpavidus et primus in-
cessens admotos[3] iam exercitus Alpibus civilique
se bello ferens obvium, non alium illi adsignaverim
70 vultum, non alium habitum. Altius certe nemo
ingredi potuit quam qui simul contra Caesarem

---

[1] *iconismos* cod. Velz.; *iconismo* BA.
[2] *sit* added by Hermes.
[3] *admotos* Pinc.; *admotus* BA.

---

a For the same figure, similarly applied, see *Ep.* lxxx. 9 and note.
b Vergil, *Georg.* iii. 75 ff.

term, these *samples*, have, I confess, a certain utility; just put them up for exhibition well recommended, and you will find men to copy them. Would you, for instance, deem it a useful thing to have evidence given you by which you may recognize a thorough-bred horse, and not be cheated in your purchase or waste your time over a low-bred animal? [a] But how much more useful it is to know the marks of a surpassingly fine soul—marks which one may appropriate from another for oneself!

Straightway the foal of the high-bred drove, nursed up in the
    pastures,
Marches with spirited step, and treads with a delicate motion;
First on the dangerous pathway and into the threatening
    river,
Trusting himself to the unknown bridge, without fear at its
    creakings,
Neck thrown high in the air, and clear-cut head, and a belly
Spare, back rounded, and breast abounding in courage and
    muscle.
He, when the clashing of weapons is heard to resound in the
    distance,
Leaps from his place, and pricks up his ears, and all in a
    tremble
Pours forth the pent-up fire that lay close-shut in his nostrils. [b]

Vergil's description, though referring to something else, might perfectly well be the portrayal of a brave man; at any rate, I myself should select no other simile for a hero. If I had to describe Cato, who was unterrified amid the din of civil war, who was first to attack the armies that were already making for the Alps, who plunged face-forward into the civil conflict, this is exactly the sort of expression and attitude which I should give him. Surely none could " march with more spirited step " than one who rose against Caesar and Pompey at the same

101

Pompeiumque se sustulit et aliis Caesareanas opes,
aliis Pompeianas foventibus [1] utrumque provocavit
ostenditque aliquas esse et rei publicae partes. Nam
parum est in Catone dicere : " nec vanos horret
strepitus." Quidni ? Cum veros [2] vicinosque non
horreat, cum contra decem legiones et Gallica auxilia
et mixta barbarica arma civilibus vocem liberam
mittat et rem publicam hortetur, ne pro libertate
decidat, sed omnia [3] experiatur, honestius in servi-
71 tutem casura quam itura. Quantum in illo vigoris ac
spiritus, quantum in publica trepidatione fiducia est!
Scit se unum esse, de cuius statu non agatur ; non
enim quaeri, an liber Cato, sed an inter liberos sit ;
inde periculorum gladiorumque [4] contemptus. Libet
admirantem invictam constantiam viri inter publicas
ruinas non labantis dicere : " luxuriatque toris
animosum pectus."
72   Proderit non tantum quales esse soleant boni viri
dicere formamque eorum et lineamenta deducere,
sed quales fuerint narrare et exponere, Catonis illud
ultimum ac fortissimum vulnus, per quod libertas
emisit [5] animam, Laeli sapientiam et cum suo
Scipione concordiam, alterius Catonis domi forisque
egregia facta, Tuberonis ligneos lectos, cum in publicum sternerent, haedinasque pro stragulis pelles et

[1] *foventibus* later MSS. ; *tibi foventibus* BA ; *sibi foventibus* edd.
[2] *veros* later MSS. ; *viros* BA.
[3] *omnia* cod. Harl. ; omitted by BA.
[4] *gladiorumque* later MSS. ; *gladiatorumque* BA.
[5] *emisit* Stephanus ; *amisit* BA.

[a] For example, Cato had from the first opposed any
assumption of illegal power,—objecting to the consulship
of Pompey and Crassus in 55 B.C., and to the conduct of
Caesar throughout. His disapproval of both simultaneously
is hinted in Plutarch's *Cato the Younger*, liv. 4.

time and, when some were supporting Caesar's party and others that of Pompey, issued a challenge to both leaders,[a] thus showing that the republic also had some backers. For it is not enough to say of Cato " without fear at its creakings." Of course he is not afraid ! He does not quail before real and imminent noises ; in the face of ten legions, Gallic auxiliaries, and a motley host of citizens and foreigners, he utters words fraught with freedom, encouraging the Republic not to fail in the struggle for freedom, but to try all hazards ; he declares that it is more honourable to fall into servitude than to fall in line with it. What force and energy are his ! What confidence he displays amid the general panic ! He knows that he is the only one whose standing is not in question, and that men do not ask whether Cato is free, but whether he is still *among* the free. Hence his contempt for danger and the sword. What a pleasure it is to say, in admiration of the unflinching steadiness of a hero who did not totter when the whole state was in ruins :

A breast abounding in courage and muscle !

It will be helpful not only to state what is the usual quality of good men, and to outline their figures and features, but also to relate and set forth what men there have been of this kind. We might picture that last and bravest wound of Cato's, through which Freedom breathed her last ; or the wise Laelius and his harmonious life with his friend Scipio ; or the noble deeds of the Elder Cato at home and abroad ; or the wooden couches of Tubero, spread at a public feast, goatskins instead of tapestry, and vessels of earthenware set out for

ante ipsius Iovis cellam adposita conviviis vasa fictilia
Quid aliud paupertatem in Capitolio consecrare ?
Ut nullum aliud factum eius habeam, quo illum
Catonibus inseram, hoc parum credimus ? Censura
73 fuit illa, non cena. O quam ignorant homines cupidi
gloriae, quid illa sit aut quemadmodum petenda !
Illo die populus Romanus multorum supellectilem
spectavit, unius miratus est. Omnium illorum aurum
argentumque fractum est et milliens [1] conflatum, at
omnibus saeculis Tuberonis fictilia durabunt. VALE.

XCVI.

SENECA LVCILIO SVO SALVTEM

1 Tamen tu indignaris aliquid aut quereris et non
intellegis nihil esse in istis mali nisi hoc unum, quod
indignaris et quereris ? Si me interrogas, nihil puto
viro miserum nisi aliquid esse in rerum natura, quod
putet miserum. Non feram me, quo die aliquid ferre
non potero.

Male valeo ; pars fati est. Familia decubuit,
faenus offendit, domus crepuit, damna, vulnera,
labores, metus incucurrerunt ; solet fieri. Hoc parum
2 est ; debuit fieri. Decernuntur ista, non accidunt.
Si quid credis mihi, intimos adfectus meos tibi cum
maxime detego ; in omnibus, quae adversa videntur
et dura, sic formatus sum : non pareo deo, sed

---

[1] *et milliens* later MSS. ; *et in milliens* BA.

---

[a] The Latin term can hardly be reproduced, though " he
did not regale but regulate " comes near it. Tubero's act
was that of a true *censor morum.*

the banquet before the very shrine of Jupiter! What else was this except consecrating poverty on the Capitol? Though I know no other deed of his for which to rank him with the Catos, is this one not enough? It was a censorship, not a banquet.[a] How lamentably do those who covet glory fail to understand what glory is, or in what way it should be sought! On that day the Roman populace viewed the furniture of many men; it marvelled only at that of one! The gold and silver of all the others has been broken up and melted down times without number; but Tubero's earthenware will endure throughout eternity. Farewell.

XCVI. ON FACING HARDSHIPS

Spite of all do you still chafe and complain, not understanding that, in all the evils to which you refer, there is really only one—the fact that you *do* chafe and complain? If you ask me, I think that for a *man* there is no misery unless there be something in the universe which he thinks miserable. I shall not endure myself on that day when I find anything unendurable.

I am ill; but that is a part of my lot. My slaves have fallen sick, my income has gone off, my house is rickety, I have been assailed by losses, accidents, toil, and fear; this is a common thing. Nay, that was an understatement; it was an inevitable thing. Such affairs come by order, and not by accident. If you will believe me, it is my inmost emotions that I am just now disclosing to you: when everything seems to go hard and uphill, I have trained myself not merely to obey God, but to agree with His

105

adsentior. Ex animo illum, non quia necesse est, sequor. Nihil umquam mihi incidet, quod tristis excipiam, quod malo vultu. Nullum tributum invitus conferam. Omnia autem, ad quae gemimus, quae expavescimus, tributa vitae sunt ; horum, mi Lucili, nec speraveris immunitatem nec petieris.

3 Vesicae [1] te dolor inquietavit, epistulae venerunt [2] parum dulces, detrimenta continua, propius [3] accedam, de capite timuisti. Quid, tu nesciebas haec te optare, cum optares senectutem ? Omnia ista in longa vita sunt, quomodo in longa via et pulvis et

4 lutum et pluvia. " Sed volebam vivere, carere tamen incommodis omnibus." Tam effeminata vox virum dedecet. Videris, quemadmodum hoc votum meum excipias ; ego illud magno animo, non tantum bono facio : neque di neque deae faciant, ut te fortuna

5 in deliciis habeat. Ipse te interroga, si quis potestatem tibi deus faciat, utrum velis vivere in macello an in castris.

Atqui vivere, Lucili, militare est. Itaque hi, qui iactantur et per operosa atque ardua sursum ac deorsum eunt et expeditiones periculosissimas obeunt, fortes viri sunt primoresque castrorum ; isti, quos putida [4] quies aliis laborantibus molliter habet, turturillae sunt, tuti contumeliae causa. VALE.

---

[1] *vesicae* later MSS. ; *vesica* BA.
[2] *venerunt* von Ian ; *vero erunt* BA.
[3] *propius* later MSS. ; *propitius* BA.
[4] *putida* later MSS. ; *putica* BA.

decisions. I follow Him because my soul wills it, and not because I must.[a] Nothing will ever happen to me that I shall receive with ill humour or with a wry face. I shall pay up all my taxes willingly. Now all the things which cause us to groan or recoil, are part of the tax of life—things, my dear Lucilius, which you should never hope and never seek to escape.

It was disease of the bladder that made you apprehensive; downcast letters came from you; you were continually getting worse; I will touch the truth more closely, and say that you feared for your life. But come, did you not know, when you prayed for long life, that this was what you were praying for? A long life includes all these troubles, just as a long journey includes dust and mud and rain. "But," you cry, "I wished to live, and at the same time to be immune from all ills." Such a womanish cry does no credit to a man. Consider in what attitude you shall receive this prayer of mine (I offer it not only in a good, but in a noble spirit): "May gods and goddesses alike forbid that Fortune keep you in luxury!" Ask yourself voluntarily which you would choose if some god gave you the choice—life in a café or life in a camp.

And yet life, Lucilius, is really a battle. For this reason those who are tossed about at sea, who proceed uphill and downhill over toilsome crags and heights, who go on campaigns that bring the greatest danger, are heroes and front-rank fighters; but persons who live in rotten luxury and ease while others toil, are mere turtle-doves—safe only because men despise them. Farewell.

[a] Cf. the words *ducunt volentem fata, nolentem trahunt* of *Ep.* cvii. 11.

107

XCVII.

Seneca Lvcilio svo salvtem

1 Erras, mi Lucili, si existimas nostri saeculi esse vitium luxuriam et neglegentiam boni moris et alia, quae obiecit suis quisque temporibus ; hominum sunt ista, non temporum. Nulla aetas vacavit a culpa. Et si aestimare licentiam cuiusque saeculi incipias, pudet dicere, numquam apertius quam coram Catone 2 peccatum est. Credat aliquis pecuniam esse versatam in eo iudicio, in quo reus erat P.[1] Clodius ob id adulterium, quod cum Caesaris uxore in operto [2] commiserat violatis religionibus eius sacrificii, quod pro populo fieri dicitur sic summotis extra consaeptum omnibus viris, ut picturae quoque masculorum animalium contegantur ? Atqui dati iudicibus nummi sunt et, quod hac etiamnunc pactione turpius est, stupra insuper matronarum et adulescentulorum 3 nobilium stilari loco exacta sunt. Minus crimine quam absolutione peccatum est : adulterii reus adulteria divisit nec ante fuit de salute securus, quam similes sui iudices suos reddidit. Haec in eo iudicio facta sunt, in quo, si nihil aliud, Cato testimonium dixerat.

Ipsa ponam verba Ciceronis, quia res fidem excedit:

[1] *P.* ed. Mentel. ; *A.* BA.
[2] *operto* later MSS. ; *aperto* BA.

---

[a] For the best account of this scandal see Plutarch, *Caesar,* ix. f.
[b] From *stilla,* "a drop." The phrase is equivalent to our proverbial "last straw."
[c] *Epp. ad Atticum,* i. 16.

XCVII. ON THE DEGENERACY OF THE AGE

You are mistaken, my dear Lucilius, if you think that luxury, neglect of good manners, and other vices of which each man accuses the age in which he lives, are especially characteristic of our own epoch; no, they are the vices of mankind and not of the times. No era in history has ever been free from blame. Moreover, if you once begin to take account of the irregularities belonging to any particular era, you will find—to man's shame be it spoken—that sin never stalked abroad more openly than in Cato's very presence. Would anyone believe that money changed hands in the trial when Clodius was defendant on the charge of secret adultery with Caesar's wife, when he violated [a] the ritual of that sacrifice which is said to be offered on behalf of the people when all males are so rigorously removed outside the precinct, that even pictures of all male creatures are covered up? And yet, money was given to the jury, and, baser even than such a bargain, sexual crimes were demanded of married women and noble youths as a sort of additional contribution. [b] The charge involved less sin than the acquittal; for the defendant on a charge of adultery parcelled out the adulteries, and was not sure of his own safety until he had made the jury criminals like himself. All this was done at the trial in which Cato gave evidence, although that was his sole part therein.

I shall quote Cicero's actual words, [c] because the facts are so bad as to pass belief: " He made

4 " Accersivit ad se, promisit, intercessit, dedit. Iam
vero—o di boni,[1] rem perditam !—etiam noctes certarum mulierum atque adulescentulorum nobilium
introductiones nonnullis iudicibus pro mercedis cu-
5 mulo fuerunt." Non vacat de pretio queri, plus in
accessionibus fuit. " Vis severi illius uxorem ? Dabo
illam. Vis divitis huius ? Tibi praestabo concubi-
tum. Adulterium nisi feceris, damna. Illa formonsa,
quam desideras, veniet. Illius tibi noctem promitto
nec differo ; intra comperendinationem fides promissi
mei stabit.[2] " Plus est distribuere adulteria quam
facere ; hoc vero matribus familiae denuntiare est.
6 Hi iudices Clodiani a senatu petierant praesidium,
quod non erat nisi damnaturis necessarium, et in-
petraverant. Itaque eleganter illis Catulus absoluto
reo, " quid vos," inquit, " praesidium a nobis pete-
batis ? An ne nummi vobis eriperentur ? " Inter
hos tamen iocos inpune tulit ante iudicium adulter,
in iudicio leno, qui damnationem peius effugit quam
meruit.
7 Quicquam fuisse corruptius illis [3] moribus credis,
quibus libido non sacris inhiberi, non iudiciis poterat,
quibus in ea ipsa quaestione, quae extra ordinem
senatusconsulto exercebatur, plus quam quaerebatur,
admissum est ? Quaerebatur, an post adulterium
aliquis posset tutus esse ; apparuit sine adulterio

---

[1] di boni Cicero, Ad Att. i. 16. 5 ; di omitted by BA.
[2] mei stabit ed. Ven. ; me extabit BA.
[3] illis later MSS. ; illius BA.

assignations, promises, pleas, and gifts. And more than this (merciful Heavens, what an abandoned state of affairs!) upon several of the jury, to round out their reward, he even bestowed the enjoyment of certain women and meetings with noble youths." It is superfluous to be shocked at the bribe; the additions to the bribe were worse. "Will you have the wife of that prig, A.? Very good. Or of B., the millionaire? I will guarantee that you shall lie with her. If you fail to commit adultery, condemn Clodius. That beauty whom you desire shall visit you. I assure you a night in that woman's company without delay; my promise shall be carried out faithfully within the legal time of postponement." It means more to parcel out such crimes than to commit them; it means blackmailing dignified matrons. These jurymen in the Clodius trial had asked the Senate for a guard—a favour which would have been necessary only for a jury about to convict the accused; and their request had been granted. Hence the witty remark of Catulus after the defendant had been acquitted: "Why did you ask us for the guard? Were you afraid of having your money stolen from you?" And yet, amid jests like these, he got off unpunished who before the trial was an adulterer, during the trial a pander, and who escaped conviction more vilely than he deserved it.

Do you believe that anything could be more disgraceful than such moral standards—when lust could not keep its hands either from religious worship or from the courts of law, when, in the very inquiry which was held in special session by order of the Senate, more crime was committed than investigated? The question at issue was whether one could be safe after committing adultery; it was

8 tutum esse non posse. Hoc inter Pompeium et
Caesarem, inter Ciceronem Catonemque commissum
est, Catonem inquam illum, quo sedente populus
negatur permisisse sibi postulare Florales iocos
nudandarum meretricum, si credis spectasse tunc
severius homines quam iudicasse. Et fient et facta
sunt ista, et licentia urbium aliquando disciplina
metuque, numquam sponte considet.

9 Non est itaque quod credas nos [1] plurimum libidini
permisisse, legibus minimum. Longe enim frugalior
haec iuventus est quam illa, cum reus adulterium apud
iudices negaret, iudices apud reum [2] confiterentur,
cum stuprum committeretur rei iudicandae causa,
cum Clodius isdem vitiis gratiosus, quibus nocens,
conciliaturas exerceret in ipsa causae dictione.
Credat hoc quisquam ? Qui damnabatur uni adul-
10 terio, absolutus est multis. Omne tempus Clodios,
non omne Catones feret. Ad deteriora faciles sumus,
quia nec dux potest nec comes deesse, et res ipsa
etiam sine duce, sine comite procedit. Non pronum
est [3] tantum ad vitia, sed praeceps, et quod plerosque
inemendabiles facit, omnium aliarum artium peccata
artificibus pudori sunt offenduntque deerrantem,
11 vitae peccata delectant. Non gaudet navigio guber-

---

[1] *nos* Haase ; *non* BA.
[2] *reum* Pincianus ; *eum* BA.
[3] *non pronum est* Lipsius ; *non prae nuntius* BA.

---

[a] A plebeian festival, held April 28, in honour of Flora, an
Italian divinity connected with Ceres and Venus. For the
story of Cato (55 B.C.) see Valer. Max. ii. 10. 8.

shown that one could not be safe without committing adultery! All this bargaining took place in the presence of Pompey and Caesar, of Cicero and Cato, —yes, that very Cato whose presence, it is said, caused the people to refrain from demanding the usual quips and cranks of naked actresses at the Floralia,[a]—if you can believe that men were stricter in their conduct at a festival than in a court-room! Such things will be done in the future, as they have been done in the past; and the licentiousness of cities will sometimes abate through discipline and fear, never of itself.

Therefore, you need not believe that it is we who have yielded most to lust and least to law. For the young men of to-day live far more simple lives than those of an epoch when a defendant would plead not guilty to an adultery charge before his judges, and his judges admit it before the defendant, when debauchery was practised to secure a verdict, and when Clodius, befriended by the very vices of which he was guilty, played the procurer during the actual hearing of the case. Could one believe this? He to whom one adultery brought condemnation was acquitted because of many. All ages will produce men like Clodius, but not all ages men like Cato. We degenerate easily, because we lack neither guides nor associates in our wickedness, and the wickedness goes on of itself, even without guides or associates. The road to vice is not only downhill, but steep; and many men are rendered incorrigible by the fact that, while in all other crafts errors bring shame to good craftsmen and cause vexation to those who go astray, the errors of life are a positive source of pleasure. The pilot is not glad when his ship is thrown on her beam-ends; the

nator everso, non gaudet aegro medicus elato, non gaudet orator, si patroni culpa reus cedidit ; at contra omnibus crimen suum voluptati est. Laetatur ille adulterio, in quod inritatus est ipsa difficultate. Laetatur ille circumscriptione furtoque, nec ante illi culpa quam culpae fortuna displicuit. Id prava consuetudine evenit.

12 Alioquin ut scias subesse animis etiam in pessima abductis boni sensum nec ignorari turpe, sed neglegi ; omnes peccata dissimulant et, quamvis feliciter cesserint, fructu illorum utuntur, ipsa subducunt. At bona conscientia prodire vult et conspici ; ipsas

13 nequitia tenebras timet. Eleganter itaque ab Epicuro dictum puto : " potest nocenti contingere, ut lateat, latendi fides non potest," aut si hoc modo melius hunc explicari posse iudicas sensum : " ideo non prodest latere peccantibus, quia latendi etiam si felicitatem habent, fiduciam non habent." Ita est : tuta scelera esse possunt, secura esse non possunt.

14 Hoc ego repugnare sectae nostrae, si sic expediatur, non iudico. Quare ? Quia prima illa et maxima peccantium est poena peccasse, nec ullum scelus, licet illud fortuna exornet muneribus suis, licet tueatur ac vindicet, inpunitum est, quoniam sceleris

---

physician is not glad when he buries his patient; the orator is not glad when the defendant loses a case through the fault of his advocate; but on the other hand every man enjoys his own crimes. A. delights in an intrigue—for it was the very difficulty which attracted him thereto. B. delights in forgery and theft, and is only displeased with his sin when his sin has failed to hit the mark. And all this is the result of perverted habits.

Conversely, however, in order that you may know that there is an idea of good conduct present subconsciously in souls which have been led even into the most depraved ways, and that men are not ignorant of what evil is but indifferent—I say that all men hide their sins, and, even though the issue be successful, enjoy the results while concealing the sins themselves. A good conscience, however, wishes to come forth and be seen of men; wickedness fears the very shadows. Hence I hold Epicurus's saying [a] to be most apt: " That the guilty may haply remain hidden is possible, that he should be sure of remaining hidden is not possible," or, if you think that the meaning can be made more clear in this way: " The reason that it is no advantage to wrong-doers to remain hidden is that even though they have the good fortune they have not the assurance of remaining so." This is what I mean: crimes can be well guarded; free from anxiety they cannot be.

This view, I maintain, is not at variance with the principles of our school, if it be so explained. And why ? Because the first and worst penalty for sin is to have committed sin; and crime, though Fortune deck it out with her favours, though she protect and take it in her charge, can never go unpunished;

115

in scelere supplicium est. Sed nihilominus et hae illam secundae poenae premunt ac secuntur, timere semper et expavescere et securitati diffidere.

Quare ego hoc supplicio nequitiam liberem ? Quare 15 non semper illam in suspenso relinquam ? Illic dissentiamus cum Epicuro, ubi dicit nihil iustum esse natura et crimina vitanda esse, quia vitari metus non posse ; hic consentiamus mala facinora conscientia flagellari et plurimum illi tormentorum esse eo, quod perpetua illam sollicitudo urget ac verberat, quod sponsoribus securitatis suae non potest credere. Hoc enim ipsum argumentum est, Epicure,[1] natura nos a scelere abhorrere, quod nulli non etiam inter tuta timor est. Multos fortuna liberat poena, 16 metu neminem. Quare nisi quia infixa nobis eius rei aversatio est, quam natura damnavit ? Ideo numquam fides latendi fit etiam latentibus, quia coarguit illos conscientia et ipsos sibi ostendit. Proprium autem est nocentium trepidare. Male de nobis actum erat, quod multa scelera legem et vindicem effugiunt et scripta supplicia, nisi illa naturalia et gravia de praesentibus solverent et in locum patientiae timor cederet. Vale.

[1] *est Epicure* cod. Velz.; *Epicuri est* B; *Epicure* A.

since the punishment of crime lies in the crime itself.
But none the less do these second penalties press
close upon the heels of the first—constant fear,
constant terror, and distrust in one's own security.

Why, then, should I set wickedness free from such
a punishment? Why should I not always leave it
trembling in the balance? Let us disagree with
Epicurus on the one point, when he declares that
there is no natural justice, and that crime should
be avoided because one cannot escape the fear which
results therefrom; let us agree with him on the
other—that bad deeds are lashed by the whip of
conscience, and that conscience is tortured to the
greatest degree because unending anxiety drives
and whips it on, and it cannot rely upon the guarantors
of its own peace of mind. For this, Epicurus, is the
very proof that we are by nature reluctant to commit
crime, because even in circumstances of safety there
is no one who does not feel fear. Good luck frees
many men from punishment, but no man from fear.
And why should this be if it were not that we have
ingrained in us a loathing for that which Nature has
condemned? Hence even men who hide their sins
can never count upon remaining hidden; for their
conscience convicts them and reveals them to themselves. But it is the property of guilt to be in fear.
It had gone ill with us, owing to the many crimes
which escape the vengeance of the law and the
prescribed punishments, were it not that those
grievous offences against nature must pay the penalty in ready money, and that in place of suffering
the punishment comes fear. Farewell.

XCVIII.

Seneca Lvcilio svo salvtem

1 Numquam credideris felicem quemquam ex felicitate suspensum. Fragilibus innititur, qui adventicio
laetus est ; exibit gaudium, quod intravit. At illud
ex se ortum fidele firmumque est et crescit et ad
extremum usque prosequitur ; cetera, quorum admiratio est vulgo, in diem bona sunt. " Quid ergo ?
Non usui ac voluptati esse possunt ? " Quis negat ?
Sed ita, si illa ex nobis pendent, non ex illis nos.
2 Omnia, quae fortuna intuetur, ita fructifera ac
iucunda fiunt, si qui habet illa, se quoque habet
nec in rerum suarum potestate est. Errant enim,
Lucili, qui aut boni aliquid nobis aut malum iudicant
tribuere fortunam ; materiam dat bonorum ac malorum et initia rerum apud nos in malum bonumve
exiturarum. Valentior enim omni fortuna animus
est et in utramque partem ipse res suas ducit beatae-
que ac miserae vitae sibi causa est.
3 Malus omnia in malum vertit, etiam quae cum
specie optimi venerant ; rectus atque integer corrigit
prava fortunae et dura atque aspera ferendi scientia
mollit, idemque et secunda grate excipit modesteque

---

^a Compare the ἔχω ἀλλ' οὐκ ἔχομαι of Aristippus, and the
(equally Epicurean) *mihi res, non me rebus subiungere* of
Horace, *Epp.* i. 1. 19.
118

XCVIII. ON THE FICKLENESS OF FORTUNE

You need never believe that anyone who depends upon happiness is happy ! It is a fragile support— this delight in adventitious things ; the joy which entered from without will some day depart. But that joy which springs wholly from oneself is leal and sound ; it increases and attends us to the last ; while all other things which provoke the admiration of the crowd are but temporary Goods. You may reply : " What do you mean ? Cannot such things serve both for utility and for delight ? " Of course. But only if they depend on us, and not we on them. All things that Fortune looks upon become productive and pleasant, only if he who possesses them is in possession also of himself, and is not in the power of that which belongs to him.[a] For men make a mistake, my dear Lucilius, if they hold that anything good, or evil either, is bestowed upon us by Fortune ; it is simply the raw material of Goods and Ills that she gives to us—the sources of things which, in our keeping, will develop into good or ill. For the soul is more powerful than any sort of Fortune ; by its own agency it guides its affairs in either direction, and of its own power it can produce a happy life, or a wretched one.

A bad man makes everything bad—even things which had come with the appearance of what is best ; but the upright and honest man corrects the wrongs of Fortune, and softens hardship and bitterness because he knows how to endure them ; he likewise accepts prosperity with appreciation and moderation, and stands up against trouble with steadiness and

et adversa constanter ac fortiter. Qui licet prudens
sit, licet exacto faciat cuncta iudicio, licet nihil supra
vires suas temptet, non continget illi bonum illud
integrum et extra minas positum, nisi certus adversus
4 incerta est. Sive alios observare volueris—liberius
enim inter aliena iudicium est, sive te ipsum favore
seposito—et senties hoc et confiteberis, nihil ex his
optabilibus et caris utile esse, nisi te contra levitatem
casus rerumque casum sequentium instruxeris, nisi
illud frequenter et sine querella inter singula damna
5 dixeris : " dis aliter visum est." Immo mehercules
ut carmen fortius ac iustius petam, quo animum
tuum magis fulcias, hoc dicito, quotiens aliquid aliter
quam cogitabas evenerit : " di melius."

Sic composito nihil accidet. Sic autem conponetur,
si, quid humanarum rerum varietas possit, cogitaverit,
antequam senserit, si et liberos et coniugem et
patrimonium sic habuerit tamquam non utique
semper habiturus et tamquam non futurus ob hoc
miserior, si habere desierit. Calamitosus est animus
6 futuri anxius et ante miserias miser, qui sollicitus est,
ut ea, quibus delectatur, ad extremum usque per-
maneant. Nullo enim tempore conquiescet et ex-
pectatione venturi praesentia, quibus frui poterat,

---

courage. Though a man be prudent, though he conduct all his interests with well-balanced judgment, though he attempt nothing beyond his strength, he will not attain the Good which is unalloyed and beyond the reach of threats, unless he is sure in dealing with that which is unsure. For whether you prefer to observe other men (and it is easier to make up one's mind when judging the affairs of others), or whether you observe yourself, with all prejudice laid aside, you will perceive and acknowledge that there is no utility in all these desirable and beloved things, unless you equip yourself in opposition to the fickleness of chance and its consequences, and unless you repeat to yourself often and uncomplainingly, at every mishap, the words: " Heaven decreed it otherwise ! " [a] Nay rather, to adopt a phrase which is braver and nearer the truth— one on which you may more safely prop your spirit—say to yourself, whenever things turn out contrary to your expectation: " Heaven decreed *better* ! "

If you are thus poised, nothing will affect you ; and a man will be thus poised if he reflects on the possible ups and downs in human affairs before he feels their force, and if he comes to regard children, or wife, or property, with the idea that he will not necessarily possess them always and that he will not be any more wretched just because he ceases to possess them. It is tragic for the soul to be apprehensive of the future and wretched in anticipation of wretchedness, consumed with an anxious desire that the objects which give pleasure may remain in its possession to the very end. For such a soul will never be at rest ; in waiting for the future it will lose the present blessings which it might enjoy. And

amittet. In aequo est autem amissae rei miseratio [1]
et timor amittendae.

7 Nec ideo praecipio tibi neglegentiam. Tu vero
metuenda declina. Quidquid consilio prospici potest,
prospice. Quodcumque laesurum est, multo ante
quam accidat, speculare et averte. In hoc ipsum
tibi plurimum conferet fiducia et ad tolerandum
omne obfirmata mens. Potest fortunam cavere, qui
potest ferre. Certe in tranquillo non tumultuatur.
Nihil est nec miserius nec stultius quam praetimere.
Quae ista dementia est malum suum antecedere ?

8 Denique ut breviter includam quod sentio, et istos
satagios ac sibi molestos describam tibi, tam intem-
perantes in ipsis miseriis quam sunt ante illas. Plus
dolet quam necesse est, qui ante dolet quam necesse
est ; eadem enim infirmitate dolorem non aestimat,
qua non exspectat ; eadem intemperantia fingit sibi
perpetuam felicitatem suam, fingit crescere debere
quaecumque contigerunt, non tantum durare ; et
oblitus huius petauri, quo humana iactantur, sibi uni
fortuitorum constantiam spondet.

9 Egregie itaque videtur mihi Metrodorus dixisse in
ea epistula, qua sororem amisso optimae indolis filio
adloquitur : " mortale est omne mortalium bonum."
De his loquitur bonis, ad quae concurritur. Nam
illud verum bonum non moritur, certum est sempiter-
numque, sapientia et virtus ; hoc unum contingit

---

[1] *miseratio* added by Buecheler.

---

a i.e., a sort of platform for mountebanks or acrobats,—
figuratively applied to life's Vanity Fair.
b Frag. 35 Körte.
122

there is no difference between grief for something lost and the fear of losing it.

But I do not for this reason advise you to be indifferent. Rather do you turn aside from you whatever may cause fear. Be sure to foresee whatever can be foreseen by planning. Observe and avoid, long before it happens, anything that is likely to do you harm. To effect this your best assistance will be a spirit of confidence and a mind strongly resolved to endure all things. He who can bear Fortune, can also beware of Fortune. At any rate, there is no dashing of billows when the sea is calm. And there is nothing more wretched or foolish than premature fear. What madness it is to anticipate one's troubles! In fine, to express my thoughts in brief compass and portray to you those busybodies and self-tormentors —they are as uncontrolled in the midst of their troubles as they are before them. He suffers more than is necessary, who suffers before it is necessary ; such men do not weigh the amount of their suffering, by reason of the same failing which prevents them from being ready for it ; and with the same lack of restraint they fondly imagine that their luck will last for ever, and fondly imagine that their gains are bound to increase as well as merely continue. They forget this spring-board [a] on which mortal things are tossed, and they guarantee for themselves exclusively a steady continuance of the gifts of chance.

For this very reason I regard as excellent the saying [b] of Metrodorus, in a letter of consolation to his sister on the loss of her son, a lad of great promise : " All the Good of mortals is mortal." He is referring to those Goods towards which men rush in shoals. For the real Good does not perish ; it is certain and lasting, and it consists of wisdom and virtue ; it is

10 inmortale mortalibus. Ceterum tam inprobi sunt tamque obliti, quo eant, quo illos singuli dies turbent, ut mirentur aliquid ipsos amittere amissuri uno die omnia. Quicquid est, dominus inscriberis, apud te est, tuum non est; nihil firmum infirmo, nihil fragili aeternum et invictum est. Tam necesse est perire quam perdere, et hoc ipsum, si intellegimus, solacium est. Aequo animo perde, pereundum [1] est.

11 Quid ergo adversus has amissiones auxili invenimus? Hoc, ut memoria teneamus amissa nec cum ipsis fructum excidere patiamur, quem ex illis percepimus. Habere eripitur, habuisse numquam. Peringratus est, qui cum amisit, pro accepto nihil debet. Rem nobis eripit casus, usum [2] fructumque apud nos relinquit, quem nos iniquitate desiderii perdidimus.

12 Dic tibi: "Ex istis, quae terribilia videntur, nihil est invictum. Singula vicere iam multi: ignem Mucius, crucem Regulus, venenum Socrates, exilium Rutilius, mortem ferro adactam Cato; et nos vincamus aliquid."

13 Rursus ista, quae ut [3] speciosa et felicia trahunt vulgum, a multis et saepe contempta sunt. Fabricius divitias imperator reiecit, censor notavit. Tubero

---

[1] *perde, pereundum* Madvig; *perdere pereundum* BA.
[2] *usum* later MSS.; *usus* BA.
[3] *ista quae ut* later MSS.; *ita quae vis* BA.

the only immortal thing that falls to mortal lot. But men are so wayward, and so forgetful of their goal and of the point toward which every day jostles them, that they are surprised at losing anything, although some day they are bound to lose everything. Anything of which you are entitled the owner is in your possession but is not your own; for there is no strength in that which is weak, nor anything lasting and invincible in that which is frail. We must lose our lives as surely as we lose our property, and this, if we understand the truth, is itself a consolation. Lose it with equanimity; for you must lose your life also.

What resource do we find, then, in the face of these losses? Simply this—to keep in memory the things we have lost, and not to suffer the enjoyment which we have derived from them to pass away along with them. To have may be taken from us, to have had, never. A man is thankless in the highest degree if, after losing something, he feels no obligation for having received it. Chance robs us of the thing, but leaves us its use and its enjoyment—and we have lost this if we are so unfair as to regret. Just say to yourself: " Of all these experiences that seem so frightful, none is insuperable. Separate trials have been overcome by many : fire by Mucius, crucifixion by Regulus, poison by Socrates, exile by Rutilius, and a sword-inflicted death by Cato; therefore, let us also overcome something." Again, those objects which attract the crowd under the appearance of beauty and happiness, have been scorned by many men and on many occasions. Fabricius when he was general refused riches,[a] and when he was censor branded them with disapproval.

---

[a] *i.e.*, when he declined the bribe of Pyrrhus, 280 b.c.

paupertatem et se dignam et Capitolio iudicavit, cum
fictilibus in publica cena usus ostendit debere iis
hominem esse contentum, quibus di etiamnunc
uterentur. Honores reppulit pater Sextius, qui ita
natus, ut rem publicam deberet capessere, latum
clavum divo Iulio dante non recepit. Intellegebat
enim quod dari posset, et eripi posse.

Nos quoque aliquid et ipsi faciamus animose ; simus
14 inter exempla. Quare defecimus ? Quare de-
speramus ? Quicquid fieri potuit, potest, nos modo
purgemus animum sequamurque naturam, a qua
aberranti cupiendum timendumque est et fortuitis
serviendum. Licet reverti in viam, licet in integrum
restitui ; restituamur, ut possimus dolores, quocumque modo corpus invaserint, perferre et fortunae
dicere : " cum viro tibi negotium est ; quaere, quem
vincas."

15 His sermonibus [1] et his similibus lenitur illa vis
ulceris, quam opto mehercules mitigari et aut sanari
aut stare et cum ipso senescere. Sed securus de illo
sum ; de nostro damno agitur, quibus senex egregius
eripitur. Nam ipse vitae plenus est, cui adici nihil
desiderat sua causa, sed eorum, quibus utilis est.
16 Liberaliter facit, quod vivit. Alius iam hos [2] cruciatus

---

[1] The testimony of an ancient grammarian, and the change
of subject in the text, may, as Hense states, indicate that a
considerable passage is lost and that another letter begins
here. *Cf* the *senex egregius* of § 15.
[2] *hos* later MSS. ; *his* BA.

---

[a] *Cf. Ep.* xcv. 72 f. *omnibus saeculis Tuberonis fictilia
durabunt.*
[b] *Cf. Ep.* lix. 7 and note *b* (vol. i.).

Tubero deemed poverty worthy both of himself and of the deity on the Capitol when, by the use of earthenware dishes at a public festival, he showed that man should be satisfied with that which the gods could still use.[a] The elder Sextius rejected the honours of office ; [b] he was born with an obligation to take part in public affairs, and yet would not accept the broad stripe even when the deified Julius offered it to him. For he understood that what can be given can also be taken away.

Let us also, therefore, carry out some courageous act of our own accord ; let us be included among the ideal types of history. Why have we been slack ? Why do we lose heart ? That which could be done, can be done, if only we purify our souls and follow Nature ; for when one strays away from Nature one is compelled to crave, and fear, and be a slave to the things of chance. We may return to the true path ; we may be restored to our proper state ; let us therefore be so, in order that we may be able to endure pain, in whatever form it attacks our bodies, and say to Fortune : " You have to deal with a *man* ; seek someone whom you can conquer ! "

By these words, and words of a like kind, the malignity of the ulcer is quieted down ; and I hope indeed that it can be reduced, and either cured or brought to a stop, and grow old along with the patient himself. I am, however, comfortable in my mind regarding him ; what we are now discussing is our own loss—the taking-off of a most excellent old man. For he himself has lived a full life, and anything additional may be craved by him, not for his own sake, but for the sake of those who need his services. In continuing to live, he deals generously. Some other person might have put an end to these

127

finisset[1]; hic tam turpe putat mortem fugere quam
ad mortem confugere. " Quid ergo ? Non, si suadebit res, exibit ? " Quidni exeat, si nemo iam uti eo
poterit ? Si nihil aliud quam dolori operam dabit ?
17 Hoc est, mi Lucili, philosophiam in opere discere et
ad verum exerceri : videre, quid homo prudens
animi habeat contra mortem, contra dolorem, cum
illa accedat, hic premat. Quid faciendum sit, a
faciente discendum est. Adhuc argumentis actum
est, an posset aliqui dolori resistere, an mors magnos
18 quoque animos admota summittere. Quid opus est
verbis ? In rem praesentem eamus : nec mors illum
contra dolorem facit fortiorem nec dolor contra
mortem. Contra utrumque sibi fidit nec spe mortis
patienter dolet nec taedio doloris libenter moritur ;
hunc fert, illam expectat. VALE.

XCIX.

SENECA LVCILIO SVO SALVTEM

1 Epistulam, quam scripsi Marullo, cum filium par-
vulum amisisset et diceretur molliter ferre, misi tibi,
in qua non sum solitum morem secutus nec putavi
leniter illum debere tractari, cum obiurgatione esset
quam solacio dignior. Adflicto enim et magnum
vulnus male ferenti paulisper cedendum est; exsatiet

---

[1] *finisset* later MSS.; *finis est* BA.

[a] Possibly Iunius Marullus, consul *designatus* in A.D. 62
(Tac. *Ann.* xiv. 48).

sufferings ; but our friend considers it no less base to flee from death than to flee towards death. " But," comes the answer, " if circumstances warrant, shall he not take his departure ? " Of course, if he can no longer be of service to anyone, if all his business will be to deal with pain. This, my dear Lucilius, is what we mean by studying philosophy while applying it, by practising it on truth — to note what courage a prudent man possesses against death, or against pain, when the one approaches and the other weighs heavily. What ought to be done must be learned from one who does it. Up to now we have dealt with arguments—whether any man can resist pain, or whether the approach of death can cast down even great souls. Why discuss it further ? Here is an immediate fact for us to tackle—death does not make our friend braver to face pain, nor pain to face death. Rather does he trust himself in the face of both ; he does not suffer with resignation because he hopes for death, nor does he die gladly because he is tired of suffering. Pain he endures, death he awaits. Farewell.

XCIX. ON CONSOLATION TO THE BEREAVED

I enclose a copy of the letter which I wrote to Marullus [a] at the time when he had lost his little son and was reported to be rather womanish in his grief— a letter in which I have not observed the usual form of condolence : for I did not believe that he should be handled gently, since in my opinion he deserved criticism rather than consolation. When a man is stricken and is finding it most difficult to endure a grievous wound, one must humour him for a while ;

129

se aut certe primum impetum effundat ; hi, qui sibi
lugere sumpserunt, protinus castigentur et discant
quasdam etiam lacrimarum ineptias esse.

2 " Solacia expectas ? Convicia accipe. Molliter tu
fers mortem filii ; quid faceres, si amicum perdidisses?
Decessit filius incertae spei, parvulus ; pusillum tem-
3 poris periit. Causas doloris conquirimus et de fortuna etiam inique queri volumus, quasi non sit iustas
querendi causas praebitura. At mehercules satis
mihi iam videbaris animi habere etiam adversus
solida mala, nedum ad istas umbras malorum, quibus
ingemescunt homines moris causa. Quod damnorum
omnium maximum est, si amicum perdidisses, danda
opera erat, ut magis gauderes, quod habueras, quam
maereres, quod amiseras.

4 " Sed plerique non computant, quanta perceperint,
quantum gavisi sint. Hoc habet inter reliqua mali
dolor iste : non supervacuus tantum, sed ingratus
est. Ergo quod habuisti talem amicum, periit opera?
Tot annis, tanta coniunctione vitae, tam familiari
studiorum societate nil actum est ? Cum amico
effers amicitiam ? Et quid doles amisisse, si habuisse
non prodest ? Mihi crede, magna pars ex iis, quos
amavimus, licet ipsos casus abstulerit, apud nos manet.
Nostrum est, quod praeteriit, tempus nec quicquam
5 est loco tutiore quam quod fuit. Ingrati adversus

---

^a As Lipsius pointed out, the remainder of Seneca's letter
consists of the quoted epistle to Marullus.

^b The Roman view differs from the modern view, just as
this Letter is rather more severe than *Ep.* lxiii. (on the death
of Lucilius's friend Flaccus).

let him satisfy his grief or at any rate work off the first shock ; but those who have assumed an indulgence in grief should be rebuked forthwith, and should learn that there are certain follies even in tears.

[a] " Is it solace that you look for ? Let me give you a scolding instead ! You are like a woman in the way you take your son's death ; what would you do if you had lost an intimate friend ? A son, a little child of unknown promise, is dead ; a fragment of time has been lost. We hunt out excuses for grief ; we would even utter unfair complaints about Fortune, as if Fortune would never give us just reason for complaining ! But I had really thought that you possessed spirit enough to deal with concrete troubles, to say nothing of the shadowy troubles over which men make moan through force of habit. Had you lost a friend (which is the greatest blow of all),[b] you would have had to endeavour rather to rejoice because you had possessed him than to mourn because you had lost him.

" But many men fail to count up how manifold their gains have been, how great their rejoicings. Grief like yours has this among other evils : it is not only useless, but thankless. Has it then all been for nothing that you have had such a friend ? During so many years, amid such close associations, after such intimate communion of personal interests, has nothing been accomplished ? Do you bury friendship along with a friend ? And why lament having lost him, if it be of no avail to have possessed him ? Believe me, a great part of those we have loved, though chance has removed their persons, still abides with us. The past is ours, and there is nothing more secure for us than that which has been. We are

percepta spe futuri sumus, quasi non quod futurum
est, si modo successerit nobis, cito in praeterita
transiturum sit. Anguste fructus rerum determinat,
qui tantum praesentibus laetus est ; et futura et
praeterita delectant, haec exspectatione, illa memoria, sed alterum pendet et non fieri potest,
alterum non potest non fuisse.

"Quis ergo furor est certissimo excidere ? Ad-
quiescamus iis, quae iam hausimus, si modo non per-
forato animo hauriebamus et transmittente quicquid
6 acceperat. Innumerabilia sunt exempla eorum, qui
liberos iuvenes sine lacrimis extulerint, qui in sena-
tum aut in aliquod publicum officium a rogo redierint
et statim aliud egerint. Nec inmerito ; nam primum
supervacuum est dolere, si nihil dolendo proficias.
Deinde iniquum est queri de eo, quod uni accidit,
omnibus restat. Deinde desiderii stulta conquestio
est, ubi minimum interest inter amissum et desiderantem. Eo itaque aequiore animo esse debemus, quod
quos amisimus, sequimur.

7 " Respice celeritatem rapidissimi temporis, cogita
brevitatem huius spatii, per quod citatissimi currimus,
observa hunc comitatum generis humani eodem
tendentis minimis intervallis distinctum, etiam ubi
maxima videntur ; quem putas perisse, praemissus
est. Quid autem dementius quam, cum idem tibi

---

[a] Almost identical language with the closing words of
Ep. lxiii. : *quem putamus perisse, praemissus est.*

ungrateful for past gains, because we hope for the future, as if the future—if so be that any future is ours—will not be quickly blended with the past. People set a narrow limit to their enjoyments if they take pleasure only in the present; both the future and the past serve for our delight—the one with anticipation, and the other with memories— but the one is contingent and may not come to pass, while the other must have been.

"What madness it is, therefore, to lose our grip on that which is the surest thing of all? Let us rest content with the pleasures we have quaffed in past days, if only, while we quaffed them, the soul was not pierced like a sieve, only to lose again whatever it had received. There are countless cases of men who have without tears buried sons in the prime of manhood—men who have returned from the funeral pyre to the Senate chamber, or to any other official duties, and have straightway busied themselves with something else. And rightly; for in the first place it is idle to grieve if you get no help from grief. In the second place, it is unfair to complain about what has happened to one man but is in store for all. Again, it is foolish to lament one's loss, when there is such a slight interval between the lost and the loser. Hence we should be more resigned in spirit, because we follow closely those whom we have lost.

"Note the rapidity of Time—that swiftest of things; consider the shortness of the course along which we hasten at top speed; mark this throng of humanity, all straining toward the same point with briefest intervals between them—even when they seem longest; he whom you count as passed away has simply posted on ahead.[a] And what is more irrational than to bewail your predecessor, when

133

iter emetiendum sit, flere eum, qui antecessit ? Flet
aliquis factum, quod non ignoravit futurum ? Aut
8 si mortem in homine non cogitavit, sibi inposuit.
Flet aliquis factum, quod aiebat non posse non fieri ?
Quisquis aliquem queritur mortuum esse, queritur[1]
hominem fuisse. Omnis eadem condicio devinxit: cui
9 nasci contigit, mori restat. Intervallis distinguimur,
exitu aequamur. Hoc quod inter primum diem et
ultimum iacet, varium incertumque est : si molestias
aestimes, etiam puero longum, si velocitatem, etiam
seni angustum. Nihil non lubricum et fallax et
omni tempestate mobilius.[2] Iactantur cuncta et in
contrarium transeunt iubente fortuna, et in tanta
volutatione rerum humanarum nihil cuiquam nisi
mors certum est. Tamen de eo queruntur omnes,
in quo uno nemo decipitur. ' Sed puer decessit.'
Nondum dico melius agi cum eo, qui cito[3] vita
defungitur ; ad eum transeamus, qui consenuit.
10 Quantulo vincit infantem ! Propone temporis pro-
fundi vastitatem et universum complectere, deinde
hoc, quod aetatem vocamus humanam, conpara im-
menso ; videbis, quam exiguum sit, quod optamus,
quod extendimus. Ex hoc quantum lacrimae, quan-
11 tum sollicitudines occupant ! Quantum mors, antequam veniat, optata, quantum valitudo, quantum
timor ! Quantum tenent aut rudes aut inutiles

[1] *mortuum esse queritur* later MSS. : om. by B and A[1].
[2] *mobilius* later MSS. ; *mobilibus* BA.
[3] *cito* added by Gertz.

134

you yourself must travel on the same journey? Does a man bewail an event which he knew would take place? Or, if he did not think of death as man's lot, he has but cheated himself. Does a man bewail an event which he has been admitting to be unavoidable? Whoever complains about the death of anyone, is complaining that he was a man. Everyone is bound by the same terms: he who is privileged to be born, is destined to die. Periods of time separate us, but death levels us. The period which lies between our first day and our last is shifting and uncertain: if you reckon it by its troubles, it is long even to a lad, if by its speed, it is scanty even to a greybeard. Everything is slippery, treacherous, and more shifting than any weather. All things are tossed about and shift into their opposites at the bidding of Fortune; amid such a turmoil of mortal affairs nothing but death is surely in store for anyone. And yet all men complain about the one thing wherein none of them is deceived. 'But he died in boyhood.' I am not yet prepared to say that he who quickly comes to the end of his life has the better of the bargain; let us turn to consider the case of him who has grown to old age. How very little is he superior to the child! [a] Place before your mind's eye the vast spread of time's abyss, and consider the universe; and then contrast our so-called human life with infinity: you will then see how scant is that for which we pray, and which we seek to lengthen. How much of this time is taken up with weeping, how much with worry! How much with prayers for death before death arrives, how much with our health, how much with our fears! How much is occupied by our years of inexperience

[a] For a similar argument see *Ep.* xii. 6 f.

135

anni ! Dimidium ex hoc edormitur. Adice labores, luctus, pericula, et intelleges etiam in longissima
12 vita minimum esse, quod vivitur. Sed quis tibi concedet non melius se habere eum, cui cito reverti licet, cui ante lassitudinem peractum est iter ? Vita nec bonum nec malum est ; boni ac mali locus est. Ita nihil ille perdidit nisi aleam in damnum certiorem. Potuit evadere modestus et prudens, potuit sub cura tua in meliora formari, sed, quod iustius timetur,
13 potuit fieri pluribus similis. Aspice illos iuvenes, quos ex nobilissimis domibus in harenam luxuria proiecit ; aspice illos, qui suam alienamque libidinem exercent mutuo inpudici, quorum nullus sine ebrietate, nullus sine aliquo insigni flagitio dies exit ; plus timeri quam sperari potuisse manifestum erit.

"Non debes itaque causas doloris accersere nec
14 levia incommoda indignando cumulare. Non hortor, ut nitaris et surgas ; non tam male de te iudico, ut tibi adversus hoc totam putem virtutem advocandam. Non est dolor iste, sed morsus ; tu illum dolorem facis.

"Sine dubio multum philosophia profecit, si puerum nutrici adhuc quam patri notiorem animo forti
15 desideras. Quid ? Nunc ego duritiam suadeo et in

---

a i.e., who have had to turn gladiators.

or of useless endeavour! And half of all this time is wasted in sleeping. Add, besides, our toils, our griefs, our dangers—and you will comprehend that even in the longest life real living is the least portion thereof. Nevertheless, who will make such an admission as: 'A man is *not* better off who is allowed to return home quickly, whose journey is accomplished before he is wearied out'? Life is neither a Good nor an Evil; it is simply the place where good and evil exist. Hence this little boy has lost nothing except a hazard where loss was more assured than gain. He might have turned out temperate and prudent; he might, with your fostering care, have been moulded to a better standard; but (and this fear is more reasonable) he might have become just like the many. Note the youths of the noblest lineage whose extravagance has flung them into the arena *a*; note those men who cater to the passions of themselves and others in mutual lust, whose days never pass without drunkenness or some signal act of shame; it will thus be clear to you that there was more to fear than to hope for.

" For this reason you ought not to invite excuses for grief or aggravate slight burdens by getting indignant. I am not exhorting you to make an effort and rise to great heights; for my opinion of you is not so low as to make me think that it is necessary for you to summon every bit of your virtue to face this trouble. Yours is not pain; it is a mere sting—and it is you yourself who are turning it into pain.

" Of a surety philosophy has done you much service if you can bear courageously the loss of a boy who was as yet better known to his nurse than to his father! And what, then? Now, at this time, am I

137

funere ipso rigere vultum volo et animum ne contrahi
quidem patior? Minime. Inhumanitas est ista, non
virtus, funera suorum isdem oculis, quibus ipsos,
videre nec commoveri ad primam familiarium divul-
sionem. Puta autem me vetare; quaedam sunt sui
iuris. Excidunt etiam retinentibus lacrimae et
16 animum profusae levant. Quid ergo est? Per-
mittamus illis cadere, non imperemus; fluat, quantum adfectus eiecerit, non quantum poscet imitatio.
Nihil vero maerori adiciamus nec illum ad alienum
augeamus exemplum. Plus ostentatio doloris exigit
quam dolor: quotus quisque sibi tristis est! Clarius,
cum audiuntur, gemunt et taciti quietique dum
secretum est, cum aliquos videre, in fletus novos
excitantur. Tunc capiti suo manus ingerunt, quod
potuerant facere nullo prohibente liberius, tunc
mortem comprecantur sibi, tunc lectulo devolvuntur;
17 sine spectatore cessat dolor. Sequitur nos ut in aliis
rebus, ita in hac quoque hoc vitium, ad plurium
exempla componi nec quid oporteat, sed quid soleat,
aspicere. A natura discedimus, populo nos damus
nullius rei bono auctori et in hac re sicut in aliis [1]
omnibus inconstantissimo. Videt aliquem fortem in

[1] *aliis* Hermes; *his* MSS.

138

advising you to be hard-hearted, desiring you to keep your countenance unmoved at the very funeral ceremony, and not allowing your soul even to feel the pinch of pain? By no means. That would mean lack of feeling rather than virtue—to behold the burial ceremonies of those near and dear to you with the same expression as you beheld their living forms, and to show no emotion over the first bereavement in your family. But suppose that I forbade you to show emotion; there are certain feelings which claim their own rights. Tears fall, no matter how we try to check them, and by being shed they ease the soul. What, then, shall we do? Let us allow them to fall, but let us not command them do so; let us weep according as emotion floods our eyes, but not as much as mere imitation shall demand. Let us, indeed, add nothing to natural grief, nor augment it by following the example of others. The display of grief makes more demands than grief itself: how few men are sad in their own company! They lament the louder for being heard; persons who are reserved and silent when alone are stirred to new paroxysms of tears when they behold others near them! At such times they lay violent hands upon their own persons,—though they might have done this more easily if no one were present to check them; at such times they pray for death; at such times they toss themselves from their couches. But their grief slackens with the departure of onlookers. In this matter, as in others also, we are obsessed by this fault—conforming to the pattern of the many, and regarding convention rather than duty. We abandon nature and surrender to the mob—who are never good advisers in anything, and in this respect as in all others are most inconsistent. People see a man

luctu suo : impium vocat et efferatum ; videt aliquem
conlabentem et corpori adfusum : effeminatum ait
18 et enervem. Omnia itaque ad rationem revocanda
sunt. Stultius vero nihil est quam famam captare
tristitiae et lacrimas adprobare, quas iudico sapienti
viro alias permissas cadere, alias vi sua latas.

"Dicam quid intersit. Cum primus nos nuntius
acerbi funeris perculit, cum tenemus corpus e com-
plexu nostro in ignem transiturum, lacrimas naturalis
necessitas exprimit et spiritus ictu doloris inpulsus
quemadmodum totum corpus quatit, ita oculos, quibus
19 adiacentem umorem perpremit et expellit. Hae
lacrimae per elisionem cadunt nolentibus nobis ; aliae
sunt, quibus exitum damus, cum memoria eorum, quos
amisimus, retractatur. Et inest quiddam dulce tristitiae, cum occurrunt sermones eorum iucundi, conversatio hilaris, officiosa pietas ; tunc oculi velut in
gaudio relaxantur. His indulgemus, illis vincimur.
20 "Non est itaque, quod lacrimas propter circulum
adstantem[1] adsidentemque aut contineas aut ex-
primas ; nec cessant nec fluunt umquam tam turpiter
quam finguntur ; eant sua sponte. Ire autem possunt placidis atque compositis. Saepe salva sapientis
auctoritate fluxerunt tanto temperamento, ut illis
nec humanitas nec dignitas deesset. Licet, inquam,

[1] *circulum adstantem* Rossbach ; *circum stantem* A.

EPISTLE XCIX.

who bears his grief bravely : they call him undutiful and savage-hearted ; they see a man who collapses and clings to his dead : they call him womanish and weak. Everything, therefore, should be referred to reason. But nothing is more foolish than to court a reputation for sadness and to sanction tears ; for I hold that with a wise man some tears fall by consent, others by their own force.

" I shall explain the difference as follows : When the first news of some bitter loss has shocked us, when we embrace the form that will soon pass from our arms to the funeral flames—then tears are wrung from us by the necessity of Nature, and the life-force, smitten by the stroke of grief, shakes both the whole body, and the eyes also, from which it presses out and causes to flow the moisture that lies within. Tears like these fall by a forcing-out process, against our will ; but different are the tears which we allow to escape when we muse in memory upon those whom we have lost. And there is in them a certain sweet sadness when we remember the sound of a pleasant voice, a genial conversation, and the busy duties of yore ; at such a time the eyes are loosened, as it were, with joy. This sort of weeping we indulge ; the former sort overcomes us.

" There is, then, no reason why, just because a group of persons is standing in your presence or sitting at your side, you should either check or pour forth your tears ; whether restrained or outpoured, they are never so disgraceful as when feigned. Let them flow naturally. But it is possible for tears to flow from the eyes of those who are quiet and at peace. They often flow without impairing the influence of the wise man—with such restraint that they show no want either of feeling or of self-respect.

141

21 naturae obsequi gravitate servata. Vidi ego in
funere suorum verendos, in quorum ore amor emine-
bat remota omni lugentium scaena, nihil erat nisi
quod veris dabatur adfectibus. Est aliquis et dolendi
decor ; hic sapienti servandus est et quemadmodum
in ceteris rebus, ita etiam in lacrimis aliquid sat est ;
inprudentium [1] ut gaudia sic dolores exundavere.

22 "Aequo animo excipe necessaria. Quid incredibile,
quid novum evenit ? Quam multis cum maxime
funus locatur, quam multis vitalia emuntur,[a] quam
multi post luctum tuum lugent ! Quotiens cogitaveris puerum fuisse, cogita et hominem, cui nihil certi
promittitur, quem fortuna non utique perducit ad
23 senectutem ; unde visum est, dimittit. Ceterum
frequenter de illo loquere et memoriam eius, quantum
potes, celebra. Quae ad te saepius revertetur, si erit
sine acerbitate [2] ventura ; nemo enim libenter tristi
conversatur, nedum tristitiae. Si quos sermones eius,
si quos quamvis parvoli iocos cum voluptate [3] audi-
eras, saepius repete ; potuisse illum implere spes
tuas, quas paterna mente conceperas, audacter ad-
24 firma. Oblivisci quidem suorum ac memoriam cum

---

[1] *imprudentium* later MSS. ; *ut prudentium* BA.
[2] *sine acerbitate* later MSS. ; *inea cervitate* BA.
[3] *voluptate* later MSS. ; *voluntate* BA.

---

[a] *i.e.*, a shroud for the funeral couch, *lectus vitalis.*

EPISTLE XCIX.

We may, I assure you, obey Nature and yet maintain our dignity. I have seen men worthy of reverence, during the burial of those near and dear, with countenances upon which love was written clear even after the whole apparatus of mourning was removed, and who showed no other conduct than that which was allowed to genuine emotion. There is a comeliness even in grief. This should be cultivated by the wise man; even in tears, just as in other matters also, there is a certain sufficiency; it is with the unwise that sorrows, like joys, gush over.

"Accept in an unruffled spirit that which is inevitable. What can happen that is beyond belief? Or what that is new? How many men at this very moment are making arrangements for funerals! How many are purchasing grave-clothes[a]! How many are mourning, when you yourself have finished mourning! As often as you reflect that your boy has ceased to be, reflect also upon man, who has no sure promise of anything, whom Fortune does not inevitably escort to the confines of old age, but lets him go at whatever point she sees fit. You may, however, speak often concerning the departed, and cherish his memory to the extent of your power. This memory will return to you all the more often if you welcome its coming without bitterness; for no man enjoys converse with one who is sorrowful, much less with sorrow itself. And whatever words, whatever jests of his, no matter how much of a child he was, may have given you pleasure to hear—these I would have you recall again and again; assure yourself confidently that he might have fulfilled the hopes which you, his father, had entertained. Indeed, to forget the beloved dead, to bury their memory along with their bodies, to

143

corporibus efferre et effusissime flere, meminisse [1]
parcissime,—inhumani animi est. Sic aves, sic ferae
suos diligunt, quarum concitatus [2] est amor et paene
rabidus, sed cum [3] amissis totus extinguitur. Hoc
prudentem virum non decet ; meminisse perseveret,
25 lugere desinat. Illud nullo modo probo, quod [4] ait
Metrodorus : esse aliquam cognatam tristitiae voluptatem, hanc esse captandam in eiusmodi tempore.
Ipsa Metrodori verba subscripsi. Μητροδώρου ἐπι-
στολῶν πρὸς τὴν ἀδελφήν.[5] ἔστιν γάρ τις ἡδονὴ λύπῃ
26 συγγενής, ἣν χρὴ θηρεύειν κατὰ τοῦτον τὸν καιρόν. De
quibus non dubito quid sis sensurus. Quid enim est
turpius quam captare in ipso luctu voluptatem,
immo per luctum, et inter lacrimas quoque quod
iuvet, quaerere ? Hi sunt, qui nobis obiciunt nimium
rigorem et infamant praecepta nostra duritiae,[6] quod
dicamus dolorem aut admittendum in animum non
esse aut cito expellendum. Utrum [7] tandem est aut
incredibilius aut inhumanius non sentire amisso
amico dolorem an voluptatem in ipso dolore aucupari ?
27 Nos quod praecipimus, honestum est ; cum aliquid
lacrimarum adfectus effuderit et, ut ita dicam,
despumaverit, non esse tradendum animum dolori.
Quid, tu dicis miscendam ipsi dolori voluptatem ?

---

[1] *meminisse* later MSS.; *memisse* BA.
[2] *quarum concitatus* later MSS.; *quorum contria concitatus actus* BA.
[3] *cum* later MSS.; *eum* BA.
[4] *quod* later MSS.; *quid* BA.
[5] Rossbach holds that these five words belong in the
margin.
[6] *duritiae* Madvig; *duritia* BA.
[7] *utrum* later MSS.; *virum* BA.

bewail them bounteously and afterwards think of
them but scantily — this is the mark of a soul
below that of man. For that is the way in which
birds and beasts love their young ; their affection is
quickly roused and almost reaches madness, but it
cools away entirely when its object dies. This
quality does not befit a man of sense ; he should
continue to remember, but should cease to mourn.
And in no wise do I approve of the remark of
Metrodorus—that there is a certain pleasure akin
to sadness, and that one should give chase thereto at
such times as these. I am quoting the actual words
of Metrodorus.[a] I have no doubt what your feelings
will be in these matters ; for what is baser than to
'chase after' pleasure in the very midst of mourning
— nay rather by means of mourning — and even
amid one's tears to hunt out that which will give
pleasure ? These [b] are the men who accuse us [c] of
too great strictness, slandering our precepts because
of supposed harshness—because (say they) we
declare that grief should either not be given place
in the soul at all, or else should be driven out forthwith. But which is the more incredible or inhuman—
to feel no grief at the loss of one's friend, or to go
a-hawking after pleasure in the midst of grief ?
That which we Stoics advise, is honourable ; when
emotion has prompted a moderate flow of tears, and
has, so to speak, ceased to effervesce, the soul should
not be surrendered to grief. But what do you mean,
Metrodorus, by saying that with our very grief
there should be a blending of pleasure ? That is

[a] This passage, which Buecheler corrected in several
places, is omitted in the English, because Seneca has already
translated it literally. M. was addressing his sister.
[b] *i.e.*, men like Metrodorus.   [c] *i.e.*, the Stoics.

Sic consolamur crustulo pueros, sic infantium fletum
infuso lacte conpescimus.

" Ne illo quidem tempore, quo filius ardet aut amicus
expirat, cessare pateris voluptatem, sed ipsum vis
titillare maerorem ? Utrum honestius dolor ab
animo summovetur an voluptas ad dolorem quoque
admittitur ? ' Admittitur ' dico ? Captatur et qui-
28 dem ex ipso. ' Est aliqua ' inquit ' voluptas cognata
tristitiae.' Istuc nobis licet dicere, vobis quidem
non licet. Unum bonum nostis voluptatem, unum
malum dolorem ; quae potest inter bonum et malum
esse cognatio ? Sed puta esse ; nunc potissimum
eruitur ? Et ipsum dolorem scrutamur, an quid [1]
29 habeat iucundum circa se et voluptarium ? Quaedam
remedia aliis partibus corporis salutaria velut foeda
et indecora adhiberi aliis nequeunt, et quod aliubi
prodesset sine damno verecundiae, id fit inhonestum
loco vulneris. Non te pudet luctum voluptate sanare ? Severius ista plaga curanda est. Illud potius
admone, nullum mali sensum ad eum, qui periit,
30 pervenire ; nam si pervenit, non periit. Nulla,
inquam, res eum laedit, qui nullus est ; vivit, si
laeditur. Utrum putas illi male esse, quod nullus
est, an quod est adhuc aliquis ? Atqui nec ex eo

[1] *an quid* Buecheler ; *aliquid* BA ; *an aliquid* later MSS.

---

[a] *i.e.*, the Epicureans.
[b] *i.e.*, grief should not be replaced by pleasure ; otherwise
grief will cease to exist.

the sweetmeat method of pacifying children; that is the way we still the cries of infants, by pouring milk down their throats!

"Even at the moment when your son's body is on the pyre, or your friend breathing his last, will you not suffer your pleasure to cease, rather than tickle your very grief with pleasure? Which is the more honourable—to remove grief from your soul, or to admit pleasure even into the company of grief? Did I say 'admit'? Nay, I mean 'chase after,' and from the hands, too, of grief itself. Metrodorus says: 'There is a certain pleasure which is related to sadness.' We Stoics may say that, but you may not. The only Good which you[a] recognize, is pleasure, and the only Evil, pain; and what relationship can there be between a Good and an Evil? But suppose that such a relationship does exist; now, of all times, is it to be rooted out?[b] Shall we examine grief also, and see with what elements of delight and pleasure it is surrounded? Certain remedies, which are beneficial for some parts of the body, cannot be applied to other parts because these are, in a way, revolting and unfit; and that which in certain cases would work to a good purpose without any loss to one's self-respect, may become unseemly because of the situation of the wound. Are you not, similarly, ashamed to cure sorrow by pleasure? No, this sore spot must be treated in a more drastic way. This is what you should preferably advise: that no sensation of evil can reach one who is dead; for if it can reach him, he is not dead. And I say that nothing can hurt him who is as naught; for if a man can be hurt, he is alive. Do you think him to be badly off because he is no more, or because he still exists as somebody? And

147

potest ei tormentum esse, quod non est ; quis enim
nullius sensus est ? Nec ex eo, quod est ; effugit
enim maximum mortis incommodum, non esse.

31 "Illud quoque dicamus ei, qui deflet ac desiderat in
aetate prima raptum : omnes, quantum ad brevitatem aevi, si universo conpares, et iuvenes et senes,
in aequo sumus. Minus enim ad nos ex aetate
omni venit quam quod minimum esse quis dixerit,
quoniam quidem minimum aliqua pars est. Hoc
quod vivimus, proximum nihilost ; et tamen, o
dementiam nostram, late disponitur.

32 "Haec tibi scripsi, non tamquam expectaturus esses
remedium tam serum, liquet enim mihi te locutum
tecum quicquid lecturus es, sed ut castigarem exi-
guam illam moram, qua a te recessisti, et in reliquom
adhortarer, contra fortunam tolleres animos et omnia
eius tela, non tamquam possent venire, sed tamquam
utique essent ventura, prospiceres." VALE.

C.

SENECA LVCILIO SVO SALVTEM

1 Fabiani Papiri libros, qui inscribuntur Civilium,
legisse te cupidissime scribis, et non respondisse
expectationi tuae, deinde oblitus de philosopho agi
conpositionem eius accusas.

148

yet no torment can come to him from the fact that he is no more—for what feeling can belong to one who does not exist?—nor from the fact that he exists; for he has escaped the greatest disadvantage that death has in it—namely, non-existence.

"Let us say this also to him who mourns and misses the untimely dead: that all of us, whether young or old, live, in comparison with eternity, on the same level as regards our shortness of life. For out of all time there comes to us less than what any one could call least, since 'least' is at any rate some part; but this life of ours is next to nothing, and yet (fools that we are!), we marshal it in broad array!

"These words I have written to you, not with the idea that you should expect a cure from me at such a late date—for it is clear to me that you have told yourself everything that you will read in my letter—but with the idea that I should rebuke you even for the slight delay during which you lapsed from your true self, and should encourage you for the future, to rouse your spirit against Fortune and to be on the watch for all her missiles, not as if they might possibly come, but as if they were bound to come." Farewell.

C. ON THE WRITINGS OF FABIANUS

You write me that you have read with the greatest eagerness the work by Fabianus Papirius entitled *The Duties of a Citizen*, and that it did not come up to your expectations; then, forgetting that you are dealing with a philosopher, you proceed to criticize his style.

THE EPISTLES OF SENECA

Puta esse quod dicis et effundi verba, non figi ;
primum habet ista res suam gratiam et est decor
proprius orationis leniter lapsae. Multum enim
interesse existimo, utrum exciderit an fluxerit.
Adice [1] nunc, quod in hoc quoque, quod dicturus
2 sum, ingens [2] differentia est : Fabianus mihi non
effundere videtur orationem, sed fundere ; adeo
larga est et sine perturbatione, non sine cursu tamen
veniens. Illud plane fatetur et praefert, non esse [3]
tractatam nec diu tortam. Sed ita, ut vis, esse
credamus ; mores ille, non verba conposuit et animis
3 scripsit ista, non auribus. Praeterea ipso dicente non
vacasset tibi partes intueri, adeo te summa rapuisset ;
et fere quae inpetu placent, minus praestant ad
manum relata.

Sed illud quoque multum est primo aspectu oculos
occupasse, etiam si contemplatio diligens inventura
4 est quod arguat. Si me interrogas, maior ille est,
qui iudicium abstulit quam qui meruit ; et scio hunc
tutiorem esse, scio audacius sibi de futuro promittere.
Oratio sollicita philosophum non decet ; ubi tandem
erit fortis et constans, ubi periculum sui faciet, qui
5 timet verbis ? Fabianus non erat neglegens in
oratione, sed securus. Itaque nihil invenies sordi-

---

[1] *adice* added by Hense.
[2] *ingens* later MSS. ; *indigens* BA.
[3] *esse* Muretus ; *esset* BA.

---

a i.e., his style is like a river rather than a torrent.

EPISTLE C.

Suppose, now, that your statement is true—that he pours forth rather than places his words ; let me, however, tell you at the start that this trait of which you speak has a peculiar charm, and that it is a grace appropriate to a smoothly-gliding style. For, I maintain, it matters a great deal whether it tumbles forth, or flows along. Moreover, there is a deal of difference in this regard also—as I shall make clear to you : Fabianus seems to me to have not so much an "efflux" as a "flow" of words :[a] so copious is it, without confusion, and yet not without speed. This is indeed what his style declares and announces—that he has not spent a long time in working his matter over and twisting it into shape. But even supposing the facts are as you would have them ; the man was building up character rather than words, and was writing those words for the mind rather than for the ear. Besides, had he been speaking them in his own person, you would not have had time to consider the details—the whole work would have so swept you along. For as a rule that which pleases by its swiftness is of less value when taken in hand for reading.

Nevertheless, this very quality, too, of attracting at first sight is a great advantage, no matter whether careful investigation may discover something to criticize. If you ask me, I should say that he who has forced approval is greater than he who has earned it ; and yet I know that the latter is safer, I know that he can give more confident guarantees for the future. A meticulous manner of writing does not suit the philosopher ; if he is timid as to words, when will he ever be brave and steadfast, when will he ever really show his worth ? Fabianus's style was not careless, it was assured. That is why

151

dum : electa verba sunt, non captata nec huius
saeculi more contra naturam suam posita et inversa,
splendida tamen, quamvis sumantur e[1] medio.
Sensus honestos et magnificos habes, non coactos in
sententiam, sed latius dictos. Videbimus, quid
parum recisum sit, quid parum structum, quid non[2]
huius recentis politurae ; cum circumspexeris omnia,
6 nullas videbis angustias inanis. Desit sane varietas
marmorum et concisura aquarum cubiculis interfluen-
tium et pauperis cella et quicquid aliud luxuria non
contenta decore simplici miscet ; quod dici solet,
domus recta est.

Adice nunc, quod de compositione non constat.
Quidam illam volunt esse ex horrido comptam,
quidam usque eo aspera gaudent, ut etiam quae
mollius casus explicuit, ex industria dissipent et
clausulas abrumpant, ne ad expectatum respon-
7 deant. Lege Ciceronem : compositio eius una est,
pedem curvat lenta et sine infamia mollis. At contra
Pollionis Asinii salebrosa et exiliens et ubi minime
exspectes, relictura. Denique omnia apud Ciceronem desinunt, aput Pollionem cadunt exceptis
paucissimis, quae ad certum modum et ad unum
exemplar adstricta sunt.

---

[1] *e* later MSS. ; *a* BA.   [2] *non* later MSS. ; om. BA.

---

[a] *Concisura* : from *concido*, to " cut into sections," " dis-
tribute " (of water-pipes).
[b] *Cf. Ep.* xviii. 7, and Martial iii. 48 :

> Pauperis extruxit cellam, sed vendidit Olus
> praedia ; nunc cellam pauperis Olus habet.

Rich men sometimes fitted up in their palaces an imitation
" poor man's cabin " by way of contrast to their other
rooms or as a gesture towards simple living ; Seneca uses
the phrase figuratively for certain devices in composition.
[c] Quintilian x. 1. 113 says : *multa in Asinio Pollione
inventio, summa diligentia, adeo ut quibusdam etiam nimia*

you will find nothing shoddy in his work : his words
are well chosen and yet not hunted for ; they are
not unnaturally inserted and inverted, according to
the present-day fashion ; but they possess distinction,
even though they are taken from ordinary speech.
There you have honourable and splendid ideas, not
fettered into aphorisms, but spoken with greater
freedom. We shall of course notice passages that
are not sufficiently pruned, not constructed with
sufficient care, and lacking the polish which is in
vogue nowadays ; but after regarding the whole,
you will see that there are no futile subtleties of
argument. There may, doubtless, be no variety of
marbles, no water-supply [a] which flows from one
apartment to another, no " pauper - rooms," [b] or
any other device that luxury adds when ill content
with simple charms ; but, in the vulgar phrase, it is
" a good house to live in."

Furthermore, opinions vary with regard to the
style. Some wish it to be polished down from all
roughness ; and some take so great a pleasure in the
abrupt manner that they would intentionally break
up any passage which may by chance spread itself
out more smoothly, scattering the closing words in
such a way that the sentences may result unexpectedly. Read Cicero : his style has unity ; it moves
with a modulated pace, and is gentle without being
degenerate. The style of Asinius Pollio, on the
other hand, is " bumpy," jerky, leaving off when
you least expect it. [c] And finally, Cicero always
stops gradually ; while Pollio breaks off, except in
the very few cases where he cleaves to a definite
rhythm and a single pattern.

videatur ; et consilii et animi satis ; a nitore et iucunditate
Ciceronis ita longe abest, ut videri possit saeculo prior.

8 Humilia praeterea tibi videri dicis omnia et parum
erecta; quo vitio carere eum iudico. Non sunt
enim humilia illa sed placida et ad animi tenorem [1]
quietum compositumque formata, nec depressa sed
plana. Deest illis oratorius vigor stimulique, quos
quaeris, et subiti ictus sententiarum. Sed totum
corpus videris quam sit comptum; honestum est.
Non habet oratio eius, sed dabit,[2] dignitatem.

9 Adfer, quem Fabiano possis praeponere. Dic
Ciceronem, cuius libri ad philosophiam pertinentes
paene totidem sunt, quot Fabiani; cedam, sed non
statim pusillum est, si quid maximo minus est. Dic
Asinium Pollionem; cedam, et respondeamus: in
re tanta eminere est post duos esse. Nomina adhuc
T. Livium, scripsit enim et dialogos, quos non magis
philosophiae adnumerare possis quam historiae, et
ex professo philosophiam continentis libros; huic
quoque dabo locum. Vide tamen, quam multos
antecedat, qui a tribus vincitur et tribus eloquentis-
simis.

10 Sed non praestat omnia: non est fortis oratio eius,
quamvis elata sit; non est violenta nec torrens,
quamvis effusa sit; non est perspicua, sed pura.
" Desideres," inquis, " contra vitia aliquid aspere dici,
contra pericula animose, contra fortunam superbe,

---

[1] *enim humilia illa sed placida et ad animi tenorem* later
MSS. and Harl.; *enim tenorem* BA.
[2] *dabit* Lipsius: *debet* BA.

---

[a] The wording here resembles strikingly that of the
Elder Seneca, *Controv.* ii. pr. *2 deerat illi* (sc. *Fabiano*)
oratorium robur et ille pugnatorius mucro.

EPISTLE C.

In addition to this, you say that everything in Fabianus seems to you commonplace and lacking in elevation; but I myself hold that he is free from such a fault. For that style of his is not commonplace, but simply calm and adjusted to his peaceful and well-ordered mind —not on a low level but on an even plane. There is lacking the verve and spur of the orator (for which you are looking), and a sudden shock of epigrams.[a] But look, please, at the whole work, how well-ordered it is: there is a distinction in it. His style does not possess, but will suggest, dignity.

Mention someone whom you may rank ahead of Fabianus. Cicero, let us say, whose books on philosophy are almost as numerous as those of Fabianus. I will concede this point; but it is no slight thing to be less than the greatest. Or Asinius Pollio, let us say. I will yield again, and content myself by replying: " It is a distinction to be third in so great a field." You may also include Livy; for Livy wrote both dialogues (which should be ranked as history no less than as philosophy), and works which professedly deal with philosophy. I shall yield in the case of Livy also. But consider how many writers Fabianus outranks, if he is surpassed by three only—and those three the greatest masters of eloquence!

But, it may be said, he does not offer everything: though his style is elevated, it is not strong; though it flows forth copiously, it lacks force and sweep; it is not translucent, but it is lucid. "One would fail," you urge, "to find therein any rugged denunciation of vice, any courageous words in the face of danger, any proud defiance of Fortune, any scornful threats

155

contra ambitionem contumeliose. Volo luxuriam obiurgari, libidinem traduci, inpotentiam frangi. Si aliquid oratorie acre, tragice grande, comice exile.' Vis illum adsidere pusillae rei, verbis ; ille rerum se magnitudini addixit,[1] eloquentiam velut umbram non hoc agens trahit.

11   Non erunt sine dubio singula circumspecta nec in se collecta nec omne verbum excitabit ac punget,[2] fateor. Exibunt multa nec ferient et interdum otiosa praeterlabetur oratio, sed multum erit in omnibus lucis, sed ingens sine taedio spatium. Denique illud praestabit, ut liqueat tibi illum sensisse quae scripsit. Intelleges hoc actum, ut tu scires quid illi placeret, non ut ille placeret tibi. Ad profectum omnia tendunt, ad bonam mentem, non quaeritur plausus.

12   Talia esse scripta eius non dubito, etiam si magis reminiscor quam teneo haeretque mihi color eorum non ex recenti conversatione familiariter, sed summatim, ut solet ex vetere notitia. Cum audirem certe illum, talia mihi videbantur, non solida, sed plena, quae adulescentem indolis bonae attollerent et ad imitationem sui evocarent sine desperatione vincendi, quae mihi adhortatio videtur efficacissima. Deterret enim qui imitandi cupiditatem fecit, spem abstulit.

---

[1] *addixit* later MSS. ; *adduxit* BA.
[2] *ac punget* later MSS. ; *ag pugnet* BA.

EPISTLE C.

against self-seeking. I wish to see luxury rebuked, lust condemned, waywardness crushed out. Let him show us the keenness of oratory, the loftiness of tragedy, the subtlety of comedy." You wish him to rely on that pettiest of things, phraseology; but he has sworn allegiance to the greatness of his subject and draws eloquence after him as a sort of shadow, but not of set purpose.

Our author will doubtless not investigate every detail, nor subject it to analysis, nor inspect and emphasize each separate word. This I admit. Many phrases will fall short, or will fail to strike home, and at times the style will slip along indolently; but there will be plenty of light throughout the work; there will be long stretches which will not weary the reader. And, finally, he will offer this quality— of making it clear to you that he meant what he wrote. You will understand that his aim was to have you know what pleased him, rather than that he should please you. All his work makes for progress and for sanity, without any search for applause.

I do not doubt that his writings are of the kind I have described, although I am harking back to him rather than retaining a sure memory of him, and although the general tone of his writings remains in my mind, not from a careful and recent perusal, but in outline, as is natural after an acquaintance of long ago. But certainly, whenever I heard him lecture, such did his work seem to me—not solid but full, the kind which would inspire young men of promise and rouse their ambition to become like him, without making them hopeless of surpassing him;—and this method of encouragement seems to me the most helpful of all. For it is disheartening to inspire in a man the desire, and to take away from

157

Ceterum verbis abundabat, sine commendatione
partium singularum in universum magnificus. VALE.

CI.

SENECA LVCILIO SVO SALVTEM

1 Omnis dies, omnis hora quam nihil simus ostendit [1]
et aliquo argumento recenti admonet fragilitatis
oblitos; tum aeterna meditatos respicere cogit ad
mortem.

Quid sibi istud principium velit quaeris? Sene-
cionem Cornelium, equitem Romanum splendidum
et officiosum, noveras: ex tenui principio se ipse
promoverat et iam illi declivis erat cursus ad cetera.
2 Facilius enim crescit dignitas quam incipit. Pecunia
quoque circa paupertatem plurimum morae [2] habet,
dum ex illa erepat haeret. Iam [3] Senecio divitiis
imminebat, ad quas illum duae res ducebant efficacis-
simae, et quaerendi et custodiendi scientia, quarum
3 vel altera locupletem facere potuisset. Hic homo
summae frugalitatis, non minus patrimonii quam
corporis diligens, cum me ex consuetudine mane
vidisset, cum per totum diem amico graviter ad-
fecto et sine spe iacenti usque in noctem adsedisset,
cum hilaris cenasset, genere valitudinis praecipiti
arreptus, angina, vix conpressum artatis faucibus
spiritum traxit in lucem. Intra paucissimas ergo

---

[1] *simus ostendit* later MSS.; *sumostendit* BA.
[2] *morae* Pincianus; *amorem* BA.
[3] *haeret; iam* Buecheler; *hae* (or *hac*) *etiam* BA.

him the hope, of emulation. At any rate, his language was fluent, and though one might not approve every detail, the general effect was noble. Farewell.

CI. ON THE FUTILITY OF PLANNING AHEAD

Every day and every hour reveal to us what a nothing we are, and remind us with some fresh evidence that we have forgotten our weakness ; then, as we plan for eternity, they compel us to look over our shoulders at Death.

Do you ask me what this preamble means ? It refers to Cornelius Senecio, a distinguished and capable Roman knight, whom you knew : from humble beginnings he had advanced himself to fortune, and the rest of the path already lay downhill before him. For it is easier to grow in dignity than to make a start ; and money is very slow to come where there is poverty ; until it can creep out of that, it goes halting. Senecio was already bordering upon wealth, helped in that direction by two very powerful assets—knowing how to make money and how to keep it also ; either one of these gifts might have made him a rich man. Here was a person who lived most simply, careful of health and wealth alike. He had, as usual, called upon me early in the morning, and had then spent the whole day, even up to night-fall, at the bedside of a friend who was seriously and hopelessly ill. After a comfortable dinner, he was suddenly seized with an acute attack of quinsy, and, with the breath clogged tightly in his swollen throat, barely lived until daybreak. So within a very few hours after the time when he had been performing

159

horas, quam omnibus erat sani ac valentis officiis
4 functus, decessit.   Ille, qui et mari et terra pecuniam
agitabat, qui ad publica quoque nullum relinquens
inexpertum genus quaestus accesserat, in ipso actu
bene cedentium rerum, in ipso procurrentis pecuniae
impetu raptus est.

Insere nunc, Meliboee, piros, pone ordine[1] vites.

Quam stultum est aetatem disponere ne crastini
quidem dominum !   O quanta dementia est spes
longas inchoantium :   emam aedificabo, credam exi-
gam, honores geram, tum deinde lassam et plenam
5 senectutem in otium referam.   Omnia, mihi crede,
etiam felicibus dubia sunt.   Nihil sibi quisquam de
futuro debet promittere.   Id quoque, quod tenetur,
per manus exit et ipsam, quam premimus, horam
casus incidit.   Volvitur tempus rata quidem lege,
sed per obscurum ;   quid autem ad me, an naturae
certum sit quod mihi incertum est ?
6   Navigationes longas et pererratis litoribus alienis
seros in patriam reditus proponimus, militiam et
castrensium laborum tarda manipretia, procurationes
officiorumque per officia processus, cum interim ad
latus mors est, quae quoniam numquam cogitatur
nisi aliena, subinde nobis ingeruntur mortalitatis
exempla non diutius quam dum miramur haesura.
7   Quid autem stultius quam mirari id ullo die factum,

---

[1] *pone in ordine* BA.

a Vergil, *Ecl.* i. 74.
b Perhaps a hint to Lucilius, who was at this time
procurator in Sicily.

all the duties of a sound and healthy man, he passed away. He who was venturing investments by land and sea, who had also entered public life and left no type of business untried, during the very realization of financial success and during the very onrush of the money that flowed into his coffers, was snatched from the world !

Graft now thy pears, Meliboeus, and set out thy vines in their order ! *a*

But how foolish it is to set out one's life, when one is not even owner of the morrow ! O what madness it is to plot out far-reaching hopes ! To say : " I will buy and build, loan and call in money, win titles of honour, and then, old and full of years, I will surrender myself to a life of ease." Believe me when I say that everything is doubtful, even for those who are prosperous. No one has any right to draw for himself upon the future. The very thing that we grasp slips through our hands, and chance cuts into the actual hour which we are crowding so full. Time does indeed roll along by fixed law, but as in darkness ; and what is it to me whether Nature's course is sure, when my own is unsure ?

We plan distant voyages and long-postponed home-comings after roaming over foreign shores, we plan for military service and the slow rewards of hard campaigns, we canvass for governorships *b* and the promotions of one office after another—and all the while death stands at our side ; but since we never think of it except as it affects our neighbour, instances of mortality press upon us day by day, to remain in our minds only as long as they stir our wonder.

Yet what is more foolish than to wonder that something which may happen every day has happened

161

quod omni potest fieri? Stat quidem terminus
nobis, ubi illum inexorabilis fatorum necessitas fixit,
sed nemo scit nostrum, quam prope versetur terminum.[1] Sic itaque formemus animum, tamquam
ad extrema ventum sit. Nihil differamus. Cotidie
8 cum vita paria faciamus. Maximum vitae vitium
est, quod inperfecta semper est, quod aliquid [2] ex illa
differtur. Qui cotidie vitae suae summam manum
inposuit, non indiget tempore. Ex hac autem in-
digentia timor nascitur et cupiditas futuri exedens
animum. Nihil est miserius dubitatione venientium
quorsus evadant; quantum sit illud quod restat
aut quale, sollicita [3] mens inexplicabili formidine
agitatur.
9 Quo modo effugiemus hanc volutationem? Uno,
si vita nostra non prominebit, si in se colligitur.
Ille enim ex futuro suspenditur, cui inritum est
praesens. Ubi vero, quidquid mihi debui, redditum
est, ubi stabilita mens scit nihil interesse inter diem
et saeculum, quicquid deinceps dierum rerumque
venturum est, ex alto prospicit et cum multo risu
seriem temporum cogitat. Quid enim varietas
mobilitasque casuum perturbabit, si certus sis adversus incerta?
10 Ideo propera, Lucili mi, vivere et singulos dies
singulas vitas puta. Qui hoc modo se aptavit,[4]
cui vita sua cotidie fuit tota, securus est; in spem [5]
viventibus proximum quodque tempus elabitur subit-

---

[1] *terminum* Buecheler; *terminus* BA.
[2] *in aliquid* BA. The best solution, in spite of several
emendations, is to drop *in*.
[3] *sollicita* Buecheler; *collecta* BA.
[4] *aptavit* Stephanus; *aptabit* BA.
[5] *spem* later MSS.; *spe* BA.

on any one day ? There is indeed a limit fixed for us, just where the remorseless law of Fate has fixed it ; but none of us knows how near he is to this limit. Therefore, let us so order our minds as if we had come to the very end. Let us postpone nothing. Let us balance life's account every day. The greatest flaw in life is that it is always imperfect, and that a certain part of it is postponed. One who daily puts the finishing touches to his life is never in want of time. And yet, from this want arise fear and a craving for the future which eats away the mind. There is nothing more wretched than worry over the outcome of future events ; as to the amount or the nature of that which remains, our troubled minds are set a-flutter with unaccountable fear.

How, then, shall we avoid this vacillation ? In one way only,—if there be no reaching forward in our life, if it is withdrawn into itself. For he only is anxious about the future, to whom the present is unprofitable. But when I have paid my soul its due, when a soundly-balanced mind knows that a day differs not a whit from eternity—whatever days or problems the future may bring—then the soul looks forth from lofty heights and laughs heartily to itself when it thinks upon the ceaseless succession of the ages. For what disturbance can result from the changes and the instability of Chance, if you are sure in the face of that which is unsure ?

Therefore, my dear Lucilius, begin at once to live, and count each separate day as a separate life. He who has thus prepared himself, he whose daily life has been a rounded whole, is easy in his mind ; but those who live for hope alone find that the immediate future always slips from their grasp and that greed

que aviditas et miserrimus ac miserrima omnia effi-
ciens metus mortis. Inde illud Maecenatis turpissimum votum, quo et debilitatem non recusat
et deformitatem et novissime acutam crucem, dummodo inter haec mala spiritus prorogetur:

11   Debilem facito manu, debilem pede coxo,
     Tuber adstrue gibberum, lubricos quate dentes;
     Vita dum superest, benest; hanc[1] mihi, vel acuta
     Si sedeam cruce, sustine.

12   Quod miserrimum erat, si incidisset, optatur et
tamquam vita petitur supplici mora. Contemptis-
simum putarem, si vivere vellet usque ad crucem:
" Tu vero " inquit, " me debilites licet, dum spiritus
in corpore fracto et inutili maneat. Depraves licet,
dum monstroso et distorto[2] temporis aliquid accedat.
Suffigas licet et acutam sessuro crucem subdas." Est
tanti vulnus suum premere et patibulo pendere di-
strictum, dum differat id, quod est in malis optimum,
supplicii finem ? Est tanti habere animam, ut agam ?
13 Quid huic optes nisi deos faciles ? Quid sibi vult ista
carminis effeminati turpitudo ? Quid timoris demen-

---

[1] *hanc* later MSS.; *hac* BA.
[2] *distorto* Erasmus; *detorto* Haase; *deserto* BA.

[a] Frag. 1, p. 35 Lunderstedt.
[b] Horace, his intimate friend, wrote *Od.* ii. 17 to cheer the
despondent Maecenas; and Pliny (*N.H.* vii. 54) mentions
his fevers and his insomnia—*perpetua febris. . . . Eidem
triennio supremo nullo horae momento contigit somnus.*

EPISTLE CI.

steals along in its place, and the fear of death, a curse
which lays a curse upon everything else. Thence
came that most debased of prayers, in which
Maecenas [a] does not refuse to suffer weakness,
deformity, and as a climax the pain of crucifixion—
provided only that he may prolong the breath of life
amid these sufferings : [b]

> Fashion me with a palsied hand,
> Weak of foot, and a cripple ;
> Build upon me a crook-backed hump ;
> Shake my teeth till they rattle ;
> All is well, if my life remains.
> Save, oh, save it, I pray you,
> Though I sit on the piercing cross !

There he is, praying for that which, if it had be-
fallen him, would be the most pitiable thing in the
world ! And seeking a postponement of suffering, as
if he were asking for life ! I should deem him most
despicable had he wished to live up to the very time of
crucifixion : " Nay," he cries, " you may weaken my
body if you will only leave the breath of life in my
battered and ineffective carcase ! " " Maim me if
you will, but allow me, misshapen and deformed as I
may be, just a little more time in the world ! You
may nail me up and set my seat upon the piercing
cross ! " Is it worth while to weigh down upon
one's own wound, and hang impaled upon a gibbet,
that one may but postpone something which is the
balm of troubles, the end of punishment ? Is it
worth all this to possess the breath of life only to give
it up ? What would you ask for Maecenas but the
indulgence of Heaven ? What does he mean by
such womanish and indecent verse ? What does he
mean by making terms with panic fear ? What does

165

tissimi pactio ? Quid tam foeda vitae mendicatio ?
Huic [1] putes umquam recitasse Vergilium :

Usque adeone mori miserum est?

Optat ultima malorum, et quae pati gravissimum est
extendi ac sustineri cupit ; qua mercede ? Scilicet
vitae longioris. Quod autem vivere est diu mori ?
14 Invenitur aliquis, qui velit inter supplicia tabescere
et perire membratim et totiens per stilicidia emittere
animam quam semel exhalare ? Invenitur, qui velit
adactus ad illud infelix lignum, iam debilis, iam
pravus et in foedum scapularum ac pectoris [2] tuber
elisus, cui multae moriendi causae etiam citra crucem
fuerant, trahere animam tot tormenta tracturam ?

Nega nunc magnum beneficium esse naturae, quod
necesse est mori. Multi peiora adhuc pacisci parati
15 sunt : etiam amicum prodere, ut diutius vivant, et
liberos ad stuprum manu sua tradere, ut contingat
lucem videre tot consciam scelerum. Excutienda
vitae cupido [3] est discendumque nihil interesse,
quando patiaris, quod quandoque patiendum est.
Quam bene vivas refert, non quam diu ; saepe autem
in hoc est [4] bene, ne diu. VALE.

[1] *huic* Muretus ; *cui* BA.
[2] *ac pectoris* later MSS. ; *acceptoris* BA.
[3] *cupido* later MSS. ; *cui pido* BA.
[4] *est* Gruter ; *esse* BA.

he mean by begging so vilely for life ? He cannot ever have heard Vergil read the words :

> Tell me, is Death so wretched as that ? [a]

He asks for the climax of suffering, and—what is still harder to bear — prolongation and extension of suffering ; and what does he gain thereby ? Merely the boon of a longer existence. But what sort of life is a lingering death ? Can anyone be found who would prefer wasting away in pain, dying limb by limb, or letting out his life drop by drop, rather than expiring once for all ? Can any man be found willing to be fastened to the accursed tree,[b] long sickly, already deformed, swelling with ugly tumours on chest and shoulders, and draw the breath of life amid long-drawn-out agony ? I think he would have many excuses for dying even before mounting the cross !

Deny, now, if you can, that Nature is very generous in making death inevitable. Many men have been prepared to enter upon still more shameful bargains : to betray friends in order to live longer themselves, or voluntarily to debase their children and so enjoy the light of day which is witness of all their sins, We must get rid of this craving for life, and learn that it makes no difference when your suffering comes, because at some time you are bound to suffer. The point is, not how long you live, but how nobly you live. And often this living nobly means that you cannot live long. Farewell.

[a] *Aeneid* xii. 646.
[b] *Infelix lignum* (or *arbor*) is the cross.

CII.

1 Quomodo molestus est iucundum somnium videnti
qui excitat, aufert enim voluptatem, etiam si falsam,
effectum tamen verae habentem ; sic epistula tua
mihi fecit iniuriam. Revocavit enim me cogitationi
aptae traditum et iturum, si licuisset, ulterius.

2 Iuvabat de aeternitate animarum quaerere, immo
mehercules credere. Praebebam[1] enim me facilem
opinionibus magnorum virorum rem gratissimam
promittentium magis quam probantium. Dabam
me spei tantae. Iam eram fastidio mihi, iam
reliquias aetatis infractae contemnebam in immensum
illud tempus et in possessionem omnis aevi transiturus ; cum subito experrectus[2] sum epistula tua
accepta et tam bellum somnium perdidi. Quod
repetam, si te dimisero, et redimam.

3 Negat me epistula prima totam quaestionem ex-
plicuisse, in qua probare conabar id quod nostris
placet, claritatem, quae post mortem contingit,
bonum esse. Id enim me non solvisse, quod opponitur nobis : " Nullum," inquiunt, " bonum ex
distantibus. Hoc autem ex distantibus constat."

4 Quod interrogas, mi Lucili, eiusdem quaestionis est

---

[1] *praebebam* Buecheler ; *credebam* BA.
[2] *experrectus* later MSS. ; *experfectus* BA.

---

[a] Seneca, worn out by his political experiences, was at
this time not less than sixty-seven years of age.

CII. ON THE INTIMATIONS OF OUR IMMORTALITY

Just as a man is annoying when he rouses a dreamer of pleasant dreams (for he is spoiling a pleasure which may be unreal but nevertheless has the appearance of reality), even so your letter has done me an injury. For it brought me back abruptly, absorbed as I was in agreeable meditation and ready to proceed still further if it had been permitted me. I was taking pleasure in investigating the immortality of souls, nay, in believing that doctrine. For I was lending a ready ear to the opinions of the great authors, who not only approve but promise this most pleasing condition. I was giving myself over to such a noble hope; for I was already weary of myself, beginning already to despise the fragments of my shattered existence,[a] and feeling that I was destined to pass over into that infinity of time and the heritage of eternity, when I was suddenly awakened by the receipt of your letter, and lost my lovely dream. But, if I can once dispose of you, I shall reseek and rescue it.

There was a remark, at the beginning of your letter, that I had not explained the whole problem—wherein I was endeavouring to prove one of the beliefs of our school, that the renown which falls to one's lot after death is a good; for I had not solved the problem with which we are usually confronted : " No good can consist of things that are distinct and separate ; yet renown consists of such things." What you are asking about, my dear Lucilius, belongs to another topic of the same subject, and that

loci alterius, et ideo non hoc [1] tantum, sed alia quoque
eodem [2] pertinentia distuleram. Quaedam enim,
ut scis, moralibus [3] rationalia inmixta sunt. Itaque
illam partem rectam et ad mores pertinentem trac-
tavi : numquid stultum sit ac supervacuum ultra
extremum diem curas transmittere, an cadant bona
nostra nobiscum nihilque sit eius, qui nullus est,
an ex eo, quod, cum erit, sensuri non sumus, antequam sit, aliquis fructus percipi [4] aut peti possit.

5   Haec omnia mores spectant ; itaque suo loco posita
sunt. At quae a dialecticis contra hanc opinionem
dicuntur, segreganda fuerunt et ideo seposita sunt.
Nunc, quia omnia exigis, omnia quae dicunt per-
6 sequar, deinde singulis occurram. Nisi aliquid prae-
dixero, intellegi non poterunt quae refellentur.
Quid est, quod praedicere [5] velim ? Quaedam continua corpora esse, ut hominem ; quaedam esse
composita, ut navem, domum, omnia denique,
quorum diversae partes iunctura in unum coactae
sunt ; quaedam ex distantibus, quorum adhuc
membra separata sunt, tamquam exercitus, populus,
senatus. Illi enim, per quos ista corpora efficiuntur,
iure aut officio cohaerent, natura diducti et singuli
sunt. Quid est, quod etiamnunc praedicere velim ?
7 Nullum bonum putamus esse, quod ex distantibus
constat. Uno [6] enim spiritu unum bonum contineri

---

[1] *hoc* added in later MSS.
[2] *eodem* later MSS. ; om. BA.
[3] *moralibus* later MSS. ; *moralia* BA.
[4] *percipi* later MSS. ; *percipit* BA.
[5] *praedicere* later MSS. ; *praecidere* BA.
[6] *uno* later MSS. ; *unde* BA.

---

[a] Seneca is perhaps popularizing the Stoic *combinations*,—
παράθεσις (juxtaposition), μῖξις (mixture) or κρᾶσις (fusion), and
σύγχυσις (chemical mixture). *Cf.* E. V. Arnold, *Roman
Stoicism*, p. 169.

is why I had postponed the arguments, not only on this one topic, but on other topics which also covered the same ground. For, as you know, certain logical questions are mingled with ethical ones. Accordingly, I handled the essential part of my subject which has to do with conduct—as to whether it is foolish and useless to be concerned with what lies beyond our last day, or whether our goods die with us and there is nothing left of him who is no more, or whether any profit can be attained or attempted beforehand out of that which, when it comes, we shall not be capable of feeling.

All these things have a view to conduct, and therefore they have been inserted under the proper topic. But the remarks of dialecticians in opposition to this idea had to be sifted out, and were accordingly laid aside. Now that you demand an answer to them all, I shall examine all their statements, and then refute them singly. Unless, however, I make a preliminary remark, it will be impossible to understand my rebuttals. And what is that preliminary remark ? Simply this : there are certain continuous bodies, such as a man ; there are certain composite bodies,—as ships, houses, and everything which is the result of joining separate parts into one sum total : there are certain others made up of things that are distinct,[a] each member remaining separate—like an army, a populace, or a senate. For the persons who go to make up such bodies are united by virtue of law or function ; but by their nature they are distinct and individual. Well, what further prefatory remarks do I still wish to make ? Simply this : we believe that nothing is a good, if it be composed of things that are distinct. For a single good should be checked and controlled by a single soul ; and the

171

ac regi debet, unum esse unius boni principale. Hoc
si quando desideraveris, per se probatur; interim
ponendum fuit, quia in nos [1] nostra tela mittuntur.

8 "Dicitis," inquit, "nullum bonum ex distantibus
esse? Claritas autem ista bonorum virorum secunda
opinio est. Nam quomodo fama non est unius sermo
nec infamia unius mala existimatio, sic nec claritas
uni bono placuisse. Consentire in hoc plures insignes
et spectabiles viri debent, ut claritas sit. Haec autem
ex iudiciis plurium [2] efficitur, id est distantium;

9 ergo non est bonum. Claritas," inquit, "laus est a
bonis bono reddita; laus oratio, vox est aliquid signi-
ficans; vox est autem, licet virorum sit bonorum, non [3]
bonum. Nec enim quicquid vir bonus facit, bonum
est. Nam et plaudit et sibilat, sed nec plausum
quisquam nec sibilum, licet omnia eius admiretur
et laudet, bonum dicit, non magis quam sternu-
mentum aut tussim. Ergo claritas bonum non est.

10 Ad summam dicite nobis, utrum laudantis an laudati
bonum sit: si laudati [4] bonum esse dicitis, tam
ridiculam rem facitis, quam si adfirmetis meum esse,
quod alius bene valeat. Sed laudare dignos honesta
actio est; ita laudantis bonum est, cuius actio est,

[1] *nos* added by Schweighaeuser.
[2] *plurium* later MSS.; *plurimum* BA.
[3] *bonorum non* inserted by Erasmus.
[4] *laudati* Madvig; *laudantis* BA.

[a] *i.e.*, the arguments of the Stoics.

essential quality of each single good should be single. This can be proved of itself whenever you desire; in the meanwhile, however, it had to be laid aside, because our own weapons [a] are being hurled at us.

Opponents speak thus: "You say, do you, that no good can be made up of things that are distinct? Yet this renown, of which you speak, is simply the favourable opinion of good men. For just as reputation does not consist of one person's remarks, and as ill repute does not consist of one person's disapproval, so renown does not mean that we have merely pleased one good person. In order to constitute renown, the agreement of many distinguished and praiseworthy men is necessary. But this results from the decision of a number—in other words, of persons who are distinct. Therefore, it is not a good. You say, again, that renown is the praise rendered to a good man by good men. Praise means speech: now speech is utterance with a particular meaning; and utterance, even from the lips of good men, is not a good in itself. For any act of a good man is not necessarily a good; he shouts his applause and hisses his disapproval, but one does not call the shouting or the hissing good—although his entire conduct may be admired and praised—any more than one would applaud a sneeze or a cough. Therefore, renown is not a good. Finally, tell us whether the good belongs to him who praises, or to him who is praised: if you say that the good belongs to him who is praised, you are on as foolish a quest as if you were to maintain that my neighbour's good health is my own. But to praise worthy men is an honourable action; thus the good is exclusively that of the man who does the praising, of the man who performs the action, and not of us, who are

173

non nostrum, qui laudamur. Atqui hoc quaerebatur."

11 Respondebo nunc singulis cursim. Primum, an sit
aliquod ex distantibus bonum, etiamnunc quaeritur
et pars utraque sententias habet. Deinde claritas
desiderat multa suffragia ? Potest et unius boni viri
iudicio esse contenta ; unus nos[1] bonus bonos iudicat.

12 " Quid ergo ? " inquit, " et fama erit unius hominis
existimatio et infamia unius malignus sermo ?
Gloriam quoque," inquit, " latius fusam intellego,
consensum enim multorum exigit." Diversa horum
condicio est et illius. Quare ? Quia, si de me bene
vir bonus sentit, eodem loco sum, quo si omnes
boni idem sentirent ; omnes enim, si me cognoverint,
idem sentient. Par illis idemque iudicium est,
aeque vero inficiscitur. Dissidere non possunt ; ita
pro eo est, ac si omnes idem sentiant, quia aliud
13 sentire non possunt. " Ad gloriam aut famam non
est satis unius opinio." Illic idem potest una sententia, quod omnium, quia omnium, si perrogetur,
una erit ; hic diversa dissimilium iudicia sunt.
Difficiles adfectus, dubia omnia invenies, levia,
suspecta. Putas tu posse unam omnium esse sententiam ? Non est unius una sententia. Illi placet
verum, veritatis una vis, una facies est ; apud hos

---

[1] *unus nos* Hense ; *nos* BA.

---

[a] *i.e.*, of the *unus vir bonus*, as contrasted with the many.
174

being praised. And yet this was the question under discussion."

I shall now answer the separate objections hurriedly. The first question still is, whether any good can consist of things that are distinct—and there are votes cast on both sides. Again, does renown need many votes? Renown can be satisfied with the decision of one good man : it is one good man who decides that we are good. Then the retort is : " What ! Would you define reputation as the esteem of one individual, and ill-repute as the rancorous chatter of one man? Glory, too, we take to be more widespread, for it demands the agreement of many men." But the position of the "many" is different from that of "the one." And why ? Because, if the good man thinks well of me, it practically amounts to my being thought well of by all good men ; for they will all think the same, if they know me. Their judgment is alike and identical; the effect of truth on it is equal. They cannot disagree, which means that they would all hold the same view, being unable to hold different views. "One man's opinion," you say, "is not enough to create glory or reputation." In the former case,[a] one judgment is a universal judgment, because all, if they were asked, would hold one opinion ; in the other case, however, men of dissimilar character give divergent judgments. You will find perplexing emotions—everything doubtful, inconstant, untrustworthy. And can you suppose that all men are able to hold one opinion ? Even an individual does not hold to a single opinion. With the good man it is truth that causes belief, and truth has but one function and one likeness ; while among the second class of which I spoke, the ideas with which they

falsa sunt, quibus adsentiuntur. Numquam autem
14 falsis constantia est : variantur et dissident. " Sed
laus," inquit, " nihil aliud quam vox est, vox autem
bonum non est." Cum dicunt[1] claritatem esse
laudem bonorum a bonis redditam,[2] non ad vocem
referunt, sed ad sententiam. Licet enim vir bonus
taceat, sed aliquem iudicet dignum laude esse,
15 laudatus est. Praeterea aliud est laus, aliud laudatio,
haec et vocem exigit. Itaque nemo dicit laudem
funebrem, sed laudationem, cuius officium oratione
constat. Cum dicimus aliquem laude dignum, non
verba illi benigna hominum, sed iudicia promittimus.
Ergo laus etiam taciti est bene sentientis ac bonum
virum apud se laudantis.
16   Deinde, ut dixi, ad animum refertur laus, non ad
verba, quae conceptam laudem egerunt et in notitiam[3] plurium emittunt. Laudat qui laudandum
esse iudicat. Cum tragicus ille apud nos ait magnificum esse " laudari a laudato viro," laude digno ait.
Et cum aeque antiquus poeta ait " laus alit artis,"[4]
non laudationem dicit, quae corrumpit artes. Nihil
enim aeque et eloquentiam et omne aliud studium
auribus deditum vitiavit quam popularis adsensio.
17 Fama vocem utique desiderat, claritas potest etiam[5]
citra vocem contingere contenta iudicio. Plena

[1] *dicunt* Lipsius ; *dicant* BA.
[2] *redditam* later MSS. ; *reddi iam* BA.
[3] *in notitiam* later MSS. ; *innocentiam* BA.
[4] *alit artes* Erasmus ; *alitteris* BA.
[5] *etiam* Buecheler ; *enim* BA.

[a] i.e., the Stoics.
[b] Naevius, quoted by Cicero, *Tusc. Disp.* iv. 31 (of Hector):

> laetus sum
> laudari me abs te, pater, laudato viro.

[c] A commonplace sentiment, found, *e.g.*, in Cicero,
Tusc. Disp. i. 2. 4.

agree are unsound. Moreover, those who are false are never steadfast: they are irregular and discordant. " But praise," says the objector, " is nothing but an utterance, and an utterance is not a good." When they [a] say that renown is praise bestowed on the good by the good, what they refer to is not an utterance but a judgment. For a good man may remain silent; but if he decides that a certain person is worthy of praise, that person is the object of praise. Besides, praise is one thing, and the giving of praise another; the latter demands utterance also. Hence no one speaks of " a funeral praise," but says " praise - giving " — for its function depends upon speech. And when we say that a man is worthy of praise, we assure human kindness to him, not in words, but in judgment. So the good opinion, even of one who in silence feels inward approval of a good man, is praise.

Again, as I have said, praise is a matter of the mind rather than of the speech; for speech brings out the praise that the mind has conceived, and publishes it forth to the attention of the many. To judge a man worthy of praise, is to praise him. And when our tragic poet [b] sings to us that it is wonderful " to be praised by a well-praised hero," he means, " by one who is worthy of praise." Again, when an equally venerable bard says: [c] " Praise nurtureth the arts," he does not mean the giving of praise, for that spoils the arts. Nothing has corrupted oratory and all other studies that depend on hearing so much as popular approval.[d] Reputation necessarily demands words, but renown can be content with men's judgments, and suffice without the spoken

[d] *Cf. Ep.* xl. 4 *haec popularis (oratio) nihil habet veri.*

est non tantum inter tacentis, sed etiam inter re-
clamantis. Quid intersit inter claritatem et gloriam
dicam : gloria multorum iudiciis constat, claritas
18 bonorum. "Cuius," inquit, "bonum est claritas, id
est laus bono a bonis reddita ? Utrum laudati an
laudantis ? " Utriusque. Meum, qui laudor ; quia
natura me¹ amantem omnium genuit, et bene
fecisse gaudeo, et gratos me invenisse virtutum
interpretes laetor ; hoc plurium² bonum est, quod
grati sunt, sed et meum. Ita enim animo conpositus
sum, ut³ aliorum bonum meum iudicem, utique
19 eorum, quibus ipse⁴ sum boni causa. Est istud
laudantium bonum, virtute enim geritur ; omnis
autem virtutis actio bonum est. Hoc contingere
illis non potuisset, nisi ego talis essem. Itaque
utriusque bonum est merito laudari, tam mehercules
quam bene iudicasse iudicantis bonum est et eius,
secundum quem iudicatum est. Numquid dubitas,
quin iustitia et habentis bonum sit et autem sit eius,
cui debitum solvit ? Merentem laudare iustitia est ;
ergo utriusque bonum est.
20 Cavillatoribus istis abunde responderimus.⁵ Sed
non debet hoc nobis esse propositum arguta disserere
et philosophiam in has angustias ex sua maiestate
detrahere ; quanto satius est ire aperta⁶ via et recta
quam sibi ipsum flexus disponere, quos cum magna

---

¹ *natura me* later MSS. ; *naturam mea* BA.
² *plurium* later MSS. ; *plurimum* BA.
³ *ut* later MSS. ; *et* BA.
⁴ *ipse* or *istius* later MSS. ; *iste* BA.
⁵ *responderimus* Pincianus ; *respondebimus* BA
⁶ *aperta* later MSS. ; *aperte* BA¹.

word. It is satisfied not only amid silent approval, but even in the face of open protest. There is, in my opinion, this difference between renown and glory—the latter depends upon the judgments of the many ; but renown on the judgments of good men. The retort comes : " But whose good is this renown, this praise rendered to a good man by good men ? Is it of the one praised, or of the one who praises ? " Of both, I say. It is my own good, in that I am praised, because I am naturally born to love all men, and I rejoice in having done good deeds and congratulate myself on having found men who express their ideas of my virtues with gratitude ; that they are grateful, is a good to the many, but it is a good to me also. For my spirit is so ordered that I can regard the good of other men as my own—in any case those of whose good I am myself the cause. This good is also the good of those who render the praise, for it is applied by means of virtue ; and every act of virtue is a good. My friends could not have found this blessing if I had not been a man of the right stamp. It is therefore a good belonging to both sides,—this being praised when one deserves it—just as truly as a good decision is the good of him who makes the decision and also of him in whose favour the decision was given. Do you doubt that justice is a blessing to its possessor, as well as to the man to whom the just due was paid ? To praise the deserving is justice ; therefore, the good belongs to both sides.

This will be a sufficient answer to such dealers in subtleties. But it should not be our purpose to discuss things cleverly and to drag Philosophy down from her majesty to such petty quibbles. How much better it is to follow the open and direct road, rather than to map out for yourself a circuitous route

THE EPISTLES OF SENECA

molestia debeas relegere? Neque enim quicquam
aliud istae disputationes sunt quam inter se perite
21 captantium lusus. Dic potius, quam naturale sit in
immensum mentem suam extendere. Magna et
generosa res est humanus animus : nullos sibi poni nisi
communes et cum deo terminos patitur. Primum
humilem non accipit patriam, Ephesum aut Alexan-
driam aut si quod est etiamnunc frequentius accolis [1]
laetiusve tectis [2] solum ; patria est illi quodcumque
suprema et universa circuitu suo cingit, hoc omne
convexum, intra quod iacent maria cum terris, intra
quod aer humanis divina secernens etiam [3] coniungit,
in quo [4] disposita tot lumina [5] in actus suos excubant.
22 Deinde artam aetatem sibi dari non sinit : " omnes,"
inquit, " anni [6] mei sunt. Nullum saeculum magnis
ingeniis clusum est, nullum non cogitationi pervium
tempus. Cum venerit dies ille, qui mixtum hoc
divini humanique secernat, corpus [7] hic, ubi inveni,
relinquam, ipse me dis [8] reddam. Nec nunc sine
23 illis sum, sed gravi terrenoque detineor." Per has
mortalis aevi moras illi meliori vitae longiorique
proluditur. Quemadmodum decem [9] mensibus tenet
nos maternus uterus et praeparat non sibi, sed [10] illi
loco, in quem videmur emitti iam idonei spiritum
trahere et in aperto durare ; sic per hoc spatium,
quod ab infantia patet in senectutem, in alium
maturescimus partum. Alia origo nos expectat,

---

[1] *accolis* Pincianus; *oculis* BA; *incolis* or *occulis* later MSS.
[2] *laetiusve tectis* Windhaus; *laetius vectis* BA.
[3] *etiam* Pincianus; *iam* BA.
[4] *quo* Schweighaeuser; *quod* BA.
[5] *lumina* Haase; *numina* BA.   [6] *anni* Pinc.; *ante* BA.
[7] *corpus* Pinc.; *tempus* BA.
[8] *diis* later MSS.: *diei* BA.
[9] *decem* later MSS.; *invicem* BA.
[10] *sed* later MSS.; *et* BA.

180

which you must retrace with infinite trouble ! For such argumentation is nothing else than the sport of men who are skilfully juggling with each other. Tell me rather how closely in accord with nature it is to let one's mind reach out into the boundless universe ! The human soul is a great and noble thing; it permits of no limits except those which can be shared even by the gods. First of all, it does not consent to a lowly birthplace, like Ephesus or Alexandria, or any land that is even more thickly populated than these, and more richly spread with dwellings. The soul's homeland is the whole space that encircles the height and breadth of the firmament, the whole rounded dome within which lie land and sea, within which the upper air that sunders the human from the divine also unites them, and where all the sentinel stars are taking their turn on duty. Again, the soul will not put up with a narrow span of existence. " All the years," says the soul, " are mine ; no epoch is closed to great minds ; all Time is open for the progress of thought. When the day comes to separate the heavenly from its earthly blend, I shall leave the body here where I found it, and shall of my own volition betake myself to the gods. I am not apart from them now, but am merely detained in a heavy and earthly prison." These delays of mortal existence are a prelude to the longer and better life. As the mother's womb holds us for ten months, making us ready, not for the womb itself, but for the existence into which we seem to be sent forth when at last we are fitted to draw breath and live in the open ; just so, throughout the years extending between infancy and old age, we are making ourselves ready for another birth. A different beginning, a different condition, await us.

alius rerum status. Nondum caelum nisi ex inter-
24 vallo pati possumus; proinde intrepidus horam illam
decretoriam prospice : non est animo suprema, sed
corpori. Quidquid circa te iacet rerum, tamquam
hospitalis loci sarcinas specta : transeundum est.
25 Excutit redeuntem natura sicut intrantem. Non
licet plus efferre quam intuleris, immo etiam ex eo,
quod ad vitam adtulisti, pars magna ponenda est :
detrahetur tibi haec circumiecta, novissimum vela-
mentum tui, cutis ; detrahetur caro et suffusus
sanguis discurrensque per totum ; detrahentur ossa
nervique, firmamenta fluidorum ac labentium.

26 Dies iste, quem tamquam extremum reformidas,
aeterni natalis est. Depone onus ; quid cunctaris,
tamquam non prius quoque relicto, in quo latebas,
corpore exieris ? Haeres, reluctaris ; tum quoque
magno nisu matris expulsus es. Gemis, ploras ; et
hoc ipsum flere nascentis est, sed tunc debebat
ignosci : rudis et imperitus omnium veneras. Ex
maternorum viscerum calido mollique fomento
emissum adflavit aura liberior, deinde offendit durae
manus tactus, tenerque adhuc et nullius rei gnarus
obstipuisti inter ignota.

27 Nunc tibi non est novum separari ab eo, cuius ante
pars fueris ; aequo animo membra iam supervacua
dimitte et istuc corpus inhabitatum diu pone.

---

a A metaphor from the arena: *decretoria* were real
decisive weapons with which death was faced, as opposed
to *lusoria*, " sham " weapons. *Cf.* Sen. *Ep.* cxvii. 25.

EPISTLE CII.

We cannot yet, except at rare intervals, endure the light of heaven; therefore, look forward without fearing to that appointed hour,[a]—the last hour of the body but not of the soul. Survey everything that lies about you, as if it were luggage in a guest-chamber: you must travel on. Nature strips you as bare at your departure as at your entrance. You may take away no more than you brought in; what is more, you must throw away the major portion of that which you brought with you into life: you will be stripped of the very skin which covers you—that which has been your last protection; you will be stripped of the flesh, and lose the blood which is suffused and circulated through your body; you will be stripped of bones and sinews, the frame-work of these transitory and feeble parts.

That day, which you fear as being the end of all things, is the birthday of your eternity. Lay aside your burden—why delay?—just as if you had not previously left the body which was your hiding-place! You cling to your burden, you struggle; at your birth also great effort was necessary on your mother's part to set you free. You weep and wail; and yet this very weeping happens at birth also; but then it was to be excused: for you came into the world wholly ignorant and inexperienced. When you left the warm and cherishing protection of your mother's womb, a freer air breathed into your face; then you winced at the touch of a rough hand, and you looked in amaze at unfamiliar objects, still delicate and ignorant of all things.

But now it is no new thing for you to be sundered from that of which you have previously been a part; let go your already useless limbs with resignation and dispense with that body in which you have dwelt for

183

Scindetur, obruetur, abolebitur. Quid contristaris?
Ita solet fieri : pereunt semper[1] velamenta nascen-
tium. Quid ista sic diligis quasi tua? Istis opertus
es. Veniet, qui te revellat dies et ex contubernio
28 foedi atque olidi ventris educat. Huic nunc quoque
tu, quantum potes, subduc te voluptatique,[2] nisi quae
necessariis seriisque[3] cohaerebit; alienus iam hinc
altius aliquid sublimiusque meditare. Aliquando
naturae tibi arcana retegentur, discutietur ista caligo
et lux undique clara percutiet.

Imaginare tecum, quantus ille sit fulgor tot si-
deribus inter se lumen miscentibus; nulla serenum
umbra turbabit. Aequaliter splendebit omne caeli
latus; dies et nox aëris infimi vices sunt. Tunc in
tenebris vixisse-te dices, cum totam lucem et totus
aspexeris, quam nunc per angustissimas oculorum vias
obscure intueris. Et tamen admiraris illam iam
procul; quid tibi videbitur divina lux, cum illam
suo loco videris?

29 Haec cogitatio nihil sordidum animo subsidere
sinit, nihil humile, nihil crudele. Deos rerum
omnium esse testes ait. Illis nos adprobari, illis in
futurum parari iubet et aeternitatem proponere.
Quam qui mente concepit, nullos horret exercitus,
non terretur tuba, nullis ad timorem minis agitur.

---

[1] *semper* Pincianus ; *saepe* BA.
[2] *subduc te voluptatique* Bartsch and Hense ; *subvoluptari-
quae* BA.
[3] *necessariis seriisque* Hense ; *necessariisque* BA.

---

[a] The departure from life is compared to the release from
the womb. There is also possibly a double meaning implied
in the word *venter*.

so long. It will be torn asunder, buried out of sight, and wasted away. Why be downcast? This is what ordinarily happens: when we are born, the afterbirth always perishes. Why love such a thing as if it were your own possession? It was merely your covering. The day will come which will tear you forth and lead you away from the company of the foul and noisome womb. Withdraw from it now too [a] as much as you can, and withdraw from pleasure, except such as may be bound up with essential and important things; estrange yourself from it even now, and ponder on something nobler and loftier. Some day the secrets of nature shall be disclosed to you, the haze will be shaken from your eyes, and the bright light will stream in upon you from all sides.

Picture to yourself how great is the glow when all the stars mingle their fires; no shadows will disturb the clear sky. The whole expanse of heaven will shine evenly; for day and night are interchanged only in the lowest atmosphere. Then you will say that you have lived in darkness, after you have seen, in your perfect state, the perfect light—that light which now you behold darkly with vision that is cramped to the last degree. And yet, far off as it is, you already look upon it in wonder; what do you think the heavenly light will be when you have seen it in its proper sphere?

Such thoughts permit nothing mean to settle in the soul, nothing low, nothing cruel. They maintain that the gods are witnesses of everything. They order us to meet the gods' approval, to prepare ourselves to join them at some future time, and to plan for immortality. He that has grasped this idea shrinks from no attacking army, is not terrified by the trumpet-blast, and is intimidated by no threats.

30 Quidni non timeat qui mori sperat? Is quoque,[1]
qui animum tamdiu iudicat manere, quamdiu retine-
tur corporis vinculo, solutum statim spargit, ut
etiam post mortem utilis esse possit. Quamvis enim
ipse ereptus sit oculis, tamen

> Multa viri virtus animo multusque recursat
> Gentis honos.

Cogita, quantum nobis exempla bona prosint; scies
magnorum virorum non minus praesentiam esse
utilem quam memoriam. VALE.

CIII.

SENECA LVCILIO SVO SALVTEM

1 Quid ista circumspicis, quae tibi possunt fortasse
evenire, sed possunt et non evenire? Incendium
dico, ruinam, alia, quae[2] nobis incidunt, non in-
sidiantur; illa potius vide, illa devita, quae[3] nos
observant, quae captant. Rariores sunt[4] casus,
etiam si graves, naufragium facere, vehiculo everti;
ab homine homini cotidianum periculum. Adversus
hoc te expedi, hoc intentis oculis intuere. Nullum
est malum frequentius, nullum pertinacius, nullum
2 blandius. Ac[5] tempestas minatur antequam surgat,
crepant aedificia antequam corruant, praenuntiat

---

[1] *qui mori sperat? is quoque* Buecheler; *qui mori speriat.
Se quoque* BA.
[2] *incendium . . . alia quae* Pincianus; *incidentium . . .
aliqua* BA.
[3] *illa de vita quae* later MSS.; *illa videvita illa quae* BA.
[4] *rariores sunt* Gruter; *pari essunt* BA.
[5] *ac* Buecheler; *ab* BA.

How should it not be that a man feels no fear, if he looks forward to death ? He also who believes that the soul abides only as long as it is fettered in the body, scatters it abroad forthwith when dissolved, so that it may be useful even after death. For though he is taken from men's sight, still

Often our thoughts run back to the hero, and often the glory
Won by his race recurs to the mind. *a*

Consider how much we are helped by good example ; you will thus understand that the presence of a noble man is of no less service than his memory. Farewell.

CIII. ON THE DANGERS OF ASSOCIATION WITH OUR FELLOW-MEN *b*

Why are you looking about for troubles which may perhaps come your way, but which may indeed not come your way at all ? I mean fires, falling buildings, and other accidents of the sort that are mere events rather than plots against us. Rather beware and shun those troubles which dog our steps and reach out their hands against us. Accidents, though they may be serious, are few—such as being shipwrecked or thrown from one's carriage ; but it is from his fellow-man that a man's everyday danger comes. Equip yourself against that ; watch that with an attentive eye. There is no evil more frequent, no evil more persistent, no evil more insinuating. Even the storm, before it gathers, gives a warning ; houses crack before they crash ; and smoke is the forerunner

a Vergil, *Aen.* iv. 3 f.
b Compare this with the Seventh letter (vol. i.).

fumus incendium ; subita est ex homine pernicies et
eo diligentius tegitur, quo propius accedit.

Erras, si istorum tibi qui occurrunt vultibus credis ;
hominum effigies habent, animos ferarum, nisi quod
illarum perniciosus[1] est primus incursus ; quos trans-
iere, non quaerunt.   Numquam enim illas ad nocendum nisi necessitas incitat ; aut[2] fame aut timore
coguntur ad pugnam ; homini perdere hominem
libet.

3   Tu tamen ita cogita, quod ex homine periculum
sit, ut cogites, quod sit hominis officium.   Alterum
intuere, ne laedaris, alterum ne laedas.   Commodis
omnium laeteris, movearis incommodis et memineris,
4 quae praestare debeas, quae cavere.   Sic vivendo
quid consequaris ?   Non te ne noceant, sed ne
fallant.   Quantum potes autem, in philosophiam
recede : illa te sinu[3] suo proteget, in huius sacrario
eris aut tutus aut tutior.   Non arietant inter se nisi
5 in eadem ambulantes via.[4]   Ipsam autem philosophiam non debebis iactare ; multis fuit periculi
causa insolenter tractata et contumaciter.   Tibi vitia
detrahat, non aliis exprobret.   Non abhorreat a
publicis moribus nec hoc agat, ut quicquid non facit,
damnare videatur.   Licet sapere sine pompa, sine
invidia.   VALE.

[1] *perniciosus* von Ian ; *perniciosius* BA.
[2] *incitat* : *aut* Buecheler ; *inicit, hae aut* BA.
[3] *te sinu* Erasmus ; *te nisu* BA.
[4] *via* Madvig ; *quia* BA.

EPISTLE CIII.

of fire. But damage from man is instantaneous, and the nearer it comes the more carefully it is concealed.

You are wrong to trust the countenances of those you meet. They have the aspect of men, but the souls of brutes; the difference is that only beasts damage you at the first encounter; those whom they have passed by they do not pursue. For nothing ever goads them to do harm except when need compels them: it is hunger or fear that forces them into a fight. But man delights to ruin man.

You must, however, reflect thus what danger you run at the hands of man, in order that you may deduce what is the duty of man. Try, in your dealings with others, to harm not, in order that you be not harmed. You should rejoice with all in their joys and sympathize with them in their troubles, remembering what you should offer and what you should withhold. And what may you attain by living such a life? Not necessarily freedom from harm at their hands, but at least freedom from deceit. In so far, however, as you are able, take refuge with philosophy: she will cherish you in her bosom, and in her sanctuary you shall be safe, or, at any rate, safer than before. People collide only when they are travelling the same path. But this very philosophy must never be vaunted by you; for philosophy when employed with insolence and arrogance has been perilous to many. Let her strip off your faults, rather than assist you to decry the faults of others. Let her not hold aloof from the customs of mankind, nor make it her business to condemn whatever she herself does not do. A man may be wise without parade and without arousing enmity. Farewell.

THE EPISTLES OF SENECA

CIV.

1 In Nomentanum meum fugi, quid putas ? Urbem ?
Immo febrem et quidem subrepentem. Iam manum
mihi iniecerat. Medicus initia esse dicebat motis
venis et incertis et naturalem turbantibus modum.
Protinus itaque parari vehiculum iussi ; Paulina mea
retinente exire perseveravi ; illud mihi ore erat
domini mei Gallionis, qui cum in Achaia febrem
habere coepisset, protinus navem ascendit clamitans
2 non corporis esse, sed loci morbum. Hoc ego
Paulinae meae dixi, quae mihi valitudinem meam
commendat. Nam cum sciam[1] spiritum illius in
meo verti, incipio, ut illi consulam, mihi consulere.
Et cum me fortiorem senectus ad multa reddiderit,
hoc beneficium aetatis amitto. Venit enim mihi in
mentem, in hoc sene et adulescentem esse, cui
parcitur. Itaque quoniam ego ab illa non impetro,
ut me fortius amet, a me[2] impetrat illa, ut me
3 diligentius amem. Indulgendum est enim honestis
adfectibus ; et interdum, etiam si premunt causae,
spiritus in honorem suorum vel cum tormento re-
vocandus et in ipso ore retinendus est, cum bono
viro vivendum sit non quamdiu iuvat sed quamdiu

---

[1] *sciam* later MSS. ; *scias* BA.

[2] *a me* was inserted by Gertz at this point ; Muretus
placed it after *illa.*

---

[a] Pompeia Paulina, the second wife of Seneca ; *cf.* Tac.
Ann. xv. 60. Though much younger than her husband, she
was a model of devotion, and remained loyal to him through
all the Neronian persecution.

[b] Elder brother of Seneca, whose name before his adop-
tion by Lucius Iunius Gallio was Annaeus Novatus. He
was governor of Achaia from A.D. July 1, 51 to July 1, 52.

EPISTLE CIV

CIV. ON CARE OF HEALTH AND PEACE OF MIND

I have run off to my villa at Nomentum, for what purpose, do you suppose? To escape the city? No; to shake off a fever which was surely working its way into my system. It had already got a grip upon me. My physician kept insisting that when the circulation was upset and irregular, disturbing the natural poise, the disease was under way. I therefore ordered my carriage to be made ready at once, and insisted on departing, in spite of my wife Paulina's *a* efforts to stop me; for I remembered my master Gallio's *b* words, when he began to develop a fever in Achaia and took ship at once, insisting that the disease was not of the body but of the place. That is what I remarked to my dear Paulina, who always urges me to take care of my health. I know that her very life-breath comes and goes with my own, and I am beginning, in my solicitude for her, to be solicitous for myself. And although old age has made me braver to bear many things, I am gradually losing this boon that old age bestows. For it comes into my mind that in this old man there is a youth also, and youth needs tenderness. Therefore, since I cannot prevail upon her to love me any more heroically, she prevails upon me to cherish myself more carefully. For one must indulge genuine emotions; sometimes, even in spite of weighty reasons, the breath of life must be called back and kept at our very lips even at the price of great suffering, for the sake of those whom we hold dear; because the good man should not live as long

See Acts xviii. 11 ff., and Duff, *Three Dialogues of Seneca*, p. xliii.

oportet. Ille, qui non uxorem, non amicum tanti putat, ut diutius in vita commoretur, qui perseverabit mori, delicatus est.

Hoc quoque imperet sibi animus, ubi utilitas suorum exigit, nec tantum, si vult mori, sed si coepit,

4 intermittat et suis se[1] commodet. Ingentis animi est aliena causa ad vitam reverti, quod magni viri saepe fecerunt. Sed hoc quoque summae humanitatis existimo, senectutem suam, cuius maximus fructus est securior sui tutela et vitae usus animosior, attentius custodire,[2] si scias alicui[3] tuorum esse dulce,

5 utile, optabile. Habet praeterea in se non mediocre ista res gaudium et mercedem ; quid enim iucundius quam uxori tam carum esse, ut[4] propter hoc tibi carior fias ? Potest itaque Paulina mea non tantum suum mihi timorem inputare, sed etiam meum.

6 Quaeris ergo, quomodo mihi consilium profectionis cesserit ? Ut primum gravitatem urbis excessi et illum odorem culinarum fumantium, quae motae quicquid pestiferi vaporis obferunt,[5] cum pulvere effundunt, protinus mutatam valitudinem sensi. Quantum deinde adiectum putas viribus, postquam vineas attigi ? In pascuum emissus cibum meum invasi. Repetivi ergo iam me ; non permansit marcor ille corporis dubii et male cogitantis. Incipio toto animo studere.

---

1 *suis se* later MSS. ; *suis* BA.
2 *attentius custodire* (*curare*) later MSS. ; *attentius* BA.
3 *alicui* later MSS. ; *aliquid* BA.
4 *ut* later MSS. ; om. BA.
5 *obferunt* F. Gloeckner ; *obruent* BA.

as it pleases him, but as long as he ought. He who does not value his wife, or his friend, highly enough to linger longer in life—he who obstinately persists in dying—is a voluptuary.

The soul should also enforce this command upon itself whenever the needs of one's relatives require ; it should pause and humour those near and dear, not only when it desires, but even when it has begun, to die. It gives proof of a great heart to return to life for the sake of others ; and noble men have often done this. But this procedure also, I believe, indicates the highest type of kindness : that although the greatest advantage of old age is the opportunity to be more negligent regarding self-preservation and to use life more adventurously, one should watch over one's old age with still greater care if one knows that such action is pleasing, useful, or desirable in the eyes of a person whom one holds dear. This is also a source of no mean joy and profit ; for what is sweeter than to be so valued by one's wife that one becomes more valuable to oneself for this reason ? Hence my dear Paulina is able to make me responsible, not only for her fears, but also for my own.

So you are curious to know the outcome of this prescription of travel ? As soon as I escaped from the oppressive atmosphere of the city, and from that awful odour of reeking kitchens which, when in use, pour forth a ruinous mess of steam and soot, I perceived at once that my health was mending. And how much stronger do you think I felt when I reached my vineyards ! Being, so to speak, let out to pasture, I regularly walked into my meals ! So I am my old self again, feeling now no wavering languor in my system, and no sluggishness in my brain. I am beginning to work with all my energy.

7 Non multum ad hoc locus confert, nisi se sibi praestat animus, qui secretum in occupationibus mediis, si volet, habebit ; at ille, qui regiones eligit et otium captat, ubique, quo distringatur, inveniet. Nam Socraten querenti cuidam, quod nihil sibi peregrinationes profuissent, respondisse ferunt : "non inmerito hoc tibi evenit ; tecum enim peregrina-

8 baris." O quam bene cum quibusdam ageretur, si a se aberrarent ! Nunc premunt[1] se ipsi,[2] sollicitant, corrumpunt, territant. Quid prodest mare traicere et urbes mutare ? Si vis ista, quibus urgueris, effugere, non aliubi sis oportet, sed alius. Puta venisse te Athenas, puta Rhodon ; elige arbitrio tuo civitatem : quid ad rem pertinet, quos illa mores habeat ? Tuos adferes.

9 Divitias iudicabis bonum : torquebit te paupertas, quod est miserrimum, falsa. Quamvis enim multum possideas, tamen, quia aliquis plus habet, tanto[3] tibi videris defici, quanto vinceris. Honores iudicabis[4] bonum : male te habebit ille consul factus, ille etiam refectus, invidebis,[5] quotiens aliquem in fastis saepius legeris. Tantus erit ambitionis furor, ut nemo tibi post te videatur, si aliquis ante te

10 fuerit. Maximum malum iudicabis mortem, cum in[6] illa nihil sit mali, nisi quod ante ipsam est, timeri.

---

[1] *premunt* Bartsch ; *primum* BA.
[2] *ipsi* Hense ; *ipsos* BA.
[3] *tanto* later MSS. ; *quanto* BA.
[4] *iudicabis* Cod. Velz. ; *iudicatus* BA.
[5] *invidebis* later MSS. ; *videberis* BA.
[6] *cum in* later MSS. ; *cum* BA.

---

[a] *Cf. Ep.* x. 1 " *Mecum loquor.*" " *Cave, rogo, et diligenter adtende ; cum homine malo loqueris.*"
194

But the mere place avails little for this purpose, unless the mind is fully master of itself, and can, at its pleasure, find seclusion even in the midst of business; the man, however, who is always selecting resorts and hunting for leisure, will find something to distract his mind in every place. Socrates is reported to have replied, when a certain person complained of having received no benefit from his travels: "It serves you right! You travelled in your own company!"[a] O what a blessing it would be for some men to wander away from themselves! As it is, they cause themselves vexation, worry, demoralization, and fear! What profit is there in crossing the sea and in going from one city to another? If you would escape your troubles, you need not another place but another personality. Perhaps you have reached Athens, or perhaps Rhodes; choose any state you fancy, how does it matter what its character may be? You will be bringing to it your own.

Suppose that you hold wealth to be a good: poverty will then distress you, and,—which is most pitiable,—it will be an imaginary poverty. For you may be rich, and nevertheless, because your neighbour is richer, you suppose yourself to be poor exactly by the same amount in which you fall short of your neighbour. You may deem official position a good; you will be vexed at another's appointment or re-appointment to the consulship; you will be jealous whenever you see a name several times in the state records. Your ambition will be so frenzied that you will regard yourself last in the race if there is anyone in front of you. Or you may rate death as the worst of evils, although there is really no evil therein except that which precedes death's coming—

Exterrebunt te non tantum pericula, sed suspiciones ;
vanis semper agitaberis.   Quid enim proderit

evasisse tot urbes
Argolicas mediosque fugam tenuisse per hostis ?

Ipsa pax timores sumministrabit. Ne tutis quidem
habebitur fides consternata semel mente ; quae ubi
consuetudinem pavoris inprovidi fecit, etiam ad tutelam salutis suae inhabilis est.[1] Non enim vitat, sed
fugit.   Magis autem periculis patemus aversi.

11   Gravissimum iudicabis malum, aliquem ex his,
quos amabis, amittere, cum interim hoc tam ineptum
erit quam flere, quod arboribus amoenis et domum
tuam ornantibus decidant folia.   Quicquid te delectat, aeque vide ut flores virides ; dum virent, utere ;[2]
alium alio die casus excutiet.   Sed quemadmodum
frondium iactura facilis est, quia renascuntur, sic
istorum, quos amas quosque oblectamenta vitae putas
esse, damnum, quia reparantur, etiam si non renas-
12 cuntur. "Sed non erunt idem." Ne tu quidem idem
eris.   Omnis dies, omnis hora te mutat ; sed in aliis
rapina facilius apparet, hic latet, quia non ex aperto
fiet.   Alii auferuntur, at ipsi nobis furto subducimur.
Horum nihil cogitabis nec remedia vulneribus op-
pones, sed ipse tibi seres sollicitudinum causas alia

---

[1] *est* later MSS. ; *es* BA.
[2] *ut . . . utere* Haase ; *ut videres dum* $\begin{Bmatrix} vireret \\ vireret \end{Bmatrix}$ *uter* BA.

---

[a] Vergil, *Aen.* iii. 282 f.

fear. You will be frightened out of your wits, not only by real, but by fancied dangers, and will be tossed for ever on the sea of illusion. What benefit will it be to

> Have threaded all the towns of Argolis,
> A fugitive through midmost press of foes ? [a]

For peace itself will furnish further apprehension. Even in the midst of safety you will have no confidence if your mind has once been given a shock ; once it has acquired the habit of blind panic, it is incapable of providing even for its own safety. For it does not avoid danger, but runs away. Yet we are more exposed to danger when we turn our backs.

You may judge it the most grievous of ills to lose any of those you love ; while all the same this would be no less foolish than weeping because the trees which charm your eye and adorn your home lose their foliage. Regard everything that pleases you as if it were a flourishing plant ; make the most of it while it is in leaf, for different plants at different seasons must fall and die. But just as the loss of leaves is a light thing, because they are born afresh, so it is with the loss of those whom you love and regard as the delight of your life ; for they can be replaced even though they cannot be born afresh. "New friends, however, will not be the same." No, nor will you yourself remain the same ; you change with every day and every hour. But in other men you more readily see what time plunders ; in your own case the change is hidden, because it will not take place visibly. Others are snatched from sight ; we ourselves are being stealthily filched away from ourselves. You will not think about any of these problems, nor will you apply remedies to these wounds. You will of your own volition be sowing a crop of

sperando, alia desperando. Si sapis,[1] alterum alteri
misce [2] : nec speraveris sine desperatione nec desperaveris [3] sine spe.

13 Quid per se peregrinatio prodesse cuiquam potuit ?
Non voluptates illa temperavit, non cupiditates re-
frenavit, non iras repressit, non indomitos amoris
impetus fregit, nulla denique animo mala eduxit.
Non iudicium dedit, non discussit errorem, sed
ut puerum ignota mirantem ad breve tempus
14 rerum aliqua novitate detinuit. Ceterum incon-
stantia mentis, quae maxime aegra est, lacessit,
mobiliorem levioremque reddit ipsa iactatio. Itaque,
quae petierant cupidissime loca, cupidius deserunt et
avium modo transvolant citiusque quam venerant,
15 abeunt. Peregrinatio notitiam dabit gentium, novas
tibi montium formas ostendet, invisitata spatia cam-
porum et inriguas perennibus aquis valles, alicuius
fluminis sub observatione naturam, sive ut Nilus
aestivo incremento tumet, sive ut Tigris eripitur ex
oculis et acto per occulta cursu integrae magnitudini
redditur, sive ut Maeander, poetarum omnium exer-
citatio et ludus, implicatur crebris anfractibus et
saepe in vicinum alveo suo admotus, antequam sibi
influat, flectitur ; ceterum neque meliorem faciet
neque saniorem.

16 Inter studia versandum est et inter auctores
sapientiae, ut quaesita discamus, nondum inventa

---

[1] *sapis* later MSS. ; *satis* BA.
[2] *misce* later MSS. ; *misces* BA.
[3] *sine desperatione nec desperaveris* later MSS. ; *sine
speratione nec speraveris* BA.

---

[a] See Index of Proper Names.
[b] Although Seneca was deeply interested in such matters,
as is proved by *Ep.* lxxix., the *Naturales Quaestiones,* and
an early work on the geography of Egypt.

trouble by alternate hoping and despairing. If you are wise, mingle these two elements : do not hope without despair, or despair without hope.

What benefit has travel of itself ever been able to give anyone ? No restraint upon pleasure, no bridling of desire, no checking of bad temper, no crushing of the wild assaults of passion, no opportunity to rid the soul of evil. Travelling cannot give us judgment, or shake off our errors ; it merely holds our attention for a moment by a certain novelty, as children pause to wonder at something unfamiliar. Besides, it irritates us, through the wavering of a mind which is suffering from an acute attack of sickness ; the very motion makes it more fitful and nervous. Hence the spots we had sought most eagerly we quit still more eagerly, like birds that flit and are off as soon as they have alighted. What travel will give is familiarity with other nations : it will reveal to you mountains of strange shape, or unfamiliar tracts of plain, or valleys that are watered by ever-flowing springs, or the characteristics of some river that comes to our attention. We observe how the Nile rises and swells in summer, or how the Tigris disappears, runs underground through hidden spaces, and then appears with unabated sweep ; or how the Maeander,[a] that oft-rehearsed theme and plaything of the poets, turns in frequent bendings, and often in winding comes close to its own channel before resuming its course. But this sort of information will not make better or sounder men of us.[b]

We ought rather to spend our time in study, and to cultivate those who are masters of wisdom, learning something which has been investigated, but not

199

quaeramus; sic eximendus animus ex miserrima
servitute in libertatem adseritur. Quamdiu quidem
nescieris, quid fugiendum quid petendum, quid
necessarium quid supervacuum, quid iustum quid
iniustum [1] sit, non erit hoc peregrinari, sed errare.

17 Nullam [2] tibi opem feret iste discursus, peregrinaris
enim cum adfectibus tuis et mala te tua sequuntur.
Utinam quidem sequerentur. Longius abessent;
nunc fers illa, non ducis. Itaque ubique te premunt
et paribus incommodis urunt.[3] Medicina aegro, non

18 regio, quaerenda est. Fregit aliquis crus aut extorsit
articulum : non vehiculum navemque conscendit, sed
advocat medicum, ut fracta pars iungatur, ut luxata
in locum reponatur. Quid ergo ? Animum tot locis
fractum et extortum credis locorum mutatione posse
sanari ? Maius est istud malum, quam ut gestatione

19 curetur. Peregrinatio non facit medicum, non ora-
torem, nulla ars loco discitur.

Quid ergo ? Sapientia, ars [4] omnium maxima, in
itinere colligitur ? Nullum est, mihi crede, iter,
quod te [5] extra cupiditates, extra iras, extra metus
sistat ; aut si quod esset, agmine facto gens illuc
humana pergeret. Tamdiu ista urguebunt mala
macerabuntque per terras ac maria vagum, quamdiu

20 malorum gestaveris causas. Fugam tibi non prodesse

---

[1] *iniustum* Cornelissen ; *honestum* BA.
[2] *nullam* later MSS. ; *nullum* BA.
[3] *urunt* later MSS. ; *erunt* BA.
[4] *sapientia, ars* Hense ; *sapientia, res* BA.
[5] *te* Erasmus ; *se* BA.

settled; by this means the mind can be relieved of a most wretched serfdom, and won over to freedom. Indeed, as long as you are ignorant of what you should avoid or seek, or of what is necessary or superfluous, or of what is right or wrong, you will not be travelling, but merely wandering. There will be no benefit to you in this hurrying to and fro; for you are travelling with your emotions and are followed by your afflictions. Would that they were indeed following you! In that case, they would be farther away; as it is, you are carrying and not leading them. Hence they press about you on all sides, continually chafing and annoying you. It is medicine, not scenery, for which the sick man must go a-searching. Suppose that someone has broken a leg or dislocated a joint: he does not take carriage or ship for other regions, but he calls in the physician to set the fractured limb, or to move it back to its proper place in the socket. What then? When the spirit is broken or wrenched in so many places, do you think that change of place can heal it? The complaint is too deep-seated to be cured by a journey. Travel does not make a physician or an orator; no art is acquired by merely living in a certain place.

Where lies the truth, then? Can wisdom, the greatest of all the arts, be picked up on a journey? I assure you, travel as far as you like, you can never establish yourself beyond the reach of desire, beyond the reach of bad temper, or beyond the reach of fear; had it been so, the human race would long ago have banded together and made a pilgrimage to the spot. Such ills, as long as you carry with you their causes, will load you down and worry you to skin and bone in your wanderings over land and sea. Do you wonder that it is of no use to run away

miraris ? Tecum sunt, quae fugis. Te igitur emenda,
onera tibi detrahe et demenda [1] desideria intra
salutarem [2] modum contine. Omnem ex animo
erade nequitiam. Si vis peregrinationes habere
iucundas, comitem tuum sana. Haerebit tibi avaritia,
quamdiu avaro sordidoque convixeris ; haerebit
tumor,[3] quamdiu superbo conversaberis. Numquam
saevitiam in tortoris contubernio pones. Incendent
21 libidines tuas adulterorum sodalicia. Si velis vitiis
exui, longe a vitiorum exemplis recedendum est.
Avarus, corruptor, saevus, fraudulentus, multum
nocituri, si prope a te fuissent, intra te sunt.

Ad meliores transi : cum Catonibus vive, cum
Laelio, cum Tuberone. Quod si convivere etiam
Graecis iuvat, cum Socrate, cum Zenone versare ;
alter te docebit mori, si necesse erit, alter, antequam
22 necesse erit. Vive cum Chrysippo, cum Posidonio :
hi tibi tradent humanorum divinorumque notitiam,
hi iubebunt in opere esse nec tantum scite loqui et
in oblectationem audientium verba iactare, sed animum indurare et adversus minas erigere. Unus est
enim huius vitae fluctuantis et turbidae portus
eventura contemnere, stare fidenter ac paratum [4] tela
fortunae adverso pectore excipere, non latitantem nec
23 tergiversantem. Magnanimos nos natura produxit et
ut quibusdam animalibus ferum dedit, quibusdam

---

[1] *demenda* Hense ; *emenda* BA.
[2] *salutarem* Haase ; *salutem* BA.
[3] *haerebit tumor* later MSS. ; *habebit timor* BA.
[4] *ac paratum* Gemoll ; *ad partum* BA.

---

[a] These men are patterns or interpreters of the virtues.
The first-named three represent courage, justice, and self-
restraint respectively. Socrates is the ideal wise man, Zeno,
Chrysippus, and Posidonius are in turn the founder, the
classifier, and the modernizer of Stoicism.

from them ? That from which you are running, is within you. Accordingly, reform your own self, get the burden off your own shoulders, and keep within safe limits the cravings which ought to be removed. Wipe out from your soul all trace of sin. If you would enjoy your travels, make healthy the companion of your travels. As long as this companion is avaricious and mean, greed will stick to you ; and while you consort with an overbearing man, your puffed-up ways will also stick close. Live with a hangman, and you will never be rid of your cruelty. If an adulterer be your club-mate, he will kindle the baser passions. If you would be stripped of your faults, leave far behind you the patterns of the faults. The miser, the swindler, the bully, the cheat, who will do you much harm merely by being near you, are *within* you.

Change therefore to better associations : live with the Catos, with Laelius, with Tubero. Or, if you enjoy living with Greeks also, spend your time with Socrates and with Zeno : the former will show you how to die if it be necessary ; the latter how to die before it is necessary. Live with Chrysippus, with Posidonius : [a] they will make you acquainted with things earthly and things heavenly ; they will bid you work hard over something more than neat turns of language and phrases mouthed forth for the entertainment of listeners ; they will bid you be stout of heart and rise superior to threats. The only harbour safe from the seething storms of this life is scorn of the future, a firm stand, a readiness to receive Fortune's missiles full in the breast, neither skulking nor turning the back. Nature has brought us forth brave of spirit, and, as she has implanted in certain animals a spirit of ferocity, in others craft,

subdolum, quibusdam pavidum, ita nobis gloriosum
et excelsum spiritum, quaerentem ubi honestissime,
non ubi tutissime vivat, simillimum mundo, quem
quantum mortalium passibus[1] licet, sequitur aemula-
turque. Profert se, laudari et aspici credit. Dominus[2]
24 omnium est, supra omnia est; itaque nulli se rei
summittat, nihil illi videatur grave, nihil quod virum
incurvet.

Terribiles visu formae letumque labosque;

minime quidem, si quis rectis oculis intueri illa
possit et tenebras perrumpere. Multa per noctem
habita terrori dies vertit ad risum. " Terribiles visu
formae letumque labosque ": egregie Vergilius
noster non[3] re dixit terribiles esse, sed visu, id est
25 videri, non esse.[4] Quid, inquam, in istis est tam
formidabile quam fama vulgavit ? Quid est, obsecro
te, Lucili, cur timeat laborem vir, mortem homo ?
Totiens mihi occurrunt isti, qui non putant fieri posse
quicquid facere non possunt, et aiunt nos loqui maiora
26 quam quae humana natura sustineat. At quanto
ego de illis melius existimo ! Ipsi quoque haec
possunt facere, sed nolunt. Denique quem umquam
ista destituere temptantem ? Cui non faciliora ap-
paruere in actu ? Non quia difficilia sunt, non
audemus, sed quia non audemus, difficilia sunt.
27 Si tamen exemplum desideratis, accipite Socraten,

[1] *passibus* later MSS. ; *passus* BA.
[2] *dominus* later MSS. ; om. BA.
[3] *non* later MSS. ; *in* BA.
[4] *esse* later MSS. ; *posse* BA.

[a] *Aeneid*, vi. 277.

in others terror, so she has gifted us with an aspiring and lofty spirit, which prompts us to seek a life of the greatest honour, and not of the greatest security, that most resembles the soul of the universe, which it follows and imitates as far as our mortal steps permit. This spirit thrusts itself forward, confident of commendation and esteem. It is superior to all, monarch of all it surveys ; hence it should be subservient to nothing, finding no task too heavy, and nothing strong enough to weigh down the shoulders of a man.

> Shapes dread to look upon, of toil or death [a]

are not in the least dreadful, if one is able to look upon them with unflinching gaze, and is able to pierce the shadows. Many a sight that is held a terror in the night-time, is turned to ridicule by day. " Shapes dread to look upon, of toil or death " : our Vergil has excellently said that these shapes are dread, not in reality, but only " to look upon "—in other words, they seem terrible, but are not. And in these visions what is there, I say, as fear-inspiring as rumour has proclaimed ? Why, pray, my dear Lucilius, should a man fear toil, or a mortal death ? Countless cases occur to my mind of men who think that what they themselves are unable to do is impossible, who maintain that we utter words which are too big for man's nature to carry out. But how much more highly do I think of these men ! They *can* do these things, but decline to do them. To whom that ever tried have these tasks proved false ? To what man did they not seem easier in the doing ? Our lack of confidence is not the result of difficulty ; the difficulty comes from our lack of confidence.

If, however, you desire a pattern, take Socrates,

perpessicium senem, per omnia aspera iactatum, invictum tamen et paupertate, quam graviorem illi
domestica onera faciebant, et laboribus, quos mili-
tares quoque pertulit. Quibus ille domi exercitus
est,[1] sive uxorem eius reminiscimur[2] moribus feram,
lingua petulantem, sive liberos indociles et matri
quam patri similiores. Si vere reputes,[3] aut in bello
fuit aut in tyrannide aut in libertate bellis ac tyrannis
28 saeviore. Viginti et septem annis pugnatum est ; post
finita arma triginta tyrannis noxae dedita est civitas,
ex quibus plerique inimici erant. Novissima damnatio
est sub gravissimis nominibus[4] impleta : obiecta est
et religionum violatio et iuventutis corruptela, quam
inmittere in deos, in patres, in rem publicam dictus
est. Post haec carcer et venenum. Haec usque eo
animum Socratis non moverant, ut ne vultum quidem
moverent. O illam[5] mirabilem laudem et singula-
rem ! Usque ad extremum nec hilariorem quisquam
nec tristiorem Socraten vidit. Aequalis fuit in tanta
inaequalitate fortunae.
29 Vis alterum exemplum ? Accipe hunc M. Catonem
recentiorem, cum quo et infestius fortuna egit et
pertinacius. Cui cum omnibus locis obstitisset, novis-

[1] *est* later MSS. ; om. BA.
[2] *reminiscimur* added by Hense.
[3] *reputes* added by Hense.
[4] *nominibus* Lipsius ; *hominibus* BA.
[5] *moverent. o illam* Buecheler ; *moverint. Illam* BA.

[a] At first a sculptor, then an independent seeker after
truth, whose wants were reduced to a minimum. Husband
of the shrewish Xanthippe and father of the dull and worthless Lamprocles. Brave soldier at Potidaea, Delium, and
Amphipolis.

a long-suffering old man, who was sea-tossed amid every hardship and yet was unconquered both by poverty (which his troubles at home made more burdensome) and by toil, including the drudgery of military service. He was much tried at home, whether we think of his wife, a woman of rough manners and shrewish tongue, or of the children whose intractability showed them to be more like their mother than their father.[a] And if you consider the facts, he lived either in time of war, or under tyrants, or under a democracy, which is more cruel than wars and tyrants. The war lasted for twenty-seven years;[b] then the state became the victim of the Thirty Tyrants, of whom many were his personal enemies. At the last came that climax of condemnation under the gravest of charges: they accused him of disturbing the state religion and corrupting the youth,[c] for they declared that he had influenced the youth to defy the gods, to defy the council, and to defy the state in general. Next came the prison, and the cup of poison.[d] But all these measures changed the soul of Socrates so little that they did not even change his features. What wonderful and rare distinction! He maintained this attitude up to the very end, and no man ever saw Socrates too much elated or too much depressed. Amid all the disturbance of Fortune, he was undisturbed.

Do you desire another case? Take that of the younger Marcus Cato, with whom Fortune dealt in a more hostile and more persistent fashion. But he withstood her, on all occasions, and in his last

---

[b] 431-404 B.C. (the Peloponnesian War).
[c] See Plato's *Apology*, 23 D. They had previously aimed at him a law forbidding the teaching of dialectic.
[d] 399 B.C.

207

sime et in morte, ostendit tamen virum fortem posse
invita fortuna vivere, invita mori. Tota illi aetas
aut in armis est exacta civilibus aut in toga [1] con-
cipiente iam civile bellum. Et hunc licet dicas non
minus quam Socraten in servis se libertati addixisse,[2]
nisi forte Cn. Pompeium et Caesarem et Crassum
30 putas libertatis socios fuisse. Nemo mutatum Catonem totiens mutata re publica vidit: eundem se
in omni statu praestitit, in praetura, in repulsa, in
accusatione, in provincia, in contione, in exercitu, in
morte. Denique in illa rei publicae trepidatione,
cum illinc Caesar esset decem legionibus pugnacis-
simis subnixus, totis exterarum gentium praesidiis,
hinc Cn. Pompeius, satis unus adversus omnia, cum
alii ad Caesarem inclinarent, alii ad Pompeium,
31 solus Cato fecit aliquas et rei publicae partes. Si
animo complecti volueris illius imaginem temporis,
videbis illinc plebem et omne erectum ad res novas
vulgum, hinc optumates et equestrem ordinem,
quicquid erat in civitate sancti et electi, duos in
medio relictos, rem publicam et Catonem.

Miraberis, inquam, cum animadverteris

Atriden [3] Priamumque et saevom ambobus Achillen.

32 Utrumque enim improbat, utrumque exarmat. Hanc
fert de utroque sententiam: ait se, si Caesar vicerit,

---

[1] *in toga* Kronenberg; *intacta* BA.
[2] *in servis se libertati addixisse*, suggested by Hense;
inseruisse dixisse BA.
[3] *Atriden* MSS.; *Atridas* Vergil.

---

[a] Triumvirs in 60 B.C. and rivals in acquiring unconstitu-
tional power.
[b] 54 B.C.

moments, at the point of death, showed that a
brave man can live in spite of Fortune, can die in
spite of her. His whole life was passed either in
civil warfare, or under a political régime which was
soon to breed civil war. And you may say that he,
just as much as Socrates, declared allegiance to
liberty in the midst of slavery—unless perchance
you think that Pompey, Caesar, and Crassus [a] were
the allies of liberty ! No one ever saw Cato change,
no matter how often the state changed : he kept
himself the same in all circumstances—in the praetor-
ship,[b] in defeat, under accusation,[c] in his province,
on the platform, in the army, in death. Furthermore, when the republic was in a crisis of terror,
when Caesar was on one side with ten embattled
legions at his call, aided by so many foreign nations,
and when Pompey was on the other, satisfied to
stand alone against all comers, and when the citizens
were leaning towards either Caesar or Pompey, Cato
alone established a definite party for the Republic.
If you would obtain a mental picture of that period,
you may imagine on one side the people and the
whole proletariat eager for revolution—on the other
the senators and knights, the chosen and honoured
men of the commonwealth ; and there were left
between them but these two—the Republic and
Cato.

I tell you, you will marvel when you see

Atreus' son, and Priam, and Achilles, wroth at both.[d]

Like Achilles, he scorns and disarms each faction.
And this is the vote which he casts concerning them

[c] Perhaps a reference to his mission in Cyprus (58-56 B.C.),
and his subsequent arraignment by Clodius.
[d] Vergil, *Aen.* i. 458.

209

moriturum, si Pompeius, exulaturum. Quid habebat, quod timeret, qui ipse [1] sibi et victo et victori
constituerat, quae constituta esse ab hostibus ira-
tissimis poterant ? Periit itaque ex decreto suo.

33 Vides posse homines laborem pati : per medias
Africae solitudines pedes duxit exercitum. Vides
posse tolerari sitim : in collibus arentibus sine ullis
inpedimentis victi exercitus reliquias trahens inopiam
umoris loricatus tulit et, quotiens aquae fuerat
occasio, novissimus bibit. Vides honorem et notam
posse contemni : eodem quo repulsus est die in
comitio pila lusit. Vides posse non timeri potentiam
superiorum : et Pompeium et Caesarem, quorum
nemo alterum offendere audebat nisi ut alterum
demereretur, simul provocavit. Vides tam mortem
posse contemni quam exilium : et exilium sibi indixit
et mortem et interim bellum.

34 Possumus itaque adversus ista tantum habere
animi, libeat modo subducere iugo collum. In primis
autem respuendae voluptates ; enervant et effe-
minant et multum petunt, multum autem a fortuna
petendum est. Deinde spernendae [2] opes : auctora-
menta sunt servitutum. Aurum et argentum et
quicquid aliud felices domos onerat, relinquatur ;
non potest gratis constare libertas. Hanc si magno
aestimas, omnia parvo aestimanda sunt. VALE.

---

[1] *ipse* Hense ; *id* BA.
[2] *spernendae* later MSS. ; *sperandae* BA.

---

[a] At Utica, in 46 B.C.

both : " If Caesar wins, I slay myself ; if Pompey, I go into exile." What was there for a man to fear who, whether in defeat or in victory, had assigned to himself a doom which might have been assigned to him by his enemies in their utmost rage ? So he died by his own decision.

You see that man can endure toil : Cato, on foot, led an army through African deserts. You see that thirst can be endured : he marched over sun-baked hills, dragging the remains of a beaten army and with no train of supplies, undergoing lack of water and wearing a heavy suit of armour ; always the last to drink of the few springs which they chanced to find. You see that honour, and dishonour too, can be despised : for they report that on the very day when Cato was defeated at the elections, he played a game of ball. You see also that man can be free from fear of those above him in rank : for Cato attacked Caesar and Pompey simultaneously, at a time when none dared fall foul of the one without endeavouring to oblige the other. You see that death can be scorned as well as exile : Cato inflicted exile upon himself and finally death,[a] and war all the while.

And so, if only we are willing to withdraw our necks from the yoke, we can keep as stout a heart against such terrors as these. But first and foremost, we must reject pleasures ; they render us weak and womanish ; they make great demands upon us, and, moreover, cause us to make great demands upon Fortune. Second, we must spurn wealth : wealth is the diploma of slavery. Abandon gold and silver, and whatever else is a burden upon our richly-furnished homes ; liberty cannot be gained for nothing. If you set a high value on liberty, you must set a low value on everything else. Farewell.

211

CV.

SENECA LVCILIO SVO SALVTEM

1 Quae observanda tibi sint, ut tutior vivas, dicam.
Tu tamen sic audias censeo ista praecepta, quomodo
si tibi praeciperem, qua ratione bonam valitudinem
in Ardeatino tuereris.

Considera, quae sint, quae hominem in perniciem
hominis instigent : invenies spem, invidiam, odium,
2 metum, contemptum. Ex omnibus istis adeo levis-
simum est contemptus, ut multi in illo remedii causa
delituerint. Quem quis contemnit, violat [1] sine
dubio, sed transit ; nemo homini contempto per-
tinaciter, nemo diligenter nocet. Etiam in acie
3 iacens praeteritur, cum stante pugnatur. Spem in-
proborum vitabis, si nihil habueris, quod cupiditatem
alienam et inprobam inritet, si nihil insigne possederis.
Concupiscuntur enim etiam parva, si notabilia sunt,
si rara. [2]

Invidiam effugies, si te non ingesseris oculis, si
bona tua non iactaveris, si scieris in sinu gaudere.
4 Odium aut est [3] ex offensa : hoc vitabis neminem
lacessendo ; aut gratuitum : a quo te sensus communis tuebitur. Fuit hoc multis periculosum ; quidam odium habuerunt nec inimicum. Illud, ne
timearis, praestabit tibi et fortunae mediocritas et

[1] *violat* Buecheler ; *vincit* BA.
[2] This is Madvig's conjecture ; *etiam pars innotarum
sunt, sic raro* BA.
[3] *aut est* Haase ; *autem* BA.

EPISTLE CV.

CV. ON FACING THE WORLD WITH CONFIDENCE

I shall now tell you certain things to which you should pay attention in order to live more safely. Do you however,—such is my judgment,—hearken to my precepts just as if I were counselling you to keep safe your health in your country-place at Ardea.

Reflect on the things which goad man into destroying man : you will find that they are hope, envy, hatred, fear, and contempt. Now, of all these, contempt is the least harmful, so much so that many have skulked behind it as a sort of cure. When a man despises you, he works you injury, to be sure, but he passes on ; and no one persistently or of set purpose does hurt to a person whom he despises. Even in battle, prostrate soldiers are neglected : men fight with those who stand their ground. And you can avoid the envious hopes of the wicked so long as you have nothing which can stir the evil desires of others, and so long as you possess nothing remarkable. For people crave even little things, if these catch the attention or are of rare occurrence.

You will escape envy if you do not force yourself upon the public view, if you do not boast your possessions, if you understand how to enjoy things privately. Hatred comes either from running foul of others : and this can be avoided by never provoking anyone ; or else it is uncalled for : and common-sense *a* will keep you safe from it. Yet it has been dangerous to many ; some people have been hated without having had an enemy. As to not being feared, a moderate fortune and an easy

---

a *i.e.*, tact.

ingenii lenitas; eum esse te homines sciant, quem
offendere sine periculo possint; reconciliatio tua et
facilis sit et certa. Timeri autem tam domi molestum
est quam foris, tam a servis quam a liberis. Nulli
non ad nocendum satis virium est. Adice nunc,
quod qui timetur, timet; nemo potuit terribilis
esse secure.

5   Contemptus superest, cuius modum in sua potestate habet, qui illum sibi adiunxit, qui contemnitur
quia voluit, non quia debuit. Huius incommodum et
artes bonae discutiunt et amicitiae eorum, qui apud
aliquem potentem potentes sunt, quibus adplicari
expediet, non inplicari, ne pluris remedium quam
6 periculum constet. Nihil tamen aeque proderit quam
quiescere et minimum cum aliis loqui, plurimum
secum. Est quaedam dulcedo sermonis, quae inrepit
et eblanditur [1] et non aliter quam ebrietas aut amor
secreta producit. Nemo quod audierit, tacebit.
Nemo quantum audierit, loquetur. Qui rem non
tacuerit, non tacebit auctorem. Habet unusquisque
aliquem, cui tantum credat, quantum ipsi creditum
est. Ut garrulitatem suam custodiat et contentus
sit unius auribus, populum faciet, si [2] quod modo
secretum erat, rumor est.

7   Securitatis magna portio est nihil inique facere.
Confusam vitam et perturbatam inpotentes agunt;

---

[1] *inrepit et eblanditur* Pincianus; *inrepitete blanditur* BA.
[2] *si* Buecheler; *sic* BA.

disposition will guarantee you that; men should know that you are the sort of person who can be offended without danger; and your reconciliation should be easy and sure. Moreover, it is as troublesome to be feared at home as abroad; it is as bad to be feared by a slave as by a gentleman. For every one has strength enough to do you some harm. Besides, he who is feared, fears also; no one has been able to arouse terror and live in peace of mind.

Contempt remains to be discussed. He who has made this quality an adjunct of his own personality, who is despised because he wishes to be despised and not because he *must* be despised, has the measure of contempt under his control. Any inconveniences in this respect can be dispelled by honourable occupations and by friendships with men who have influence with an influential person; with these men it will profit you to engage but not to entangle yourself, lest the cure may cost you more than the risk. Nothing, however, will help you so much as keeping still—talking very little with others, and as much as may be with yourself. For there is a sort of charm about conversation, something very subtle and coaxing, which, like intoxication or love, draws secrets from us. No man will keep to himself what he hears. No one will tell another only as much as he has heard. And he who tells tales will tell names, too. Everyone has someone to whom he entrusts exactly what has been entrusted to him. Though he checks his own garrulity, and is content with one hearer, he will bring about him a nation, if that which was a secret shortly before becomes common talk.

The most important contribution to peace of mind is never to do wrong. Those who lack self-control lead disturbed and tumultuous lives; their crimes

215

tantum metuunt, quantum nocent, nec ullo tempore
vacant. Trepidant enim, cum fecerunt, haerent;
conscientia aliud agere non patitur ac subinde respon-
dere ad se cogit. Dat poenas quisquis expectat;
8 quisquis autem meruit, expectat. Tutum aliqua res
in mala conscientia praestat, nulla securum; putat
enim se, etiam si non deprenditur, posse deprendi.
Et inter somnos movetur et, quotiens alicuius scelus
loquitur, de suo cogitat; non satis illi obliteratum
videtur, non satis tectum. Nocens habuit aliquando
latendi fortunam, numquam fiduciam. VALE.

CVI.

SENECA LVCILIO SVO SALVTEM

1 Tardius rescribo ad epistulas tuas, non quia
districtus occupationibus sum. Hanc excusationem
cave audias; vaco et omnes vacant, qui volunt.
Neminem res secuntur. Ipsi illas amplexantur et
argumentum esse felicitatis occupationem putant.
Quid ergo fuit, quare non protinus rescriberem?
Id,[1] de quo quaerebas, veniebat in contextum operis
2 mei. Scis enim me moralem philosophiam velle
conplecti et omnes ad eam pertinentis quaestiones
explicare. Itaque dubitavi utrum differrem te, donec

[1] *id* Madvig; *ei* BA[1].

---

[a] Presumably (*cf. Ep.* cviii. § 1) into this collection of
Epistles.

are balanced by their fears, and they are never at ease. For they tremble after the deed, and they are embarrassed; their consciences do not allow them to busy themselves with other matters, and continually compel them to give an answer. Whoever expects punishment, receives it, but whoever deserves it, expects it. Where there is an evil conscience something may bring safety, but nothing can bring ease; for a man imagines that, even if he is not under arrest, he may soon be arrested. His sleep is troubled; when he speaks of another man's crime, he reflects upon his own, which seems to him not sufficiently blotted out, not sufficiently hidden from view. A wrongdoer sometimes has the luck to escape notice but never the assurance thereof. Farewell.

CVI. ON THE CORPOREALITY OF VIRTUE

My tardiness in answering your letter was not due to press of business. Do not listen to that sort of excuse; I am at liberty, and so is anyone else who wishes to be at liberty. No man is at the mercy of affairs. He gets entangled in them of his own accord, and then flatters himself that being busy is a proof of happiness. Very well; you no doubt want to know why I did not answer the letter sooner? The matter about which you consulted me was being gathered into the fabric of my volume.[a] For you know that I am planning to cover the whole of moral philosophy and to settle all the problems which concern it. Therefore I hesitated whether to make you wait until the proper time came for

suus isti rei veniret locus, an[1] ius tibi extra ordinem
dicerem ; humanius visum est tam longe venientem
3 non detinere. Itaque et hoc ex illa serie rerum
cohaerentium excerpam et, si qua erunt eiusmodi,
non quaerenti tibi ultro mittam.

Quae sint haec interrogas ? Quae scire magis
iuvat quam prodest, sicut hoc, de quo quaeris :
4 bonum an corpus sit ? Bonum facit : prodest enim.[2]
Quod facit, corpus est. Bonum agitat animum et
quodammodo format et continet, quae propria[3] sunt
corporis. Quae corporis bona sunt, corpora sunt ;
5 ergo et quae animi sunt. Nam et hoc corpus est.
Bonum hominis necesse est corpus sit, cum ipse sit
corporalis. Mentior, nisi et quae alunt illum et
quae valitudinem eius vel custodiunt vel restituunt,
corpora sunt ; ergo et bonum eius corpus est. Non
puto te dubitaturum, an adfectus corpora sint—ut
aliud quoque, de quo non quaeris, infulciam—tamquam ira, amor, tristitia, nisi[4] dubitas, an vultum nobis
mutent, an frontem adstringant, an faciem diffundant,
an ruborem evocent, an fugent sanguinem. Quid
ergo ? Tam manifestas notas corporis credis inprimi[5]
6 nisi a corpore ? Si adfectus corpora sunt, et morbi
animorum, ut[6] avaritia, crudelitas, indurata vitia
et in statum inemendabilem adducta ; ergo et malitia

---

[1] *an* after *differrem te* BA ; after *locus* Eisele.
[2] *facit : prodest enim* Schweighaeuser ; *prodest. facile enim* BA.
[3] *ergo propria* MSS. ; *propria* Schweighaeuser.
[4] *nisi* Gertz ; *si* BA.
[5] *inprimi* later MSS. : *incrimine* BA.
[6] *ut* Windhaus and Gertz, with cod. Velz. ; *et* BA.

---

[a] As Lucilius, in his letter, has come from far away.
[b] This subject is discussed more fully in *Ep.* cxiii. For

this subject, or to pronounce judgment out of the logical order; but it seemed more kindly not to keep waiting one who comes from such a distance.[a] So I propose both to pick this out of the proper sequence of correlated matter, and also to send you, without waiting to be asked, whatever has to do with questions of the same sort.

Do you ask what these are? Questions regarding which knowledge pleases rather than profits; for instance, your question whether the good is corporeal.[b] Now the good is active: for it is beneficial; and what is active is corporeal. The good stimulates the mind and, in a way, moulds and embraces that which is essential to the body. The goods of the body are bodily; so therefore must be the goods of the soul. For the soul, too, is corporeal. *Ergo*, man's good must be corporeal, since man himself is corporeal. I am sadly astray if the elements which support man and preserve or restore his health, are not bodily; therefore, his good is a body. You will have no doubt, I am sure, that emotions are bodily things (if I may be allowed to wedge in another subject not under immediate discussion), like wrath, love, sternness; unless you doubt whether they change our features, knot our foreheads, relax the countenance, spread blushes, or drive away the blood? What, then? Do you think that such evident marks of the body are stamped upon us by anything else than body? And if emotions are corporeal, so are the diseases of the spirit—such as greed, cruelty, and all the faults which harden in our souls, to such an extent that they get into an incurable state. Therefore evil is also, and all

a clear account of the whole question of "body" see Arnold, *Roman Stoicism*, pp. 157 ff.

et species eius omnes, malignitas, invidia, superbia
7 ergo et bona, primum quia contraria istis sunt, deinde
quia eadem tibi indicia praestabunt. An non vides,
quantum oculis det vigorem fortitudo? Quantam
intentionem prudentia? Quantam modestiam et
quietem reverentia? Quantam serenitatem laetitia?
Quantum rigorem severitas? Quantam remissionem
lenitas? Corpora ergo sunt, quae colorem habitum-
que corporum mutant, quae in illis regnum suum
exercent.

Omnes autem, quas rettuli, virtutes bona[1] sunt, et
quicquid ex illis est. Numquid est dubium, an id,
8 quo quid tangi potest, corpus sit?

> Tangere enim et tangi nisi corpus nulla potest res,

ut ait Lucretius. Omnia autem ista, quae dixi, non
mutarent corpus, nisi tangerent; ergo corpora sunt.
9 Etiam nunc cui tanta vis est, ut inpellat et cogat et
retineat et inhibeat,[2] corpus est. Quid ergo? Non
timor retinet? Non audacia inpellit? Non fortitudo inmittit et impetum dat? Non moderatio
refrenat ac revocat? Non gaudium extollit? Non
10 tristitia adducit? Denique quidquid facimus, aut
malitiae aut virtutis gerimus imperio. Quod imperat
corpori, corpus est,[3] quod vim corpori adfert, corpus.
Bonum corporis corporalest,[4] bonum hominis et corporis bonum est; itaque corporale[5] est.
11 Quoniam, ut voluisti, morem gessi tibi, nunc ipse
dicam mihi, quod dicturum esse te video: latrunculis

[1] *bona* later MSS.; *bonae* BA.
[2] *inhibeat* Gertz; *iubeat* BA.
[3] *est* later MSS.; *sit* BA.
[4] *corporalest* Windhaus; *corporalis* BA; *corporalis res est* later MSS.
[5] *corporale* later MSS.; *corporalis* BA.

its branches—spite, hatred, pride; and so also are goods, first because they are opposite poles of the bad, and second because they will manifest to you the same symptoms. Do you not see how a spirit of bravery makes the eye flash? How prudence tends towards concentration? How reverence produces moderation and tranquillity? How joy produces calm? How sternness begets stiffness? How gentleness produces relaxation? These qualities are therefore bodily; for they change the tones and the shapes of substances, exercising their own power in their own kingdoms.

Now all the virtues which I have mentioned are goods, and so are their results. Have you any doubt that whatever can touch is corporeal?

Nothing but body can touch or be touched,

as Lucretius[a] says. Moreover, such changes as I have mentioned could not affect the body without touching it. Therefore, they are bodily. Furthermore, any object that has power to move, force, restrain, or control, is corporeal. Come now! Does not fear hold us back? Does not boldness drive us ahead? Bravery spur us on, and give us momentum? Restraint rein us in and call us back? Joy raise our spirits? Sadness cast us down? In short, any act on our part is performed at the bidding of wickedness or virtue. Only a body can control or forcefully affect another body. The good of the body is corporeal; a man's good is related to his bodily good; therefore, it is bodily.

Now that I have humoured your wishes, I shall anticipate your remark, when you say: " What a

---

[a] *De Rerum Nat.* i. 304.

ludimus. In supervacuis subtilitas teritur ; non
faciunt bonos ista, sed doctos. Apertior res est
12 sapere, immo simpliciter satius [1] est ad mentem
bonam uti litteris, sed nos ut cetera in supervacuum diffundimus, ita philosophiam ipsam. Quemadmodum omnium rerum, sic litterarum quoque
intemperantia laboramus ; non vitae sed scholae
discimus. VALE.

CVII.

SENECA LVCILIO SVO SALVTEM

1 Ubi illa prudentia tua ? Ubi in dispiciendis rebus
subtilitas ? Ubi magnitudo ? Iam pusilla te res
angit [2] ? Servi occupationes tuas occasionem fugae
putaverunt. Si amici deciperent—habeant enim sane
nomen, quod illis noster error [3] inposuit, et vocentur,
quo turpius non sint—omnibus rebus tuis desset
aliquid ; nunc [4] desunt illi, qui et operam tuam
conterebant et te aliis molestum esse credebant.
2 Nihil horum insolitum, nihil inexpectatum est.
Offendi rebus istis tam ridiculum est quam queri,
quod spargaris in publico aut inquineris in luto.
Eadem vitae condicio est, quae balnei, turbae,
itineris: quaedam in te mittentur,[5] quaedam incident.

---

[1] *satius* Buecheler ; *faucis* BA.
[2] *te res angit* later MSS.; *tangit* BA ; *pusilla tangunt*
Erasmus.
[3] *error* Madvig ; *e priori* or *epicurus* BA.
[4] *desset aliquid* ; *nunc* inserted by Hense.
[5] *in te mittentur* Lipsius ; *intermittentur* BA.

---

[a] The Romans had a *ludus latrunculorum*, with features
resembling both draughts and chess. The pieces (*calculi*)
were perhaps of different values : the *latrunculus* may have
been a sort of " rover," *cf.* Martial, *Epig.* vii. 72.

game of pawns ! " [a] We dull our fine edge by such
superfluous pursuits ; these things make men clever,
but not good. Wisdom is a plainer thing than that ;
nay, it is clearly better to use literature for the
improvement of the mind, instead of wasting philosophy itself as we waste other efforts on superfluous
things. Just as we suffer from excess in all things, so
we suffer from excess in literature ; thus we learn
our lessons, not for life, but for the lecture-room.
Farewell.

CVII. ON OBEDIENCE TO THE UNIVERSAL WILL

Where is that common-sense of yours ? Where
that deftness in examining things ? That greatness
of soul ? Have you come to be tormented by a trifle ?
Your slaves regarded your absorption in business
as an opportunity for them to run away. Well, if
your friends deceived you (for by all means let them
have the name which we mistakenly bestowed upon
them, and so call them, that they may incur more
shame by not being such friends)—if your friends, I
repeat, deceived you, all your affairs would lack something ; as it is, you merely lack men who damaged
your own endeavours and considered you burdensome
to your neighbours. None of these things is unusual
or unexpected. It is as nonsensical to be put out
by such events as to complain of being spattered in
the street or at getting befouled in the mud. The
programme of life is the same as that of a bathing
establishment, a crowd, or a journey : sometimes
things will be thrown at you, and sometimes they

Non est delicata res vivere. Longam viam ingressus
es ; et labaris oportet et arietes et cadas et lasseris
et exclames : " O mors ! " id est mentiaris. Alio
loco comitem relinques, alio efferes, alio timebis ; per
eiusmodi offensas emetiendum est confragosum hoc
iter.

3 Mori vult ? Praeparetur animus contra omnia ;
sciat se venisse, ubi tonat fulmen. Sciat se venisse,
ubi

> Luctus et ultrices posuere cubilia curae
> Pallentesque habitant morbi tristisque senectus.

In hoc contubernio vita degenda est. Effugere ista
non potes, contemnere potes. Contemnes autem, si
4 saepe cogitaveris et futura praesumpseris. Nemo
non fortius ad id, cui se diu conposuerat, accessit
et duris quoque, si praemeditata erant, obstitit. At
contra inparatus etiam levissima expavit. Id agendum est, ne quid nobis inopinatum sit. Et quia
omnia novitate graviora sunt, hoc cogitatio adsidua
praestabit, ut nulli sis malo tiro.

5 " Servi me reliquerunt." Alium compilaverunt,
alium accusaverunt, alium occiderunt, alium pro-
diderunt, alium calcaverunt, alium veneno, alium
criminatione petierunt ; quicquid dixeris, multis
accidit. Deinceps quae multa et varia sunt, in nos

---

will strike you by accident. Life is not a dainty business. You have started on a long journey; you are bound to slip, collide, fall, become weary, and cry out: " O for Death ! "—or in other words, tell lies. At one stage you will leave a comrade behind you, at another you will bury someone, at another you will be apprehensive. It is amid stumblings of this sort that you must travel out this rugged journey.

Does one wish to die ? Let the mind be prepared to meet everything; let it know that it has reached the heights round which the thunder plays. Let it know that it has arrived where—

> Grief and avenging Care have set their couch,
> And pallid sickness dwells, and drear Old Age.ᵃ

With such messmates must you spend your days. Avoid them you cannot, but despise them you can. And you will despise them, if you often take thought and anticipate the future. Everyone approaches courageously a danger which he has prepared himself to meet long before, and withstands even hardships if he has previously practised how to meet them. But, contrariwise, the unprepared are panic-stricken even at the most trifling things. We must see to it that nothing shall come upon us unforeseen. And since things are all the more serious when they are unfamiliar, continual reflection will give you the power, no matter what the evil may be, not to play the unschooled boy.

" My slaves have run away from me ! " Yes, other men have been robbed, blackmailed, slain, betrayed, stamped under foot, attacked by poison or by slander; no matter what trouble you mention, it has happened to many. Again, there are manifold

225

tela deriguntur.[1]   Quaedam in nos fixa sunt, quaedam vibrant et cum maxime veniunt, quaedam
6 in alios perventura nos stringunt.   Nihil miremur
eorum, ad quae nati sumus, quae ideo nulli querenda,
quia paria sunt omnibus.   Ita dico, paria sunt ; nam
etiam quod effugit aliquis, pati potuit.   Aequum
autem ius est non quo omnes usi sunt, sed quod
omnibus latum est.   Imperetur aequitas animo et sine
querella mortalitatis tributa pendamus.

7   Hiems frigora adducit : algendum est.   Aestas
calores refert : aestuandum est.   Intemperies caeli
valitudinem temptat : aegrotandum est.   Et fera
nobis aliquo loco occurret et homo perniciosior feris
omnibus.   Aliud aqua, aliud ignis eripiet.   Hanc
rerum condicionem mutare non possumus ; illud
possumus, magnum sumere animum et viro bono
dignum, quo fortiter fortuita patiamur et naturae
8 consentiamus.   Natura autem hoc, quod vides, regnum mutationibus temperat ; nubilo serena succedunt ; turbantur maria, cum quieverunt ; flant in
vicem venti ; noctem dies sequitur ; pars caeli con-
surgit, pars mergitur.   Contrariis rerum aeternitas
constat.

9   Ad hanc legem animus noster aptandus est ; hanc
sequatur, huic pareat.   Et quaecumque fiunt, de-
buisse fieri putet nec velit obiurgare naturam.
Optimum est pati, quod emendare non possis, et

---

[1] *varia sunt, in nos tela deriguntur* Hense ; B and A
omit *tela* and read *diriguntur.*

kinds of missiles which are hurled at us. Some are planted in us, some are being brandished and at this very moment are on the way, some which were destined for other men graze us instead. We should not manifest surprise at any sort of condition into which we are born, and which should be lamented by no one, simply because it is equally ordained for all. Yes, I say, equally ordained; for a man might have experienced even that which he has escaped. And an equal law consists, not of that which all have experienced, but of that which is laid down for all. Be sure to prescribe for your mind this sense of equity; we should pay without complaint the tax of our mortality.

Winter brings on cold weather; and we must shiver. Summer returns, with its heat; and we must sweat. Unseasonable weather upsets the health; and we must fall ill. In certain places we may meet with wild beasts, or with men who are more destructive than any beasts. Floods, or fires, will cause us loss. And we cannot change this order of things; but what we can do is to acquire stout hearts, worthy of good men, thereby courageously enduring chance and placing ourselves in harmony with Nature. And Nature moderates this world-kingdom which you see, by her changing seasons: clear weather follows cloudy; after a calm, comes the storm; the winds blow by turns; day succeeds night; some of the heavenly bodies rise, and some set. Eternity consists of opposites.

It is to this law that our souls must adjust themselves, this they should follow, this they should obey. Whatever happens, assume that it was bound to happen, and do not be willing to rail at Nature. That which you cannot reform, it is best to endure,

deum, quo auctore cuncta proveniunt, sine murmuratione comitari ; malus miles est qui imperatorem
10 gemens sequitur. Quare inpigri atque alacres excipiamus imperia nec deseramus [1] hunc operis pulcherrimi cursum, cui quidquid patiemur, intextum est.

Et sic adloquamur Iovem, cuius gubernaculo [2] moles ista derigitur, quemadmodum Cleanthes noster versibus disertissimis adloquitur, quos mihi in nostrum sermonem mutare permittitur Ciceronis, disertissimi viri, exemplo. Si placuerint, boni consules ; si displicuerint, scies me in hoc secutum Ciceronis exemplum :

11
    Duc, o parens celsique dominator poli,
    Quocumque placuit ; nulla parendi mora est.
    Adsum inpiger. Fac nolle, comitabor gemens
    Malusque patiar, facere quod licuit bono.
    Ducunt volentem fata, nolentem trahunt.

12 Sic vivamus, sic loquamur ; paratos nos inveniat atque inpigros fatum. Hic est magnus animus, qui se ei tradidit ; at contra ille pusillus et degener, qui obluctatur et de ordine mundi male existimat et emendare mavult deos quam se. VALE.

CVIII.

1   Id, de quo quaeris, ex his est, quae scire tantum

[1] *deseramus* later MSS. ; *desimus* BA.
[2] *gubernaculo* later MSS. ; *tabernaculo* BA.

[a] Cleanthes, Frag. 527 von Arnim. In Epictetus (*Ench.* 53) these verses are assigned to Cleanthes (omitting the last line) ; while St. Augustine (*Civ. Dei*, v. 8) quotes them as Seneca's : *Annaei Senecae sunt, nisi fallor, hi versus.* Wilamowitz and others follow the latter view.
228

and to attend uncomplainingly upon the God under whose guidance everything progresses ; for it is a bad soldier who grumbles when following his commander. For this reason we should welcome our orders with energy and vigour, nor should we cease to follow the natural course of this most beautiful universe, into which all our future sufferings are woven.

Let us address Jupiter, the pilot of this world-mass, as did our great Cleanthes in those most eloquent lines — lines which I shall allow myself to render in Latin, after the example of the eloquent Cicero. If you like them, make the most of them ; if they displease you, you will understand that I have simply been following the practice of Cicero :

> Lead me, O Master of the lofty heavens,
> My Father, whithersoever thou shalt wish.
> I shall not falter, but obey with speed.
> And though I would not, I shall go, and suffer,
> In sin and sorrow what I might have done
> In noble virtue. Aye, the willing soul
> Fate leads, but the unwilling drags along.[a]

Let us live thus, and speak thus ; let Fate find us ready and alert. Here is your great soul—the man who has given himself over to Fate ; on the other hand, that man is a weakling and a degenerate who struggles and maligns the order of the universe and would rather reform the gods than reform himself. Farewell.

CVIII. ON THE APPROACHES TO PHILOSOPHY

The topic about which you ask me is one of those where our only concern with knowledge is to have the

eo, ut scias, pertinet. Sed nihilominus, quia pertinet, properas nec vis exspectare libros, quos cum maxime ordino continentes totam moralem philosophiae partem. Statim expediam, illud tamen prius scribam, quemadmodum tibi ista cupiditas discendi, qua flagrare te video, digerenda sit, ne ipsa se inpediat. Nec passim carpenda sunt nec avide invadenda universa; per partes pervenietur ad totum. Aptari onus viribus debet nec plus occupari quam cui sufficere possimus. Non quantum vis, sed quantum capis, hauriendum est. Bonum tantum habe animum; capies quantum voles. Quo plus recipit animus, hoc se magis laxat.

3 Haec nobis praecipere Attalum memini, cum scholam eius opsideremus et primi veniremus et novissimi exiremus, ambulantem quoque illum ad aliquas disputationes evocaremus, non tantum paratum discentibus, sed obvium. "Idem," inquit, "et docenti et discenti debet esse propositum: ut ille prodesse velit, hic proficere." Qui ad philosophum venit, cotidie aliquid secum boni ferat: aut sanior domum redeat aut sanabilior. Redibit autem; ea philosophiae vis est, ut non studentes, sed etiam conversantes iuvet. Qui in solem venit, licet non in

---

[a] *Cf. Ep.* cvi. 2 *scis enim me moralem philosophiam velle conplecti*, etc.

[b] Seneca's first and most convincing teacher of Stoicism, to whom this letter is a tribute. The ablest of contemporary philosophers, he was banished during the reign of Tiberius. See Indexes to Vols. I. and II.

knowledge. Nevertheless, because it does so far concern us, you are in a hurry; you are not willing to wait for the books which I am at this moment arranging for you, and which embrace the whole department of moral philosophy.[a] I shall send you the books at once; but I shall, before doing that, write and tell you how this eagerness to learn, with which I see you are aflame, should be regulated, so that it may not get in its own way. Things are not to be gathered at random; nor should they be greedily attacked in the mass; one will arrive at a knowledge of the whole by studying the parts. The burden should be suited to your strength, nor should you tackle more than you can adequately handle. Absorb not all that you wish, but all that you can hold. Only be of a sound mind, and then you will be able to hold all that you wish. For the more the mind receives, the more does it expand.

This was the advice, I remember, which Attalus[b] gave me in the days when I practically laid siege to his class-room, the first to arrive and the last to leave. Even as he paced up and down, I would challenge him to various discussions; for he not only kept himself accessible to his pupils, but met them half-way. His words were: "The same purpose should possess both master and scholar—an ambition in the one case to promote, and in the other to progress." He who studies with a philosopher should take away with him some one good thing every day: he should daily return home a sounder man, or in the way to become sounder And he will thus return; for it is one of the functions of philosophy to help not only those who study her, but those also who associate with her. He that walks in the sun, though he walk not for that purpose, must needs

hoc venerit, colorabitur ; qui in unguentaria taberna
resederunt et paullo diutius commorati sunt, odorem
secum loci ferunt. Et qui ad philosophum fuerunt,
traxerint aliquid necesse est, quod prodesset etiam
neglegentibus. Attende, quid dicam : neglegentibus, non repugnantibus.

5 " Quid ergo ? Non novimus quosdam, qui multis
apud philosophum annis persederint et ne colorem
quidem duxerint ? " Quidni noverim ? Pertinacis-
simos quidem et adsiduos, quos ego non discipulos
6 philosophorum, sed inquilinos*a* voco. Quidam veniunt
ut audiant, non ut discant, sicut in theatrum voluptatis causa ad delectandas aures oratione vel voce vel
fabulis ducimur. Magnam hanc auditorum partem
videbis, cui philosophi schola deversorium otii sit.
Non id agunt, ut aliqua illo vitia deponant, ut aliquam
legem vitae accipiant, qua mores suos exigant, sed
ut oblectamento aurium perfruantur. Aliqui tamen
et cum pugillaribus veniunt, non ut res excipiant, sed
ut verba,*b* quae tam sine profectu alieno dicant quam
sine suo audiunt. Quidam ad magnificas voces excitantur et transeunt in adfectum dicentium alacres
7 vultu et animo, nec aliter concitantur quam solent
Phrygii tibicinis sono semiviri et ex imperio furentes.[1]
Rapit illos instigatque rerum pulchritudo, non ver-

---

[1] *furentes* Erasmus ; *fugientes* BA[1].

---

a Literally " tenants," " lodgers," of a temporary sort.
b *Cf.* the dangers of such *lusoria* (*Ep.* xlviii. 8) and *a
rebus studium transferendum est ad verba* (*Ep.* xl. 14).
c *i.e.*, mendicant Galli, worshippers of Cybele, the Magna
Mater.

become sunburned. He who frequents the per-
fumer's shop and lingers even for a short time, will
carry with him the scent of the place. And he who
follows a philosopher is bound to derive some benefit
therefrom, which will help him even though he be
remiss. Mark what I say: "remiss," not "re-
calcitrant."

"What then?" you say, "do we not know certain
men who have sat for many years at the feet of a
philosopher and yet have not acquired the slightest
tinge of wisdom?" Of course I know such men.
There are indeed persevering gentlemen who stick
at it; I do not call them pupils of the wise, but
merely "squatters." [a] Certain of them come to hear
and not to learn, just as we are attracted to the
theatre to satisfy the pleasures of the ear, whether
by a speech, or by a song, or by a play. This class,
as you will see, constitutes a large part of the listeners,
—who regard the philosopher's lecture-room merely
as a sort of lounging-place for their leisure. They
do not set about to lay aside any faults there, or to
receive a rule of life, by which they may test their
characters; they merely wish to enjoy to the full
the delights of the ear. And yet some arrive even
with notebooks, not to take down the matter, but
only the words,[b] that they may presently repeat
them to others with as little profit to these as they
themselves received when they heard them. A
certain number are stirred by high-sounding phrases,
and adapt themselves to the emotions of the
speaker with lively change of face and mind—just
like the emasculated Phrygian priests [c] who are
wont to be roused by the sound of the flute and go
mad to order. But the true hearer is ravished and
stirred by the beauty of the subject matter, not by

borum inanium sonitus. Si quid acriter contra
mortem dictum est, si quid contra fortunam contumaciter, iuvat protinus quae audias, facere. Ad-
ficiuntur illis et sunt quales iubentur, si illa animo
forma permaneat, si non impetum insignem protinus
populus, honesti dissuasor, excipiat; pauci illam,
quam conceperant mentem, domum perferre po-
8 tuerunt. Facile est auditorem concitare ad cupidinem
recti; omnibus enim natura fundamenta dedit
semenque virtutum. Omnes ad omnia ista nati
sumus; cum inritator accessit, tunc illa anima bona
veluti soluta excitatur. Non vides, quemadmodum
theatra consonent, quotiens aliqua dicta sunt, quae
publice adgnoscimus et consensu vera esse testamur?

9   Desunt inopiae multa, avaritiae omnia.

     In nullum avarus bonus est, in se pessimus.

Ad hos versus ille sordidissimus plaudit et vitiis suis
fieri convicium gaudet; quanto magis hoc iudicas
evenire, cum a philosopho ista dicuntur, cum salutari-
bus praeceptis versus inseruntur, efficacius eadem illa
10 demissuri in animum imperitorum? "Nam," ut
dicebat Cleanthes, "quemadmodum spiritus noster
clariorem sonum reddit, cum illum tuba per longi
canalis angustias tractum patentiore novissime exitu
effudit, sic sensus nostros clariores carminis arta
necessitas efficit." Eadem neglegentius audiuntur

---

a Syri Sententiae, Frag. 236 Ribbeck.
b Ib., Frag. 234 R.   *c* Frag. 487 von Arnim.
234

the jingle of empty words. When a bold word has been uttered in defiance of death, or a saucy fling in defiance of Fortune, we take delight in acting straightway upon that which we have heard. Men are impressed by such words, and become what they are bidden to be, should but the impression abide in the mind, and should the populace, who discourage honourable things, not immediately lie in wait to rob them of this noble impulse ; only a few can carry home the mental attitude with which they were inspired. It is easy to rouse a listener so that he will crave righteousness ; for Nature has laid the foundations and planted the seeds of virtue in us all. And we are all born to these general privileges ; hence, when the stimulus is added, the good spirit is stirred as if it were freed from bonds. Have you not noticed how the theatre re-echoes whenever any words are spoken whose truth we appreciate generally and confirm unanimously ?

> The poor lack much : the greedy man lacks all.[a]
> A greedy man does good to none ; he does
> Most evil to himself.[b]

At such verses as these, your meanest miser claps applause and rejoices to hear his own sins reviled. How much more do you think this holds true, when such things are uttered by a philosopher, when he introduces verses among his wholesome precepts, that he may thus make those verses sink more effectively into the mind of the neophyte ! Cleanthes used to say :[c] " As our breath produces a louder sound when it passes through the long and narrow opening of the trumpet and escapes by a hole which widens at the end, even so the fettering rules of poetry clarify our meaning." The very same words are more carelessly received and make less impression

235

minusque percutiunt, quamdiu soluta oratione dicuntur; ubi accessere numeri et egregium sensum adstrinxere certi pedes, eadem illa sententia velut
11 lacerto excussiore [1] torquetur. De contemptu pecuniae multa dicuntur et longissimis orationibus hoc praecipitur, ut homines in animo, non in patrimonio putent esse divitias, eum esse locupletem, qui paupertati suae aptatus est et parvo se divitem fecit; magis tamen feriuntur animi, cum carmina eiusmodi dicta sunt:

> Is minimo eget mortalis, qui minimum cupit.
> Quod vult habet, qui velle quod satis est potest.

12 Cum haec atque eiusmodi audimus, ad confessionem veritatis adducimur.

Illi enim, quibus nihil satis est, admirantur, adclamant, odium pecuniae indicunt. Hunc illorum adfectum cum [2] videris, urge, hoc preme, hoc onera [3] relictis ambiguitatibus et syllogismis et cavillationibus et ceteris acuminis inriti ludicris. Dic in avaritiam, dic in luxuriam; cum profecisse te videris et animos audientium adfeceris, insta vehementius; veri simile non est, quantum proficiat talis oratio remedio intenta et tota in bonum audientium versa. Facillime enim tenera conciliantur ingenia ad honesti rectique

---

[1] *excussiore* Gertz; *excussare* BA.
[2] *cum* later MSS.; om. BA.
[3] *onera* later MSS.; *honora* BA.

---

[a] Pall. Incert. Fab. 65 and 66 Ribbeck.

upon us, when they are spoken in prose ; but when metre is added and when regular prosody has compressed a noble idea, then the selfsame thought comes, as it were, hurtling with a fuller fling. We talk much about despising money, and we give advice on this subject in the lengthiest of speeches, that mankind may believe true riches to exist in the mind and not in one's bank account, and that the man who adapts himself to his slender means and makes himself wealthy on a little sum, is the truly rich man ; but our minds are struck more effectively when a verse like this is repeated :

> He needs but little who desires but little.

or,

> He hath his wish, whose wish includeth naught
> Save that which is enough.[a]

When we hear such words as these, we are led towards a confession of the truth.

Even men in whose opinion nothing is enough, wonder and applaud when they hear such words, and swear eternal hatred against money. When you see them thus disposed, strike home, keep at them, and charge them with this duty, dropping all double meanings, syllogisms, hair-splitting, and the other side-shows of ineffective smartness. Preach against greed, preach against high living ; and when you notice that you have made progress and impressed the minds of your hearers, lay on still harder. You cannot imagine how much progress can be brought about by an address of that nature, when you are bent on curing your hearers and are absolutely devoted to their best interests. For when the mind is young, it may most easily be won over to desire what is honourable and upright ; truth, if she

237

THE EPISTLES OF SENECA

amorem et adhuc docibilibus leviterque corruptis
inicit manum veritas, si advocatum idoneum nancta
est.

13   Ego certe cum Attalum audirem in vitia, in errores,
in mala vitae perorantem, saepe miseritus sum generis
humani et illum sublimem altioremque humano
fastigio credidi. Ipse regem se esse dicebat, sed plus
quam regnare mihi videbatur, cui liceret censuram
14 agere regnantium. Cum vero commendare paupertatem coeperat et ostendere, quam quidquid usum
excederet, pondus esset supervacuum et grave ferenti,
saepe exire e schola pauperi libuit. Cum coeperat
voluptates nostras traducere, laudare castum corpus,
sobriam mensam, puram mentem non tantum ab
inlicitis voluptatibus, sed etiam supervacuis, libebat
15 circumscribere gulam ac ventrem. Inde mihi quaedam permansere, Lucili. Magno enim in omnia
inceptu veneram. Deinde ad civitatis vitam reductus
ex bene coeptis pauca servavi. Inde ostreis boletis-
que in omnem vitam renuntiatum est; nec enim
cibi, sed oblectamenta sunt ad edendum saturos
cogentia, quod gratissimum est edacibus et se ultra
quam capiunt farcientibus, facile descensura, facile
16 reditura. Inde in omnem vitam unguento abstinemus,
quoniam optimus odor in corpore est nullus. Inde
vino carens stomachus. Inde in omnem vitam bal-
neum fugimus, decoquere corpus atque exinanire

---

^a A characteristic Stoic paradox.
^b An almost proverbial saying; *cf.* the *recte olet ubi nil olet* of Plautus (*Most.* 273), Cicero, and Martial.
238

can obtain a suitable pleader, will lay strong hands upon those who can still be taught, those who have been but superficially spoiled.

At any rate, when I used to hear Attalus denouncing sin, error, and the evils of life, I often felt sorry for mankind and regarded Attalus as a noble and majestic being,—above our mortal heights. He called himself a king,[a] but I thought him more than a king, because he was entitled to pass judgment on kings. And in truth, when he began to uphold poverty, and to show what a useless and dangerous burden was everything that passed the measure of our need, I often desired to leave his lecture-room a poor man. Whenever he castigated our pleasure-seeking lives, and extolled personal purity, moderation in diet, and a mind free from unnecessary, not to speak of unlawful, pleasures, the desire came upon me to limit my food and drink. And that is why some of these habits have stayed with me, Lucilius. For I had planned my whole life with great resolves. And later, when I returned to the duties of a citizen, I did indeed keep a few of these good resolutions. That is why I have forsaken oysters and mushrooms for ever: since they are not really food, but are relishes to bully the sated stomach into further eating, as is the fancy of gourmands and those who stuff themselves beyond their powers of digestion: down with it quickly, and up with it quickly! That is why I have also throughout my life avoided perfumes; because the best scent for the person is no scent at all.[b] That is why my stomach is unacquainted with wine. That is why throughout my life I have shunned the bath, and have believed that to emaciate the body and sweat it into thinness is

239

sudoribus inutile simul delicatumque credidimus.
Cetera proiecta redierunt, ita tamen, ut quorum
abstinentiam interrupi, modum servem et quidem
abstinentiae proximiorem, nescio an difficiliorem,
quoniam quaedam absciduntur facilius animo quam
temperantur.

17 Quoniam coepi tibi exponere, quanto maiore impetu ad philosophiam iuvenis accesserim quam senex
pergam, non pudebit fateri, quem mihi amorem
Pythagoras iniecerit. Sotion dicebat, quare ille
animalibus abstinuisset, quare postea Sextius. Dissimilis utrique causa erat, sed utrique magnifica.

18 Hic homini satis alimentorum citra sanguinem esse
credebat et crudelitatis consuetudinem fieri, ubi in
voluptatem esset adducta laceratio. Adiciebat con-
trahendam materiam esse luxuriae ; colligebat bonae
valitudini contraria esse alimenta varia et nostris

19 aliena corporibus. At Pythagoras omnium inter
omnia cognationem esse dicebat et animorum com-
mercium in alias atque alias formas transeuntium.
Nulla, si illi credas, anima interit, ne cessat quidem
nisi tempore exiguo, dum in aliud corpus trans-
funditur. Videbimus, per quas temporum vices et
quando pererratis pluribus domiciliis in hominem
revertatur ; interim sceleris hominibus ac parricidii
metum fecit, cum possent in parentis animam inscii
incurrere et ferro morsuve violare, si in quo cognatus

ᵃ Pythagorean philosopher of the Augustan age, and one
of Seneca's early teachers.

at once unprofitable and effeminate. Other resolutions have been broken, but after all in such a way that, in cases where I ceased to practice abstinence, I have observed a limit which is indeed next door to abstinence ; perhaps it is even a little more difficult, because it is easier for the will to cut off certain things utterly than to use them with restraint.

Inasmuch as I have begun to explain to you how much greater was my impulse to approach philosophy in my youth than to continue it in my old age, I shall not be ashamed to tell you what ardent zeal Pythagoras inspired in me. Sotion [a] used to tell me why Pythagoras abstained from animal food, and why, in later times, Sextius did also. In each case, the reason was different, but it was in each case a noble reason. Sextius believed that man had enough sustenance without resorting to blood, and that a habit of cruelty is formed whenever butchery is practised for pleasure. Moreover, he thought we should curtail the sources of our luxury ; he argued that a varied diet was contrary to the laws of health, and was unsuited to our constitutions. Pythagoras, on the other hand, held that all beings were interrelated, and that there was a system of exchange between souls which transmigrated from one bodily shape into another. If one may believe him, no soul perishes or ceases from its functions at all, except for a tiny interval—when it is being poured from one body into another. We may question at what time and after what seasons of change the soul returns to man, when it has wandered through many a dwelling-place ; but meantime, he made men fearful of guilt and parricide, since they might be, without knowing it, attacking the soul of a parent and injuring it with knife or with teeth—if, as is possible, the related

241

20 aliqui spiritus hospitaretur. Haec cum exposuisset
Sotion et inplesset argumentis suis, "Non credis,"
inquit, "animas in alia corpora atque alia discribi et
migrationem esse quod dicimus mortem? Non credis
in his pecudibus ferisve aut aqua mersis illum quondam
hominis animum morari? Non credis nihil perire in
hoc mundo, sed mutare regionem? Nec tantum
caelestia per certos circuitus verti, sed animalia quoque per vices ire et animos per orbem agi? Magni
21 ista crediderunt viri. Itaque iudicium quidem tuum
sustine, ceterum omnia tibi in integro serva. Si vera
sunt ista, abstinuisse animalibus innocentia est; si
falsa, frugalitas est. Quod istic credulitatis[1] tuae
damnum est? Alimenta tibi leonum et vulturum
eripio."

22   His ego instinctus abstinere animalibus coepi, et
anno peracto non tantum facilis erat mihi consuetudo,
sed dulcis. Agitatiorem mihi animum esse credebam, nec tibi hodie adfirmaverim, an fuerit. Quaeris,
quomodo desierim? In primum Tiberii Caesaris
principatum iuventae tempus inciderat. Alienigena
tum sacra movebantur, sed inter argumenta super-
stitionis ponebatur quorundam animalium absti-
nentia. Patre itaque meo rogante, qui non calum-
niam timebat, sed philosophiam oderat, ad pristinam

---

[1] *credulitatis* cod. Rhedig.; *crudelitatis* BA.

[a] A.D. 19.   *Cf.* Tacitus, *Ann.* ii. 85 *actum de sacris
Aegyptiis Iudaicisque pellendis.*

spirit be dwelling temporarily in this bit of flesh! When Sotion had set forth this doctrine, supplementing it with his own proofs, he would say: " You do not believe that souls are assigned, first to one body and then to another, and that our so-called death is merely a change of abode? You do not believe that in cattle, or in wild beasts, or in creatures of the deep, the soul of him who was once a man may linger? You do not believe that nothing on this earth is annihilated, but only changes its haunts? And that animals also have cycles of progress and, so to speak, an orbit for their souls, no less than the heavenly bodies, which revolve in fixed circuits? Great men have put faith in this idea; therefore, while holding to your own view, keep the whole question in abeyance in your mind. If the theory is true, it is a mark of purity to refrain from eating flesh; if it be false, it is economy. And what harm does it do to you to give such credence? I am merely depriving you of food which sustains lions and vultures."

I was imbued with this teaching, and began to abstain from animal food; at the end of a year the habit was as pleasant as it was easy. I was beginning to feel that my mind was more active; though I would not to-day positively state whether it really was or not. Do you ask how I came to abandon the practice? It was this way: The days of my youth coincided with the early part of the reign of Tiberius Caesar. Some foreign rites were at that time *a* being inaugurated, and abstinence from certain kinds of animal food was set down as a proof of interest in the strange cult. So at the request of my father, who did not fear prosecution, but who detested philosophy, I returned to my previous habits; and

243

consuetudinem redii. Nec difficulter mihi, ut in-
ciperem melius cenare, persuasit.

23   Laudare solebat Attalus culcitam, quae resisteret
corpori ; tali utor etiam senex, in qua vestigium
apparere non possit. Haec rettuli ut probarem tibi,
quam vehementes haberent tirunculi impetus primos
ad optima quaeque, si quis [1] exhortaretur illos, si
quis incenderet.[2] Sed aliquid praecipientium vitio
peccatur, qui nos docent disputare, non vivere, aliquid
discentium, qui propositum adferunt ad praeceptores
suos non animum excolendi, sed ingenium. Itaque
quae philosophia fuit, facta philologia est.

24   Multum autem ad rem pertinet, quo proposito ad
quamquam rem accedas. Qui grammaticus futurus
Vergilium scrutatur, non hoc animo legit illud
egregium :

fugit inreparabile tempus :

vigilandum est ; nisi properamus, relinquemur ; agit
nos agiturque velox dies ; inscii rapimur ; omnia in
futurum disponimus et inter praecipitia lenti sumus ;
sed ut observet, quotiens Vergilius de celeritate [3]
temporum dicit, hoc uti verbo illum " fugit."

Optima quaeque dies miseris mortalibus aevi
Prima fugit ; subeunt morbi tristisque senectus
Et labor, et durae rapit inclementia mortis.

25 Ille, qui ad philosophiam spectat, haec eadem quo
debet, adducit : numquam Vergilius, inquit, dies dicit

<hr>

       [1] *quis* later MSS. ; *quisque* BA.
      [2] *incenderet* Hense : *inpenderet* BA[1].
      [3] *celeritate* later MSS. ; *claritate* BA.

<hr>

   [a] In this passage Seneca differs (as also in *Ep.* lxxxviii. § 3)
from the earlier Roman idea of *grammaticus* as *poetarum
interpres* : he is thinking of one who deals with verbal
expressions and the meaning of words. *Cf.* Sandys, *Hist.
Class. Schol.* i. 8 ff.
   [b] *Georg.* iii. 284.   [c] *Georg.* iii. 66 ff.

it was no very hard matter to induce me to dine more comfortably.

Attalus used to recommend a pillow which did not give in to the body ; and now, old as I am, I use one so hard that it leaves no trace after pressure. I have mentioned all this in order to show you how zealous neophytes are with regard to their first impulses towards the highest ideals, provided that some one does his part in exhorting them and in kindling their ardour. There are indeed mistakes made, through the fault of our advisers, who teach us how to debate and not how to live ; there are also mistakes made by the pupils, who come to their teachers to develop, not their souls, but their wits. Thus the study of wisdom has become the study of words.

Now it makes a great deal of difference what you have in mind when you approach a given subject. If a man is to be a scholar,[a] and is examining the works of Vergil, he does not interpret the noble passage :

Time flies away, and cannot be restored [b]

in the following sense : " We must wake up ; unless we hasten, we shall be left behind. Time rolls swiftly ahead, and rolls us with it. We are hurried along ignorant of our destiny ; we arrange all our plans for the future, and on the edge of a precipice are at our ease." Instead of this, he brings to our attention how often Vergil, in speaking of the rapidity of time, uses the word " flies " (*fugit*).

The choicest days of hapless human life
Fly first ; disease and bitter eld succeed,
And toil, till harsh death rudely snatches all.[c]

He who considers these lines in the spirit of a philosopher comments on the words in their proper sense : " Vergil never says, ' Time goes,' but ' Time

ire, sed fugere, quod currendi genus concitatissimum
est, et optimos quosque primos rapi[1]; quid ergo
cessamus nos ipsi concitare, ut velocitatem rapidissi-
mae rei possimus aequare ? Meliora praetervolant,
26 deteriora succedunt. Quemadmodum ex amphora
primum, quod est sincerissimum, effluit, gravissimum
quodque turbidumque subsidit, sic in aetate nostra
quod est optimum, in primo est. Id exhauriri aliis[2]
potius patimur, ut nobis faecem reservemus ? In-
haereat istud animo et tamquam missum oraculo
placeat :

> Optima quaeque dies miseris mortalibus aevi
> Prima fugit.

27 Quare optima ? Quia quod restat, incertum est.
Quare optima ? Quia iuvenes possumus discere,
possumus facilem animum et adhuc tractabilem ad
meliora convertere ; quia hoc tempus idoneum est
laboribus, idoneum agitandis per studia ingeniis et[3]
exercendis per opera corporibus ; quod superest,
segnius et languidius est et propius a fine.

Itaque toto hoc agamus animo et omissis, ad quae
devertimur, in rem unam laboremus, ne hanc temporis pernicissimi celeritatem, quam retinere non
possumus, relicti demum intellegamus. Primus quisque tamquam optimus dies placeat et redigatur in
28 nostrum. Quod fugit, occupandum est. Haec non
cogitat ille, qui grammatici[4] oculis carmen istud

---

[1] *rapi* later MSS. ; *rapit* BA.
[2] *aliis* Haase ; *in aliis* BA.
[3] *et* later MSS. ; *est et* BA.
[4] *grammatici* edd. ; *grammati* BA.

flies,' because the latter is the quickest kind of movement, and in every case our best days are the first to be snatched away ; why, then, do we hesitate to bestir ourselves so that we may be able to keep pace with this swiftest of all swift things ? " The good flies past and the bad takes its place. Just as the purest wine flows from the top of the jar and the thickest dregs settle at the bottom ; so in our human life, that which is best comes first. Shall we allow other men to quaff the best, and keep the dregs for ourselves ? Let this phrase cleave to your soul ; you should be satisfied thereby as if it were uttered by an oracle :

> Each choicest day of hapless human life
> Flies first.

Why " choicest day " ? Because what's to come is unsure. Why " choicest day " ? Because in our youth we are able to learn ; we can bend to nobler purposes minds that are ready and still pliable ; because this is the time for work, the time for keeping our minds busied in study and in exercising our bodies with useful effort ; for that which remains is more sluggish and lacking in spirit—nearer the end.

Let us therefore strive with all courage, omitting attractions by the way ; let us struggle with a single purpose, lest, when we are left behind, we comprehend too late the speed of quick-flying time, whose course we cannot stay. Let every day, as soon as it comes, be welcome as being the choicest, and let it be made our own possession. We must catch that which flees. Now he who scans with a scholar's eye

legit, ideo optimum quemque primum esse diem,
quia subeunt morbi, quia senectus premit et adhuc
adulescentiam cogitantibus supra caput est ; sed ait
Vergilium semper una ponere morbos et senectutem,
non mehercules immerito.   Senectus enim insanabilis
29 morbus est.   Praeterea, inquit, hoc senectuti co-
gnomen inposuit, tristem illam vocat :

> subeunt morbi tristisque senectus.

Alio loco dicit :

> Pallentesque habitant morbi tristisque senectus.

Non est quod mireris ex eadem materia suis
quemque studiis apta colligere ; in eodem prato bos
30 herbam quaerit, canis leporem, ciconia lacertam.
Cum Ciceronis librum de Re Publica prendit[1] hinc
philologus aliquis, hinc grammaticus, hinc philosophiae
deditus, alius alio curam suam mittit.   Philosophus
admiratur contra iustitiam dici tam multa potuisse.
Cum ad hanc eandem lectionem philologus accessit,
hoc subnotat : Duos Romanos reges esse, quorum
alter patrem non habet, alter matrem.   Nam de
Servi matre dubitatur ; Anci pater nullus, Numae
31 nepotis,[2] dicitur.   Praeterea notat eum, quem nos
dictatorem dicimus et in historiis ita nominari
legimus, apud antiquos magistrum populi vocatum.
Hodieque id extat in auguralibus libris, et testimonium est, quod qui ab illo nominatur, magister
equitum est.   Aeque notat Romulum perisse solis de-

---

[1] de re p. prendit Erasmus ; deprendit BA.
[2] Numae nepotis Buecheler ; Numae (nume) nepotes BA.

[a] Aen. vi. 275.
[b] Cicero, De re publica, ii. 18 Numae Pompili nepos ex
filia rex a populo est Ancus Marcius constitutus . . . si-
quidem istius regis matrem habemus, ignoramus patrem.

248

the lines I have just quoted, does not reflect that our first days are the best because disease is approaching and old age weighs upon us and hangs over our heads while we are still thinking about our youth. He thinks rather of Vergil's usual collocation of *disease and eld*; and indeed rightly. For old age is a disease which we cannot cure. "Besides," he says to himself, "think of the epithet that accompanies *eld*; Vergil calls it *bitter*,"—

Disease and bitter eld succeed.

And elsewhere Vergil says:

There dwelleth pale disease and bitter eld.[a]

There is no reason why you should marvel that each man can collect from the same source suitable matter for his own studies; for in the same meadow the cow grazes, the dog hunts the hare, and the stork the lizard. When Cicero's book *On the State* is opened by a philologist, a scholar, or a follower of philosophy, each man pursues his investigation in his own way. The philosopher wonders that so much could have been said therein against justice. The philologist takes up the same book and comments on the text as follows: There were two Roman kings — one without a father and one without a mother. For we cannot settle who was Servius's mother, and Ancus, the grandson of Numa, has no father on record.[b] The philologist also notes that the officer whom we call dictator, and about whom we read in our histories under that title, was named in old times the *magister populi*; such is the name existing to-day in the augural records, proved by the fact that he whom the dictator chose as second in command was called *magister equitum*. He will remark, too, that Romulus

fectione; provocationem ad populum etiam a[1] regibus
fuisse; id ita in pontificalibus libris esse et alii quiqui [2]
32 putant et Fenestella. Eosdem libros cum grammaticus explicuit, primum verba expressa,[3] reapse [4]
dici a Cicerone, id est re ipsa, in commentarium
refert, nec minus sepse,[5] id est se ipse. Deinde
transit ad ea, quae consuetudo saeculi mutavit,
tamquam ait Cicero : " quoniam sumus ab ipsa calce
eius interpellatione revocati." Hanc quam nunc in
circo cretam vocamus, calcem antiqui dicebant.
Deinde Ennianos [6] colligit versus et in primis illos de
33 Africano scriptos :

cui nemo civis neque hostis
Quibit [7] pro factis reddere opis pretium.

Ex eo se ait intellegere, opem [8] aput antiquos non
tantum auxilium significasse, sed operam. Ait enim
Ennius [9] neminem potuisse Scipioni [10] neque civem
neque hostem reddere operae pretium. Felicem
34 deinde se putat, quod invenerit, unde visum sit
Vergilio dicere :

quem super ingens
porta tonat caeli.

Ennium [11] hoc ait Homero subripuisse,[12] Ennio Vergi-

[1] *etiam a* later MSS. ; *etiam* BA.
[2] *id . . . quiqui* Windhaus ; *id ita inveniri in p. l. et*
aliqui B (*aliqui* A).
[3] *expressa* later MSS. ; *expresse* BA.
[4] *reapse* Schweighaeuser ; *ab se* BA.
[5] *sepse* Muretus ; *sese* BA.
[6] *Ennianos* Pincianus ; *inanes* BA.
[7] *quibit* Pincianus ; *quivult* BA.
[8] *opem* add. Korsch.
[9] *ait enim Ennius* Vahlen and Haase ; *ait operaenim*
ineius BA.
[10] *Scipioni* Pincianus ; *Scipionem* BA.
[11] *Ennium* Pincianus ; *Ennius* BA.
[12] *subripuisse* cod. Rom. ; *se subripuisse* BA.

met his end during an eclipse ; that there was an appeal to the people even from the kings (this is so stated in the pontiffs' register and is the opinion of others, including Fenestella [a]). When the scholar unrolls this same volume, he puts down in his notebook the forms of words, noting that *reapse*, equivalent to *re ipsa*, is used by Cicero, and *sepse* [b] just as frequently, which means *se ipse*. Then he turns his attention to changes in current usage. Cicero, for example, says : " Inasmuch as we are summoned back from the very *calx* by his interruption." Now the line in the circus which we call the *creta*, [c] was called the *calx* by men of old time. Again, he puts together some verses by Ennius, especially those which referred to Africanus :

> A man to whom nor friend nor foe could give
> Due meed for all his efforts and his deeds. [d]

From this passage the scholar declares that he infers the word *opem* to have meant formerly not merely *assistance*, but *efforts*. For Ennius must mean that neither friend nor foe could pay Scipio a reward worthy of his efforts. Next, he congratulates himself on finding the source of Vergil's words :

> Over whose head the mighty gate of Heaven
> Thunders, [e]

remarking that Ennius stole the idea from Homer,

---

[a] *Fl.* in the Augustan Age. *Provocatio* is defined by Greenidge (*Rom. Pub. Life*, p. 64) as " a challenge by an accused to a magistrate to appear before another tribunal."
[b] A suffix, probably related to the intensive *-pte*.
[c] Literally, the chalk-marked, or lime-marked, goal-line.
[d] Vahlen's *Ennius*, p. 215.
[e] *Georg.* iii. 260 f.

lium. Esse enim apud Ciceronem in his ipsis de R<
Publica hoc epigramma Enni

> Si fas endo plagas caelestum ascendere cuiquam est,
> Mi soli caeli maxima porta patet.

35 Sed ne et ipse, dum aliud ago, in philologum au⟨
grammaticum delabar, illud admoneo, auditionem
philosophorum lectionemque ad propositum beatae
vitae trahendam, non ut verba prisca aut ficta
captemus et translationes inprobas figurasque dicendi, sed ut profutura praecepta et magnificas voces
et animosas, quae mox in rem transferantur. Sic
ista ediscamus, ut quae fuerint verba, sint opera.

36 Nullos autem peius mereri de omnibus mortalibus
iudico quam qui philosophiam velut aliquod artificium
venale didicerunt, qui aliter vivunt quam vivendum
esse praecipiunt. Exempla enim se ipsos inutilis
disciplinae circumferunt nulli non vitio, quod in-

37 sequuntur, obnoxii. Non magis mihi potest quisquam
talis prodesse praeceptor quam gubernator in tempestate nauseabundus. Tenendum rapiente fluctu
gubernaculum, luctandum cum ipso mari, eripienda
sunt vento vela ; quid me potest adiuvare rector
navigii attonitus et vomitans ? Quanto maiore putas
vitam tempestate iactari quam ullam ratem ? Non est
loquendum, sed gubernandum.

38 Omnia quae dicunt, quae turba audiente iactant,
aliena sunt ; dixit illa Platon, dixit Zenon, dixit
Chrysippus et Posidonius et ingens agmen nostrorum[1]
tot ac talium. Quomodo probare possint sua esse,

---

[1] *nostrorum* Buecheler ; *non* BA.

[a] Vahlen's *Ennius*, p. 216.

and Vergil from Ennius. For there is a couplet by
Ennius, preserved in this same book of Cicero's, *On
the State* : [a]

> If it be right for a mortal to scale the regions of Heaven,
> Then the huge gate of the sky opens in glory to *me*.

But that I, too, while engaged upon another task,
may not slip into the department of the philologist
or the scholar, my advice is this—that all study of
philosophy and all reading should be applied to the
idea of living the happy life, that we should not
hunt out archaic or far-fetched words and eccentric
metaphors and figures of speech, but that we should
seek precepts which will help us, utterances of
courage and spirit which may at once be turned
into facts. We should so learn them that words
may become deeds. And I hold that no man has
treated mankind worse than he who has studied
philosophy as if it were some marketable trade, who
lives in a different manner from that which he advises.
For those who are liable to every fault which they
castigate advertise themselves as patterns of useless
training. A teacher like that can help me no more
than a sea-sick pilot can be efficient in a storm. He
must hold the tiller when the waves are tossing him ;
he must wrestle, as it were, with the sea ; he must
furl his sails when the storm rages ; what good is
a frightened and vomiting steersman to *me* ? And
how much greater, think you, is the storm of life
than that which tosses any ship ! One must steer,
not talk.

All the words that these men utter and juggle
before a listening crowd, belong to others. They
have been spoken by Plato, spoken by Zeno, spoken
by Chrysippus or by Posidonius, and by a whole host
of Stoics as numerous as excellent. I shall show you

39 monstrabo : faciant, quae dixerint. Quoniam quae
volueram ad te perferre, iam dixi, nunc desiderio
tuo satis faciam et in [1] alteram epistulam integrum,
quod exegeras, transferam, ne ad rem spinosam et
auribus erectis curiosisque audiendam lassus accedas.
Vale.

CIX.

Seneca Lvcilio svo salvtem

1   An sapiens sapienti prosit scire desideras. Dicimus plenum omni bono esse sapientem et summa
adeptum ; quomodo prodesse aliqui possit summum
habenti bonum, quaeritur.

Prosunt inter se boni ; exercent enim virtutes et
sapientiam in suo statu continent. Desiderat uterque
2 aliquem, cum quo conferat, cum quo quaerat. Peritos luctandi usus exercet ; musicum, qui paria
didicit, movet. Opus est et sapienti agitatione [2]
virtutum : ita quemadmodum ipse se movet, sic
3 movetur ab alio sapiente. Quid sapiens sapienti
proderit ? Impetum illi dabit, occasiones actionum
honestarum commonstrabit. Praeter haec aliquas
cogitationes suas exprimet : docebit, quae invenerit.
Semper enim etiam a sapiente restabit, quod inveniat
et quo animus eius excurrat.

[1] *in* later MSS. ; *inter* BA.
[2] *sapienti agitatione* later MSS.; *sapientia cogitatione*
BA.

how men can prove their words to be their own : it is by doing what they have been talking about. Since therefore I have given you the message I wished to pass on to you, I shall now satisfy your craving and shall reserve for a new letter a complete answer to your summons ; so that you may not approach in a condition of weariness a subject which is thorny and which should be followed with an attentive and painstaking ear. Farewell.

CIX. ON THE FELLOWSHIP OF WISE MEN

You expressed a wish to know whether a wise man can help a wise man. For we say that the wise man is completely endowed with every good, and has attained perfection ; accordingly, the question arises how it is possible for anyone to help a person who possesses the Supreme Good.

Good men are mutually helpful ; for each gives practice to the other's virtues and thus maintains wisdom at its proper level. Each needs someone with whom he may make comparisons and investigations. Skilled wrestlers are kept up to the mark by practice ; a musician is stirred to action by one of equal proficiency. The wise man also needs to have his virtues kept in action ; and as he prompts himself to do things, so is he prompted by another wise man. How can a wise man help another wise man ? He can quicken his impulses, and point out to him opportunities for honourable action. Besides, he can develop some of his own ideas ; he can impart what he has discovered. For even in the case of the wise man something will always remain to discover, something towards which his mind may make new ventures.

255

4 Malus malo nocet facitque peiorem, iram eius[1]
incitando, tristitiae adsentiendo, voluptates laudando,
et tunc maxime laborant mali, ubi plurimum vitia
miscuere, et in unum conlata nequitia est. Ergo ex
contrario bonus bono proderit. "Quomodo?" in-
5 quis. Gaudium illi adferet, fiduciam confirmabit,
ex conspectu mutuae tranquillitatis crescet utriusque
laetitia. Praeterea quarumdam illi rerum scientiam
tradet; non enim omnia sapiens scit. Etiam si
sciret, breviores vias rerum aliqui excogitare posset
et has indicare, per quas facilius totum opus circum-
6 fertur. Proderit sapienti sapiens, non scilicet tantum
suis viribus, sed ipsius, quem adiuvat. Potest quidem
ille etiam relictus sibi explicare partes suas; nihilominus adiuvat etiam currentem hortator.

"Non prodest sapienti sapiens, sed sibi ipse.
Hoc scias: detrahe illi vim propriam, et ille nihil
7 aget." Illo[2] modo dicas licet non esse in melle
dulcedinem: nam ipse ille, qui esse debeat, ita
aptatus lingua palatoque est ad eiusmodi gustum, ut
illa talis sapor capiat, aut[3] offendetur. Sunt enim
quidam, quibus morbi vitio mel amarum videatur.
Oportet utrumque valere,[4] ut et ille prodesse possit
8 et hic profuturo idonea materia sit. "Si[5] in summum," inquit, "perducto[6] calorem calefieri super-

---

[1] *eius* later MSS.; *metus* BA.
[2] *illo* Windhaus; *uno* BA.
[3] *aut* add. Klammer.
[4] *valere* Haase; *colore* or *calere* MSS.
[5] *si* add. Gertz.
[6] *perducto* Pincianus; *perductum* BA.

---

[a] *i.e.*, in possession of a perfect, an encyclopaedic, wisdom.

Evil men harm evil men ; each debases the other by rousing his wrath, by approving his churlishness, and praising his pleasures ; bad men are at their worst stage when their faults are most thoroughly intermingled, and their wickedness has been, so to speak, pooled in partnership. Conversely, therefore, a good man will help another good man. " How ? " you ask. Because he will bring joy to the other, he will strengthen his faith, and from the contemplation of their mutual tranquillity the delight of both will be increased. Moreover, they will communicate to each other a knowledge of certain facts ; for the wise man is not all-knowing.[a] And even if he were all-knowing, someone might be able to devise and point out short cuts, by which the whole matter is more readily disseminated. The wise will help the wise, not, mark you, because of his own strength merely, but because of the strength of the man whom he assists. The latter, it is true, can by himself develop his own parts ; nevertheless, even one who is running well is helped by one who cheers him on.

" But the wise man does not really help the wise ; he helps himself. Let me tell you this : strip the one of his special powers, and the other will accomplish nothing." You might as well, on that basis, say that sweetness is not in the honey : for it is the person himself who is to eat it, that is so equipped, as to tongue and palate, for tasting this kind of food that the special flavour appeals to him, and anything else displeases. For there are certain men so affected by disease that they regard honey as bitter. Both men should be in good health, that the one may be helpful and the other a proper subject for help. Again they say : " When the highest degree of heat has been attained, it is superfluous to apply more

vacuum est, et in summum perducto bonum supervacuum est si[1] qui prosit. Numquid instructus
omnibus rebus agricola ab alio instrui quaerit?
Numquid armatus miles, quantum in aciem exituro
satis est tuti,[2] amplius arma desiderat? Ergo nec
sapiens; satis enim vitae instructus, satis armatus
9 est." Ad haec respondeo: et qui in summo est
calore, opus est calore adiecto,[3] ut summum teneat.
"Sed ipse se," inquit, "calor continet." Primum
multum interest inter ista, quae comparas; calor
enim unus est, prodesse varium est. Deinde calor
non adiuvatur adiectione caloris, ut caleat; sapiens
non potest in habitu mentis suae stare, nisi amicos
aliquos similes sui admisit, cum quibus virtutes suas
10 communicet. Adice nunc, quod omnibus inter se
virtutibus amicitia est. Itaque prodest, qui virtutes
alicuius paris sui[4] amat amandasque invicem praestat. Similia delectant, utique ubi honesta sunt et
11 probare ac probari sciunt. Etiamnunc sapientis
animum perite movere nemo alius potest quam
sapiens, sicut hominem movere rationaliter non potest
nisi homo. Quomodo ergo ad rationem movendam
ratione opus est, sic ut moveatur ratio perfecta, opus
est ratione perfecta.
12   Prodesse dicuntur et qui media nobis largiuntur,
pecuniam, gratiam, incolumitatem, alia in usus vitae

---

[1] *si* add. Buecheler.
[2] *tuti* Buecheler; *uti* BA.
[3] *in . . . adiecto* Madvig; *in summa motus est calore
adiecto* BA.
[4] *paris sui* Buecheler; *partes sui* BA; *pares suis* later
MSS.

---

[a] In other words, Wisdom, Justice, Courage, and Self-
Restraint, together with the other qualities of simplicity,
kindness, etc., being "avatars" of Virtue herself, are interrelated.

heat; and when the Supreme Good has been attained, it is superfluous to have a helper. Does a completely stocked farmer ask for further supplies from his neighbours ? Does a soldier who is sufficiently armed for going well-equipped into action need any more weapons ? Very well, neither does the wise man ; for he is sufficiently equipped and sufficiently armed for life." My answer to this is, that when one is heated to the highest degree, one must have continued heat to maintain the highest temperature. And if it be objected that heat is self-maintaining, I say that there are great distinctions among the things that you are comparing ; for heat is a single thing, but helpfulness is of many kinds. Again, heat is not helped by the addition of further heat, in order to be hot ; but the wise man cannot maintain his mental standard without intercourse with friends of his own kind—with whom he may share his goodness. Moreover, there is a sort of mutual friendship among all the virtues.[a] Thus, he who loves the virtues of certain among his peers, and in turn exhibits his own to be loved, is helpful. Like things give pleasure, especially when they are honourable and when men know that there is mutual approval. And besides, none but a wise man can prompt another wise man's soul in an intelligent way, just as man can be prompted in a rational way by man only. As, therefore, reason is necessary for the prompting of reason, so, in order to prompt perfect reason, there is need of perfect reason.

Some say that we are helped even by those [b] who bestow on us the so-called " indifferent " benefits, such as money, influence, security, and all the other

[b] *e.g.*, certain of the Peripatetic school.

cara aut necessaria. In his dicetur etiam stultus
prodesse sapienti. Prodesse autem est animum
secundum naturam movere virtute sua ut eius, qui
movebitur. Hoc non sine ipsius quoque, qui proderit,
bono fiet. Necesse enim alienam virtutem exercendo
13 exerceat et suam. Sed ut removeas ista, quae aut
summa bona sunt aut summorum efficientia, nihilominus prodesse inter se sapientes possunt. Invenire
enim sapientem sapienti per se res expetenda[1] est,
quia natura bonum omne carum est bono et sic
quisque conciliatur bono quemadmodum sibi.

14 Necesse est ex hac quaestione argumenti causa in
alteram transeam. Quaeritur enim, an deliberaturus
sit sapiens, an in consilium aliquem advocaturus.
Quod facere illi necessarium est, cum ad haec civilia
et domestica venitur et, ut ita dicam, mortalia. In
his sic illi opus est alieno consilio quomodo medico,
quomodo gubernatori, quomodo advocato et litis
ordinatori. Proderit ergo sapiens aliquando sapienti,
suadebit enim. Sed in illis quoque magnis ac divinis,
ut diximus, communiter honesta tractando et animos
15 cogitationesque miscendo utilis erit. Praeterea
secundum naturam est et amicos complecti et
amicorum auctu[2] ut suo proprioque laetari. Nam
nisi hoc fecerimus, ne virtus quidem nobis per-
manebit, quae exercendo sensu valet. Virtus autem

---

[1] *expetenda* later MSS. ; *excedenda* BA[1].
[2] *auctu* Haase ; *actu* BA.

valued or essential aids to living. If we argue in this way, the veriest fool will be said to help a wise man. Helping, however, really means prompting the soul in accordance with Nature, both by the prompter's excellence and by the excellence of him who is thus prompted. And this cannot take place without advantage to the helper also. For in training the excellence of another, a man must necessarily train his own. But, to omit from discussion supreme goods or the things which produce them, wise men can none the less be mutually helpful. For the mere discovery of a sage by a sage is in itself a desirable event; since everything good is naturally dear to the good man, and for this reason one feels congenial with a good man as one feels congenial with oneself.

It is necessary for me to pass from this topic to another, in order to prove my point. For the question is asked, whether the wise man will weigh his opinions, or whether he will apply to others for advice. Now he is compelled to do this when he approaches state and home duties—everything, so to speak, that is mortal. He needs outside advice on such matters, as does the physician, the pilot, the attorney, or the pleader of cases. Hence, the wise will sometimes help the wise; for they will persuade each other. But in these matters of great import also,—aye, of divine import, as I have termed them,—the wise man can also be useful by discussing honourable things in common, and by contributing his thoughts and ideas. Moreover, it is in accordance with Nature to show affection for our friends, and to rejoice in their advancement as if it were absolutely our own. For if we have not done this, even virtue, which grows strong only through exercising our perceptions, will not abide with us. Now virtue advises us to

suadet praesentia bene conlocare, in futurum consulere, deliberare et intendere animum; facilius intendet explicabitque qui aliquem sibi adsumpserit.

Quaeret itaque aut perfectum virum aut proficientem vicinumque perfecto. Proderit autem ille perfectus, si consilium communi prudentia iuverit.

16 Aiunt homines plus in alieno negotio videre. Vitio[1] hoc illis evenit, quos amor sui excaecat quibusque dispectum utilitatis timor in periculis excutit; incipiet sapere securior et extra metum positus. Sed nihilominus quaedam sunt, quae etiam sapientes in alio quam in se diligentius vident. Praeterea illud dulcissimum et honestissimum " idem velle atque idem nolle " sapiens sapienti praestabit; egregium opus pari iugo ducet.

17 Persolvi id[2] quod exegeras, quamquam in ordine rerum erat, quas moralis philosophiae voluminibus complectimur. Cogita, quod soleo frequenter tibi dicere, in istis nos nihil aliud quam acumen exercere. Totiens enim illo revertor: quid ista me res iuvat? Fortiorem fac iam, iustiorem, temperantiorem. Nondum exerceri vacat; adhuc medico mihi opus

18 est. Quid me poscis scientiam inutilem? Magna promisisti; exige, vide. Dicebas intrepidum fore,

---

[1] *vitio* later MSS.; *initio* BA.
[2] *persolvi id* Windhaus; *persolvit* BA.

---

[a] Sallust, *Cat.* xx. 4 *idem velle atque idem nolle, ea demum firma amicitia est.* *Cf.* the Greek " ἴσῳ ζυγῷ," " yoked equally together." [b] *Cf. Ep.* cviii. 1 and note.

arrange the present well, to take thought regarding the future, to deliberate and apply our minds; and one who takes a friend into council with him, can more easily apply his mind and think out his problem.

Therefore he will seek either the perfect wise man or one who has progressed to a point bordering on perfection. The perfect wise man, moreover, will help us if he aids our counsels with ordinary good sense. They say that men see farther in the affairs of others than in their own. A defect of character causes this in those who are blinded by self-love, and whose fear in the hour of peril takes away their clear view of that which is useful; it is when a man is more at ease and freed from fear that he will begin to be wise. Nevertheless, there are certain matters where even wise men see the facts more clearly in the case of others than in their own. Moreover, the wise man will, in company with his fellow sage, confirm the truth of that most sweet and honourable proverb—" always desiring and always refusing the same things ": it will be a noble result when they draw the load " with equal yoke." [a]

I have thus answered your demand, although it came under the head of subjects which I include in my volumes *On Moral Philosophy*.[b] Reflect, as I am often wont to tell you, that there is nothing in such topics for us except mental gymnastics. For I return again and again to the thought: " What good does this do me? Make me more brave now, more just, more restrained! I have not yet the opportunity to make use of my training; for I still need the physician. Why do you ask of me a useless knowledge? You have promised great things; test me, watch me! You assured me that I should be

etiam si circa me gladii micarent, etiam si mucro
tangeret iugulum ; dicebas securum fore, etiam si
circa me flagrarent incendia, etiam si subitus turbo
toto navem meam mari raperet. Hanc mihi praesta
curam, ut[1] voluptatem, ut gloriam contemnam.
Postea docebis inplicta solvere, ambigua distinguere,
obscura perspicere ; nunc doce quod necesse est.
Vale.

CX.

Seneca Lvcilio svo salvtem

1 Ex Nomentano meo te saluto et iubeo habere
mentem bonam, hoc est propitios deos omnis, quos
habet placatos et faventes, quisquis sibi se propitiavit.
Sepone in praesentia, quae quibusdam placent, unicuique nostrum paedagogum dari deum, non quidem
ordinarium, sed hunc inferioris notae ex eorum
numero, quos Ovidius ait "de plebe deos." Ita
tamen hoc seponas volo, ut memineris maiores nostros,
qui crediderunt, Stoicos fuisse ; singulis enim et
2 Genium et Iunonem dederunt. Postea videbimus,
an tantum dis vacet, ut privatorum negotia pro-
curent ; interim illud scito, sive adsignati sumus,
sive neglecti et fortunae dati, nulli te posse inprecari

---

[1] *praesta curam ut* Hense ; *praestaturum* BA.

---

[a] *Cf. Ep.* civ. 1.
[b] *Metam.* i. 595,—a Roman interpretation, along the lines
of the *Di Indigetes.*
[c] Every man had his Genius, and every woman her Juno.
In the case of the Stoics, God dwelt in every soul.

unterrified though swords were flashing round me, though the point of the blade were grazing my throat; you assured me that I should be at ease though fires were blazing round me, or though a sudden whirlwind should snatch up my ship and carry it over all the sea. Now make good for me such a course of treatment that I may despise pleasure and glory. Thereafter you shall teach me to work out complicated problems, to settle doubtful points, to see through that which is not clear; teach me now what it is necessary for me to know!" Farewell.

CX. ON TRUE AND FALSE RICHES

From my villa at Nomentum,[a] I send you greeting and bid you keep a sound spirit within you—in other words, gain the blessing of all the gods, for he is assured of their grace and favour who has become a blessing to himself. Lay aside for the present the belief of certain persons—that a god is assigned to each one of us as a sort of attendant—not a god of regular rank, but one of a lower grade —one of those whom Ovid calls "plebeian gods."[b] Yet, while laying aside this belief, I would have you remember that our ancestors, who followed such a creed, have become Stoics; for they have assigned a Genius or a Juno to every individual.[c] Later on we shall investigate whether the gods have enough time on their hands to care for the concerns of private individuals; in the meantime, you must know that whether we are allotted to special guardians, or whether we are neglected and consigned to Fortune, you can curse a man with no heavier

265

quicquam gravius, quam si inprecatus fueris, ut se
habeat iratum.

Sed non est quare cuiquam, quem poena putaveris
dignum, optes, ut infestos deos habeat; habet,
inquam, etiam si videtur eorum favore produci.

3 Adhibe diligentiam tuam et intuere, quid sint res
nostrae, non quid vocentur; et scies plura mala
contingere nobis quam accidere. Quotiens enim
felicitatis et [1] causa et initium fuit, quod calamitas
vocabatur? Quotiens magna gratulatione excepta
res gradum sibi struxit in praeceps et aliquem iam
eminentem adlevavit etiamnunc, tamquam adhuc ibi
4 staret, unde tuto cadunt? Sed ipsum illud cadere
non habet in se mali quidquam, si exitum spectes,
ultra quem natura neminem deiecit. Prope est
rerum omnium terminus, prope est, inquam, et illud,
unde felix eicitur, et illud, unde infelix emittitur;
nos utraque extendimus et longa spe ac metu
facimus.

Sed si sapis, omnia humana condicione metire;
simul et quod gaudes et quod times, contrahe. Est
autem tanti nihil diu gaudere, ne quid diu timeas.

5 Sed quare istuc malum adstringo? Non est quod
quicquam timendum putes. Vana sunt ista, quae
nos movent, quae attonitos habent. Nemo nostrum
quid veri esset, excussit, sed metum alter alteri
tradidit; nemo ausus est ad id, quo perturbabatur,

----

[1] *et* Schweighaeuser; *est* BA.

[a] *i.e.*, death, in Stoic language.

curse than to pray that he may be at enmity with himself.

There is no reason, however, why you should ask the gods to be hostile to anyone whom you regard as deserving of punishment ; they *are* hostile to such a person, I maintain, even though he seems to be advanced by their favour. Apply careful investigation, considering how our affairs actually stand, and not what men say of them ; you will then understand that evils are more likely to help us than to harm us. For how often has so-called affliction been the source and the beginning of happiness ! How often have privileges which we welcomed with deep thanksgiving built steps for themselves to the top of a precipice, still uplifting men who were already distinguished—just as if they had previously stood in a position whence they could fall in safety ! But this very fall has in it nothing evil, if you consider the end,[a] after which nature lays no man lower. The universal limit is near ; yes, there is near us the point where the prosperous man is upset, and the point where the unfortunate is set free. It is we ourselves that extend both these limits, lengthening them by our hopes and by our fears.

If, however, you are wise, measure all things according to the state of man ; restrict at the same time both your joys and your fears. Moreover, it is worth while not to rejoice at anything for long, so that you may not fear anything for long. But why do I confine the scope of this evil ? There is no reason why you should suppose that anything is to be feared. All these things which stir us and keep us a-flutter, are empty things. None of us has sifted out the truth ; we have passed fear on to one another ; none has dared to approach the object which

267

accedere et naturam ac bonum timoris sui nosse.
Itaque res falsa et inanis habet adhuc fidem, quia
6 non coarguitur.   Tanti putemus oculos intendere ;
iam apparebit, quam brevia, quam incerta, quam tuta
timeantur.   Talis est animorum nostrorum confusio,
qualis Lucretio visa est :

> Nam veluti pueri trepidant atque omnia caecis
> In tenebris metuunt, ita nos in luce timemus.

Quid ergo ? Non omni puero stultiores sumus qui
7 in luce timemus ?   Sed falsum est, Lucreti, non
timemus in luce ; omnia nobis fecimus tenebras.
Nihil videmus, nec quid noceat nec quid expediat ;
tota vita incursitamus nec ob hoc resistimus aut
circumspectius pedem ponimus.   Vides autem, quam
sit furiosa res in tenebris impetus.   At mehercules
id agimus, ut longius revocandi simus, et cum
ignoremus, quo feramur, velociter tamen illo, quo
intendimus, perseveramus.
8   Sed lucescere, si velimus, potest.   Uno autem
modo potest, si quis hanc humanorum divinorumque
notitiam scientia acceperit, si illa se non perfuderit,
sed infecerit, si eadem, quamvis sciat, retractaverit
et ad se saepe rettulerit, si quaesierit, quae sint bona,
quae mala, quibus hoc falso sit nomen adscriptum,
si quaesierit de honestis et turpibus, de providentia.
9 Nec [1] intra haec humani ingenii sagacitas sistitur ;

---

[1] *nec* later MSS. ; *et* BA.

[a] *De Rerum Nat.* ii. 55 f.
[b] *i.e.*, to the starting-point.

EPISTLE CX.

caused his dread, and to understand the nature of his fear—aye, the good behind it. That is why falsehood and vanity still gain credit—because they are not refuted. Let us account it worth while to look closely at the matter; then it will be clear how fleeting, how unsure, and how harmless are the things which we fear. The disturbance in our spirits is similar to that which Lucretius detected:

> Like boys who cower frightened in the dark,
> So grown-ups in the light of day feel fear.[a]

What, then? Are we not more foolish than any child, we who "in the light of day feel fear"? But you were wrong, Lucretius; we are not afraid in the daylight; we have turned everything into a state of darkness. We see neither what injures nor what profits us; all our lives through we blunder along, neither stopping nor treading more carefully on this account. But you see what madness it is to rush ahead in the dark. Indeed, we are bent on getting ourselves called back[b] from a greater distance; and though we do not know our goal, yet we hasten with wild speed in the direction whither we are straining.

The light, however, may begin to shine, provided we are willing. But such a result can come about only in one way—if we acquire by knowledge this familiarity with things divine and human, if we not only flood ourselves but steep ourselves therein, if a man reviews the same principles even though he understands them and applies them again and again to himself, if he has investigated what is good, what is evil, and what has falsely been so entitled; and, finally, if he has investigated honour and baseness, and Providence. The range of the human intelligence is not

269

prospicere et ultra mundum libet, quo feratur, unde surrexerit, in quem exitum tanta rerum velocitas properet. Ab hac divina contemplatione abductum animum in sordida et humilia pertraximus, ut avaritiae serviret, ut relicto mundo terminisque eius et dominis cuncta versantibus terram rimaretur et quaereret, quid ex illa mali effoderet, non contentus oblatis.

10 Quidquid nobis bono futurum erat, deus et parens noster in proximo posuit; non expectavit inquisitionem nostram et ultro dedit. Nocitura altissime pressit. Nihil nisi de nobis queri possumus; ea, quibus periremus, nolente rerum natura et abscondente protulimus. Addiximus animum voluptati, cui indulgere initium omnium malorum est, tradidimus ambitioni et famae, ceteris aeque vanis et inanibus.

11 Quid ergo nunc te hortor ut facias? Nihil novi—nec enim novis malis remedia quaeruntur—sed hoc primum, ut tecum ipse dispicias, quid sit necessarium, quid supervacuum. Necessaria tibi ubique occurrent; supervacua et semper et [1] toto animo quaerenda sunt.

12 Non est autem quod te nimis laudes, si contempseris aureos lectos et gemmeam supellectilem. Quae est enim virtus supervacua contemnere? Tunc te ad-

---

[1] *et* later MSS.; om. BA[1].

confined within these limits ; it may also explore outside the universe—its destination and its source, and the ruin towards which all nature hastens so rapidly. We have withdrawn the soul from this divine contemplation and dragged it into mean and lowly tasks, so that it might be a slave to greed, so that it might forsake the universe and its confines, and, under the command of masters who try all possible schemes, pry beneath the earth and seek what evil it can dig up therefrom—discontented with that which was freely offered to it.

Now God, who is the Father of us all, has placed ready to our hands those things which he intended for our own good ; he did not wait for any search on our part, and he gave them to us voluntarily. But that which would be injurious, he buried deep in the earth. We can complain of nothing but ourselves ; for we have brought to light the materials for our destruction, against the will of Nature, who hid them from us. We have bound over our souls to pleasure, whose service is the source of all evil ; we have surrendered ourselves to self-seeking and reputation, and to other aims which are equally idle and useless.

What, then, do I now encourage you to do ? Nothing new—we are not trying to find cures for new evils—but this first of all : namely, to see clearly for yourself what is necessary and what is superfluous. What is necessary will meet you everywhere ; what is superfluous has always to be hunted out—and with great endeavour. But there is no reason why you should flatter yourself over-much if you despise gilded couches and jewelled furniture. For what virtue lies in despising useless things ? The time to admire your own conduct is when you

mirare, cum contempseris necessaria. Non magnam rem facis, quod vivere sine regio [1] apparatu potes, quod non desideras milliarios apros nec linguas phoenicopterorum et alia portenta luxuriae iam tota animalia fastidientis et certa membra ex singulis eligentis ; tunc te admirabor, si contempseris etiam sordidum panem, si tibi persuaseris herbam, ubi necesse est, non pecori tantum, sed homini nasci, si scieris cacumina arborum explementum esse ventris, in quem sic pretiosa congerimus tamquam recepta servantem. Sine fastidio inplendus est. Quid enim ad rem pertinet, quid accipiat perditurus quicquid

13 acceperit ? Delectant te disposita, quae terra mari- que capiuntur, alia eo gratiora, si recentia perferuntur ad mensam, alia, si diu pasta et coacta pinguescere fluunt ac vix saginam continent suam. Delectat te nidor [2] horum arte quaesitus. At mehercules ista sollicite scrutata varieque condita cum subierint ven- trem, una atque eadem foeditas occupabit. Vis ciborum voluptatem contemnere ? Exitum specta.

14 Attalum memini cum magna admiratione omnium haec dicere :

"Diu," inquit, "mihi inposuere divitiae. Stupe- bam, ubi aliquid ex illis alio atque alio loco fulserat. Existimabam similia esse quae laterent, his, quae ostenderentur. Sed in quodam apparatu vidi totas opes urbis caelatas et auro et argento et iis, quae

---

[1] *regio* later MSS. ; *recto* BA.
[2] *nidor* codd. Pinc. ; *nitor* BA.

---

[a] *i.e.*, acorns, etc.

have come to despise the necessities. You are doing
no great thing if you can live without royal pomp, if
you feel no craving for boars which weigh a thousand
pounds, or for flamingo tongues, or for the other
absurdities of a luxury that already wearies of game
cooked whole, and chooses different bits from separate
animals; I shall admire you only when you have
learned to scorn even the common sort of bread,
when you have made yourself believe that grass
grows for the needs of men as well as of cattle,
when you have found out that food from the tree-
top *a* can fill the belly—into which we cram things
of value as if it could keep what it has received.
We should satisfy our stomachs without being over-
nice. How does it matter what the stomach receives,
since it must lose whatever it has received? You
enjoy the carefully arranged dainties which are
caught on land and sea ; some are more pleasing if
they are brought fresh to the table, others, if after
long feeding and forced fattening they almost melt
and can hardly retain their own grease. You like
the subtly devised flavour of these dishes. But I
assure you that such carefully chosen and variously
seasoned dishes, once they have entered the belly,
will be overtaken alike by one and the same corrup-
tion. Would you despise the pleasures of eating ?
Then consider its result ! I remember some words
of Attalus, which elicited general applause:

" Riches long deceived me. I used to be dazed
when I caught some gleam of them here and there.
I used to think that their hidden influence matched
their visible show. But once, at a certain elaborate
entertainment, I saw embossed work in silver and
gold equalling the wealth of a whole city, and colours
and tapestry devised to match objects which sur-

pretium auri argentique vicerunt, exquisitos colores
et vestes ultra non tantum nostrum, sed ultra finem
hostium advectas; hinc puerorum perspicuos cultu
atque forma greges, hinc feminarum, et alia, quae
res suas recognoscens summi imperii fortuna pro-
15 tulerat. Quid hoc est, inquam, aliud nisi[1] inritare
cupiditates hominum per se incitatas? Quid sibi
vult ista pecuniae pompa? Ad discendam avaritiam
convenimus? At mehercules minus cupiditatis istinc
effero quam adtuleram. Contempsi divitias, non quia
16 supervacuae, sed quia pusillae sunt. Vidistine, quam
intra paucas horas ille ordo quamvis lentus dis-
positusque transierit? Hoc totam vitam nostram
occupavit, quod totum diem occupare non potuit?

"Accessit illud quoque: tam supervacuae mihi visae
17 sunt habentibus quam fuerunt spectantibus. Hoc
itaque ipse mihi dico, quotiens tale aliquid praestrin-
xerit oculos meos, quotiens occurrit domus splendida,
cohors culta servorum, lectica formonsis inposita
calonibus: Quid miraris? Quid stupes? Pompa
est. Ostenduntur istae res, non possidentur, et dum
18 placent, transeunt. Ad veras potius te converte
divitias. Disce parvo esse contentus et illam vocem
magnus atque animosus exclama : ' habemus aquam,
habemus polentam, Iovi ipsi controversiam de felicitate[2] faciamus.' Faciamus, oro te, etiam si ista
defuerint. Turpe est beatam vitam in auro et

---

[1] *aliud nisi* later MSS.; *aliud* BA.
[2] *felicitate* later MSS.; *facilitate* BA.

passed the value of gold or of silver—brought not only from beyond our own borders, but from beyond the borders of our enemies ; on one side were slave-boys notable for their training and beauty, on the other were throngs of slave-women, and all the other resources that a prosperous and mighty empire could offer after reviewing its possessions. What else is this, I said to myself, than a stirring-up of man's cravings, which are in themselves provocative of lust ? What is the meaning of all this display of money ? Did we gather merely to learn what greed was ? For my own part I left the place with less craving than I had when I entered. I came to despise riches, not because of their uselessness, but because of their pettiness. Have you noticed how, inside a few hours, that programme, however slow-moving and carefully arranged, was over and done ? Has a business filled up this whole life of ours, which could not fill up a whole day ?

" I had another thought also : the riches seemed to me to be as useless to the possessors as they were to the onlookers. Accordingly, I say to myself, whenever a show of that sort dazzles my eyes, whenever I see a splendid palace with a well-groomed corps of attendants and beautiful bearers carrying a litter : Why wonder ? Why gape in astonishment ? It is all show ; such things are displayed, not possessed ; while they please they pass away. Turn thyself rather to the true riches. Learn to be content with little, and cry out with courage and with greatness of soul : ' We have water, we have porridge ; let us compete in happiness with Jupiter himself.' And why not, I pray thee, make this challenge even without porridge and water ? For it is base to make the happy life depend upon silver and gold, and

argento reponere, aeque turpe in aqua et polenta.
19 'Quid ergo faciam, si ista non fuerint?' Quaeris,
quod sit remedium inopiae? Famem fames finit;
alioquin quid interest, magna sint an exigua, quae
servire te cogant? Quid refert, quantulum sit, quod
20 tibi possit negare fortuna? Haec ipsa aqua et
polenta in alienum arbitrium cadit. Liber est autem
non in quem parum licet fortunae, sed in quem nihil.
Ita¹ est : nihil desideres oportet, si vis Iovem
provocare nihil desiderantem."

Haec nobis Attalus dixit² ; quae si voles frequenter cogitare, id ages, ut sis felix, non ut videaris,
et ut tibi videaris, non aliis. VALE.

CXI.

SENECA LVCILIO SVO SALVTEM

1 Quid vocentur Latine sophismata, quaesisti a me.
Multi temptaverunt illis nomen inponere, nullum
haesit. Videlicet, quia res ipsa non recipiebatur a
nobis nec in usu erat, nomini quoque repugnatum
est. Aptissimum tamen videtur mihi, quo Cicero
2 usus est : cavillationes vocat. Quibus quisquis se
tradidit, quaestiunculas quidem vafras nectit, ceterum
ad vitam nihil proficit, neque fortior fit neque
temperantior neque elatior.

¹ *ita* later MSS. ; *ista* BA.
² After *dixit* later MSS. have *natura omnibus dixit* ; om.
BA.

just as base to make it depend upon water and porridge. 'But,' some will say, 'what could I do without such things?' Do you ask what is the cure for want? It is to make hunger satisfy hunger; for, all else being equal, what difference is there in the smallness or the largeness of the things that force you to be a slave? What matter how little it is that Fortune can refuse to you? Your very porridge and water can fall under another's jurisdiction; and besides, freedom comes, not to him over whom Fortune has slight power, but to him over whom she has no power at all. This is what I mean: you must crave nothing, if you would vie with Jupiter; for Jupiter craves nothing."

This is what Attalus told us. If you are willing to think often of these things, you will strive not to *seem* happy, but to *be* happy, and, in addition, to seem happy to yourself rather than to others. Farewell.

CXI. ON THE VANITY OF MENTAL GYMNASTICS

You have asked me to give you a Latin word for the Greek *sophismata*. Many have tried to define the term, but no name has stuck. This is natural, inasmuch as the thing itself has not been admitted to general use by us; the name, too, has met with opposition. But the word which Cicero used seems to me most suitable: he calls them *cavillationes*. If a man has surrendered himself to them, he weaves many a tricky subtlety, but makes no progress toward real living; he does not thereby become braver, or more restrained, or loftier of spirit.

At ille, qui philosophiam in remedium suum
exercuit, ingens fit animo, plenus fiduciae, inex-
3 superabilis et maior adeunti.   Quod in magnis evenit
montibus, quorum proceritas minus apparet longe
intuentibus ; cum accesseris, tunc manifestum fit,
quo in arduo summa sint ; talis est, mi Lucili, verus
et rebus, non artificiis philosophus.   In edito stat
admirabilis, celsus, magnitudinis verae.   Non exsurgit
in plantas nec summis ambulat digitis eorum more,
qui mendacio staturam adiuvant longioresque quam
sunt, videri volunt ; contentus est magnitudine sua.
4 Quidni contentus sit eo usque crevisse, quo manus
fortuna non porrigit ?   Ergo et supra humana est
et par sibi in omni statu rerum, sive secundo cursu
vita procedit, sive fluctuatur et it[1] per adversa ac
difficilia ; hanc constantiam cavillationes istae, de
quibus paulo ante loquebar, praestare non possunt.
Ludit istis animus, non proficit, et philosophiam a
fastigio suo deducit in planum.
5   Nec te prohibuerim aliquando ista agere, sed tunc,
cum voles nihil agere.   Hoc tamen habent in se
pessimum : dulcedinem quandam sui faciunt et
animum specie subtilitatis inductum tenent ac
morantur, cum tanta rerum moles vocet, cum vix
tota vita sufficiat, ut hoc unum discas, vitam contemnere.   " Quid ? Regere," inquis.   Secundum opus

[1] *it* added by Rossbach.

He, however, who has practised philosophy to effect his own cure, becomes high-souled, full of confidence, invincible, and greater as you draw near him. This phenomenon is seen in the case of high mountains, which appear less lofty when beheld from afar, but which prove clearly how high the peaks are when you come near them ; such, my dear Lucilius, is our true philosopher, true by his acts and not by his tricks. He stands in a high place, worthy of admiration, lofty, and really great. He does not stretch himself or walk on tiptoe like those who seek to improve their height by deceit, wishing to seem taller than they really are ; he is content with his own greatness. And why should he not be content with having grown to such a height that Fortune cannot reach her hands to it ? He is therefore above earthly things, equal to himself under all conditions, —whether the current of life runs free, or whether he is tossed and travels on troubled and desperate seas ; but this steadfastness cannot be gained through such hair-splittings as I have just mentioned. The mind plays with them, but profits not a whit ; the mind in such cases is simply dragging philosophy down from her heights to the level ground.

I would not forbid you to practise such exercises occasionally ; but let it be at a time when you wish to do nothing. The worst feature, however, that these indulgences present is that they acquire a sort of self-made charm, occupying and holding the soul by a show of subtlety ; although such weighty matters claim our attention, and a whole life seems scarcely sufficient to learn the single principle of despising life. "What? Did you not mean 'control' instead of 'despise'"? No; "controlling"

est ; nam nemo illam bene rexit nisi qui contemp-
serat. VALE.

CXII.

SENECA LVCILIO SVO SALVTEM

1 Cupio mehercules amicum tuum formari, ut desideras, et institui ; sed valde durus capitur, immo,
quod est molestius, valde mollis capitur et consuetudine mala ac diutina fractus.

Volo tibi ex nostro artificio exemplum referre.[a]
2 Non quaelibet insitionem vitis patitur ; si vetus et
exesa est, si infirma gracilisque, aut non recipiet
surculum aut non alet nec adplicabit sibi nec in
qualitatem eius naturamque transibit. Itaque solemus supra terram praecidere, ut si non respondit,
temptari possit secunda fortuna, et iterum repetita
infra terram inseratur.

3 Hic, de quo scribis et mandas, non habet vires ;
indulsit vitiis. Simul et emarcuit et induruit. Non
potest recipere rationem, non potest nutrire. " At
cupit ipse." Noli credere. Non dico illum mentiri
tibi ; putat se cupere. Stomachum illi fecit luxuria ;
4 cito cum illa redibit in gratiam. " Sed dicit se
offendi vita sua." Non negaverim. Quis enim non
offenditur ? Homines vitia sua et amant simul et
oderunt. Tunc itaque de illo feremus sententiam,

---

[a] Seneca was an extensive and prosperous vine-grower.
Compare *Ep.* civ. 6 f. for his description of his hobby at
the country-place near Nomentum. There are many figures
which deal with the vine scattered through the Letters.

is the second task; for no one has controlled his life aright unless he has first learned to despise it. Farewell.

CXII. ON REFORMING HARDENED SINNERS

I am indeed anxious that your friend be moulded and trained, according to your desire. But he has been taken in a very hardened state, or rather (and this is a more difficult problem), in a very soft state, broken down by bad and inveterate habits.

I should like to give you an illustration from my own handicraft.[a] It is not every vine that admits the grafting process; if it be old and decayed, or if it be weak and slender, the vine either will not receive the cutting, or will not nourish it and make it a part of itself, nor will it accommodate itself to the qualities and nature of the grafted part. Hence we usually cut off the vine above ground, so that if we do not get results at first, we may try a second venture, and on a second trial graft it below the ground.

Now this person, concerning whom you have sent me your message in writing, has no strength; for he has pampered his vices. He has at one and the same time become flabby and hardened. He cannot receive reason, nor can he nourish it. "But," you say, "he desires reason of his own free will." Don't believe him. Of course I do not mean that he is lying to you; for he really thinks that he desires it. Luxury has merely upset his stomach; he will soon become reconciled to it again. "But he says that he is put out with his former way of living." Very likely. Who is not? Men love and hate their vices at the same time. It will be the proper season to pass judgment on him when he has given us a

cum fidem nobis fecerit invisam iam sibi esse luxuriam; nunc illis male convenit. VALE.

CXIII.

SENECA LVCILIO SVO SALVTEM

1 Desideras tibi scribi a me, quid sentiam de hac quaestione iactata[1] apud nostros: an iustitia, fortitudo, prudentia ceteraeque virtutes animalia sint. Hac subtilitate effecimus, Lucili carissime, ut exercere ingenium inter inrita videremur et disputationibus nihil profuturis otium terere. Faciam quod desideras, et quid nostris videatur, exponam. Sed me in alia esse sententia profiteor: puto quaedam esse, quae deceant phaecasiatum palliatumque. Quae sint ergo quae antiquos moverint, vel quae sint quae antiqui moverint, dicam.

2 Animum constat animal esse, cum ipse efficiat, ut simus animalia, cum ab illo animalia nomen hoc traxerint. Virtus autem nihil aliud est quam animus quodammodo se habens; ergo animal est. Deinde virtus agit aliquid; agi autem nihil sine impetu potest. Si impetum habet, qui nulli est nisi animali, animal est. "Si animal est," inquit, "virtus, habet ipsa virtutem." Quidni habeat se ipsam? Quo-
3 modo sapiens omnia per virtutem gerit, sic virtus per

---

[1] *iactata* Hense; *iacta* BA.

---

[a] The fulfilment of the promise made in *Ep.* cvi. 3 (see note *ad loc.*).

[b] The allusion. s sarcastic. The *phaecasium* was a white shoe worn by Greek priests and Athenian gymnasiarchs,—sometimes aped by Romans.

[c] *i.e., animal* from *animus, anima* (" breath of life ").

guarantee that he really hates luxury; as it is now, luxury and he are merely not on speaking terms. Farewell.

CXIII. ON THE VITALITY OF THE SOUL AND ITS ATTRIBUTES

You wish me to write to you my opinion concerning this question, which has been mooted by our school—whether justice, courage, foresight, and the other virtues, are living things.[a] By such niceties as this, my beloved Lucilius, we have made people think that we sharpen our wits on useless objects, and waste our leisure time in discussions that will be unprofitable. I shall, however, do as you ask, and shall set forth the subject as viewed by our school. For myself, I confess to another belief: I hold that there are certain things which befit a wearer of white shoes and a Greek mantle.[b] But what the beliefs are that have stirred the ancients, or those which the ancients have stirred up for discussion, I shall explain to you.

The soul, men are agreed, is a living thing, because of itself it can make us living things, and because " living things "[c] have derived their name therefrom. But virtue is nothing else than a soul in a certain condition; therefore it is a living thing. Again, virtue is active, and no action can take place without impulse. And if a thing has impulse, it must be a living thing; for none except a living thing possesses impulse. A reply to this is: " If virtue is a living thing, then virtue itself possesses virtue." Of course it possesses its own self! Just as the wise man does everything by reason of virtue, so virtue accomplishes everything by reason

283

se. "Ergo," inquit, "et omnes artes animalia sunt
et omnia, quae cogitamus quaeque mente con-
plectimur. Sequitur, ut multa millia animalium
habitent in his angustiis pectoris, et singuli multa
simus animalia aut multa habeamus animalia."

Quaeris, quid adversus istud respondeatur? Una-
quaeque ex istis res animal erit; multa animalia non
erunt. Quare? Dicam, si mihi accommodaveris
4 subtilitatem et intentionem tuam. Singula animalia
singulas habere debent substantias; ista omnia unum
animum habent; itaque singula esse possunt, multa
esse non possunt. Ego et animal sum et homo, non
tamen duos esse nos dices. Quare? Quia separati
debent esse. Ita dico: alter ab altero debet esse
diductus, ut duo sint. Quicquid in uno multiplex
est, sub unam naturam cadit; itaque unum est.
5 Et animus meus animal est et ego animal sum, duo
tamen non sumus. Quare? Quia animus mei pars
est. Tunc aliquid per se numerabitur, cum per se
stabit. Ubi vero alterius membrum erit, non poterit
videri aliud. Quare? Dicam: quia quod aliud est,
suum oportet esse et proprium et totum et intra se
6 absolutum. Ego in alia esse me sententia professus
sum. Non enim tantum virtutes animalia erunt, si
hoc recipitur, sed opposita quoque illis vitia et

ᵃ i.e., from those who hold that the man, the soul, and
the functions of the soul, can be classed as separate entities;
or even from those who believe that it is worth while to
discuss the matter at all. See § 1 of this Letter.

of itself. "In that case," say they, "all the arts also are living things, and all our thoughts and all that the mind comprehends. It therefore follows that many thousands of living things dwell in man's tiny heart, and that each individual among us consists of, or at least contains, many living beings."

Are you gravelled for an answer to this remark? Each of these will be a living thing; but they will not be many separate living things. And why? I shall explain, if you will apply your subtlety and your concentration to my words. Each living thing must have a separate substance; but since all the things mentioned above have a single soul, consequently they can be separate living things but without plurality. I myself am a living thing, and a man; but you cannot say that there are two of me for that reason. And why? Because, if that were so, they would have to be two separate existences. This is what I mean: one would have to be sundered from the other so as to produce two. But whenever you have that which is manifold in one whole, it falls into the category of a single nature, and is therefore single.

My soul is a living thing, and so am I; but we are not two separate persons. And why? Because the soul is part of myself. It will only be reckoned as a definite thing in itself, when it shall exist by itself. But as long as it shall be part of another, it cannot be regarded as different. And why? I will tell you: it is because that which is different, must be personal and peculiar to itself, a whole, and complete within itself. I myself have gone on record as being of a different opinion;[a] for if one adopts this belief, not only the virtues will be living things, but so will their contrary vices, and the emotions, like

285

adfectus, tamquam ira, timor, luctus, suspicio. Ultra
res ista procedet; omnes sententiae, omnes cogitationes animalia erunt. Quod nullo modo recipiendum
est. Non enim quicquid ab homine fit, homo est.
7 "Iustitia quid est?" inquit. Animus quodammodo
se habens. "Itaque si animus animal est, et iustitia."
Minime.[1] Haec enim habitus animi est et quaedam
vis; idem animus in varias figuras convertitur et non
totiens animal aliud [2] est, quotiens aliud facit. Nec
8 illud, quod fit ab animo, animal est. Si [3] iustitia
animal est, si [3] fortitudo, si ceterae [4] virtutes, utrum
desinunt esse animalia, subinde autem [5] rursus incipiunt, an semper sunt?

Desinere virtutes non possunt. Ergo multa animalia, immo innumerabilia, in hoc animo versantur.
9 "Non sunt," inquit, "multa, quia ex uno religata
sunt et partes unius ac membra sunt." Talem ergo
faciem animi nobis proponimus, qualis est hydrae
multa habentis capita, quorum unumquodque per se
pugnat, per se nocet. Atqui nullum ex illis capitibus
animal est, sed animalis caput, ceterum ipsa unum
animal est. Nemo in Chimaera leonem animal esse
dixit aut draconem; hae partes erant eius; partes
autem non sunt animalia. Quid est, quo colligas
10 iustitiam animal esse? "Agit," inquit, "aliquid et
prodest. Quod autem agit et prodest, impetum

---

[1] *iustitia minime* later MSS.; *iustitiam in me* BA.
[2] *aliud* later MSS.; *alius* BA.
[3] *si* before *iustitia* and *fortitudo* added by Muretus.
[4] *si ceterae* Muretus; *sic ceterae* (*cetetre*) BA.
[5] *autem* edd.; *aut* or *ut* MSS.

---

[a] Homer, *Il.* vi. 181 πρόσθε λέων, ὄπιθεν δὲ δράκων, μέσση

wrath, fear, grief, and suspicion. Nay, the argument will carry us still further—all opinions and all thoughts will be living things. This is by no means admissible ; since anything that man does is not necessarily the man himself. " What is Justice ? " people say. Justice is a soul that maintains itself in a certain attitude. " Then if the soul is a living being, so is Justice." By no means. For Justice is really a state, a kind of power, of the soul ; and this same soul is transformed into various likenesses and does not become a different kind of living thing as often as it acts differently. Nor is the result of soul-action a living thing. If Justice, Bravery, and the other virtues have actual life, do they cease to be living things and then begin life over again, or are they *always* living things ?

But the virtues cannot cease to be. Therefore, there are many, nay countless, living things, sojourning in this one soul. " No," is the answer, " not many, because they are all attached to the one, being parts and members of a single whole." We are then portraying for ourselves an image of the soul like that of a many-headed hydra—each separate head fighting and destroying independently. And yet there is no separate living thing to each head ; it is the head of a living thing, and the hydra itself is one single living thing. No one ever believed that the Chimaera contained a living lion or a living serpent ;[a] these were merely parts of the whole Chimaera ; and parts are not living things. Then how can you infer that Justice is a living thing ? " Justice," people reply, " is active and helpful ; that which acts and is helpful, possesses impulse ;

δὲ χίμαιρα. This is a frequent illustration of the " whole and the parts " among ancient philosophers.

THE EPISTLES OF SENECA

habet ; quod autem impetum habet,[1] animal est."
Verum est, si suum impetum habet ; suum autem non
11 habet,[2] sed animi.   Omne animal, donec moriatur, id
est, quod coepit ; homo, donec moriatur, homo est,
equus equus, canis canis.[3]   Transire in aliud non
potest. Iustitia, id est animus quodammodo se habens,
animal est.   Credamus ; deinde animal est fortitudo,
id est animus quodammodo se habens.   Quis animus ?
Ille, qui modo iustitia erat? Tenetur in priore animali,
in aliud animal transire ei non licet ; in eo illi, in quo
12 primum esse coepit, perseverandum est.   Praeterea
unus animus duorum esse animalium non potest,
multo minus plurium.   Si iustitia, fortitudo, temperantia ceteraeque virtutes animalia sunt, quo modo
unum animum habebunt ?   Singulos habeant oportet,
13 aut non sunt animalia.   Non potest unum corpus
plurium animalium esse.   Hoc et ipsi fatentur.
Iustitiae quod est corpus ?   " Animus."   Quid ?   Fortitudinis quod est corpus ?   " Idem animus."   Atqui
unum corpus esse duorum animalium non potest.
14 "Sed idem animus," inquit, "iustitiae habitum induit[4]
et fortitudinis et temperantiae."   Hoc fieri posset, si
quo tempore iustitia esset, fortitudo non esset, quo
tempore fortitudo esset, temperantia non esset ;
nunc vero omnes virtutes simul sunt.   Ita quomodo
singulae erunt animalia, cum unus animus sit, qui
plus quam unum animal non potest facere ?

---

[1] *quod . . . habet* added by later MSS. ; om. BA.
[2] *suum . . . habet* later MSS. ; om. BA.
[3] *equus equus, canis canis* edd. ; *equus canis* BA.
[4] *induit* later MSS. ; *inbuit* BA.

---

[a] *i.e.*, the form in which it is contained.
[b] The soul is " body," " world-stuff " (not " matter " in
the modern sense).   It is therefore, according to the Stoics,
a living entity, a unit ; and Virtue is a διάθεσις ψυχῆς,—
a " permanent disposition of the soul."

and that which possesses impulse is a living thing."
True, if the impulse is its own ; (but in the case of
justice it is not its own ;) the impulse comes from
the soul. Every living thing exists as it began, until
death ; a man, until he dies, is a man, a horse is a
horse, a dog a dog. They cannot change into anything else. Now let us grant that Justice—which
is defined as " a soul in a certain attitude," is a living
thing. Let us suppose this to be so. Then Bravery
also is alive, being " a soul in a certain attitude."
But which soul ? That which was but now defined
as Justice ? The soul is kept within the first-named
being, and cannot cross over into another ; it must
last out its existence in the medium where it had its
origin. Besides, there cannot be one soul to two
living things, much less to many living things. And
if Justice, Bravery, Restraint, and all the other
virtues, are living things, how will they have one
soul ? They must possess separate souls, or else
they are not living things. Several living things
cannot have one body ; this is admitted by our very
opponents. Now what is the " body " *a* of justice ?
" The soul," they admit. And of bravery ? " The
soul also." And yet there cannot be one body of
two living things. " The same soul, however," they
answer, " assumes the guise of Justice, or Bravery,
or Restraint." This would be possible if Bravery
were absent when Justice was present, and if Restraint were absent when Bravery was present; as
the case stands now, all the virtues exist at the same
time. Hence, how can the separate virtues be living
things, if you grant that there is one single soul,*b* which
cannot create more than one single living thing ?

289

15   Denique nullum animal pars est alterius animalis.
Iustitia autem pars est animi ; non est ergo animal.
Videor mihi in re confessa perdere operam ; magis
enim indignandum de isto quam disputandum est.
Nullum animal alteri par est. Circumspice omnium
corpora : nulli non et color proprius est et figura sua
16 et magnitudo. Inter cetera, propter quae mirabile
divini artificis ingenium est, hoc quoque existimo, et
quod in tanta copia rerum numquam in idem incidit ;
etiam quae similia videntur, cum contuleris, diversa
sunt. Tot fecit genera foliorum : nullum non sua
proprietate signatum. Tot animalia : nullius magnitudo cum altero convenit, utique aliquid interest.
Exegit a se, ut quae alia erant, et dissimilia essent
et inparia ; virtutes omnes, ut dicitis, pares sunt.
Ergo non sunt animalia.

17   Nullum non animal per se agit. Virtus autem per
se nihil agit, sed cum homine. Omnia animalia aut
rationalia sunt, ut homines, ut di, aut inrationalia, ut
ferae, ut pecora.[1] Virtutes utique rationales sunt ;
atqui nec homines sunt nec di ; ergo non sunt
18 animalia. Omne rationale animal nihil agit, nisi
primum specie alicuius rei inritatum est, deinde
impetum cepit, deinde adsensio confirmavit hunc
impetum. Quid sit adsensio, dicam. Oportet me
ambulare : tunc demum ambulo, cum hoc mihi dixi
et adprobavi hanc opinionem meam. Oportet me
sedere : tunc demum sedeo. Haec adsensio in

----

[1] *aut . . . pecora* later MSS. ; om. BA.

----

[a] The usual progression was αἴσθησις (*sensus*), φαντασία
(*species*, " external impression "), συγκατάθεσις (*adsensus*),
and κατάληψις (*comprehensio*). See *Ep.* xcv. 62 note.

EPISTLE CXIII.

Again, no living thing is part of another living thing. But Justice is a part of the soul; therefore Justice is not a living thing. It looks as if I were wasting time over something that is an acknowledged fact; for one ought to decry such a topic rather than debate it. And no two living things are equal. Consider the bodies of all beings: every one has its particular colour, shape, and size. And among the other reasons for marvelling at the genius of the Divine Creator is, I believe, this,—that amid all this abundance there is no repetition; even seemingly similar things are, on comparison, unlike. God has created all the great number of leaves that we behold: each, however, is stamped with its special pattern. All the many animals: none resembles another in size — always some difference! The Creator has set himself the task of making unlike and unequal things that are different; but all the virtues, as your argument states, are equal. Therefore, they are not living things.

Every living thing acts of itself; but virtue does nothing of itself; it must act in conjunction with man. All living things either are gifted with reason, like men and gods, or else are irrational, like beasts and cattle. Virtues, in any case, are rational; and yet they are neither men nor gods; therefore they are not living things. Every living thing possessed of reason is inactive if it is not first stirred by some external impression; then the impulse comes, and finally assent confirms the impulse.[a] Now what *assent* is, I shall explain. Suppose that I ought to take a walk: I *do* walk, but only after uttering the command to myself and approving this opinion of mine. Or suppose that I ought to seat myself; I *do* seat myself, but only after the same process.

291

19 virtute non est. Puta enim prudentiam esse ; quomodo adsentietur " oportet me ambulare " ? Hoc natura non recipit. Prudentia enim ei, cuius est, prospicit, non sibi. Nam nec ambulare potest nec sedere. Ergo adsensionem non habet, rationale animal non est. Virtus si animal est, rationale est.

20 Rationale autem non est ; ergo nec animal. Si virtus animal est, virtus autem bonum, non est omne bonum animal ? Est. Hoc nostri fatentur.

Patrem servare bonum est, et sententiam prudenter in senatu dicere bonum est, et iuste decernere bonum est ; ergo et [1] patrem servare animal est et prudenter sententiam dicere animal est. Eo usque res exegit, ut risum tenere non possis : prudenter tacere bonum est, frugaliter cenare bonum est [2] ; ita et tacere et

21 cenare animal est. Ego mehercules titillare non desinam et ludos mihi ex istis subtilibus ineptiis facere. Iustitia et fortitudo, si animalia sunt, certe terrestria sunt. Omne animal terrestre alget, esurit, sitit ; ergo iustitia alget, fortitudo esurit, clementia sitit.

22 Quid porro ? Non interrogabo illos, quam figuram habeant ista animalia ? Hominis an equi an ferae ? Si rotundam illis qualem deo dederint, quaeram, an et avaritia et luxuria et dementia aeque rotundae sint. Sunt enim et ipsae animalia. Si has quoque

[1] *et* later MSS. ; *ut* BA.
[2] *frugaliter (bene) cenare bonum est* Hense and later MSS.; om. BA.

---

[a] This problem is discussed from another angle in *Ep.* lviii. 16.
[b] *i.e.*, the virtues.

This assent is not a part of virtue. For let us suppose that it is Prudence; how will Prudence assent to the opinion: " I must take a walk " ? Nature does not allow this. For Prudence looks after the interests of its possessor, and not of its own self. Prudence cannot walk or be seated. Accordingly, it does not possess the power of assent, and it is not a living thing possessed of reason. But if virtue is a living thing, it is rational. But it is not rational; therefore it is not a living thing. If virtue is a living thing, and virtue is a Good—is not, then, every Good a living thing? It is. Our school professes it.

Now to save a father's life is a Good; it is also a Good to pronounce one's opinion judiciously in the senate, and it is a Good to hand down just opinions; therefore the act of saving a father's life is a living thing, also the act of pronouncing judicious opinions. We have carried this absurd argument so far that you cannot keep from laughing outright: wise silence is a Good, and so is a frugal dinner; therefore silence and dining are living things.[a] Indeed I shall never cease to tickle my mind and to make sport for myself by means of this nice nonsense. Justice and Bravery, if they are living things, are certainly of the earth. Now every earthly living thing gets cold or hungry or thirsty; therefore, Justice goes a-cold, Bravery is hungry, and Kindness craves a drink!

And what next? Should I not ask our honourable opponents what shape these living beings[b] have? Is it that of man, or horse, or wild beast? If they are given a round shape, like that of a god, I shall ask whether greed and luxury and madness are equally round. For these, too, are " living things." If I find that they give a rounded shape to these also, I

conrotundaverint, etiamnunc interrogabo, an prudens
ambulatio animal sit. Necesse est confiteantur,
deinde dicant ambulationem animal esse et quidem
rotundum.

23 Ne putes autem primum me [1] ex nostris non ex
praescripto loqui, sed meae sententiae esse : inter
Cleanthen et discipulum eius Chrysippum non convenit, quid sit ambulatio. Cleanthes ait spiritum
esse a principali usque in pedes permissum, Chrysippus ipsum principale. Quid [2] est ergo, cur non
ipsius Chrysippi exemplo sibi quisque se vindicet et
ista tot animalia, quot mundus ipse non potest
24 capere, derideat ? "Non sunt," inquit, "virtutes
multa animalia, et tamen animalia sunt. Nam quemadmodum aliquis et poeta est et orator, et tamen
unus, sic virtutes istae animalia sunt, sed multa non
sunt. Idem est animus et animus [3] et iustus et
prudens et fortis, ad singulas virtutes quodammodo
25 se habens." Sublata controversia [4] convenit nobis.
Nam et ego interim fateor animum animal esse,
postea visurus, quam de ista re sententiam feram ;
actiones eius animalia esse nego. Alioqui et omnia
verba erunt animalia et omnes versus ; nam si
prudens sermo bonum est, bonum autem omne
animal est, sermo animal est. [5] Prudens versus bonum
est, bonum autem omne animal est ; versus ergo
animal est. Ita "arma virumque cano," animal est,
quod non possunt rotundum dicere, cum sex pedes

[1] *me* added by Hermes.   [2] *quid* later MSS. ; *quod* BA.
[3] *et animus* MSS. ; del. vulg.
[4] *sublata controversia* Brakman ; *sublata* MSS.
[5] *sermo animal est* vulg. ; om. MSS.

---

[a] Cleanthes, Frag. 525 von Arnim ; Chrysippus, Frag.
836 von Arnim. The former would seem to be more in
accord with general Stoic views.

shall go so far as to ask whether a modest gait is a living thing ; they must admit it, according to their argument, and proceed to say that a gait is a living thing, and a rounded living thing, at that !

Now do not imagine that I am the first one of our school who does not speak from rules but has his own opinion : Cleanthes and his pupil Chrysippus could not agree in defining the act of walking. Cleanthes held that it was spirit transmitted to the feet from the primal essence, while Chrysippus maintained that it was the primal essence in itself.[a] Why, then, following the example of Chrysippus himself, should not every man claim his own freedom, and laugh down all these " living things,"— so numerous that the universe itself cannot contain them ? One might say : " The virtues are not many living things, and yet they are living things. For just as an individual may be both poet and orator in one, even so these virtues are living things, but they are not many. The soul is the same ; it can be at the same time just and prudent and brave, maintaining itself in a certain attitude towards each virtue." The dispute is settled, and we are therefore agreed. For I shall admit, meanwhile, that the soul is a living thing with the proviso that later on I may cast my final vote ; but I deny that the acts of the soul are living beings. Otherwise, all words and all verses would be alive ; for if prudent speech is a Good, and every Good a living thing, then speech is a living thing. A prudent line of poetry is a Good ; everything alive is a Good ; therefore, the line of poetry is a living thing. And so " Arms and the man I sing," is a living thing ; but they cannot call it rounded, because it has six

295

26 habeat. " Textorium," inquis, " totum mehercules
istud, quod cum maxime agitur." Dissilio risu, cum
mihi propono soloecismum animal esse et bar-
barismum et synlogismum et aptas illis facies tamquam pictor adsigno. Haec disputamus attractis
superciliis, fronte rugosa? Non possum hoc loco
dicere illud Caelianum : " O tristes ineptias ! "
Ridiculae sunt. Quin itaque potius aliquid utile
nobis ac salutare tractamus et quaerimus, quomodo
ad virtutes pervenire possimus, quae nos ad illas via
adducat.

27 Doce me non an fortitudo animal sit, sed nullum
animal felix esse sine fortitudine, nisi contra fortuita
convaluit et omnis casus,[1] antequam exciperet,
meditando praedomuit. Quid est fortitudo ? Muni-
mentum humanae imbecillitatis inexpugnabile, quod
qui circumdedit sibi, securus in hac vitae obsidione
28 perdurat ; utitur enim suis viribus, suis telis. Hoc
loco tibi Posidonii nostri referre sententiam volo :
" Non est quod umquam fortunae armis putes esse
te tutum ; tuis pugna. Contra ipsam fortuna non
armat ; itaque contra hostes instructi, contra ipsam
inermes sunt."

29 Alexander Persas quidem et Hyrcanos et Indos et
quicquid gentium usque in oceanum extendit oriens,
vastabat fugabatque, sed ipse modo occiso amico,
modo amisso iacebat in tenebris, alias scelus, alias

---

[1] *casus* later MSS. ; *causas* BA.

[a] *Caecilianum* (the reading of later MSS.) would refer to
Statius Caecilius, the comic writer of the second century B.C.
Caelianum (B and A) would indicate M. Caelius Rufus, the
orator and contemporary of Cicero and Catullus.
[b] 334–330 B.C.
[c] See *Ep.* xciv. 63 f., and notes.
[d] *e.g.*, the execution of Parmenio in Media and the murder
of Cleitus in Samarkand.

feet! "This whole proposition," you say, "which we are at this moment discussing, is a puzzling fabric." I split with laughter whenever I reflect that solecisms and barbarisms and syllogisms are living things, and, like an artist, I give to each a fitting likeness. Is this what we discuss with contracted brow and wrinkled forehead? I cannot say now, after Caelius,[a] "What melancholy trifling!" It is more than this; it is absurd. Why do we not rather discuss something which is useful and wholesome to ourselves, seeking how we may attain the virtues, and finding the path which will take us in that direction?

Teach me, not whether Bravery be a living thing, but prove that no living thing is happy without bravery, that is, unless it has grown strong to oppose hazards and has overcome all the strokes of chance by rehearsing and anticipating their attack. And what is Bravery? It is the impregnable fortress for our mortal weakness; when a man has surrounded himself therewith, he can hold out free from anxiety during life's siege; for he is using his own strength and his own weapons. At this point I would quote you a saying of our philosopher Posidonius: "There are never any occasions when you need think yourself safe because you wield the weapons of Fortune; fight with your own! Fortune does not furnish arms against herself; hence men equipped against their foes are unarmed against Fortune herself."

Alexander, to be sure, harried and put to flight the Persians,[b] the Hyrcanians, the Indians, and all the other races that the Orient spreads even to the Ocean;[c] but he himself, as he slew one friend or lost another, would lie in the darkness lamenting sometimes his crime, and sometimes his loss;[d]

desiderium suum maerens, victor tot regum atque
populorum irae tristitiaeque succumbens. Id enim
egerat, ut omnia potius haberet in potestate quam
30 adfectus. O quam magnis homines tenentur erro-
ribus, qui ius dominandi trans maria cupiunt per-
mittere felicissimosque se iudicant, si multas [1] milite [2]
provincias optinent et novas veteribus adiungunt,
ignari, quod sit illud ingens parque dis regnum.
31 Imperare sibi maximum imperium est. Doceat me,
quam sacra res sit iustitia alienum bonum spectans,
nihil ex se petens nisi usum sui. Nihil sit illi cum
ambitione famaque; sibi placeat.

Hoc ante omnia sibi quisque persuadeat : me
iustum esse gratis oportet. Parum est ; adhuc illud
persuadeat sibi : me in hanc pulcherrimam virtutem
ultro etiam inpendere iuvet. Tota cogitatio a pri-
vatis commodis quam longissime aversa sit. Non est
quod spectes, quod sit iustae rei praemium ; maius
in iusto [3] est. Illud adhuc tibi adfige, quod paulo
32 ante dicebam : nihil ad rem pertinere, quam multi
aequitatem tuam noverint. Qui virtutem suam
publicari vult, non virtuti laborat, sed gloriae. Non
vis esse iustus [4] sine gloria ? At mehercules saepe
iustus esse debebis cum infamia. Et tunc, si sapis,
mala opinio bene parta delectet. VALE.

---

[1] *si multas* later MSS. ; *simulatas* BA.
[2] *milite* Buecheler ; *pro milite* BA.
[3] *in iusto* Schweighaeuser and Madvig ; *iniustae* BA ;
in iustitia later MSS.
[4] *iustus* later MSS. ; *intus* BA.

he, the conqueror of so many kings and nations, was laid low by anger and grief! For he had made it his aim to win control over everything except his emotions. Oh with what great mistakes are men obsessed, who desire to push their limits of empire beyond the seas, who judge themselves most prosperous when they occupy many provinces with their soldiery and join new territory to the old! Little do they know of that kingdom which is on an equality with the heavens in greatness! Self-Command is the greatest command of all. Let her teach me what a hallowed thing is the Justice which ever regards another's good and seeks nothing for itself except its own employment. It should have nothing to do with ambition and reputation; it should satisfy itself.

Let each man convince himself of this before all else—" I must be just without reward." And that is not enough; let him convince himself also of this: " May I take pleasure in devoting myself of my own free will to uphold this noblest of virtues." Let all his thoughts be turned as far as possible from personal interests. You need not look about for the reward of a just deed; a just deed in itself offers a still greater return. Fasten deep in your mind that which I remarked a short space above: that it makes no difference how many persons are acquainted with your uprightness. Those who wish their virtue to be advertised are not striving for virtue but for renown. Are you not willing to be just without being renowned? Nay, indeed you must often be just and be at the same time disgraced. And then, if you are wise, let ill repute, well won, be a delight. Farewell.

CXIV.

1   Quare quibusdam temporibus provenerit corrupti
generis oratio quaeris, et quomodo in quaedam vitia
inclinatio ingeniorum facta sit, ut aliquando inflata
explicatio vigeret, aliquando infracta et in morem
cantici ducta ? Quare alias sensus audaces et fidem
egressi placuerint, alias abruptae sententiae et suspi-
ciosae, in quibus plus intellegendum esset quam
audiendum ? Quare aliqua aetas fuerit, quae trans-
lationis iure uteretur inverecunde ? Hoc quod audire
vulgo soles, quod apud Graecos in proverbium cessit :
2 talis hominibus fuit oratio qualis vita. Quemadmodum autem uniuscuiusque actio dicenti similis
est, sic genus dicendi aliquando imitatur publicos
mores, si¹ disciplina civitatis laboravit et se in delicias
dedit. Argumentum est luxuriae publicae orationis
3 lascivia, si modo non in uno aut in altero fuit, sed
adprobata est et recepta. Non potest alius esse
ingenio, alius animo color. Si ille sanus est, si compositus, gravis, temperans, ingenium quoque siccum
ac sobrium est ; illo vitiato hoc quoque adflatur.
Non vides, si animus elanguit, trahi membra et
pigre moveri pedes ? Si ille effeminatus est, in

---

¹ *si* later MSS. ; *sic* BA.

ᵃ οἷος ὁ βίος, τοιοῦτος καὶ ὁ λόγος. The saying is referred
to Socrates by Cicero (*Tusc.* v. 47).
  ᵇ *i.e.*, that inborn quality which is compounded of character and intelligence.

CXIV. ON STYLE AS A MIRROR OF CHARACTER

You have been asking me why, during certain periods, a degenerate style of speech comes to the fore, and how it is that men's wits have gone downhill into certain vices—in such a way that exposition at one time has taken on a kind of puffed-up strength, and at another has become mincing and modulated like the music of a concert piece. You wonder why sometimes bold ideas—bolder than one could believe —have been held in favour, and why at other times one meets with phrases that are disconnected and full of innuendo, into which one must read more meaning than was intended to meet the ear. Or why there have been epochs which maintained the right to a shameless use of metaphor. For answer, here is a phrase which you are wont to notice in the popular speech—one which the Greeks have made into a proverb : " Man's speech is just like his life." [a] Exactly as each individual man's actions seem to speak, so people's style of speaking often reproduces the general character of the time, if the morale of the public has relaxed and has given itself over to effeminacy. Wantonness in speech is proof of public luxury, if it is popular and fashionable, and not confined to one or two individual instances. A man's ability [b] cannot possibly be of one sort and his soul of another. If his soul be wholesome, well-ordered, serious, and restrained, his ability also is sound and sober. Conversely, when the one degenerates, the other is also contaminated. Do you not see that if a man's soul has become sluggish, his limbs drag and his feet move indolently ? If it is womanish, that

ipso incessu adparere mollitiam ? Si ille acer est
et ferox, concitari gradum ? Si furit aut, quod furori
simile est, irascitur, turbatum esse corporis motum
nec ire, sed ferri ?

Quanto hoc magis accidere ingenio putas, quod
totum animo permixtum est ; ab illo fingitur, illi
4 paret, inde legem petit. Quomodo Maecenas vixerit
notius est, quam ut narrari nunc debeat, quomodo
ambulaverit, quam delicatus fuerit, quam cupierit
videri, quam vitia sua latere noluerit. Quid ergo ?
Non oratio eius aeque soluta est quam ipse discinctus ?
Non tam insignita illius verba sunt quam cultus, quam
comitatus, quam domus, quam uxor ? Magni vir
ingenii fuerat, si illud egisset via rectiore, si non
vitasset intellegi, si non etiam in oratione difflueret.
Videbis itaque eloquentiam ebrii hominis involutam
et errantem et licentiae plenam.[1]
5 Quid turpius " amne silvisque ripa comantibus ? "
Vide ut " alveum lintribus arent versoque vado [2]
remittant hortos." Quid ? Si quis " feminae cinno
crispat et labris columbatur incipitque suspirans, ut
cervice lassa fanantur nemoris tyranni." " Inreme-
diabilis factio rimantur epulis lagonaque temptant

---

[1] After *plenam* BA give *Maecenas de cultu suo* ; an
interpolation (Gruter). See Summers in *C.Q.* ii. 170 ff.,
and O. Hense, p. 548 (ed. of 1914), for a discussion of the
quoted passages.
[2] *vado* later MSS. ; *vada* BA.

---

[a] *Cf.* Suetonius, *Aug.* 86, where the Emperor *Maecenatem
suum, cuius " myrobrechis," ut ait, " cincinnos "* (" unguent-
dripping curls " (Rolfe)) *usque quaque persequitur et imi-
tando per iocum irridet.* Augustus here refers especially to
the style of Maecenas as a writer.
[b] Terentia. For her charms see Horace, *Od.* ii. 12 ; for

EPISTLE CXIV.

one can detect the effeminacy by his very gait?
That a keen and confident soul quickens the step?
That madness in the soul, or anger (which resembles
madness), hastens our bodily movements from walking to rushing?

And how much more do you think that this affects
one's ability, which is entirely interwoven with
the soul,—being moulded thereby, obeying its commands, and deriving therefrom its laws! How
Maecenas lived is too well-known for present com-
ment. We know how he walked, how effeminate he
was, and how he desired to display himself; also,
how unwilling he was that his vices should escape
notice. What, then? Does not the looseness of his
speech match his ungirt attire? [a] Are his habits,
his attendants, his house, his wife, [b] any less clearly
marked than his words? He would have been a
man of great powers, had he set himself to his task
by a straight path, had he not shrunk from making
himself understood, had he not been so loose in his
style of speech also. You will therefore see that his
eloquence was that of an intoxicated man—twisting,
turning, unlimited in its slackness.

What is more unbecoming than the words: [c] " A
stream and a bank covered with long-tressed woods "?
And see how " men plough the channel with boats
and, turning up the shallows, leave gardens behind
them." Or, " He curls his lady-locks, and bills and
coos, and starts a-sighing, like a forest lord who
offers prayers with down-bent neck." Or, " An
unregenerate crew, they search out people at feasts,
and assail households with the wine-cup, and, by hope,

her faults see *De prov.* iii. 10, where Seneca calls her
" petulant."
[c] Maecenas, Frag. 11 Lunderstedt.

303

domos et spe mortem exigunt." " Genium festo vix
suo testem. Tenuisve cerei fila et crepacem molam.
Focum mater aut uxor investiunt."

6 Non statim, cum haec legeris, hoc tibi occurret,
hunc esse, qui solutis tunicis in urbe semper in-
cesserit ? Nam etiam cum absentis Caesaris partibus
fungeretur, signum a discincto petebatur. Hunc esse,
qui in [1] tribunali, in rostris, in omni publico coetu sic
apparuerit, ut pallio velaretur caput exclusis utrimque
auribus, non aliter quam in mimo fugitivi divitis
solent ? Hunc esse, cui tunc maxime civilibus bellis
strepentibus et sollicita urbe et armata comitatus hic
fuerit in publico spadones duo, magis tamen viri
quam ipse ? Hunc esse, qui uxorem milliens duxit,
cum unam habuerit ? Haec verba tam improbe
7 structa, tam neglegenter abiecta, tam contra consuetudinem omnium posita ostendunt mores quoque
non minus novos et pravos et singulares fuisse.
Maxima laus illi tribuitur mansuetudinis, pepercit
gladio, sanguine abstinuit nec ulla alia re, quid posset,
quam licentia ostendit ; hanc ipsam laudem suam
corrupit istis orationis portentosissimae deliciis.
8 Apparet enim mollem fuisse, non mitem. Hoc istae
ambages compositionis, hoc verba transversa, hoc
sensus miri,[2] magni quidem saepe, sed enervati dum

---

[1] *in* later MSS.; *om.* BA.
[2] *miri* Buecheler ; *mihi* BA.

---

[a] Instead of properly girt up—a mark of slackness
[b] For a similar mark of slovenliness, in Pompey's freed-
man Demetrius, see Plutarch, *Pompey*, xl. 4.
[c] *i.e.*, often repulsed by his wife Terentia, and then restored to grace.
[d] *e.g.*, in the Treaty of Brundisium (37 B.C.), and often
during the Triumvirate.

exact death." Or, "A Genius could hardly bear witness to his own festival"; or "threads of tiny tapers and crackling meal"; "mothers or wives clothing the hearth."

Can you not at once imagine, on reading through these words, that this was the man who always paraded through the city with a flowing [a] tunic? For even if he was discharging the absent emperor's duties, he was always in undress when they asked him for the countersign. Or that this was the man who, as judge on the bench, or as an orator, or at any public function, appeared with his cloak wrapped about his head, leaving only the ears exposed,[b] like the millionaire's runaway slaves in the farce? Or that this was the man who, at the very time when the state was embroiled in civil strife, when the city was in difficulties and under martial law, was attended in public by two eunuchs—both of them more men than himself? Or that this was the man who had but one wife, and yet was married countless times? [c] These words of his, put together so faultily, thrown off so carelessly, and arranged in such marked contrast to the usual practice, declare that the character of their writer was equally unusual, unsound, and eccentric. To be sure, we bestow upon him the highest praise for his humanity; he was sparing with the sword and refrained from bloodshed; [d] and he made a show of his power only in the course of his loose living; but he spoiled, by such preposterous finickiness of style, this genuine praise, which was his due. For it is evident that he was not really gentle, but effeminate, as is proved by his misleading word-order, his inverted expressions, and the surprising thoughts which frequently contain something great,

exeunt, cuivis manifestum facient. Motum illi felicitate nimia caput.

Quod vitium hominis esse interdum, interdum
9 temporis solet. Ubi luxuriam late felicitas fudit,
cultus[1] primum corporum esse diligentior incipit.
Deinde supellectili laboratur. Deinde in ipsas domos
inpenditur cura, ut in laxitatem ruris excurrant, ut
parietes advectis trans maria marmoribus fulgeant, ut
tecta varientur auro, ut lacunaribus pavimentorum
respondeat nitor. Deinde ad cenas lautitia trans-
fertur, et illic commendatio ex novitate et soliti
ordinis commutatione captatur, ut ea, quae includere
solent cenam, prima ponantur, ut quae advenientibus
dabantur, exeuntibus dentur.

10 Cum adsuevit animus fastidire, quae ex more sunt,
et illi pro sordidis solita sunt, etiam in oratione, quod
novum est, quaerit et modo antiqua verba atque
exsoleta revocat ac profert, modo fingit et ignota ac
deflectit, modo, id quod nuper increbruit, pro cultu
11 habetur audax translatio ac frequens. Sunt qui
sensus praecidant et hoc gratiam sperent, si sententia
pependerit et audienti suspicionem sui fecerit. Sunt
qui illos[2] detineant et porrigant. Sunt qui non
usque ad vitium accedant, necesse est enim hoc

---

[1] *cultus* Muretus ; *luxus* BA.
[2] *illos* later MSS. ; *illo* BA.

but in finding expression have become nerveless. One would say that his head was turned by too great success.

This fault is due sometimes to the man, and sometimes to his epoch. When prosperity has spread luxury far and wide, men begin by paying closer attention to their personal appearance. Then they go crazy over furniture. Next, they devote attention to their houses—how to take up more space with them, as if they were country-houses, how to make the walls glitter with marble that has been imported over seas, how to adorn a roof with gold, so that it may match the brightness of the inlaid floors. After that, they transfer their exquisite taste to the dinner-table, attempting to court approval by novelty and by departures from the customary order of dishes, so that the courses which we are accustomed to serve at the end of the meal may be served first, and so that the departing guests may partake of the kind of food which in former days was set before them on their arrival.

When the mind has acquired the habit of scorning the usual things of life, and regarding as mean that which was once customary, it begins to hunt for novelties in speech also ; now it summons and displays obsolete and old-fashioned words ; now it coins even unknown words or misshapes them ; and now a bold and frequent metaphorical usage is made a special feature of style, according to the fashion which has just become prevalent. Some cut the thoughts short, hoping to make a good impression by leaving the meaning in doubt and causing the hearer to suspect his own lack of wit. Some dwell upon them and lengthen them out. Others, too, approach just short of a fault—for a man must

facere aliquid grande temptanti, sed qui ipsum
vitium ament. Itaque ubicumque videris orationem
corruptam placere, ibi mores quoque a recto descivisse
non erit dubium.

Quomodo conviviorum luxuria, quomodo vestium
aegrae civitatis indicia sunt, sic orationis licentia, si
modo frequens est, ostendit animos quoque, a quibus
12 verba exeunt, procidisse. Mirari quidem non debes
corrupta excipi non tantum a [1] corona sordidiore, sed
ab hac quoque turba cultiore, togis enim inter se
isti, non iudiciis distant. Hoc magis mirari potes,
quod non tantum vitiosa, sed vitia laudentur. Nam
illud semper factum est : nullum sine venia placuit
ingenium. Da mihi quemcumque vis, magni no-
minis virum [2] ; dicam, quid illi aetas sua ignoverit,
quid in illo sciens dissimulaverit. Multos tibi dabo,
quibus vitia non nocuerint, quosdam, quibus pro-
fuerint. Dabo, inquam, maximae famae et inter
admiranda propositos, quos si quis corrigit, delet ; sic
enim vitia virtutibus inmissa sunt, ut illas secum
13 tractura sint. Adice nunc, quod oratio certam regu-
lam non habet ; consuetudo illam civitatis, quae
numquam in eodem diu stetit, versat. Multi ex
alieno saeculo petunt verba, duodecim tabulas loquuntur. Gracchus illis et Crassus et Curio nimis culti
et recentes sunt, ad Appium usque et Coruncanium
redeunt. Quidam contra, dum nihil nisi tritum et

---

[1] *a* later MSS. ; om. BA.
[2] *virum* later MSS. ; *utrum* BA.

---

[a] *i.e.*, the " ring " of onlookers, the " pit."
[b] Fifth century B.C.
[c] *i.e.*, from the second and first centuries B.C., back to
the third century.

really do this if he hopes to attain an imposing effect—but actually love the fault for its own sake. In short, whenever you notice that a degenerate style pleases the critics, you may be sure that character also has deviated from the right standard.

Just as luxurious banquets and elaborate dress are indications of disease in the state, similarly a lax style, if it be popular, shows that the mind (which is the source of the word) has lost its balance. Indeed you ought not to wonder that corrupt speech is welcomed not merely by the more squalid mob *a* but also by our more cultured throng; for it is only in their dress and not in their judgments that they differ. You may rather wonder that not only the effects of vices, but even vices themselves, meet with approval. For it has ever been thus: no man's ability has ever been approved without something being pardoned. Show me any man, however famous; I can tell you what it was that his age forgave in him, and what it was that his age purposely overlooked. I can show you many men whose vices have caused them no harm, and not a few who have been even helped by these vices. Yes, I will show you persons of the highest reputation, set up as models for our admiration; and yet if you seek to correct their errors, you destroy them; for vices are so intertwined with virtues that they drag the virtues along with them. Moreover, style has no fixed laws; it is changed by the usage of the people, never the same for any length of time. Many orators hark back to earlier epochs for their vocabulary, speaking in the language of the Twelve Tables.*b* Gracchus, Crassus, and Curio, in their eyes, are too refined and too modern; so back to Appius and Coruncanius!*c* Conversely, certain men, in their endeavour to main-

14 usitatum volunt, in sordes incidunt. Utrumque diverso genere corruptum est, tam mehercules quam nolle nisi splendidis uti ac sonantibus et poeticis, necessaria atque in usu posita vitare. Tam hunc dicam peccare quam illum : alter se plus iusto colit, alter plus iusto neglegit ; ille et crura, hic ne alas quidem vellit.

15 Ad compositionem transeamus. Quot genera tibi in hac dabo, quibus peccetur ? Quidam praefractam et asperam probant ; disturbant de industria, si quid placidius effluxit. Nolunt sine salebra esse iuncturam ; virilem putant et fortem, quae aurem inaequalitate percutiat. Quorundam non est compositio, modula-

16 tio est; adeo blanditur et molliter labitur. Quid de illa loquar, in qua verba differuntur et diu expectata vix ad clausulas redeunt ? Quid illa in exitu lenta, qualis Ciceronis est, devexa et molliter detinens nec aliter quam solet, ad morem suum pedemque respondens ? Non tantum in genere sententiarum vitium est, si aut pusillae sunt et pueriles aut improbae et plus ausae quam pudore salvo licet, si floridae sunt et nimis dulces, si in vanum exeunt et sine effectu nihil amplius quam sonant.

17 Haec vitia unus aliquis inducit, sub quo tunc eloquentia est, ceteri imitantur et alter alteri tradunt.

ᵃ The latter a reasonable mark of good breeding, the former an ostentatious bit of effeminacy. Summers cites Ovid, *A.A.* i. 506 " don't rub your legs smooth with the tight-scraping pumice-stone."

ᵇ As Cicero (see *Ep.* xl. 11) was an example of the rhythmical in style, so Pollio is the representative of the " bumpy " (*salebrosa*) manner (*Ep.* c. 7).

tain nothing but well-worn and common usages, fall into a humdrum style. These two classes, each in its own way, are degenerate; and it is no less degenerate to use no words except those which are conspicuous, high-sounding, and poetical, avoiding what is familiar and in ordinary usage. One is, I believe, as faulty as the other: the one class are unreasonably elaborate, the other are unreasonably negligent; the former depilate the leg, the latter not even the armpit.[a]

Let us now turn to the arrangement of words. In this department, what countless varieties of fault I can show you! Some are all for abruptness and unevenness of style, purposely disarranging anything which seems to have a smooth flow of language. They would have jolts in all their transitions; they regard as strong and manly whatever makes an uneven impression on the ear. With some others it is not so much an " arrangement " of words as it is a setting to music; so wheedling and soft is their gliding style. And what shall I say of that arrangement in which words are put off and, after being long waited for, just manage to come in at the end of a period? Or again of that softly-concluding style, Cicero-fashion,[b] with a gradual and gently poised descent, always the same and always with the customary arrangement of the rhythm! Nor is the fault only in the style of the sentences, if they are either petty and childish, or debasing, with more daring than modesty should allow, or if they are flowery and cloying, or if they end in emptiness, accomplishing mere sound and nothing more.

Some individual makes these vices fashionable—some person who controls the eloquence of the day; the rest follow his lead and communicate the habit

Sic Sallustio vigente anputatae sententiae et verba ante exspectatum cadentia et obscura brevitas fuere pro cultu. L. Arruntius, vir rarae frugalitatis, qui historias belli Punici scripsit, fuit Sallustianus et in illud genus nitens. Est apud Sallustium : " exercitum argento fecit," id est, pecunia paravit. Hoc Arruntius amare coepit ; posuit illud omnibus paginis. Dicit quodam loco : " fugam nostris fecere." Alio loco : " Hiero, rex Syracusanorum, bellum fecit." Et alio loco : " quae audita Panhormitanos dedere
18 Romanis fecere." Gustum tibi dare volui ; totus his contexitur liber. Quae apud Sallustium rara fuerunt, apud hunc crebra sunt et paene continua, nec sine causa ; ille enim in haec incidebat, at hic illa quaerebat. Vides autem, quid sequatur, ubi alicui vitium
19 pro exemplo est. Dixit Sallustius : " aquis hiemantibus." Arruntius in primo libro belli Punici ait : " repente hiemavit tempestas." Et alio loco cum dicere vellet frigidum annum fuisse, ait : " totus hiemavit annus." Et alio loco : " inde sexaginta onerarias leves praeter militem et necessarios nautarum hiemante aquilone misit." Non desinit omnibus locis hoc verbum infulcire. Quodam loco dicit Sallustius : " inter arma civilia aequi bonique famas petit." Arruntius non temperavit, quo minus primo

---

[a] *Flor.* 40 B.C.

[b] For these Sallust fragments see the edition of Kritz, Nos. 33, *Jug.* 37. 4, and 42 ; for Arruntius see H. Peter, *Frag. Hist. Rom.* ii. pp. 41 f.

[c] Literally, " created," " made."

[d] " Brought to pass flight for our men "; "Hiero, king of the Syracusans, brought about war "; "The news brought the men of Panormus " (now Palermo, Sicily) " to the point of surrendering to the Romans."

[e] " Amid the wintry waters "; "The storm suddenly grew wintry "; "The whole year was like winter "; "Then he

to each other. Thus when Sallust [a] was in his glory, phrases were lopped off, words came to a close unexpectedly, and obscure conciseness was equivalent to elegance.   L. Arruntius, a man of rare simplicity, author of a historical work on the Punic War, was a member and a strong supporter of the Sallust school. There is a phrase in Sallust : *exercitum argento fecit,*[b] meaning thereby that he *recruited* [c] an army by means of money. Arruntius began to like this idea ; he therefore inserted the verb *facio* all through his book. Hence, in one passage, *fugam nostris fecere* [d] ; in another, *Hiero, rex Syracusanorum, bellum fecit* [d] ; and, in another, *quae audita Panhormitanos dedere Romanis fecere.*[d] I merely desired to give you a taste ; his whole book is interwoven with such stuff as this. What Sallust reserved for occasional use, Arruntius makes into a frequent and almost continual habit—and there was a reason : for Sallust used the words as they occurred to his mind, while the other writer went afield in search of them. So you see the results of copying another man's vices. Again, Sallust said : *aquis hiemantibus.*[e] Arruntius, in his first book on the Punic War, uses the words : *repente hiemavit tempestas.*[e] And elsewhere, wishing to describe an exceptionally cold year, he says : *totus hiemavit annus.*[e] And in another passage : *inde sexaginta onerarias leves praeter militem et necessarios nautarum hiemante aquilone misit* [e] ; and he continues to bolster many passages with this metaphor. In a certain place, Sallust gives the words : *inter arma civilia aequi bonique famas* [f] *petit* ; and Arruntius cannot restrain himself from men-

dispatched sixty transports of light draught besides the soldiers and the necessary sailors amid a wintry storm."
  [f] The peculiarity here is the use of the plural instead of the singular form.   " Amid civil war he seeks reminders of justice and virtue."

statim libro poneret ingentes esse "famas" de Regulo.

20   Haec ergo et eiusmodi vitia, quae alicui inpressit imitatio, non sunt indicia luxuriae nec animi corrupti; propria enim esse debent et ex ipso nata, ex quibus tu aestimes alicuius adfectus. Iracundi hominis iracunda oratio est, commoti nimis incitata, delicati

21 tenera et fluxa. Quod vides istos sequi, qui aut vellunt barbam aut intervellunt, qui labra pressius tondent et adradunt servata et summissa cetera parte, qui lacernas coloris improbi sumunt, qui perlucentem togam, qui nolunt facere quicquam, quod hominum oculis transire liceat; inritant illos et in se advertunt; volunt vel reprehendi, dum conspici. Talis est oratio Maecenatis omniumque aliorum, qui non casu errant

22 sed scientes volentesque. Hoc a magno animi malo oritur. Quomodo in vino non ante lingua titubat quam mens cessit oneri et inclinata vel prodita est, ita ista orationis [1] quid aliud quam ebrietas nulli molesta est, nisi animus labat? Ideo ille curetur; ab illo sensus, ab illo verba exeunt, ab illo nobis est habitus, vultus, incessus. Illo sano ac valente oratio quoque robusta, fortis, virilis est; si ille procubuit, et cetera ruinam sequuntur.

[1] *orationis* Buecheler; *oratio nisi* BA; *oratio* later MSS.

tioning at once, in the first book, that there were extensive " reminders " concerning Regulus.

These and similar faults, which imitation stamps upon one's style, are not necessarily indications of loose standards or of debased mind ; for they are bound to be personal and peculiar to the writer, enabling one to judge thereby of a particular author's temperament ; just as an angry man will talk in an angry way, an excitable man in a flurried way, and an effeminate man in a style that is soft and un-resisting. You note this tendency in those who pluck out, or thin out, their beards, or who closely shear and shave the upper lip while preserving the rest of the hair and allowing it to grow, or in those who wear cloaks of outlandish colours, who wear transparent togas, and who never deign to do any-thing which will escape general notice ; they en-deavour to excite and attract men's attention, and they put up even with censure, provided that they can advertise themselves. That is the style of Maecenas and all the others who stray from the path, not by hazard, but consciously and voluntarily. This is the result of great evil in the soul. As in the case of drink, the tongue does not trip until the mind is overcome beneath its load and gives way or betrays itself ; so that intoxication of style—for what else than this can I call it ?—never gives trouble to anyone unless the soul begins to totter. Therefore, I say, take care of the soul ; for from the soul issue our thoughts, from the soul our words, from the soul our dispositions, our expres-sions, and our very gait. When the soul is sound and strong, the style too is vigorous, energetic, manly ; but if the soul lose its balance, down comes all the rest in ruins.

23   Rege incolumi mens omnibus una est;
      Amisso rupere fidem.

Rex noster est animus. Hoc incolumi cetera manent
in officio, parent, optemperant; cum ille paulum
vaccillavit, simul dubitant. Cum vero cessit voluptati, artes quoque eius actusque marcent et omnis ex
24 languido fluidoque conatus est. Quoniam hac simili-
tudine usus sum, perseverabo : animus noster modo
rex est, modo tyrannus. Rex, cum honesta intuetur,
salutem commissi sibi corporis curat, et illi nihil
imperat turpe, nihil sordidum. Ubi vero inpotens,
cupidus, delicatus est, transit in nomen detestabile ac
dirum et fit tyrannus; tunc illum excipiunt adfectus
inpotentes et instant, qui initio quidem gaudent, ut
solet populus largitione nocitura frustra plenus, et
25 quae non potest haurire, contrectat. Cum vero
magis ac magis vires morbus exedit et in medullas
nervosque descendere deliciae, conspectu eorum,
quibus se nimia aviditate inutilem reddidit, laetus,
pro suis voluptatibus habet alienarum spectaculum,
sumministrator libidinum testisque, quarum usum sibi
ingerendo abstulit. Nec illi tam gratum est abun-
dare iucundis quam acerbum, quod non omnem illum
apparatum per gulam ventremque transmittit, quod
non cum omni exoletorum feminarumque turba con-
volutatur, maeretque, quod magna pars suae felicitatis exclusa corporis angustiis cessat.

---

        [a] Vergil, *Georg.* iv. 212 f.

EPISTLE CXIV.

> If but the king be safe, your swarm will live
> Harmonious; if he die, the bees revolt.[a]

The soul is our king. If it be safe, the other functions remain on duty and serve with obedience; but the slightest lack of equilibrium in the soul causes them to waver along with it. And when the soul has yielded to pleasure, its functions and actions grow weak, and any undertaking comes from a nerveless and unsteady source. To persist in my use of this simile—our soul is at one time a king, at another a tyrant. The king, in that he respects things honourable, watches over the welfare of the body which is entrusted to his charge, and gives that body no base, no ignoble commands. But an uncontrolled, passionate, and effeminate soul changes kingship into that most dread and detestable quality—tyranny; then it becomes a prey to the uncontrolled emotions, which dog its steps, elated at first, to be sure, like a populace idly sated with a largess which will ultimately be its undoing, and spoiling what it cannot consume. But when the disease has gradually eaten away the strength, and luxurious habits have penetrated the marrow and the sinews, such a soul exults at the sight of limbs which, through its over-indulgence, it has made useless; instead of its own pleasures, it views those of others; it becomes the go-between and witness of the passions which, as the result of self-gratification, it can no longer feel. Abundance of delights is not so pleasing a thing to that soul as it is bitter, because it cannot send all the dainties of yore down through the over-worked throat and stomach, because it can no longer whirl in the maze of eunuchs and mistresses, and it is melancholy because a great part of its happiness is shut off, through the limitations of the body.

26 Numquid enim, mi Lucili, in hoc furor est, quod
nemo nostrum mortalem se cogitat, quod nemo
inbecillum ? In illo, quod nemo nostrum unum esse
se cogitat ! Aspice culinas nostras et concursantis
inter tot ignes cocos ; unum videri putas ventrem,
cui tanto tumultu comparatur cibus ? Aspice vete-
raria nostra et plena multorum saeculorum vindemiis
horrea ; unum putas videri ventrem, cui tot consulum
regionumque vina cluduntur ? Aspice, quot locis
terra vertatur, quot millia colonorum arent, fodiant ;
unum videri putas ventrem, cui et in Sicilia et in
27 Africa seritur ? Sani erimus et modica concupiscemus, si unusquisque se numeret, metiatur simul
corpus, sciat, quam nec multum capere nec diu possit.
Nihil tamen aeque tibi profuerit ad temperantiam
omnium rerum quam frequens cogitatio brevis aevi et
huius incerti ; quidquid facies, respice ad mortem.
Vale.

CXV.

Seneca Lvcilio svo salvtem

1 Nimis anxium esse te circa verba et compositionem,
mi Lucili, nolo ; habeo maiora, quae cures. Quaere,
quid scribas, non quemadmodum ; et hoc ipsum,
non ut scribas, sed ut sentias, ut illa, quae senseris,
magis adplices tibi et velut signes. Cuiuscumque

Now is it not madness, Lucilius, for none of us to reflect that he is mortal? Or frail? Or again that he is but one individual? Look at our kitchens, and the cooks, who bustle about over so many fires; is it, think you, for a single belly that all this bustle and preparation of food takes place? Look at the old brands of wine and store-houses filled with the vintages of many ages; is it, think you, a single belly that is to receive the stored wine, sealed with the names of so many consuls, and gathered from so many vineyards? Look, and mark in how many regions men plough the earth, and how many thousands of farmers are tilling and digging; is it, think you, for a single belly that crops are planted in Sicily and Africa? We should be sensible, and our wants more reasonable, if each of us were to take stock of himself, and to measure his bodily needs also, and understand how little he can consume, and for how short a time! But nothing will give you so much help toward moderation as the frequent thought that life is short and uncertain here below; whatever you are doing, have regard to death. Farewell.

CXV. ON THE SUPERFICIAL BLESSINGS

I wish, my dear Lucilius, that you would not be too particular with regard to words and their arrangement; I have greater matters than these to commend to your care. You should seek what to write, rather than how to write it—and even that not for the purpose of writing but of feeling it, that you may thus make what you have felt more your own and, as it were, set a seal on it. Whenever

2 orationem videris sollicitam et politam, scito animum quoque non minus esse pusillis occupatum. Magnus ille remissius loquitur et securius; quaecumque dicit, plus habent fiduciae quam curae.

Nosti comptulos [1] iuvenes, barba et coma nitidos, de capsula totos; nihil ab illis speraveris forte, nihil solidum. Oratio cultus animi est: si circumtonsa est et [2] fucata et manu facta, ostendit illum quoque non esse sincerum et habere aliquid fracti. Non est 3 ornamentum virile concinnitas. Si nobis animum boni viri liceret inspicere, o quam pulchram faciem, quam sanctam, quam ex magnifico placidoque fulgentem videremus, hinc iustitia, illinc fortitudine, hinc temperantia prudentiaque lucentibus! Praeter has frugalitas et continentia et tolerantia et liberalitas comitasque et—quis credat?—in homine rarum humanitas bonum, splendorem illi suum adfunderent. Tunc providentia cum elegantia et ex istis magnanimitas eminentissima quantum, di boni, decoris illi, quantum ponderis gravitatisque adderent! Quanta esset cum gratia auctoritas! Nemo illam 4 amabilem, qui non simul venerabilem diceret. Si quis viderit hanc faciem altiorem fulgentioremque quam cerni inter humana consuevit, nonne velut numinis occursu obstupefactus resistat et, ut " fas sit vidisse," tacitus precetur? Tum evocante ipsa vultus benignitate productus adoret ac supplicet, et diu

---

[1] *comptulos* Buecheler; *complutos* BA.
[2] *est et* later MSS.; *esset* B; *esse* A[1].

---

[a] Elsewhere (*Epp.* lxxvi. 2 and lxxxvii. 9) called *trossuli,* " fops."

you notice a style that is too careful and too polished,
you may be sure that the mind also is no less absorbed
in petty things. The really great man speaks in-
formally and easily ; whatever he says, he speaks
with assurance rather than with pains.

You are familiar with the young dandies,[4] natty
as to their beards and locks, fresh from the bandbox ;
you can never expect from them any strength or
any soundness. Style is the garb of thought : if it
be trimmed, or dyed, or treated, it shows that there
are defects and a certain amount of flaws in the
mind. Elaborate elegance is not a manly garb. If
we had the privilege of looking into a good man's
soul, oh what a fair, holy, magnificent, gracious, and
shining face should we behold—radiant on the one
side with justice and temperance, on another with
bravery and wisdom ! And, besides these, thriftiness,
moderation, endurance, refinement, affability, and—
though hard to believe—love of one's fellow-men,
that Good which is so rare in man, all these would
be shedding their own glory over that soul. There,
too, forethought combined with elegance and, resulting from these, a most excellent greatness of soul
(the noblest of all these virtues)—indeed what charm,
O ye heavens, what authority and dignity would they
contribute ! What a wonderful combination of sweetness and power ! No one could call such a face
lovable without also calling it worshipful. If one
might behold such a face, more exalted and more
radiant than the mortal eye is wont to behold,
would not one pause as if struck dumb by a visitation
from above, and utter a silent prayer, saying : " May
it be lawful to have looked upon it !"? And then, led
on by the encouraging kindliness of his expression,
should we not bow down and worship ? Should we

contemplatus multum extantem superque mensuram
solitorum inter nos aspici elatam, oculis mite quiddam,
sed nihilominus vivido igne flagrantibus, tunc deinde
illam Vergili nostri vocem verens atque attonitus
emittat ?

5   O quam te memorem, virgo ? Namque haut tibi vultus
     Mortalis nec vox hominem sonat.

      .   .   .   .

     Sis felix, nostrumque leves quaecumque laborem.

Aderit levabitque, si colere eam voluerimus.   Colitur
autem non taurorum opimis corporibus contrucidatis
nec auro argentoque suspenso nec in thensauros stipe
infusa, sed pia et recta voluntate.

6   Nemo, inquam, non amore eius arderet, si nobis
illam videre contingeret ; nunc enim multa obstrigill-
ant et aciem nostram aut splendore nimio repercu-
tiunt aut obscuro [1] retinent.   Sed si, quemadmodum
visus oculorum quibusdam medicamentis acui solet
et repurgari, sic nos aciem animi liberare inpedimentis voluerimus, poterimus perspicere virtutem
etiam obrutam corpore, etiam paupertate opposita,
etiam humilitate et infamia obiacentibus.   Cernemus,
7 inquam, pulchritudinem illam quamvis sordido ob-
tectam.   Rursus aeque malitiam et aerumnosi animi
veternum perspiciemus, quamvis multus circa divitiarum radiantium splendor inpediat et intuentem

----

¹ *obscuro* Muretus ; *obscure* BA.

ª *Aen.* i. 327 ff.

not, after much contemplation of a far superior countenance, surpassing those which we are wont to look upon, mild-eyed and yet flashing with life-giving fire—should we not then, I say, in reverence and awe, give utterance to those famous lines of our poet Vergil :

> O maiden, words are weak ! Thy face is more
> Than mortal, and thy voice rings sweeter far
> Than mortal man's ; . . . .
> Blest be thou ; and, whoe'er thou art, relieve
> Our heavy burdens.[a]

And such a vision will indeed be a present help and relief to us, if we are willing to worship it. But this worship does not consist in slaughtering fattened bulls, or in hanging up offerings of gold or silver, or in pouring coins into a temple treasury ; rather does it consist in a will that is reverent and upright.

There is none of us, I declare to you, who would not burn with love for this vision of virtue, if only he had the privilege of beholding it ; for now there are many things that cut off our vision, piercing it with too strong a light, or clogging it with too much darkness. If, however, as certain drugs are wont to be used for sharpening and clearing the eyesight, we are likewise willing to free our mind's eye from hindrances, we shall then be able to perceive virtue, though it be buried in the body — even though poverty stand in the way, and even though lowliness and disgrace block the path. We shall then, I say, behold that true beauty, no matter if it be smothered by unloveliness. Conversely, we shall get a view of evil and the deadening influences of a sorrow-laden soul—in spite of the hindrance that results from the widespread gleam of riches that flash round about, and in spite of the false light—of official position

323

hinc honorum, illinc magnarum potestatium falsa lux
verberet.

8 Tunc intellegere nobis licebit, quam contemnenda
miremur, simillimi pueris, quibus omne ludicrum in
pretio est ; parentibus quippe nec minus fratribus
praeferunt parvo aere empta monilia.[1] Quid ergo
inter nos et illos interest, ut Ariston ait, nisi quod
nos circa tabulas et statuas insanimus carius inepti ?
Illos reperti in litore calculi leves et aliquid habentes
varietatis delectant, nos ingentium maculae colum-
narum, sive ex Aegyptiis harenis sive[2] ex Africae
solitudinibus advectae porticum aliquam vel capacem
9 populi cenationem ferunt. Miramur parietes tenui
marmore inductos, cum sciamus, quale sit quod
absconditur. Oculis nostris inponimus, et cum auro
tecta perfudimus, quid aliud quam mendacio gau-
demus ? Scimus enim sub illo auro foeda ligna lati-
tare.

Nec tantum parietibus aut lacunaribus ornamentum
tenue praetenditur ; omnium istorum, quos incedere
altos vides, bratteata felicitas est. Inspice, et scies,
sub ista tenui membrana dignitatis quantum mali
10 iaceat. Haec ipsa res, quae tot magistratus, tot
iudices detinet, quae et magistratus et iudices facit,
pecunia, ex quo in honore esse coepit, verus rerum
honor cecidit, mercatoresque et venales in vicem

[1] *monilia* Erasmus ; *mobilia* B ; *mobiba* A.
[2] *harenis sive* later MSS. ; *harent. sive* BA.

[a] Frag. 372 von Arnim.

on the one side or great power on the other—which beats pitilessly upon the beholder.

Then it will be in our power to understand how contemptible are the things we admire—like children who regard every toy as a thing of value, who cherish necklaces bought at the price of a mere penny as more dear than their parents or than their brothers. And what, then, as Aristo says,[a] is the difference between ourselves and these children, except that we elders go crazy over paintings and sculpture, and that our folly costs us dearer? Children are pleased by the smooth and variegated pebbles which they pick up on the beach, while we take delight in tall columns of veined marble brought either from Egyptian sands or from African deserts to hold up a colonnade or a dining-hall large enough to contain a city crowd; we admire walls veneered with a thin layer of marble, although we know the while what defects the marble conceals. We cheat our own eyesight, and when we have overlaid our ceilings with gold, what else is it but a lie in which we take such delight? For we know that beneath all this gilding there lurks some ugly wood.

Nor is such superficial decoration spread merely over walls and ceilings; nay, all the famous men whom you see strutting about with head in air, have nothing but a gold-leaf prosperity. Look beneath, and you will know how much evil lies under that thin coating of titles. Note that very commodity which holds the attention of so many magistrates and so many judges, and which creates both magistrates and judges—that money, I say, which ever since it began to be regarded with respect, has caused the ruin of the true honour of things; we become alternately merchants and merchandise, and

facti quaerimus non quale sit quidque, sed quanti ;
ad mercedem pii sumus, ad mercedem impii, et
honesta, quamdiu aliqua illis spes inest, sequimur,
in contrarium transituri, si plus scelera promittent.

11 Admirationem nobis parentes auri argentique fecerunt, et teneris infusa cupiditas altius sedit crevitque
nobiscum. Deinde totus populus in alia discors in
hoc convenit ; hoc suspiciunt, hoc suis optant, hoc
dis velut rerum humanarum maximum, cum grati
videri volunt, consecrant. Denique eo mores redacti
sunt, ut paupertas maledicto probroque sit, contempta divitibus, invisa pauperibus.

12 Accedunt deinde carmina poetarum, quae adfectibus nostris facem subdant, quibus divitiae velut
unicum vitae decus ornamentumque laudantur. Nihil
illis melius nec dare videntur di immortales posse
nec habere.

13   Regia Solis erat sublimibus alta columnis
        Clara micante auro.

Eiusdem currum aspice :

        Aureus axis erat, temo aureus, aurea summae
        Curvatura rotae, radiorum argenteus ordo.

Denique quod optimum videri volunt saeculum,
14 aureum appellant. Nec apud Graecos tragicos
desunt, qui lucro innocentiam, salutem, opinionem
bonam mutent.

---

a Ovid, *Metam.* ii. 1 f.   b *Id. ib.* ii. 107 ff.

we ask, not what a thing truly is, but what it costs ; we fulfil duties if it pays, or neglect them if it pays, and we follow an honourable course as long as it encourages our expectations, ready to veer across to the opposite course if crooked conduct shall promise more. Our parents have instilled into us a respect for gold and silver ; in our early years the craving has been implanted, settling deep within us and growing with our growth. Then too the whole nation, though at odds on every other subject, agrees upon this ; this is what they regard, this is what they ask for their children, this is what they dedicate to the gods when they wish to show their gratitude—as if it were the greatest of all man's possessions ! And finally, public opinion has come to such a pass that poverty is a hissing and a reproach, despised by the rich and loathed by the poor.

Verses of poets also are added to the account—verses which lend fuel to our passions, verses in which wealth is praised as if it were the only credit and glory of mortal man. People seem to think that the immortal gods cannot give any better gift than wealth—or even possess anything better :

> The Sun-god's palace, set with pillars tall,
> And flashing bright with gold.[a]

Or they describe the chariot of the Sun[b] :

> Gold was the axle, golden eke the pole,
> And gold the tires that bound the circling wheels,
> And silver all the spokes within the wheels.

And finally, when they would praise an epoch as the best, they call it the " Golden Age." Even among the Greek tragic poets there are some who regard pelf as better than purity, soundness, or good report :

327

Sine me vocari pessimum, ut [1] dives vocer.

An dives, omnes quaerimus, nemo, an bonus.

Non quare et unde, quid habeas, tantum rogant.

Ubique tanti quisque, quantum habuit, fuit.

Quid habere nobis turpe sit quaeris ?   Nihil.

Aut dives opto vivere aut pauper mori.

Bene moritur, quisquis moritur dum lucrum facit.

Pecunia, ingens generis humani bonum,
Cui non voluptas matris aut blandae potest
Par esse prolis, non sacer meritis parens ;
Tam dulce si quid Veneris in vultu micat,
Merito illa amores caelitum atque hominum movet.

15 Cum hi novissimi versus in tragoedia Euripidis
pronuntiati essent, totus populus ad eiciendum et
actorem et carmen consurrexit uno impetu, donec
Euripides in medium ipse prosilivit petens, ut ex-
pectarent [2] viderentque, quem admirator auri exitum
faceret.   Dabat in illa fabula poenas Bellerophontes,
16 quas in sua quisque dat.   Nulla enim avaritia sine
poena est, quamvis satis sit ipsa poenarum.   O quantum lacrimarum, quantum laborum exigit !   Quam
misera desiderat esse, quam misera e partis est !
Adice cotidianas sollicitudines, quae pro modo habendi quemque discruciant.   Maiore tormento pecunia
possidetur quam quaeritur.   Quantum damnis in-

---

[1] *ut* Hense ; *simul ut* MSS.
[2] *exspectarent* Muretus ; *spectarent* BA.

---

[a] *Cf.* Nauck, *Trag. Gr. fragg. adesp.* 181. 1 and 461.
[b] *Cf. id.*, *Eurip. Danaë*, *Frag.* 324, and Hense's note (ed.
of 1914, p. 559).

Call me a scoundrel, only call me rich !

All ask how great my riches are, but none
Whether my soul is good.

None asks the means or source of your estate,
But merely how it totals.

All men are worth as much as what they own

What is most shameful for us to possess ?
Nothing !

If riches bless me, I should love to live ;
Yet I would rather die, if poor.

A man dies nobly in pursuit of wealth.[a]

Money, that blessing to the race of man,
Cannot be matched by mother's love, or lisp
Of children, or the honour due one's sire.
And if the sweetness of the lover's glance
Be half so charming, Love will rightly stir
The hearts of gods and men to adoration.[b]

When these last-quoted lines were spoken at a performance of one of the tragedies of Euripides, the
whole audience rose with one accord to hiss the actor
and the play off the stage.   But Euripides jumped to
his feet, claimed a hearing, and asked them to wait for
the conclusion and see the destiny that was in store
for this man who gaped after gold.   Bellerophon, in
that particular drama, was to pay the penalty which
is exacted of all men in the drama of life.   For one
must pay the penalty for all greedy acts ; although
the greed is enough of a penalty in itself.   What
tears and toil does money wring from us !   Greed is
wretched in that which it craves and wretched in
that which it wins !   Think besides of the daily
worry which afflicts every possessor in proportion to
the measure of his gain !   The possession of riches
means even greater agony of spirit than the acquisition of riches.   And how we sorrow over our losses—

gemescunt, quae et magna incidunt et videntur
maiora! Denique ut illis fortuna nihil detrahat,
quidquid non adquiritur, damnum est.

17 "At felicem illum homines et divitem vocant et
consequi optant, quantum ille possidet." Fateor.
Quid ergo? Tu ullos esse condicionis peioris existimas quam qui habent et miseriam et invidiam?
Utinam qui divitias optaturi essent, cum divitibus
deliberarent! Utinam honores petituri cum am-
bitiosis et summum adeptis dignitatis statum! Pro-
fecto vota mutassent, cum interim illi nova suscipiunt,[1] cum priora damnaverint. Nemo enim est,
cui felicitas sua, etiam si cursu venit, satis faciat.
Queruntur et de consiliis et de processibus suis
maluntque semper quae reliquerunt.

18 Itaque hoc tibi philosophia praestabit, quo equidem
nihil maius existimo : numquam te paenitebit tui.
Ad hanc tam solidam felicitatem, quam tempestas
nulla concutiat, non perducent te apte verba contexta
et oratio fluens leniter. Eant, ut volent, dum animo
compositio sua constet, dum sit magnus et opinionum
securus et ob ipsa, quae aliis displicent, sibi placens,
qui profectum suum vita aestimet et tantum scire se
iudicet, quantum non cupit quantum non timet.
VALE.

---

[1] *suscipiunt* codd., Gruter; *suspiciunt* BA.

[a] A play on the *compositio* of rhetoric.

losses which fall heavily upon us, and yet seem still more heavy! And finally, though Fortune may leave our property intact, whatever we cannot gain in addition, is sheer loss!

"But," you will say to me, "people call yonder man happy and rich; they pray that some day they may equal him in possessions." Very true. What, then? Do you think that there is any more pitiable lot in life than to possess misery and hatred also? Would that those who are bound to crave wealth could compare notes with the rich man! Would that those who are bound to seek political office could confer with ambitious men who have reached the most sought-after honours! They would then surely alter their prayers, seeing that these grandees are always gaping after new gain, condemning what is already behind them. For there is no one in the world who is contented with his prosperity, even if it comes to him on the run. Men complain about their plans and the outcome of their plans; they always prefer what they have failed to win.

So philosophy can settle this problem for you, and afford you, to my mind, the greatest boon that exists — absence of regret for your own conduct. This is a sure happiness; no storm can ruffle it; but you cannot be steered safely through by any subtly woven words, or any gently flowing language. Let words proceed as they please, provided only your soul keeps its own sure order,[a] provided your soul is great and holds unruffled to its ideals, pleased with itself on account of the very things which displease others, a soul that makes life the test of its progress, and believes that its knowledge is in exact proportion to its freedom from desire and its freedom from fear. Farewell.

331

CXVI.

SENECA LVCILIO SVO SALVTEM

1 Utrum satius sit modicos habere adfectus an nullos, saepe quaesitum est. Nostri illos expellunt, Peripatetici temperant. Ego non video, quomodo salubris esse aut utilis possit ulla mediocritas morbi. Noli timere ; nihil eorum, quae tibi non vis negari, eripio. Facilem me indulgentemque praebebo rebus, ad quas tendis et quas aut necessarias vitae aut utiles aut iucundas putas ; detraham vitium. Nam cum tibi cupere interdixero, velle permittam, ut eadem illa intrepidus facias, ut certiore consilio, ut voluptates ipsas magis sentias ; quidni ad te magis perventurae sint, si illis imperabis, quam si servies ?

2 "Sed naturale est," inquis, "ut desiderio amici torquear ; da ius[1] lacrimis tam iuste cadentibus. Naturale est opinionibus hominum tangi et adversis contristari ; quare mihi non permittas hunc tam honestum malae opinionis metum ? "

Nullum est vitium sine patrocinio ; nulli non initium verecundum est et exorabile, sed ab hoc latius funditur. Non obtinebis, ut desinat, si incipere 3 permiseris. Inbecillus est primo omnis adfectus. Deinde ipse se concitat et vires, dum procedit, parat ; excluditur facilius quam expellitur. Quis negat

---

[1] *da ius* Lipsius ; *datus* BA.

---

[a] For a discussion of ἀπάθεια see *Epp.* ix. 2 ff. and lxxxv. 3 ff.

CXVI. ON SELF-CONTROL

The question has often been raised whether it is better to have moderate emotions, or none at all.[a] Philosophers of our school reject the emotions; the Peripatetics keep them in check. I, however, do not understand how any half-way disease can be either wholesome or helpful. Do not fear; I am not robbing you of any privileges which you are unwilling to lose! I shall be kindly and indulgent towards the objects for which you strive — those which you hold to be necessary to our existence, or useful, or pleasant; I shall simply strip away the vice. For after I have issued my prohibition against the desires, I shall still allow you to wish that you may do the same things fearlessly and with greater accuracy of judgment, and to feel even the pleasures more than before; and how can these pleasures help coming more readily to your call, if you are their lord rather than their slave!

" But," you object, " it is natural for me to suffer when I am bereaved of a friend; grant some privileges to tears which have the right to flow! It is also natural to be affected by men's opinions and to be cast down when they are unfavourable; so why should you not allow me such an honourable aversion to bad opinion ? "

There is no vice which lacks some plea; there is no vice that at the start is not modest and easily entreated; but afterwards the trouble spreads more widely. If you allow it to begin, you cannot make sure of its ceasing. Every emotion at the start is weak. Afterwards, it rouses itself and gains strength by progress; it is more easy to forestall it than to forgo it. Who does not admit that all the emotions

333

omnis adfectus a quodam quasi naturali fluere principio ? Curam nobis nostri natura mandavit, sed huic ubi nimium indulseris, vitium est. Voluptatem natura necessariis rebus admiscuit, non ut illam peteremus, sed ut ea, sine quibus non possumus vivere, grata [1] nobis illius faceret accessio ; suo veniat iure, luxuria est.

Ergo intrantibus resistamus, quia facilius, ut dixi, non recipiuntur quam exeunt. " Aliquatenus," inquis, " dolere, aliquatenus timere permitte " ; sed illud " aliquatenus " longe producitur nec ubi vis, accipit finem. Sapienti non sollicite custodire se tutum est, et lacrimas suas et voluptates ubi volet sistet ; nobis quia non est regredi facile, optimum est omnino non progredi. Eleganter mihi videtur Panaetius respondisse adulescentulo cuidam quaerenti, an sapiens amaturus esset. " De sapiente," inquit, " videbimus ; mihi et tibi, qui adhuc a sapiente longe absumus, non est committendum, ut incidamus in rem commotam, inpotentem, alteri emancupatam, vilem sibi. Sive enim non respuit,[2] humanitate eius inritamur, sive contempsit, superbia accendimur. Aeque facilitas amoris quam difficultas nocet ; facilitate capimur, cum difficultate certamus. Itaque conscii nobis inbecillitatis nostrae quiescamus. Nec vino infirmum animum com-

---

[1] *grata* Windhaus and cod. Velz. ; *gratia* or *gratiora* MSS.
[2] *respuit* Buecheler ; *respicit* BA.

---

[a] Frag. 56 Fowler.
[b] Literally, " out of our possession " (from *mancipium*, " ownership ").

flow as it were from a certain natural source? We are endowed by Nature with an interest in our own well-being; but this very interest, when over-indulged, becomes a vice. Nature has intermingled pleasure with necessary things—not in order that we should seek pleasure, but in order that the addition of pleasure may make the indispensable means of existence attractive to our eyes. Should it claim rights of its own, it is luxury.

Let us therefore resist these faults when they are demanding entrance, because, as I have said, it is easier to deny them admittance than to make them depart. And if you cry: "One should be allowed a certain amount of grieving, and a certain amount of fear," I reply that the "certain amount" can be too long-drawn-out, and that it will refuse to stop short when you so desire. The wise man can safely control himself without becoming over-anxious; he can halt his tears and his pleasures at will; but in our case, because it is not easy to retrace our steps, it is best not to push ahead at all. I think that Panaetius [a] gave a very neat answer to a certain youth who asked him whether the wise man should become a lover: "As to the wise man, we shall see later; but you and I, who are as yet far removed from wisdom, should not trust ourselves to fall into a state that is disordered, uncontrolled, enslaved to another,[b] contemptible to itself. If our love be not spurned, we are excited by its kindness; if it be scorned, we are kindled by our pride. An easily-won love hurts us as much as one which is difficult to win; we are captured by that which is compliant, and we struggle with that which is hard. Therefore, knowing our weakness, let us remain quiet. Let us not expose this unstable spirit to the tempta-

335

mittamus nec formae nec adulationi nec ullis rebus blande trahentibus."

6 Quod Panaetius de amore quaerenti respondit, hoc ego de omnibus adfectibus dico. Quantum possumus, nos a lubrico recedamus ; in sicco quoque
7 parum fortiter stamus. Occurres hoc loco mihi illa publica contra Stoicos voce : " Nimis magna promittitis, nimis dura praecipitis. Nos homunciones sumus, omnia nobis negare non possumus. Dolebimus, sed parum ; concupiscemus, sed temperate ; irascemur, sed placabimur." Scis, quare non possu-
8 mus ista ? Quia nos posse non credimus. Immo mehercules aliud est in re : vitia nostra quia amamus, defendimus et malumus excusare illa quam excutere. Satis natura homini dedit roboris, si illo utamur, si vires nostras colligamus ac totas pro nobis, certe non contra nos concitemus. Nolle in causa est, non posse praetenditur. Vale.

CXVII.

Seneca Lvcilio svo salvtem

1 Multum mihi negotii concinnabis et, dum nescis, in magnam me litem ac molestiam inpinges, qui mihi tales quaestiunculas ponis, in quibus ego nec dissen-

tions of drink, or beauty, or flattery, or anything that coaxes and allures."

Now that which Panaetius replied to the question about love may be applied, I believe, to all the emotions. In so far as we are able, let us step back from slippery places ; even on dry ground it is hard enough to take a sturdy stand. At this point, I know, you will confront me with that common complaint against the Stoics : " Your promises are too great, and your counsels too hard. We are mere manikins, unable to deny ourselves everything. We shall sorrow, but not to any great extent ; we shall feel desires, but in moderation ; we shall give way to anger, but we shall be appeased." And do you know why we have not the power to attain this Stoic ideal ? It is because we refuse to believe in our power. Nay, of a surety, there is something else which plays a part : it is because we are in love with our vices ; we uphold them and prefer to make excuses for them rather than shake them off. We mortals have been endowed with sufficient strength by nature, if only we use this strength, if only we concentrate our powers and rouse them all to help us or at least not to hinder us. The reason is unwillingness, the excuse, inability. Farewell.

CXVII. ON REAL ETHICS AS SUPERIOR TO SYLLOGISTIC SUBTLETIES

You will be fabricating much trouble for me, and you will be unconsciously embroiling me in a great discussion, and in considerable bother, if you put such petty questions as these ; for in settling them I cannot disagree with my fellow-Stoics without

THE EPISTLES OF SENECA

tire a nostris salva gratia nec consentire salva conscientia possum. Quaeris, an verum sit, quod Stoicis
placet, sapientiam bonum esse, sapere bonum non
esse. Primum exponam, quid Stoicis videatur;
deinde tunc dicere sententiam audebo.

2   Placet nostris, quod bonum est, corpus esse, quia
quod bonum est, facit; quidquid facit, corpus est.
Quod bonum est, prodest. Faciat autem aliquid
oportet, ut prosit; si facit, corpus est. Sapientiam
bonum esse dicunt; sequitur, ut necesse sit illam
3 corporalem quoque dicere. At sapere non putant
eiusdem condicionis esse. Incorporale est et accidens
alteri, id est sapientiae; itaque nec facit quidquam
nec prodest.

"Quid ergo?" inquit, "non dicimus, bonum est
sapere?" Dicimus referentes ad id, ex quo pendet,
4 id est ad ipsam sapientiam. Adversus hos quid ab
aliis respondeatur, audi, antequam ego incipio se-
cedere et in alia parte considere. "Isto modo," inquiunt, "nec beate vivere bonum est. Velint nolint,
respondendum est beatam vitam bonum esse, beate
5 vivere bonum non esse." Etiamnunc nostris illud
quoque opponitur: "Vultis sapere. Ergo expetenda
res est sapere. Si expetenda res est, bona est."
Coguntur nostri verba torquere et unam syllabam
expetendo interponere, quam sermo noster inseri non

* For this sort of discussion see *Ep.* cxiii. 1 ff.

impairing my standing among them, nor can I sub-
scribe to such ideas without impairing my conscience.
Your query is, whether the Stoic belief is true ;
that wisdom is a Good, but that *being wise* is not a
Good.[a] I shall first set forth the Stoic view, and
then I shall be bold enough to deliver my own
opinion.

We of the Stoic school believe that the Good is
corporeal, because the Good is active, and whatever
is active is corporeal. That which is good, is helpful.
But, in order to be helpful, it must be active ; so, if
it is active, it is corporeal. They (the Stoics) declare
that wisdom is a Good ; it therefore follows that one
must also call wisdom corporeal. But they do not
think that *being wise* can be rated on the same basis.
For it is incorporeal and accessory to something
else, in other words, wisdom ; hence it is in no
respect active or helpful.

" What, then ? " is the reply ; " Why do we not say
that *being wise* is a Good ? " We do say so ; but only
by referring it to that on which it depends—in
other words, wisdom itself. Let me tell you what
answers other philosophers make to these objectors,
before I myself begin to form my own creed and to
take my place entirely on another side. " Judged
in that light," they say, " not even *living happily* is a
Good. Willy nilly, such persons ought to reply that
the happy life is a Good, but that *living happily* is not
a Good." And this objection is also raised against
our school : " You wish to be wise. Therefore,
being wise is a thing to be desired. And if it be a
thing to be desired, it is a Good." So our philosophers are forced to twist their words and insert
another syllable into the word " desired,"—a syllable
which our language does not normally allow to be

sinit. Ego illam, si pateris, adiungam. " Expetendum est," inquiunt, " quod bonum est : expetibile,
quod nobis contingit, cum bonum consecuti sumus.
Non petitur tamquam bonum, sed petito bono accedit."

6 Ego non idem sentio et nostros iudico in hoc descendere, quia iam primo vinculo tenentur et mutare
illis formulam non licet. Multum dare solemus
praesumptioni omnium hominum, et apud nos veritatis argumentum est aliquid omnibus videri. Tamquam deos esse inter alia hoc colligimus, quod
omnibus insita de dis opinio est nec ulla gens usquam
est adeo extra leges moresque proiecta, ut non
aliquos deos credat. Cum de animarum aeternitate
disserimus, non leve momentum apud nos habet
consensus hominum aut timentium inferos aut colen-
tium. Utor hac publica persuasione : neminem invenies, qui non putet et sapientiam bonum et sapere.[1]
7 Non faciam, quod victi solent, ut provocem ad
populum ; nostris incipiamus armis confligere.

Quod accidit alicui, utrum extra id, cui accidit, est
an in eo, cui accidit ? Si in eo est, cui accidit, tam
corpus est quam illud, cui accidit. Nihil enim accidere sine tactu potest ; quod tangit, corpus est. Si
extra est, posteaquam acciderat, recessit. Quod
recessit, motum habet. Quod motum habet, corpus

---

[1] *et sapientiam bonum et sapere* ed. Mentel. ; *et s. et b. s.*
B ; *et s. b. s.* A ; *et s. b. et s. bonum* later MSS.

---

[a] This adjective *expetibilis* is found in Tacitus, *Ann.*
xvi. 21, and in Boethius, *Cons.* ii. 6.
[b] *i.e.,* the Stoics as mentioned above (with whom Seneca
often disagrees on minor details).

inserted. But, with your permission, I shall add it. " That which is good," they say, " is a thing to be desired; the *desirable*[a] thing is that which falls to our lot after we have attained the Good. For the desirable is not sought as a Good; it is an accessory to the Good after the Good has been attained."

I myself do not hold the same view, and I judge that our philosophers[b] have come down to this argument because they are already bound by the first link in the chain and for that reason may not alter their definition. People are wont to concede much to the things which all men take for granted; in our eyes the fact that all men agree upon something is a proof of its truth. For instance, we infer that the gods exist, for this reason, among others—that there is implanted in everyone an idea concerning deity, and there is no people so far beyond the reach of laws and customs that it does not believe at least in gods of some sort. And when we discuss the immortality of the soul, we are influenced in no small degree by the general opinion of mankind, who either fear or worship the spirits of the lower world. I make the most of this general belief: you can find no one who does not hold that wisdom is a Good, and *being wise* also. I shall not appeal to the populace, like a conquered gladiator; let us come to close quarters, using our own weapons.

When something affects a given object, is it outside the object which it affects, or is it inside the object it affects? If it is inside the object it affects, it is as corporeal as the object which it affects. For nothing can affect another object without touching it, and that which touches is corporeal. If it is outside, it withdraws after having affected the object. And withdrawal means motion. And that which possesses

341

est. Speras me dicturum non esse aliud cursum,
8 aliud currere, nec aliud calorem, aliud calere, nec
aliud lucem, aliud lucere ; concedo ista alia esse, sed
non sortis alterius. Si valetudo indifferens est, et
valere indifferens est [1] ; si forma indifferens est, et
formonsum esse. Si iustitia bonum est, et iustum
esse. Si turpitudo malum est, et turpem esse malum
est, tam mehercules quam, si lippitudo malum est,
lippire quoque malum est. Hoc ut scias, neutrum
esse sine altero potest. Qui sapit, sapiens est ; qui
sapiens est, sapit. Adeo non potest dubitari, an
quale illud sit, tale hoc sit, ut quibusdam utrumque
unum videatur atque idem.

9 Sed illud libenter quaesierim : cum omnia aut mala
sint aut bona aut indifferentia, sapere in quo numero
sit ? Bonum negant esse, malum utique non est ;
sequitur ut medium sit. Id autem medium atque
indifferens vocamus, quod tam malo contingere quam
bono possit, tamquam pecunia, forma, nobilitas. Hoc,
ut sapiat, contingere nisi bono non potest ; ergo
indifferens non est. Atqui ne malum quidem est,
quod contingere malo non potest ; ergo bonum est.
Quod nisi bonus non habet, bonum est. Sapere non
10 nisi bonus habet ; ergo bonum est. " Accidens est,"
inquit, " sapientiae." Hoc ergo, quod vocas sapere,

---

[1] *et valere indifferens est* add. Erasmus ; *bene valere
indifferens est* later MSS.

---

[a] *i.e.*, the external things ; see *Ep.* xciii. 7 and note,—
defined more specifically in § 9 below.

motion, is corporeal. You expect me, I suppose, to deny that "race" differs from "running," that "heat" differs from "being hot," that "light" differs from "giving light." I grant that these pairs vary, but hold that they are not in separate classes. If good health is an indifferent[a] quality, then so is *being in good health*; if beauty is an indifferent quality, then so is *being beautiful*. If justice is a Good, then so is *being just*. And if baseness is an evil, then it is an evil to be base—just as much as, if sore eyes are an evil, the state of having sore eyes is also an evil. Neither quality, you may be sure, can exist without the other. He who is wise is a man of wisdom; he who is a man of wisdom is wise. So true it is that we cannot doubt the quality of the one to equal the quality of the other, that they are both regarded by certain persons as one and the same.

Here is a question, however, which I should be glad to put: granted that all things are either good or bad or indifferent—in what class does *being wise* belong? People deny that it is a Good; and, as it obviously is not an evil, it must consequently be one of the "media." But we mean by the "medium," or the "indifferent" quality that which can fall to the lot of the bad no less than to the good—such things as money, beauty, or high social position. But the quality of *being wise* can fall to the lot of the good man alone; therefore *being wise* is not an indifferent quality. Nor is it an evil, either; because it cannot fall to the lot of the bad man; therefore, it is a Good. That which the good man alone can possess, is a Good; now *being wise* is the possession of the good man only; therefore it is a Good. The objector replies: "It is only an accessory of wisdom." Very well, then, I say, this quality which you call

343

utrum facit sapientiam an patitur? Utroque modo
corpus est. Nam et quod fit et quod facit, corpus
est; si corpus est, bonum est. Unum enim illi deerat, quominus bonum esset, quod incorporale erat.

11 Peripateticis placet nihil interesse inter sapientiam
et sapere, cum in utrolibet eorum et alterum sit.
Numquid enim quemquam existimas sapere nisi qui
sapientiam habet? Numquid quemquam, qui sapit,

12 non putas habere sapientiam? Dialectici veteres ista
distinguunt; ab illis divisio usque ad Stoicos venit.
Qualis sit haec, dicam. Aliud est ager, aliud agrum
habere, quidni? Cum habere agrum ad habentem,
non ad agrum pertineat. Sic aliud est sapientia,
aliud sapere. Puto concedes duo esse haec, id, quod
habetur, et eum, qui habet; habetur sapientia, habet
qui sapit. Sapientia est mens perfecta vel ad summum optimumque perducta. Ars enim vitae est.
Sapere quid est? Non possum dicere " mens perfecta," sed id quod contingit perfectam mentem
habenti; ita alterum est mens bona, alterum quasi
habere mentem bonam.

13 " Sunt," inquit, " naturae corporum, tamquam hic
homo est, hic equus. Has deinde sequuntur motus
animorum enuntiativi corporum. Hi habent pro-

being wise—does it actively produce wisdom, or is it a passive concomitant of wisdom? It is corporeal in either case. For that which is acted upon and that which acts, are alike corporeal; and, if corporeal, each is a Good. The only quality which could prevent it from being a Good, would be incorporeality.

The Peripatetics believe that there is no distinction between *wisdom* and *being wise*, since either of these implies the other also. Now do you suppose that any man can *be wise* except one who possesses wisdom? Or that anyone who *is wise* does not possess wisdom? The old masters of dialectic, however, distinguish between these two conceptions; and from them the classification has come right down to the Stoics. What sort of a classification this is, I shall explain: A field is one thing, and the possession of the field another thing; of course, because "possessing the field" refers to the possessor rather than to the field itself. Similarly, wisdom is one thing and *being wise* another. You will grant, I suppose, that these two are separate ideas—the possessed and the possessor: wisdom being that which one possesses, and he who *is wise* its possessor. Now wisdom is Mind perfected and developed to the highest and best degree. For it is the art of life. And what is *being wise*? I cannot call it "Mind Perfected," but rather that which falls to the lot of him who possesses a "mind perfected"; thus a good mind is one thing, and the so-called possession of a good mind another.

"There are," it is said, "certain natural classes of bodies; we say: 'This is a man,' 'this is a horse.' Then there attend on the bodily natures certain movements of the mind which declare something about the body. And these have a certain essential quality

345

prium quiddam et a corporibus seductum, tamquam
video Catonem ambulantem. Hoc sensus ostendit,
animus credidit. Corpus est, quod video, cui et
oculos intendi et animum. Dico deinde : Cato ambulat. Non corpus," inquit, " est, quod nunc loquor,
sed enuntiativum quiddam de corpore, quod alii
effatum vocant, alii enuntiatum, alii dictum. Sic cum
dicimus sapientiam, corporale quiddam intellegimus ;
cum dicimus " sapit," de corpore loquimur. Plurimum autem interest, utrum illum dicas an de illo."

14 Putemus in praesentia ista duo esse,—nondum
enim, quid mihi videatur, pronuntio,—quid prohibet,
quominus aliud quidem sit,[1] sed nihilominus bonum ?
Dicebam [2] paulo ante aliud esse agrum, aliud habere
agrum. Quidni ? In alia enim natura est qui habet,
in alia quod habetur. Illa terra est, hic homo est.
At in hoc, de quo agitur, eiusdem naturae sunt
15 utraque, et qui habet sapientiam, et ipsa. Praeterea
illic aliud est, quod habetur, alius, qui habet ; hic in
eodem est et quod habetur et qui habet. Ager iure
possidetur, sapientia natura. Ille abalienari potest
et alteri tradi, haec non discedit a domino. Non est
itaque quod compares inter se dissimilia.

Coeperam dicere posse ista duo esse et tamen
utraque bona, tamquam sapientia et sapiens duo

[1] *sit* om. BA.
[2] *dicebam* Hermes ; *dicebas* BA.
346

which is sundered from body ; for example : ' I see Cato walking.' The senses indicate this, and the mind believes it. What I see, is *body*, and upon this I concentrate my eyes and my mind. Again, I say : ' Cato walks.' What I say," they continue, " is not body ; it is a certain declarative fact concerning body—called variously an ' utterance,' a ' declaration,' a ' statement.' Thus, when we say ' wisdom,' we mean something *pertaining to* body ; when we say ' *he is wise*,' we are speaking *concerning* body. And it makes considerable difference whether you mention the person directly, or speak concerning the person."

Supposing for the present that these are two separate conceptions (for I am not yet prepared to give my own opinion) ; what prevents the existence of still a third—which is none the less a Good ? I remarked a little while ago that a " field " was one thing, and the " possession of a field " another ; of course, for possessor and possessed are of different natures ; the latter is the land, and the former is the man who owns the land. But with regard to the point now under discussion, both are of the same nature—the possessor of wisdom, and wisdom itself. Besides, in the one case that which is possessed is one thing, and he who possesses it is another ; but in this case the possessed and the possessor come under the same category. The field is owned by virtue of law, wisdom by virtue of nature. The field can change hands and go into the ownership of another ; but wisdom never departs from its owner. Accordingly, there is no reason why you should try to compare things that are so unlike one another.

I had started to say that these can be two separate conceptions, and yet that both can be Goods—for instance, wisdom and the wise man being

sunt et utrumque bonum esse concedis. Quomodo nihil obstat, quominus et sapientia bonum sit et habens sapientiam, sic nihil obstat, quominus et sapientia bonum sit et habere sapientiam, id est 16 sapere. Ego in hoc volo sapiens esse, ut sapiam. Quid ergo ? Non est id bonum, sine quo nec illud bonum est ? Vos certe dicitis sapientiam, si sine usu detur, accipiendam non esse. Quid est usus sapientiae ? Sapere ; hoc est in illa pretiosissimum, quo detracto supervacua fit. Si tormenta mala sunt, torqueri malum est, adeo quidem, ut illa non sint mala, si quod sequitur detraxeris. Sapientia habitus perfectae mentis est, sapere usus perfectae mentis. Quomodo potest usus eius bonum non esse, quae 17 sine usu bonum non [1] est ? Interrogo te, an sapientia expetenda sit ; fateris. Interrogo, an usus sapientiae expetendus sit ; fateris ; negas enim te illam recepturum, si uti ea prohibearis. Quod expetendum est, bonum est. Sapere sapientiae usus est, quomodo eloquentiae eloqui, quomodo oculorum videre. Ergo sapere sapientiae usus est, usus autem sapientiae expetendus est ; sapere ergo expetendum est. Si expetendum est, bonum est.

18   Olim ipse me damno, qui illos imitor, dum accuso,

[1] *non* later MSS. ; om. BA.

two separate things and yet granted by you to be equally good. And just as there is no objection to regarding both wisdom and the possessor of wisdom as Goods, so there is no objection to regarding as a good both wisdom and the possession of wisdom, —in other words, *being wise*. For I only wish to be a wise man in order to *be wise*. And what then? Is not that thing a Good without the possession of which a certain other thing cannot be a Good? You surely admit that wisdom, if given without the right to be used, is not to be welcomed! And wherein consists the use of wisdom? In *being wise*; that is its most valuable attribute; if you withdraw this, wisdom becomes superfluous. If processes of torture are evil, then being tortured is an evil— with this reservation, indeed, that if you take away the consequences, the former are not evil. Wisdom is a condition of "mind perfected," and *being wise* is the employment of this "mind perfected." How can the employment of that thing not be a Good, which without employment is not a Good? If I ask you whether wisdom is to be desired, you admit that it is. If I ask you whether the employment of wisdom is to be desired, you also admit the fact; for you say that you will not receive wisdom if you are not allowed to employ it. Now that which is to be desired is a Good. *Being wise* is the employment of wisdom, just as it is of eloquence to make a speech, or of the eyes to see things. Therefore, *being wise* is the employment of wisdom, and the employment of wisdom is to be desired. Therefore *being wise* is a thing to be desired; and if it is a thing to be desired, it is a Good.

Lo, these many years I have been condemning myself for imitating these men at the very time

et verba apertae rei impendo. Cui enim dubium
potest esse, quin si aestus malum est, et aestuare
malum sit ? Si algor malum est, malum sit algere ?
Si vita bonum est, et vivere bonum sit ? Omnia ista
circa sapientiam, non in ipsa sunt. At nobis in ipsa
19 commorandum est. Etiam si quid evagari libet,
amplos habet illa spatiososque[1] secessus : de deorum
natura quaeramus, de siderum alimento, de his tam
variis stellarum discursibus, an ad illarum motus
nostra moveantur, an[2] corporibus omnium animisque
illinc impetus veniat, an et haec, quae fortuita
dicuntur, certa lege constricta sint nihilque in hoc
mundo repentinum aut expers ordinis volutetur. Ista
iam a formatione morum recesserunt, sed levant
animum et ad ipsarum, quas tractat, rerum magnitudinem attollunt ; haec vero, de quibus paulo ante
dicebam, minuunt et deprimunt nec, ut putatis,
20 exacuunt, sed extenuant. Obsecro vos, tam necessariam curam maioribus melioribusque debitam in re
nescio an falsa, certe inutili terimus ? Quid mihi
profuturum est scire, an aliud sit sapientia, aliud
sapere ? Quid mihi profuturum est scire illud bonum
esse, hoc non esse[3] ? Temere me geram, subibo[4]
huius voti aleam : tibi sapientia, mihi sapere contingat ; pares erimus.

[1] *spatiososque* later MSS. ; *speciososque* BA.
[2] *an* later MSS. ; *in* BA.
[3] *hoc non esse* add. Muretus.
[4] *subibo* Erasmus ; *subito* BA.

---

[a] Presumably an allusion to the syllogistic enthusiasts
rather than to Lucilius and his like.

when I am arraigning them, and of wasting words on a subject that is perfectly clear. For who can doubt that, if heat is an evil, it is also an evil to be hot? Or that, if cold is an evil, it is an evil to be cold? Or that, if life is a Good, so is *being alive*? All such matters are on the outskirts of wisdom, not in wisdom itself. But our abiding-place should be in wisdom itself. Even though one takes a fancy to roam, wisdom has large and spacious retreats: we may investigate the nature of the gods, the fuel which feeds the constellations, or all the varied courses of the stars; we may speculate whether our affairs move in harmony with those of the stars, whether the impulse to motion comes from thence into the minds and bodies of all, and whether even these events which we call fortuitous are fettered by strict laws and nothing in this universe is unforeseen or unregulated in its revolutions. Such topics have nowadays been withdrawn from instruction in morals, but they uplift the mind and raise it to the dimensions of the subject which it discusses; the matters, however, of which I was speaking a while ago, wear away and wear down the mind, not (as you and yours [a] maintain) whetting, but weakening it. And I ask you, are we to fritter away that necessary study which we owe to greater and better themes, in discussing a matter which may perhaps be wrong and is certainly of no avail? How will it profit me to know whether wisdom is one thing, and *being wise* another? How will it profit me to know that the one is, and the other is not, a Good? Suppose I take a chance, and gamble on this prayer: "Wisdom for you, and *being wise* for me!" We shall come out even.

21 Potius id age, ut mihi viam monstres, qua ad ista
perveniam. Dic, quid vitare debeam, quid adpetere,
quibus animum labantem studiis firmem, quemadmodum quae me ex transverso feriunt aguntque,
procul a me repellam, quomodo par esse tot malis
possim, quomodo istas calamitates removeam, quae
ad me inruperunt, quomodo illas, ad quas ego inrupi.
Doce, quomodo feram aerumnam sine gemitu meo,
felicitatem sine alieno, quomodo ultimum ac necessarium non expectem, sed ipsemet,[1] cum visum erit,

22 profugiam. Nihil mihi videtur turpius quam optare
mortem. Nam si vis vivere, quid optas mori ? Sive
non vis, quid deos rogas, quod tibi nascenti dederunt ?
Nam ut quandoque moriaris, etiam invito positum
est, ut cum voles, in tua manu est. Alterum tibi
necesse est, alterum licet.

23 Turpissimum his diebus principium diserti mehercules viri legi : " Ita,"[2] inquit, " quamprimum
moriar." Homo demens, optas rem tuam. " Ita
quamprimum moriar." Fortasse inter has voces
senex factus es. Alioqui quid in mora est ? Nemo
te tenet ; evade, qua visum est. Elige quamlibet
rerum naturae partem, quam tibi praebere exitum
iubeas. Haec nempe sunt elementa,[3] quibus hic
mundus administratur, aqua, terra, spiritus. Omnia

24 ista tam causae vivendi sunt quam viae mortis. " Ita

---

[1] *ipsemet* Pincianus ; *ipsemecum* BA.
[2] *ita* Pincianus ; *itaque* MSS.
[3] *elementa* later MSS. ; *et elementa* BA.

---

[a] *i.e., wisdom* or *being wise.*

EPISTLE CXVII.

Try rather to show me the way by which I may attain those ends.ᵃ Tell me what to avoid, what to seek, by what studies to strengthen my tottering mind, how I may rebuff the waves that strike me abeam and drive me from my course, by what means I may be able to cope with all my evils, and by what means I can be rid of the calamities that have plunged in upon me and those into which I myself have plunged. Teach me how to bear the burden of sorrow without a groan on my part, and how to bear prosperity without making others groan ; also, how to avoid waiting for the ultimate and inevitable end, and to beat a retreat of my own free will, when it seems proper to me to do so. I think nothing is baser than to pray for death. For if you wish to live, why do you pray for death ? And if you do not wish to live, why do you ask the gods for that which they gave you at birth ? For even as, against your will, it has been settled that you must die some day, so the time when you shall wish to die is in your own hands. The one fact is to you a necessity, the other a privilege.

I read lately a most disgraceful doctrine, uttered (more shame to him !) by a learned gentleman : " So may I die as soon as possible ! " Fool, thou art praying for something that is already thine own ! " So may I die as soon as possible ! " Perhaps thou didst grow old while uttering these very words ! At any rate, what is there to hinder ? No one detains thee ; escape by whatsoever way thou wilt ! Select any portion of Nature, and bid it provide thee with a means of departure ! These, namely, are the elements, by which the world's work is carried on— water, earth, air. All these are no more the causes of life than they are the ways of death. " So may

353

quamprimum moriar " : " quamprimum " istud quid
esse vis ? Quem illi diem ponis ? Citius fieri
quam optas, potest. Inbecillae mentis ista sunt
verba et hac detestatione misericordiam captantis ;
non vult mori qui optat. Deos vitam et salutem
roga ; si mori placuit, hic mortis est fructus, optare
desinere.

25 Haec, mi Lucili, tractemus, his formemus animum.
Hoc est sapientia, hoc est sapere, non disputatiunculis
inanibus subtilitatem vanissimam agitare. Tot quaestiones fortuna tibi posuit, nondum illas solvisti ; iam
cavillaris ? Quam stultum est, cum signum pugnae
acceperis, ventilare. Remove ista lusoria arma ; de-
cretoriis opus est. Dic, qua ratione nulla animum
tristitia, nulla formido perturbet, qua ratione hoc
secretarum cupiditatium pondus effundam. Agatur
26 aliquid. " Sapientia bonum est, sapere non est
bonum "; sic fit, ut[1] negemur sapere, ut hoc totum
studium derideatur tamquam operatum supervacuis.
Quid, si scires etiam illud quaeri, an bonum sit futura
sapientia[2] ? Quid enim dubi est, oro te, an nec
messem futuram iam sentiant horrea nec futuram
adulescentiam pueritia viribus aut ullo robore intellegat ? Aegro interim nil ventura sanitas prodest,

---

[1] *ut* add. Schweighaeuser.
[2] *sit futura sapientia* Pinc. ; *sit puta sapientia* BA.

I die as soon as possible!" And what is thy wish with regard to this "as soon as possible"? What day dost thou set for the event? It may be sooner than thy prayer requests. Words like this come from a weak mind, from one that courts pity by such cursing; he who prays for death does not wish to die. Ask the gods for life and health; if thou art resolved to die, death's reward is to have done with prayers.

It is with such problems as these, my dear Lucilius, that we should deal, by such problems that we should mould our minds. This is wisdom, this is what *being wise* means—not to bandy empty subtleties in idle and petty discussions. Fortune has set before you so many problems—which you have not yet solved—and are you still splitting hairs? How foolish it is to practise strokes after you have heard the signal for the fight! Away with all these dummy-weapons; you need armour for a fight to the finish. Tell me by what means sadness and fear may be kept from disturbing my soul, by what means I may shift off this burden of hidden cravings. Do something! "Wisdom is a Good, but *being wise* is not a Good;" such talk results for us in the judgment that we are not wise, and in making a laughing-stock of this whole field of study—on the ground that it wastes its effort on useless things. Suppose you knew that this question was also debated: whether future wisdom is a Good? For, I beseech you, how could one doubt whether barns do not feel the weight of the harvest that is to come, and that boyhood does not have premonitions of approaching young manhood by any brawn and power? The sick person, in the intervening period, is not helped by the health that is to come, any more

355

non magis quam currentem luctantemque post multos
27 secuturum menses otium reficit. Quis nescit hoc
ipso non esse bonum id, quod futurum est, quia
futurum est ? Nam quod bonum est, utique prodest.
Nisi praesentia prodesse non possunt ; si non prodest,
bonum non est ; si prodest, iam est. Futurus sum
sapiens ; hoc bonum erit, cum fuero, interim non
est. Prius aliquid esse debet, deinde quale esse.
28 Quomodo, oro te, quod adhuc nihil est, iam bonum
est ? Quomodo autem tibi magis vis probari non
esse aliquid, quam si dixero : futurum est ? Nondum
enim venisse apparet quod venit. Ver secuturum
est : scio nunc hiemem esse. Aestas secutura est :
scio aestatem non esse. Maximum argumentum
29 habeo nondum praesentis futurum esse. Sapiam,
spero, sed interim non sapio. Si illud bonum ha-
berem, iam hoc carerem malo. Futurum est, ut
sapiam ; ex hoc licet nondum sapere me intellegas.
Non possum simul et in illo bono et in hoc malo
esse ; duo ista non coeunt nec apud eundem sunt
una malum et bonum.
30   Transcurramus sollertissimas nugas et ad illa, quae
nobis aliquam opem sunt latura, properemus. Nemo,
qui obstetricem parturienti filiae sollicitus accersit,
edictum et ludorum ordinem perlegit. Nemo, qui ad
incendium domus suae currit, tabulam latrun-

---

    a *Cf. Ep.* xlviii. 10 and notes.
    b *Cf. Ep.* cvi. 11 and note.

than a runner or a wrestler is refreshed by the
period of repose that will follow many months later.
Who does not know that what is yet to be is not a
Good, for the very reason that it is yet to be? For
that which is good is necessarily helpful. And unless
things are in the present, they cannot be helpful; and
if a thing is not helpful, it is not a Good; if helpful,
it is already. I shall be a wise man some day;
and this Good will be mine when I shall be a wise
man, but in the meantime it is non-existent. A
thing must exist first, then may be of a certain
kind. How, I ask you, can that which is still
nothing be already a Good? And in what better
way do you wish it to be proved to you that
a certain thing is not, than to say: "It is yet
to be"? For it is clear that something which is on
the way has not yet arrived. "Spring will follow":
I know that winter is here now. "Summer will
follow:" I know that it is not summer. The best
proof to my mind that a thing is not yet present
is that it is yet to be. I hope some day to be wise,
but meanwhile I am not wise. For if I possessed that
Good, I should now be free from this Evil. Some
day I shall be wise; from this very fact you may
understand that I am not yet wise. I cannot at the
same time live in that state of Good and in this state
of Evil; the two ideas do not harmonize, nor do Evil
and Good exist together in the same person.

Let us rush past all this clever nonsense, and
hurry on to that which will bring us real assistance.
No man who is anxiously running after a midwife
for his daughter in her birth-pangs will stop to read
the praetor's edict [a] or the order of events at the
games. No one who is speeding to save his burning
house will scan a checker-board [b] to speculate how

culariam prospicit, ut sciat, quomodo alligatus
31 exeat calculus. At mehercule omnia tibi undique
nuntiantur, et incendium domus et periculum
liberorum et obsidio patriae et bonorum direptio;
adice isto naufragia motusque terrarum et quicquid
aliud timeri potest; inter ista districtus rebus nihil
aliud quam animum oblectantibus vacas? Quid
inter sapientiam et sapere intersit, inquiris? Nodos
nectis ac solvis tanta mole impendente capiti tuo?
32 Non tam benignum ac liberale tempus natura nobis
dedit, ut aliquid ex illo vacet perdere. Et vide,
quam multa etiam diligentissimis pereant: aliud
valetudo sua cuique abstulit, aliud suorum; aliud
necessaria negotia, aliud publica occupaverunt;
vitam nobiscum dividit somnus.

Ex[1] hoc tempore tam angusto et rapido et nos
auferente quid iuvat maiorem partem mittere in
33 vanum? Adice nunc, quod adsuescit animus de-
lectare se potius quam sanare et philosophiam
oblectamentum facere, cum remedium sit. Inter
sapientiam et sapere quid intersit nescio; scio mea
non interesse, sciam ista an nesciam. Dic mihi:
cum quid inter sapientiam et sapere intersit didicero,
sapiam[2]?

Cur ergo potius inter vocabula me sapientiae
detines quam inter opera? Fac me fortiorem, fac
securiorem, fac fortunae parem, fac superiorem.
Possum autem superior esse, si derexero eo[3] omne,
quod disco. VALE.

[1] *ex* Pinc.; *et* BA.
[2] *sapiam* later MSS.; *sapientiam* BA.
[3] *eo* added by Haase.

the imprisoned piece can be freed. But good heavens !—in your case all sorts of news are announced on all sides—your house afire, your children in danger, your country in a state of siege, your property plundered. Add to this shipwreck, earthquakes, and all other objects of dread ; harassed amid these troubles, are you taking time for matters which serve merely for mental entertainment ? Do you ask what difference there is between wisdom and *being wise* ? Do you tie and untie knots while such a ruin is hanging over your head ? Nature has not given us such a generous and free-handed space of time that we can have the leisure to waste any of it. Mark also how much is lost even when men are very careful : people are robbed of one thing by ill-health and of another thing by illness in the family ; at one time private, at another public, business absorbs the attention ; and all the while sleep shares our lives with us.

Out of this time, so short and swift, that carries us away in its flight, of what avail is it to spend the greater part on useless things ? Besides, our minds are accustomed to entertain rather than to cure themselves, to make an aesthetic pleasure out of philosophy, when philosophy should really be a remedy. What the distinction is between wisdom and *being wise* I do not know ; but I do know that it makes no difference to me whether I know such matters or am ignorant of them. Tell me : when I have found out the difference between wisdom and *being wise*, shall I be wise ?

Why then do you occupy me with the words rather than with the works of wisdom ? Make me braver, make me calmer, make me the equal of Fortune, make me her superior. And I can be her superior, if I apply to this end everything that I learn. Farewell.

CXVIII.

SENECA LVCILIO SVO SALVTEM

1 Exigis a me frequentiores epistulas. Rationes conferamus ; solvendo non eris. Convenerat quidem, ut tua priora essent, tu scriberes, ego rescriberem. Sed non ero difficilis ; bene credi tibi scio. Itaque in anticessum dabo nec faciam, quod Cicero, vir disertissimus, facere Atticum iubet, ut etiam " si rem nullam habebit, quod in buccam venerit scribat."

2 Numquam potest deesse, quod scribam, ut omnia illa, quae Ciceronis implent epistulas, transeam : quis candidatus laboret ; quis alienis, quis suis viribus pugnet ; quis consulatum fiducia Caesaris, quis Pompei, quis arcae petat ; quam durus sit faenerator Caecilius, a quo minoris centesimis propinqui nummum movere non possint.

Sua satius est mala quam aliena tractare, se excutere et videre, quam multarum rerum candidatus
3 sit, et non suffragari. Hoc est, mi Lucili, egregium, hoc securum ac liberum, nihil petere et tota fortunae comitia transire. Quam putas esse iucundum tribubus vocatis, cum candidati in templis suis pendeant et alius nummos pronuntiet, alius per sequestrem agat, alius eorum manus osculis conterat, quibus designatus contingendam manum negaturus est,

---

^a *i.e., solvendo aeri alieno,* "in a position to pay one's debts."

^b *Ad Att.* i. 12. 4.

^c *Ad Att.* i. 12. 1 : "Even his relatives can't screw a penny out of Caecilius at less than 12 per cent " (Winstedt).

CXVIII. ON THE VANITY OF PLACE-SEEKING

You have been demanding more frequent letters from me. But if we compare the accounts, you will not be on the credit side.[a] We had indeed made the agreement that your part came first, that you should write the first letters, and that I should answer. However, I shall not be disagreeable ; I know that it is safe to trust you, so I shall pay in advance, and yet not do as the eloquent Cicero bids Atticus do :[b] " Even if you have nothing to say, write whatever enters your head." For there will always be something for me to write about, even omitting all the kinds of news with which Cicero fills his correspondence : what candidate is in difficulties, who is striving on borrowed resources and who on his own ; who is a candidate for the consulship relying on Caesar, or on Pompey, or on his own strong-box ; what a merciless usurer is Caecilius,[c] out of whom his friends cannot screw a penny for less than one per cent each month.

But it is preferable to deal with one's own ills, rather than with another's—to sift oneself and see for how many vain things one is a candidate, and cast a vote for none of them. This, my dear Lucilius, is a noble thing, this brings peace and freedom—to canvass for nothing, and to pass by all the elections of Fortune. How can you call it enjoyable, when the tribes are called together and the candidates are making offerings in their favourite temples—some of them promising money gifts and others doing business by means of an agent, or wearing down their hands with the kisses of those to whom they will refuse the least finger-touch after being elected

361

omnes attoniti vocem praeconis exspectent, stare
otiosum et spectare illas nundinas nec ementem
4 quicquam nec vendentem ?   Quanto hic maiore gaudio fruitur, qui non praetoria aut consularia comitia
securus intuetur, sed magna illa, in quibus alii
honores anniversarios petunt, alii perpetuas potes-
tates, alii bellorum eventus prosperos triumphosque,
alii divitias, alii matrimonia ac liberos, alii salutem
suam suorumque !   Quanti animi res est solum nihil
petere, nulli supplicare, et dicere : " Nihil mihi
tecum, fortuna.   Non facio mei tibi copiam.   Scio
apud te Catones repelli, Vatinios fieri.   Nihil rogo."
Hoc est privatam facere fortunam.

5   Licet ergo haec in vicem scribere et hanc semper
integram egerere materiam circumspicientibus tot
milia hominum inquieta, qui ut aliquid pestiferi
consequantur, per mala nituntur in malum petuntque
6 mox fugienda aut etiam fastidienda.   Cui enim
adsecuto satis fuit, quod optanti nimium videbatur ?
Non est, ut existimant homines, avida felicitas, sed
pusilla ; itaque neminem satiat.   Tu ista credis excelsa, quia longe ab illis iaces ; ei vero, qui ad illa
pervenit, humilia sunt.   Mentior, nisi adhuc quaerit
escendere ; istud, quod tu summum putas, gradus
7 est.   Omnes autem male habet ignorantia veri ;

---

a   For the character of Vatinius see *Ep.* xciv. 25 note ; for
a similar comparison of V. with Cato see *Ep.* cxx. 19.

—when all are excitedly awaiting the announcement of the herald, do you call it enjoyable, I say, to stand idle and look on at this Vanity Fair without either buying or selling? How much greater joy does one feel who looks without concern, not merely upon the election of a praetor or of a consul, but upon that great struggle in which some are seeking yearly honours, and others permanent power, and others the triumph and the prosperous outcome of war, and others riches, or marriage and offspring, or the welfare of themselves and their relatives! What a great-souled action it is to be the only person who is canvassing for nothing, offering prayers to no man, and saying: "Fortune, I have nothing to do with you. I am not at your service. I know that men like Cato are spurned by you, and men like Vatinius made by you.[a] I ask no favours." This is the way to reduce Fortune to the ranks.

These, then, are the things about which we may write in turn, and this is the ever fresh material which we may dig out as we scan the restless multitudes of men, who, in order to attain something ruinous, struggle on through evil to evil, and seek that which they must presently shun or even find surfeiting. For who was ever satisfied, after attainment, with that which loomed up large as he prayed for it? Happiness is not, as men think, a greedy thing; it is a lowly thing; for that reason it never gluts a man's desire. You deem lofty the objects you seek, because you are on a low level and hence far away from them; but they are mean in the sight of him who has reached them. And I am very much mistaken if he does not desire to climb still higher; that which you regard as the top is merely a rung on the ladder. Now all men suffer

tamquam ad bona feruntur decepti rumoribus, deinde mala esse aut inania aut minora [1] quam speraverint, adepti ac multa passi vident. Maiorque pars miratur ex intervallo fallentia, et vulgo bona pro magnis sunt.

8 Hoc ne nobis quoque eveniat, quaeramus, quid sit bonum. Varia eius interpretatio fuit, alius illud aliter expressit. Quidam ita finiunt : " bonum est quod invitat animos, quod ad se vocat." Huic statim opponitur : quid, si invitat quidem, sed in perniciem ? Scis, quam multa mala blanda sint. Verum et veri simile inter se differunt ; ita quod bonum est, vero iungitur ; non est enim bonum nisi verum est. At quod invitat ad se et adlicefacit,[2] veri simile est ;
9 subripit, sollicitat, adtrahit. Quidam ita finierunt : " bonum est, quod petitionem sui movet, vel quod impetum animi tendentis ad se movet." Et huic idem opponitur ; multa enim impetum animi movent, quae petantur petentium malo. Melius illi, qui ita finierunt : " bonum est, quod ad se impetum animi secundum naturam movet et ita demum petendum est, cum coepit esse expetendum." Iam et honestum est ; hoc enim est perfecte petendum.
10 Locus ipse me admonet, ut quid intersit inter bonum honestumque dicam. Aliquid inter se mix-

---

[1] *minora* later MSS. ; *miro* BA.
[2] *adlicefacit* Gronovius ; *adlicer* B ; *adicer* A.

---

[a] Discussed in *Ep.* lxxi. 4 f., lxxiv. 30, lxxvi. 16 ff., and especially lxxxvii. 25 : *nam idem est honestum et bonum.* The Academic school tended to draw more of a distinction than the Stoic, as in *Ep.* lxxxv. 17 f.

from ignorance of the truth; deceived by common report, they make for these ends as if they were good, and then, after having won their wish, and suffered much, they find them evil, or empty, or less important than they had expected. Most men admire that which deceives them at a distance, and by the crowd good things are supposed to be big things.

Now, lest this happen also in our own case, let us ask what is the Good. It has been explained in various ways; different men have described it in different ways. Some define it in this way: " That which attracts and calls the spirit to itself is a Good." But the objection at once comes up— what if it does attract, but straight to ruin? You know how seductive many evils are. That which is true differs from that which looks like the truth; hence the Good is connected with the true, for it is not good unless it is also true. But that which attracts and allures, is only *like* the truth; it steals your attention, demands your interest, and draws you to itself. Therefore, some have given this definition : " That is good which inspires desire for itself, or rouses towards itself the impulse of a struggling soul." There is the same objection to this idea; for many things rouse the soul's impulses, and yet the search for them is harmful to the seeker. The following definition is better: " That is good which rouses the soul's impulse towards itself in accordance with nature, and is worth seeking only when it begins to be thoroughly worth seeking." It is by this time an honourable thing; for that is a thing completely worth seeking.

The present topic suggests that I state the difference between the Good and the honourable.[a] Now they have a certain quality which blends with

tum habent et inseparabile : nec potest bonum esse,
nisi cui aliquid honesti inest, et honestum utique
bonum est. Quid ergo inter duo interest ? Honestum [1] est perfectum bonum, quo beata vita completur,
11 cuius contactu alia quoque bona fiunt. Quod dico,
talest : sunt quaedam neque bona neque mala,
tamquam militia, legatio, iurisdictio. Haec cum
honeste administrata sunt, bona esse incipiunt et ex
dubio in bonum transeunt. Bonum societate honesti
fit, honestum per se bonum est. Bonum ex honesto
fluit, honestum ex se est. Quod bonum est, malum
esse potuit ; quod honestum est, nisi bonum esse
non potuit.
12 Hanc quidam finitionem reddiderunt : " bonum
est, quod secundum naturam est." Attende, quid
dicam : quod bonum, est secundum naturam ; non
protinus quod secundum naturam est, etiam bonum
est. Multa naturae quidem consentiunt, sed tam
pusilla sunt, ut non conveniat illis boni nomen. Levia
enim sunt, contemnenda. Nullum est minimum
contemnendum bonum ; nam quamdiu exiguum est,
bonum non est ; cum bonum esse coepit, non est
exiguum. Unde adcognoscitur bonum ? Si perfecte
secundum naturam est.
13 " Fateris," inquis, " quod bonum est, secundum
naturam esse ; haec eius proprietas est. Fateris et
alia secundum naturam quidem esse, sed bona non
esse. Quomodo ergo illud bonum est, cum haec non

---

[1] *utique b. e. q. e. i. d. i. honestum* added by later MSS.;
om. BA.

both and is inseparable from either : nothing can be good unless it contains an element of the honourable, and the honourable is necessarily good. What, then, is the difference between these two qualities? The honourable is the perfect Good, and the happy life is fulfilled thereby ; through its influence other things also are rendered good. I mean something like this : there are certain things which are neither good nor bad—as military or diplomatic service, or the pronouncing of legal decisions. When such pursuits have been honourably conducted, they begin to be good, and they change over from the " indifferent " class into the Good. The Good results from partnership with the honourable, but the honourable is good in itself. The Good springs from the honourable, but the latter from itself. What is good might have been bad ; what is honourable could never have been anything but good.

Some have defined as follows : " That is good which is according to nature." Now attend to my own statement : that which is good is according to nature, but that which is according to nature does not also become immediately good ; for many things harmonize with nature, but are so petty that it is not suitable to call them good. For they are unimportant and deserve to be despised. But there is no such thing as a very small and despicable good, for, as long as it is scanty, it is not good, and when it begins to be good, it ceases to be scanty. How, then, can the Good be recognized? Only if it is completely according to nature.

People say : " You admit that that which is good is according to nature ; for this is its peculiar quality. You admit, too, that there are other things according to nature, which, however, are not good. How then

367

sint ? Quomodo ad aliam proprietatem pervenit,
cum utrique praecipuum illud commune sit, secundum
14 naturam esse ? " Ipsa scilicet magnitudine. Nec
hoc novum est, quaedam crescendo mutari. Infans
fuit ; factus est pubes, alia eius proprietas fit. Ille
enim inrationalis est, hic rationalis. Quaedam incremento non tantum in maius exeunt, sed in aliud.
15 " Non fit," inquit, " aliud quod maius fit. Utrum
lagonam an dolium impleas vino, nihil refert ; in
utroque proprietas vini est. Et exiguum mellis pondus et magnum [1] sapore non differt." Diversa ponis
exempla ; in istis enim eadem qualitas [2] est ; quam-
16 vis augeantur, manet. Quaedam amplificata in suo
genere et in sua proprietate perdurant.

Quaedam post multa incrementa ultima demum
vertit adiectio et novam illis aliamque quam in qua
fuerunt, condicionem inprimit. Unus lapis facit
fornicem, ille, qui latera inclinata cuneavit [3] et inter-
ventu suo vinxit. Summa adiectio quare plurimum
facit vel exigua ? Quia non auget, sed implet.
17 Quaedam processu priorem exuunt formam et in
novam transeunt. Ubi aliquid animus diu protulit
et magnitudinem eius sequendo lassatus est, infinitum
coepit vocari. Quod longe aliud factum est quam

---

[1] *et magnum* later MSS. ; *ex magno* BA.
[2] *qualitas* later MSS. ; *aequalitas* BA.
[3] *cuneavit* later MSS. ; *cenavit* BA.

---

[a] This argument (that complete virtue is a sort of trans-
forming climax of life) is not to be confused with the theory
of *accessio* (a term used also in Roman law), or " addition " ;
for virtue does not permit of *accessio*, or the addition of any
external advantage. See *Ep.* lxvi. 9 *quid accedere perfecto
potest ?*

can the former be good, and the latter not ? How can there be an alteration in the peculiar quality of a thing, when each has, in common with the other, the special attribute of being in accord with nature ? " Surely because of its magnitude. It is no new idea that certain objects change as they grow. A person, once a child, becomes a youth ; his peculiar quality is transformed ; for the child could not reason, but the youth possesses reason. Certain things not only grow in size as they develop, but grow into something else. Some reply : " But that which becomes greater does not necessarily become different. It matters not at all whether you pour wine into a flask or into a vat ; the wine keeps its peculiar quality in both vessels. Small and large quantities of honey are not distinct in taste." But these are different cases which you mention ; for wine and honey have a uniform quality ; no matter how much the quantity is enlarged, the quality is the same. For some things endure according to their kind and their peculiar qualities, even when they are enlarged.

There are others, however, which, after many increments, are altered by the last addition ; there is stamped upon them a new character, different from that of yore. One stone makes an archway—the stone which wedges the leaning sides and holds the arch together by its position in the middle. And why does the last addition, although very slight, make a great deal of difference ? Because it does not increase ; it fills up. Some things, through development, put off their former shape and are altered into a new figure.[a] When the mind has for a long time developed some idea, and in the attempt to grasp its magnitude has become weary, that thing begins to be called " infinite." And

369

fuit, cum magnum videretur, sed finitum. Eodem
modo aliquid difficulter secari cogitavimus ; novissime
crescente hac difficultate insecabile inventum est.
Sic ab eo, quod vix et aegre movebatur, processimus
ad inmobile. Eadem ratione aliquid secundum naturam fuit ; hoc in aliam proprietatem magnitudo
sua transtulit et bonum fecit. VALE.

CXIX.

SENECA LVCILIO SVO SALVTEM

1 Quotiens aliquid inveni, non expecto, donec dicas
"in commune." Ipse mihi dico. Quid sit, quod
invenerim quaeris ; sinum laxa, merum lucrum est.
Docebo, quomodo fieri dives celerrime possis. Quam
valde cupis audire ! nec inmerito ; ad maximas te
divitias conpendiaria ducam. Opus erit tamen tibi
creditore ; ut negotiari possis, aes alienum facias
oportet, sed nolo per intercessorem mutueris, nolo
2 proxenetae nomen tuum iactent. Paratum tibi
creditorem dabo Catonianum illum, a te mutuum
sumes. Quantulumcumque est, satis erit, si, quidquid deerit,[1] id a nobis petierimus. Nihil enim, mi
Lucili, interest, utrum non desideres an habeas.
Summa rei in utroque eadem est : non torqueberis.

----

[1] *deerit* later MSS.; *dederit* BA.

----

[a] Seneca here reverts to the money-metaphors of *Epp.*
i.–xxxiii.—*lucellum, munusculum, diurna mercedula*, etc.
[b] Frag. p. 79 Iordan.

then this has become something far different from what it was when it seemed great but finite. In the same way we have thought of something as difficult to divide; at the very end, as the task grows more and more hard, the thing is found to be "indivisible." Similarly, from that which could scarcely or with difficulty be moved we have advanced on and on—until we reach the "immovable." By the same reasoning a certain thing was according to nature; its greatness has altered it into some other peculiar quality and has rendered it a Good. Farewell.

CXIX. ON NATURE AS OUR BEST PROVIDER

Whenever I have made a discovery, I do not wait for you to cry "Shares!" I say it to myself in your behalf. If you wish to know what it is that I have found, open your pocket; it is clear profit.[a] What I shall teach you is the ability to become rich as speedily as possible. How keen you are to hear the news! And rightly; I shall lead you by a short cut to the greatest riches. It will be necessary, however, for you to find a loan; in order to be able to do business, you must contract a debt, although I do not wish you to arrange the loan through a middle-man, nor do I wish the brokers to be discussing your rating. I shall furnish you with a ready creditor, Cato's famous one, who says:[b] "Borrow from yourself!" No matter how small it is, it will be enough if we can only make up the deficit from our own resources. For, my dear Lucilius, it does not matter whether you crave nothing, or whether you possess something. The important principle in either case is the same—freedom from worry.

THE EPISTLES OF SENECA

Nec illud praecipio, ut aliquid naturae neges—
contumax est, non potest vinci, suum poscit—sed
ut quicquid naturam excedit, scias precarium esse,
3 non necessarium. Esurio ; edendum est. Utrum
hic panis sit plebeius an siligineus, ad naturam nihil
pertinet ; illa ventrem non delectari vult, sed
impleri. Sitio ; utrum haec aqua sit, quam ex
lacu proximo excepero, an ea, quam multa nive
clusero, ut rigore refrigeretur alieno, ad naturam
nihil pertinet. Illa hoc unum iubet, sitim extingui ;
utrum sit aureum poculum an crustallinum an
murreum an Tiburtinus calix an manus concava,
4 nihil refert. Finem omnium rerum specta, et supervacua dimittes. Fames me appellat ; ad proxima
quaeque porrigatur manus ; ipsa mihi commen-
5 davit quodcumque comprendero. Nihil contemnit
esuriens.

Quid sit ergo, quod me delectaverit quaeris ?
Videtur mihi egregie dictum : sapiens divitiarum
naturalium est quaesitor acerrimus. " Inani me," [1]
inquis, "lance muneras. Quid est istud ? Ego iam
paraveram fiscos. Circumspiciebam, in quod me
mare negotiaturus inmitterem, quod publicum
agitarem, quas arcesserem merces. Decipere est
istud, docere paupertatem, cum divitias promiseris."
Ita tu pauperem iudicas, cui nihil deest ? " Suo,"
inquis, " et patientiae suae beneficio, non fortunae."
Ideo ergo illum non iudicas divitem, quia divitiae

---

[1] *inani me* later MSS. ; *inanima* BA.

---

[a] *i.e.*, "something for one's spare time"; *cf. Ep.* liii. 8 note,
non est quod precario philosopheris.
[b] *i.e.*, of common earthenware.
[c] *i.e.*, had got my coffers ready for the promised wealth.

372

But I do not counsel you to deny anything to nature—for nature is insistent and cannot be overcome; she demands her due—but you should know that anything in excess of nature's wants is a mere " extra " [a] and is not necessary. If I am hungry, I must eat. Nature does not care whether the bread is the coarse kind or the finest wheat; she does not desire the stomach to be entertained, but to be filled. And if I am thirsty, Nature does not care whether I drink water from the nearest reservoir, or whether I freeze it artificially by sinking it in large quantities of snow. Nature orders only that the thirst be quenched; and it does not matter whether it be a golden, or crystal, or murrine goblet, or a cup from Tibur,[b] or the hollow hand. Look to the end, in all matters, and then you will cast away superfluous things. Hunger calls me; let me stretch forth my hand to that which is nearest; my very hunger has made attractive in my eyes whatever I can grasp. A starving man despises nothing.

Do you ask, then, what it is that has pleased me? It is this noble saying which I have discovered: " The wise man is the keenest seeker for the riches of nature." " What," you ask, " will you present me with an empty plate? What do you mean? I had already arranged my coffers; [c] I was already looking about to see some stretch of water on which I might embark for purposes of trade, some state revenues that I might handle, and some merchandise that I might acquire. That is deceit—showing me poverty after promising me riches." But, friend, do you regard a man as poor to whom nothing is wanting? " It is, however," you reply, " thanks to himself and his endurance, and not thanks to his fortune." Do you, then, hold that such a man is not rich, just

eius desinere non possunt ? Utrum mavis habere
6 multum an satis ? Qui multum habet, plus cupit ;
quod est argumentum nondum illum satis habere ;
qui satis habet, consecutus est, quod numquam
diviti contigit, finem. An has ideo non putas esse
divitias, quia propter illas nemo proscriptus est ?
Quia propter illas nulli venenum filius, nulli uxor
inpegit ? Quia in bello tutae sunt ? Quia in pace
otiosae ? Quia nec habere illas periculosum est nec
operosum disponere ?

7 "At parum habet qui tantum non alget, non
esurit, non sitit." Plus Iuppiter non habet. Numquam parum est quod satis est, et numquam multum
est quod satis non est. Post Dareum et Indos
pauper est Alexander. Mentior ? Quaerit, quod
suum faciat, scrutatur maria ignota, in oceanum
classes novas mittit et ipsa, ut ita dicam, mundi
claustra perrumpit. Quod naturae satis est, homini
8 non est. Inventus est qui concupisceret aliquid
post omnia ; tanta est caecitas mentium et tanta
initiorum suorum unicuique, cum processit, oblivio.
Ille modo ignobilis anguli non sine controversia
dominus tacto fine terrarum per suum rediturus
9 orbem tristis est. Neminem pecunia divitem fecit,
immo contra nulli non maiorem sui cupidinem
incussit. Quaeris, quae sit huius rei causa ? Plus
incipit habere posse, qui plus habet.

---

[a] Alexander the Great.

because his wealth can never fail? Would you rather have much, or enough? He who has much desires more—a proof that he has not yet acquired enough; but he who has enough has attained that which never fell to the rich man's lot—a stopping-point. Do you think that this condition to which I refer is not riches, just because no man has ever been proscribed as a result of possessing them? Or because sons and wives have never thrust poison down one's throat for that reason? Or because in war-time these riches are unmolested? Or because they bring leisure in time of peace? Or because it is not dangerous to possess them, or troublesome to invest them?

"But one possesses too little, if one is merely free from cold and hunger and thirst." Jupiter himself however, is no better off. Enough is never too little, and not-enough is never too much. Alexander was poor even after his conquest of Darius and the Indies. Am I wrong? He seeks something which he can really make his own, exploring unknown seas, sending new fleets over the Ocean, and, so to speak, breaking down the very bars of the universe. But that which is enough for nature, is not enough for man. There have been found persons who crave something more after obtaining everything; so blind are their wits and so readily does each man forget his start after he has got under way. He who *a* was but lately the disputed lord of an unknown corner of the world, is dejected when, after reaching the limits of the globe, he must march back through a world which he has made his own. Money never made a man rich; on the contrary, it always smites men with a greater craving for itself. Do you ask the reason for this? He who possesses more begins to be able to possess still more.

Ad summam, quem voles mihi ex his, quorum nomina cum Crasso Licinoque[1] numerantur, in medium licet protrahas. Adferat censum, et quicquid habet et quicquid sperat, simul computet; iste, si mihi credis, pauper est, si tibi, potest esse.

10 At hic, qui se ad id,[2] quod exigit natura, composuit, non tantum extra sensum est paupertatis, sed extra metum. Sed ut scias, quam difficile sit res suas ad naturalem modum coartare, hic ipse, quem circa dicimus, quem tu vocas pauperem, habet aliquid et

11 supervacui. At excaecant populum et in se convertunt opes, si numerati multum ex aliqua domo effertur, si multum auri tecto quoque eius inlinitur, si familia aut corporibus electa aut spectabilis cultu est. Omnium istorum felicitas in publicum spectat; ille, quem nos et populo et fortunae sub-

12 duximus,[3] beatus introsum est. Nam quod ad illos pertinet, apud quos falso divitiarum nomen invasit occupata paupertas, sic divitias habent, quomodo habere dicimur febrem, cum illa nos habeat. E contrario dicere solemus: febris illum tenet. Eodem modo dicendum est: divitiae illum tenent. Nihil ergo monuisse te malim quam hoc, quod nemo monetur satis, ut omnia naturalibus desideriis metiaris, quibus aut gratis satis fiat aut parvo;

13 tantum miscere vitia desideriis noli. Quaeris, quali

[1] *Crasso Licinoque* Muretus; *croeso (crasso) licinioque* MSS.
[2] *ad id* later MSS.; *ad* BA.
[3] *subduximus* later MSS.; *subdiximus* BA.

---

[a] *i.e.,* a " poverty " which is never satisfied.

EPISTLE CXIX.

To sum up, you may hale forth for our inspection any of the millionaires whose names are told off when one speaks of Crassus and Licinus. Let him bring along his rating and his present property and his future expectations, and let him add them all together: such a man, according to my belief, is poor; according to yours, he may be poor some day. He, however, who has arranged his affairs according to nature's demands, is free from the fear, as well as from the sensation, of poverty. And in order that you may know how hard it is to narrow one's interests down to the limits of nature—even this very person of whom we speak, and whom you call poor, possesses something actually superfluous. Wealth, however, blinds and attracts the mob, when they see a large bulk of ready money brought out of a man's house, or even his walls crusted with abundance of gold, or a retinue that is chosen for beauty of physique, or for attractiveness of attire. The prosperity of all these men looks to public opinion; but the ideal man, whom we have snatched from the control of the people and of Fortune, is happy inwardly. For as far as those persons are concerned, in whose minds bustling *a* poverty has wrongly stolen the title of riches—these individuals have riches just as we say that we " have a fever," when really the fever has *us*. Conversely, we are accustomed to say : " A fever grips him." And in the same way we should say : " Riches grip him." There is therefore no advice—and of such advice no one can have too much—which I would rather give you than this : that you should measure all things by the demands of Nature ; for these demands can be satisfied either without cost or else very cheaply. Only, do not mix any vices with these demands. Why need you ask

377

THE EPISTLES OF SENECA

mensa, quali argento, quam paribus ministeriis et levibus adferatur cibus ? Nihil praeter cibum natura desiderat.

> Num tibi, cum fauces urit sitis, aurea quaeris
> Pocula ? Num esuriens fastidis omnia praeter
> Pavonem rhombumque ?

14 Ambitiosa non est fames, contenta desinere est ; quo desinat, non nimis curat. Infelicis luxuriae ista tormenta sunt ; quaerit, quemadmodum post saturitatem quoque esuriat, quemadmodum non impleat ventrem, sed farciat, quemadmodum sitim prima potione sedatam revocet. Egregie itaque Horatius negat ad sitim pertinere, quo poculo aqua aut quam eleganti manu ministretur. Nam si pertinere ad te iudicas, quam crinitus puer et quam perlucidum tibi poculum porrigat, non sitis.

15 Inter reliqua hoc nobis praestitit natura praecipuum, quod necessitati fastidium excussit. Recipiunt supervacua dilectum : hoc parum decens, illud parum laudatum, oculos hoc meos laedit. Id actum est ab illo mundi conditore, qui nobis vivendi iura discripsit, ut salvi essemus, non ut delicati. Ad salutem omnia parata sunt et in promptu, deliciis omnia misere ac sollicite conparantur.

16 Utamur ergo hoc naturae beneficio inter magna

ª Horace, *Sat.* i. 2. 114 ff.

how your food should be served, on what sort of table, with what sort of silver, with what well-matched and smooth-faced young servants? Nature demands nothing except mere food.

> Dost seek, when thirst inflames thy throat, a cup of gold?
> Dost scorn all else but peacock's flesh or turbot
> When the hunger comes upon thee?[a]

Hunger is not ambitious; it is quite satisfied to come to an end; nor does it care very much what food brings it to an end. Those things are but the instruments of a luxury which is not "happiness"; a luxury which seeks how it may prolong hunger even after repletion, how to stuff the stomach, not to fill it, and how to rouse a thirst that has been satisfied with the first drink. Horace's words are therefore most excellent when he says that it makes no difference to one's thirst in what costly goblet, or with what elaborate state, the water is served. For if you believe it to be of importance how curly-haired your slave is, or how transparent is the cup which he offers you, you are not thirsty.

Among other things, Nature has bestowed upon us this special boon: she relieves sheer necessity of squeamishness. The superfluous things admit of choice; we say: "That is not suitable"; "this is not well recommended"; "that hurts my eyesight." The Builder of the universe, who laid down for us the laws of life, provided that we should exist in well-being, but not in luxury. Everything conducive to our well-being is prepared and ready to our hands; but what luxury requires can never be got together except with wretchedness and anxiety.

Let us therefore use this boon of Nature by reckoning it among the things of high importance;

numerando et cogitemus nullo nomine melius illam meruisse de nobis, quam quia quicquid ex necessitate desideratur, sine fastidio sumitur. VALE.

CXX.

1 Epistula tua per plures quaestiunculas vagata est, sed in una constitit et hanc expediri desiderat, quomodo ad nos boni honestique notitia pervenerit. Haec duo apud alios diversa sunt, apud nos tantum 2 divisa. Quid sit hoc dicam. Bonum putant esse aliqui id,[1] quod utile est; itaque hoc et[2] divitiis et equo et vino et calceo nomen inponunt; tanta fit apud illos boni vilitas et adeo in sordida usque descendit. Honestum putant, cui ratio recti officii constat, tamquam pie curatam patris senectutem, adiutam amici paupertatem, fortem expeditionem, 3 prudentem moderatamque sententiam.[3] Nos[4] ista duo quidem facimus, sed ex uno. Nihil est bonum, nisi quod honestum est. Quod honestum, est utique bonum. Supervacuum iudico adicere, quid inter ista discriminis sit, cum saepe dixerim. Hoc unum dicam, nihil bonum nobis[5] videri, quo quis et male uti potest. Vides autem divitiis, nobilitate, viribus quam multi male utantur.

Nunc ergo ad id revertor, de quo desideras dici,

[1] *aliqui id* Buecheler and Windhaus; *aliquit* BA.
[2] *et* later MSS.; *et de* BA.
[3] *sententiam* later MSS.; *sentiam* BA.
[4] *nos* cod. Vat.; om. BA.
[5] *nihil bonum nobis* cod. Ottobon.; *nihil nobis* BA.

---

[a] *i.e.*, the Peripatetic and Academic schools.
[b] *Cf. Ep.* cxviii. 10 and note.

let us reflect that Nature's best title to our gratitude is that whatever we want because of sheer necessity we accept without squeamishness. Farewell.

CXX. MORE ABOUT VIRTUE

Your letter roamed over several little problems, but finally dwelt upon this alone, asking for explanation : " How do we acquire a knowledge of that which is good and that which is honourable ? " In the opinion of other schools,[a] these two qualities are distinct ; among our followers, however, they are merely divided. This is what I mean : Some believe the Good to be that which is useful ; they accordingly bestow this title upon riches, horses, wine, and shoes ; so cheaply do they view the Good, and to such base uses do they let it descend. They regard as honourable that which agrees with the principle of right conduct—such as taking dutiful care of an old father, relieving a friend's poverty, showing bravery on a campaign, and uttering prudent and well-balanced opinions. We, however, do make the Good and the honourable two things, but we make them out of one : only the honourable can be good ; also, the honourable is necessarily good. I hold it superfluous to add the distinction between these two qualities, inasmuch as I have mentioned it so many times.[b] But I shall say this one thing—that we regard nothing as good which can be put to wrong use by any person. And you see for yourself to what wrong uses many men put their riches, their high position, or their physical powers.

To return to the matter on which you desire

381

quomodo ad nos prima boni honestique notitia per-
4 venerit. Hoc nos natura docere non potuit; semina
nobis scientiae dedit, scientiam non dedit. Quidam
aiunt nos in notitiam incidisse, quod est incredibile,
virtutis alicui speciem casu occucurrisse. Nobis videtur observatio collegisse et rerum saepe factarum
inter se conlatio, per analogian nostri intellectum et
honestum et bonum iudicant. Hoc verbum cum
Latini grammatici civitate donaverint, ego damnan-
dum non puto, puto[1] in civitatem suam redigendum.
Utar ergo illo non tantum tamquam recepto, sed
tamquam usitato.

5   Quae sit haec analogia, dicam. Noveramus corporis sanitatem ; ex hac cogitavimus esse aliquam et
animi. Noveramus vires corporis ; ex his collegimus
esse et animi robur. Aliqua benigna facta, aliqua
humana, aliqua fortia nos obstupefecerant ; haec
coepimus tamquam perfecta mirari. Suberant illis
multa vitia, quae species conspicui alicuius facti
fulgorque celabat ; haec dissimulavimus. Natura
iubet augere laudanda, nemo non gloriam ultra verum
tulit ; ex his ergo speciem ingentis boni traximus.
6 Fabricius Pyrrhi regis aurum reppulit maiusque
regno iudicavit regias opes posse contemnere. Idem

___
[1] *puto* add. Buecheler.

___
a Consult Sandys, *Hist. Class. Schol.* i. pp. 148 and 175 f.
Alexandrian " analogists " opposed Pergamene " anom-
alists " with reference to the rules affecting the forms of
words. Out of the controversy arose the scientific study of
grammar.

information : " How we first acquire the knowledge of that which is good and that which is honourable." Nature could not teach us this directly ; she has given us the seeds of knowledge, but not knowledge itself. Some say that we merely happened upon this knowledge ; but it is unbelievable that a vision of virtue could have presented itself to anyone by mere chance. We believe that it is inference due to observation, a comparison of events that have occurred frequently ; our school of philosophy hold that the honourable and the good have been comprehended by analogy. Since the word " analogy " [a] has been admitted to citizen rank by Latin scholars, I do not think that it ought to be condemned, but I do think it should be brought into the citizenship which it can justly claim. I shall, therefore, make use of the word, not merely as admitted, but as established.

Now what this " analogy " is, I shall explain. We understood what bodily health was : and from this basis we deduced the existence of a certain mental health also. We knew, too, bodily strength, and from this basis we inferred the existence of mental sturdiness. Kindly deeds, humane deeds, brave deeds, had at times amazed us ; so we began to admire them as if they were perfect. Underneath, however, there were many faults, hidden by the appearance and the brilliancy of certain conspicuous acts ; to these we shut our eyes. Nature bids us amplify praiseworthy things : everyone exalts renown beyond the truth. And thus from such deeds we deduced the conception of some great good. Fabricius rejected King Pyrrhus's gold, deeming it greater than a king's crown to be able to scorn a king's money. Fabricius also, when the royal

medico Pyrrhi promittente venenum se regi daturum
monuit Pyrrhum, caveret insidias. Eiusdem animi
fuit auro non vinci, veneno non vincere. Admirati
sumus ingentem virum, quem non regis, non contra
regem promissa flexissent, boni exempli tenacem,
quod difficillimum est, in bello innocentem, qui aliquod esse crederet etiam in hostes nefas, qui in
summa paupertate, quam sibi decus fecerat, non
aliter refugit divitias quam venenum. " Vive," inquit, " beneficio meo, Pyrrhe, et gaude quod adhuc
dolebas, Fabricium non posse corrumpi."

7   Horatius Cocles solus implevit pontis angustias
adimique a tergo sibi reditum, dummodo iter hosti
auferretur, iussit et tam diu prementibus restitit,
donec revulsa ingenti ruina tigna sonuerunt. Postquam respexit et extra periculum esse patriam
periculo suo sensit, "veniat, si quis vult," inquit,
" sic euntem sequi," iecitque ¹ se in praeceps et non
minus sollicitus in illo rapido alveo fluminis ut armatus
quam ut salvus exiret, retento armorum victricium
decore tam tutus rediit, quam si ponte venisset.

8   Haec et eiusmodi facta imaginem nobis ostendere
virtutis. Adiciam, quod mirum fortasse videatur :
mala interdum speciem honesti optulere et optimum
ex contrario enituit.² Sunt enim, ut scis, virtutibus

¹ *iecitque* later MSS.; *legitque* BA¹.
² *enituit* Buecheler, with cod. Ottobon.; *emicuit* cod.
Velz.; *nituit* BA.

ª The two stories refer to the years 280 and 279 B.C.,
during the campaigns of Pyrrhus in Italy.
ᵇ See Livy, ii. 10.
ᶜ Livy (*loc. cit.*) reports him as saying : " Tiberine pater,
te sancte precor, haec arma et hunc militem propitio flumine
accipias ! " Macaulay in his ballad translates Livy's quota-
tion almost literally.

physician promised to give his master poison, warned Pyrrhus to beware of a plot. The selfsame man had the resolution to refuse either to be won over by gold or to win by poison. So we admired the hero, who could not be moved by the promises of the king or against the king, who held fast to a noble ideal, and who—is anything more difficult?—was in war sinless; for he believed that wrongs could be committed even against an enemy, and in that extreme poverty which he had made his glory, shrank from receiving riches as he shrank from using poison. " Live," he cried, " O Pyrrhus, thanks to me, and rejoice, instead of grieving as you have done till now, that Fabricius cannot be bribed ! " [a]

Horatius Cocles [b] blocked the narrow bridge alone, and ordered his retreat to be cut off, that the enemy's path might be destroyed; then he long withstood his assailants until the crash of the beams, as they collapsed with a huge fall, rang in his ears. When he looked back and saw that his country, through his own danger, was free from danger, " Whoever," he cried, " wishes to pursue me this way, let him come ! " [c] He plunged headlong, taking as great care to come out armed from the midst of the dashing river-channel as he did to come out unhurt; he returned, preserving the glory of his conquering weapons, as safely as if he had come back over the bridge.

These deeds and others of the same sort have revealed to us a picture of virtue. I will add something which may perhaps astonish you : evil things have sometimes offered the appearance of what is honourable, and that which is best has been manifested through its opposite. For there are, as you know, vices which are next-door to virtues ; and

vitia confinia, et perditis quoque ac turpibus recti similitudo est ; sic mentitur prodigus liberalem, cum plurimum intersit, utrum quis dare sciat an servare nesciat. Multi, inquam, sunt, Lucili, qui non donant, sed proiciunt ; non voco ego liberalem pecuniae suae iratum. Imitatur neglegentia facilitatem, temeritas
9 fortitudinem. Haec nos similitudo coegit attendere et distinguere specie quidem vicina, re autem plurimum inter se dissidentia, ac [1] dum observamus eos, quos insignes egregium opus fecerat, adnotare, quis rem aliquam generoso animo fecisset et magno impetu, sed semel. Hunc vidimus in bello fortem, in foro timidum, animose paupertatem ferentem, humiliter infamiam ; factum laudavimus, contemp-
10 simus virum. Alium vidimus adversus amicos benignum, adversus inimicos temperatum, et publica et privata sancte ac religiose administrantem, non deesse ei in iis quae toleranda erant, patientiam, in iis quae agenda, prudentiam. Vidimus, ubi tribuendum esset, plena manu dantem, ubi laborandum, pertinacem et obnixum [2] et lassitudinem corporis animo sublevantem. Praeterea idem erat semper et in omni actu par sibi, iam non consilio bonus, sed more eo perductus, ut non tantum recte facere posset,

---

[1] *ac* add. Gertz.
[2] *obnixum* codd. Laur. and Ottobon.; *obnoxium* BA.

even that which is lost and debased can resemble that which is upright. So the spendthrift falsely imitates the liberal man—although it matters a great deal whether a man knows how to give, or does not know how to save, his money. I assure you, my dear Lucilius, there are many who do not give, but simply throw away; and I do not call a man liberal who is out of temper with his money. Carelessness looks like ease, and rashness like bravery. This resemblance has forced us to watch carefully and to distinguish between things which are by outward appearance closely connected, but which actually are very much at odds with one another; and in watching those who have become distinguished as a result of some noble effort, we have been forced to observe what persons have done some deed with noble spirit and lofty impulse, but have done it only once. We have marked one man who is brave in war and cowardly in civil affairs, enduring poverty courageously and disgrace shame-facedly; we have praised the deed but we have despised the man. Again, we have marked another man who is kind to his friends and restrained towards his enemies, who carries on his political and his personal business with scrupulous devotion, not lacking in longsuffering where there is anything that must be endured, and not lacking in prudence when action is to be taken. We have marked him giving with lavish hand when it was his duty to make a payment, and, when he had to toil, striving resolutely and lightening his bodily weariness by his resolution. Besides, he has always been the same, consistent in all his actions, not only sound in his judgment but trained by habit to such an extent that he not only can act rightly, but cannot help

sed nisi recte facere non posset. Intelleximus in illo
perfectam esse virtutem.

11 Hanc in partes divisimus ; oportebat cupiditates
refrenari, metus comprimi, facienda provideri, red-
denda distribui ; conprehendimus temperantiam,
fortitudinem, prudentiam, iustitiam et suum cuique
dedimus officium. Ex quo ergo virtutem intelleximus ? Ostendit illam nobis ordo eius et decor et constantia et omnium inter se actionum concordia et
magnitudo super omnia efferens sese. Hinc in-
tellecta est illa beata vita secundo defluens cursu,
12 arbitrii sui tota. Quomodo ergo hoc ipsum nobis
apparuit ? Dicam. Numquam vir ille perfectus
adeptusque virtutem fortunae maledixit, numquam
accidentia tristis excepit, civem esse se universi et
militem credens labores velut imperatos subiit.
Quicquid inciderat, non tamquam malum aspernatus
est et in se casu[1] delatum, sed quasi delegatum sibi.
Hoc qualecumque est, inquit, meum est ; asperum
est, durum est, in hoc ipso navemus operam.

13 Necessario itaque magnus apparuit qui numquam
malis ingemuit, numquam de fato suo questus est ;
fecit multis intellectum sui et non aliter quam in
tenebris lumen effulsit advertitque in se omnium
animos, cum esset placidus et lenis, humanis divinis-
14 que rebus pariter aequus. Habebat perfectum animum et ad summam sui adductum, supra quam

---

[1] *casu* ed. Ven. ; *casum* B ; *cassum* A.

acting rightly. We have formed the conception
that in such a man perfect virtue exists.

We have separated this perfect virtue into its
several parts. The desires had to be reined in, fear
to be suppressed, proper actions to be arranged,
debts to be paid; we therefore included self-
restraint, bravery, prudence, and justice—assigning
to each quality its special function. How then have
we formed the conception of virtue ? Virtue has
been manifested to us by this man's order, propriety,
steadfastness, absolute harmony of action, and a
greatness of soul that rises superior to everything.
Thence has been derived our conception of the
happy life, which flows along with steady course,
completely under its own control. How then did
we discover this fact ? I will tell you : that perfect
man, who has attained virtue, never cursed his luck,
and never received the results of chance with de-
jection ; he believed that he was citizen and soldier
of the universe, accepting his tasks as if they were
his orders. Whatever happened, he did not spurn i;
as if it were evil and borne in upon him by hazard;
he accepted it as if it were assigned to be his duty.
" Whatever this may be," he says, " it is my lot ; it
is rough and it is hard, but I must work diligently at
the task."

Necessarily, therefore, the man has shown himself
great who has never grieved in evil days and never
bewailed his destiny ; he has given a clear conception of himself to many men ; he has shone forth
like a light in the darkness and has turned towards
himself the thoughts of all men, because he was
gentle and calm and equally compliant with the
orders of man and of God. He possessed perfection
of soul, developed to its highest capabilities, inferior

389

nihil est nisi mens dei, ex quo pars et in hoc pectus mortale defluxit. Quod numquam magis divinum est, quam ubi mortalitatem suam cogitat et scit in hoc natum hominem, ut vita defungeretur, nec domum esse hoc corpus, sed hospitium, et quidem breve hospitium, quod relinquendum est, ubi te
15 gravem esse hospiti videas. Maximum, inquam, mi Lucili, argumentum est animi ab altiore sede venientis, si haec, in quibus versatur, humilia iudicat et angusta, si exire non metuit. Scit enim, quo exiturus sit, qui unde venerit meminit. Non videmus quam multa nos incommoda[1] exagitent, quam male
16 nobis conveniat hoc corpus ? Nunc de capite, nunc de ventre, nunc de pectore ac faucibus querimur. Alias nervi nos, alias pedes vexant, nunc deiectio, nunc destillatio, aliquando superest sanguis, aliquando deest; hinc atque illinc temptamur et expellimur; hoc evenire solet in alieno habitantibus.
17   At nos corpus tam putre sortiti nihilominus aeterna proponimus et in quantum potest aetas humana protendi, tantum spe occupamus, nulla contenti pecunia, nulla potentia. Quid hac re fieri impudentius, quid stultius potest ? Nihil satis est morituris, immo morientibus ; cotidie enim propius ab ultimo stamus, et illo, unde nobis cadendum est,
18 hora nos omnis inpellit. Vide in quanta caecitate mens nostra sit ! Hoc quod futurum dico, cum

[1] *incommoda* later MSS. ; *commoda* BA.

---

[a] A chronic disease of Seneca himself. See the autobiographic fragment in *Ep.* lxxviii. 1 f.

only to the mind of God—from whom a part flows down even into this heart of a mortal. But this heart is never more divine than when it reflects upon its mortality, and understands that man was born for the purpose of fulfilling his life, and that the body is not a permanent dwelling, but a sort of inn (with a brief sojourn at that) which is to be left behind when one perceives that one is a burden to the host. The greatest proof, as I maintain, my dear Lucilius, that the soul proceeds from loftier heights, is if it judges its present situation lowly and narrow, and is not afraid to depart. For he who remembers whence he has come knows whither he is to depart. Do we not see how many discomforts drive us wild, and how ill-assorted is our fellowship with the flesh? We complain at one time of our headaches, at another of our bad digestions, at another of our hearts and our throats. Sometimes the nerves trouble us, sometimes the feet; now it is diarrhoea, and again it is catarrh *a*; we are at one time full-blooded, at another anaemic; now this thing troubles us, now that, and bids us move away: it is just what happens to those who dwell in the house of another.

But we, to whom such corruptible bodies have been allotted, nevertheless set eternity before our eyes, and in our hopes grasp at the utmost space of time to which the life of man can be extended, satisfied with no income and with no influence. What can be more shameless or foolish than this? Nothing is enough for us, though we must die some day, or rather, are already dying; for we stand daily nearer the brink, and every hour of time thrusts us on towards the precipice over which we must fall. See how blind our minds are! What I speak of as

391

maxime fit, et pars eius magna iam facta est, nam quod viximus. Erramus autem qui ultimum timemus diem, cum tantumdem in mortem singuli conferant. Non ille gradus lassitudinem facit, in quo deficimus, sed ille profitetur. Ad mortem dies extremus pervenit, accedit[1] omnis. Carpit nos illa, non corripit.

Ideo magnus animus conscius sibi melioris naturae dat quidem operam, ut in hac statione qua positus est, honeste se atque industrie gerat, ceterum nihil horum, quae circa sunt, suum iudicat, sed ut com-
19 modatis utitur, peregrinus et properans. Cum aliquem huius videremus constantiae, quidni subiret nos species non usitatae indolis ? Utique si hanc, ut dixi, magnitudinem veram esse ostendebat aequalitas.[2] Vero tenor permanet, falsa non durant. Quidam alternis Vatinii, alternis Catones sunt; et modo parum illis severus est Curius, parum pauper Fabricius, parum frugi et contentus vilibus Tubero; modo Licinum divitiis,[3] Apicium cenis, Maecena-
20 tem deliciis provocant. Maximum indicium est malae mentis fluctuatio et inter[4] simulationem virtutum amoremque vitiorum[5] adsidua iactatio. Aliquis[6]

> habebat saepe ducentos,
> Saepe decem servos ; modo reges atque tetrarchas,
> Omnia magna loquens, modo " sit mihi mensa tripes et

[1] *accedit* later MSS. ; *accidit* BA.
[2] *aequalitas* Gronovius ; *qualitas* BA.
[3] *Licinum divitiis* cod. Guelf. ; *linum dividitis* BA.
[4] *et inter* cod. Harl. ; *cancer* BA.
[5] *amoremque vitiorum* Pinc., and cod. Harl. ; *amorumque utiliorum* BA.
[6] *aliquis* Buecheler ; *is* BA ; *s.* (*scilicet*) Hense.

---

[a] Seneca is here developing the thought sketched in *Ep.* xii. 6 *unus autem dies gradus vitae est.*

in the future is happening at this minute, and a large portion of it has already happened; for it consists of our past lives. But we are mistaken in fearing the last day, seeing that each day, as it passes, counts just as much to the credit of death.[a] The failing step does not produce, it merely announces, weariness. The last hour reaches, but every hour approaches, death. Death wears us away, but does not whirl us away.

For this reason the noble soul, knowing its better nature, while taking care to conduct itself honourably and seriously at the post of duty where it is placed, counts none of these extraneous objects as its own, but uses them as if they were a loan, like a foreign visitor hastening on his way. When we see a person of such steadfastness, how can we help being conscious of the image of a nature so unusual? Particularly if, as I remarked, it was shown to be true greatness by its consistency. It is indeed consistency that abides; false things do not last. Some men are like Vatinius or like Cato by turns;[b] at times they do not think even Curius stern enough, or Fabricius poor enough, or Tubero sufficiently frugal and contented with simple things; while at other times they vie with Licinus in wealth, with Apicius in banqueting, or with Maecenas in daintiness. The greatest proof of an evil mind is unsteadiness, and continued wavering between pretence of virtue and love of vice.

> He'd have sometimes two hundred slaves at hand
> And sometimes ten. He'd speak of kings and grand
> Moguls and naught but greatness. Then he'd say:
> " Give me a three-legged table and a tray

[b] For the same contrast cf. Ep. cxviii. 4 (and note). For the following names see Index of Proper Names.

Concha salis puri, toga quae defendere frigus
Quamvis crassa queat " ; decies centena dedisses
Huic parco, paucis contento ; quinque diebus
Nil erat.

21 Homines[1] isti tales sunt, qualem hunc describit
Horatius Flaccus, numquam eundem, ne similem
quidem sibi ; adeo in diversum aberrat. Multos
dixi ? Prope est, ut omnes sint. Nemo non cotidie
et consilium mutat et votum. Modo uxorem vult
habere, modo amicam, modo regnare vult, modo id
agit, ne quis sit officiosior servus, modo dilatat se
usque ad invidiam, modo subsidit et contrahitur
infra humilitatem vere iacentium, nunc pecuniam
22 spargit, nunc rapit. Sic maxime coarguitur animus
inprudens ; alius prodit atque alius et, quo turpius
nihil iudico, impar sibi est. Magnam rem puta
unum hominem agere. Praeter sapientem autem
nemo unum agit, ceteri multiformes sumus. Modo
frugi tibi videbimur et graves, modo prodigi et vani.
Mutamus subinde personam et contrariam ei sumi-
mus, quam exuimus. Hoc ergo a te exige, ut,
qualem institueris praestare te, talem usque ad
exitum serves. Effice ut possis laudari, si minus,
ut adgnosci. De aliquo, quem here vidisti, merito
dici potest : " hic qui est ? " Tanta mutatio est.
VALE.

---

[1] *homines* Buecheler ; *omnes* BA.

[a] Horace, *Sat.* i. 3. 11-17.

EPISTLE CXX.

Of good clean salt, and just a coarse-wove gown
To keep the cold out." If you paid him down
(So sparing and content !) a million cool,
In five short days he'd be a penceless fool.[a]

The men I speak of are of this stamp ; they are
like the man whom Horatius Flaccus describes—
a man never the same, never even like himself ;
to such an extent does he wander off into opposites.
Did I say many are so ? It is the case with
almost all. Everyone changes his plans and prayers
day by day. Now he would have a wife, and now
a mistress ; now he would be king, and again he
strives to conduct himself so that no slave is more
cringing ; now he puffs himself up until he becomes
unpopular ; again, he shrinks and contracts into
greater humility than those who are really un-
assuming ; at one time he scatters money, at another
he steals it. That is how a foolish mind is most
clearly demonstrated : it shows first in this shape
and then in that, and is never like itself—which is,
in my opinion, the most shameful of qualities. Believe me, it is a great rôle—to play the rôle of one man.
But nobody can be one person except the wise man ;
the rest of us often shift our masks. At times you
will think us thrifty and serious, at other times
wasteful and idle. We continually change our characters and play a part contrary to that which we
have discarded. You should therefore force yourself
to maintain to the very end of life's drama the character which you assumed at the beginning. See to it
that men be able to praise you ; if not, let them at
least identify you. Indeed, with regard to the man
whom you saw but yesterday, the question may
properly be asked : "Who is he ?" So great a
change has there been ! Farewell.

CXXI.

1 Litigabis, ego video, cum tibi hodiernam quae-
stiunculam, in qua satis diu haesimus, exposuero.
Iterum enim exclamabis: " hoc quid ad mores? "
Sed exclama, dum tibi primum alios opponam, cum
quibus litiges, Posidonium et Archidemum; hi iudicium accipient. Deinde dicam: non quicquid
2 morale est, mores bonos facit. Aliud ad hominem
alendum pertinet, aliud ad exercendum, aliud ad
vestiendum, aliud ad docendum, aliud ad delectan-
dum. Omnia tamen ad hominem pertinent, etiam
si non omnia meliorem eum faciunt. Mores[1] alia
aliter attingunt: quaedam illos corrigunt et ordi-
nant, quaedam naturam eorum et originem scru-
3 tantur. Cum quaero,[2] quare hominem natura pro-
duxerit, quare praetulerit animalibus ceteris, longe
me iudicas mores reliquisse? Falsum est. Quomodo
enim scies, qui habendi sint, nisi quid homini sit optimum, inveneris, nisi naturam eius inspexeris? Tunc
demum intelleges, quid faciendum tibi, quid vitandum
sit, cum didiceris, quid naturae tuae debeas.
4   "Ego," inquis, "volo discere, quomodo minus
cupiam, minus timeam. Superstitionem mihi ex-
cute. Doce leve esse vanumque hoc, quod felicitas
dicitur, unam illi syllabam facillime accedere." De-

---

[1] *mores* later MSS. ; *timores* BA.
[2] *quaero* add. Schweighaeuser ; *quaeritur* later MSS. ;
om. BA.

---

[a] *i.e.*, in addition to myself and confirming my statement.
[b] Frag. 17 von Arnim.
[c] *i.e.*, *felicitas* becomes IN*felicitas.*

396

CXXI. ON INSTINCT IN ANIMALS

You will bring suit against me, I feel sure, when I set forth for you to-day's little problem, with which we have already fumbled long enough. You will cry out again: "What has this to do with character?" Cry out if you like, but let me first of all match you with other opponents,[a] against whom you may bring suit—such as Posidonius and Archidemus;[b] these men will stand trial. I shall then go on to say that whatever deals with character does not necessarily produce good character. Man needs one thing for his food, another for his exercise, another for his clothing, another for his instruction, and another for his pleasure. Everything, however, has reference to man's needs, although everything does not make him better. Character is affected by different things in different ways: some things serve to correct and regulate character, and others investigate its nature and origin. And when I seek the reason why Nature brought forth man, and why she set him above other animals, do you suppose that I have left character-study in the rear? No; that is wrong. For how are you to know what character is desirable, unless you have discovered what is best suited to man? Or unless you have studied his nature? You can find out what you should do and what you should avoid, only when you have learned what you owe to your own nature.

"I desire," you say, "to learn how I may crave less, and fear less. Rid me of my unreasoning beliefs. Prove to me that so-called felicity is fickle and empty, and that the word easily admits of a syllable's increase."[c] I shall fulfil your want, encouraging

397

siderio tuo satis faciam, et virtutes exhortabor et
vitia converberabo. Licet aliquis nimium in-
moderatumque in hac parte me iudicet, non desistam
persequi nequitiam et adfectus efferatissimos in-
hibere et voluptates ituras in dolorem compescere
et votis opstrepere. Quidni? Cum maxima malorum optaverimus, et ex gratulatione natum sit
quidquid adloquimur.

5 Interim permitte mihi ea, quae paulo remotiora
videntur, excutere. Quaerebamus, an esset omnibus animalibus constitutionis suae sensus? Esse
autem ex eo maxime apparet, quod membra apte
et expedite movent non aliter quam in hoc erudita.
Nulli non partium suarum agilitas est. Artifex
instrumenta sua tractat ex facili, rector navis scite[1]
gubernaculum flectit, pictor colores, quos ad red-
dendam similitudinem multos variosque ante se
posuit, celerrime denotat et inter ceram opusque
facili vultu ac manu commeat; sic animal in omnem
6 usum sui mobilest. Mirari solemus saltandi[2] peritos,
quod in omnem significationem rerum et adfectuum
parata illorum est manus, et verborum velocitatem
gestus adsequitur. Quod illis ars praestat, his
natura. Nemo aegre molitur artus suos, nemo in
usu sui haesitat. Hoc[3] edita protinus faciunt. Cum
hac scientia prodeunt; instituta nascuntur.

7 " Ideo," inquit, " partes suas animalia apte movent,

---

[1] *scite* Windhaus; *scit* BA.
[2] *saltandi* Gronovius; *satiant* BA; *satiant saltandi* cod.
Harl.
[3] *haesitat. hoc* Madvig; *haesit. ad hoc* BA.

---

a *i.e.*, their physical make-up, the elements of their physical
being.

your virtues and lashing your vices. People may decide that I am too zealous and reckless in this particular; but I shall never cease to hound wickedness, to check the most unbridled emotions, to soften the force of pleasures which will result in pain, and to cry down men's prayers. Of course I shall do this; for it is the greatest evils that we have prayed for, and from that which has made us give thanks comes all that demands consolation.

Meanwhile, allow me to discuss thoroughly some points which may seem now to be rather remote from the present inquiry. We were once debating whether all animals had any feelings about their "constitution."[a] That this is the case is proved particularly by their making motions of such fitness and nimbleness that they seem to be trained for the purpose. Every being is clever in its own line. The skilled workman handles his tools with an ease born of experience; the pilot knows how to steer his ship skilfully; the artist can quickly lay on the colours which he has prepared in great variety for the purpose of rendering the likeness, and passes with ready eye and hand from palette to canvas. In the same way an animal is agile in all that pertains to the use of its body. We are apt to wonder at skilled dancers because their gestures are perfectly adapted to the meaning of the piece and its accompanying emotions, and their movements match the speed of the dialogue. But that which art gives to the craftsman, is given to the animal by nature. No animal handles its limbs with difficulty, no animal is at a loss how to use its body. This function they exercise immediately at birth. They come into the world with this knowledge; they are born full-trained.

But people reply: "The reason why animals are

quia si aliter moverint, dolorem sensura sunt. Ita,
ut vos dicitis, coguntur, metusque illa in rectum,
non voluntas movet." Quod est falsum. Tarda
enim sunt, quae necessitate inpelluntur, agilitas
sponte motis est. Adeo autem non adigit illa ad
hoc doloris timor, ut in naturalem motum etiam
8 dolore prohibente nitantur. Sic infans, qui stare
meditatur et ferre se adsuescit, simul temptare vires
suas coepit, cadit et cum fletu totiens resurgit, donec
se per dolorem ad id, quod natura poscit, exercuit.
Animalia quaedam tergi durioris inversa tam diu
se torquent ac pedes exerunt et obliquant, donec
ad locum reponantur. Nullum tormentum sentit
supina testudo,[1] inquieta est tamen desiderio
naturalis status nec ante desinit[2] quatere se, quam
in pedes constitit.

9 Ergo omnibus constitutionis suae sensus est et
inde membrorum tam expedita tractatio, nec ullum
maius indicium habemus cum hac illa[3] ad vivendum
venire notitia, quam quod nullum animal ad usum
10 sui rude est. "Constitutio," inquit, "est, ut vos
dicitis, principale animi quodam modo se habens
erga corpus. Hoc tam perplexum et subtile et
vobis quoque vix enarrabile quomodo infans intellegit? Omnia animalia dialectica nasci oportet, ut

[1] supina testudo later MSS.; supinate studio BA.
[2] After desinit Haase removed niti.
[3] illa later MSS.; illam BA.

---

[a] i.e., the " soul of the world," of which each living soul
is a part. The Stoics believed that it was situated in the
heart. Zeno called it ἡγεμονικόν, " ruling power " ; while
the Romans used the term principale or principatus. The
principle described above is ὁρμή (impulse) or τόνος (tension).

so dexterous in the use of their limbs is that if they move them unnaturally, they will feel pain. They are *compelled* to do thus, according to your school, and it is fear rather than will-power which moves them in the right direction." This idea is wrong. Bodies driven by a compelling force move slowly; but those which move of their own accord possess alertness. The proof that it is not fear of pain which prompts them thus, is, that even when pain checks them they struggle to carry out their natural motions. Thus the child who is trying to stand and is becoming used to carry his own weight, on beginning to test his strength, falls and rises again and again with tears until through painful effort he has trained himself to the demands of nature. And certain animals with hard shells, when turned on their backs, twist and grope with their feet and make motions side-ways until they are restored to their proper position. The tortoise on his back feels no suffering; but he is restless because he misses his natural condition, and does not cease to shake himself about until he stands once more upon his feet.

So all these animals have a consciousness of their physical constitution, and for that reason can manage their limbs as readily as they do; nor have we any better proof that they come into being equipped with this knowledge than the fact that no animal is unskilled in the use of its body. But some object as follows: " According to your account, one's constitution consists of a ruling power [a] in the soul which has a certain relation towards the body. But how can a child comprehend this intricate and subtle principle, which I can scarcely explain even to you? All living creatures should be born logicians, so as to

401

istam finitionem magnae parti hominum togatorum obscuram intellegant." Verum erat quod opponis,

11 si ego ab animalibus constitutionis finitionem intellegi dicerem, non ipsam constitutionem. Facilius natura intellegitur quam enarratur ; itaque infans ille quid sit constitutio non novit, constitutionem suam novit. Et quid sit animal, nescit, animal esse

12 se sentit. Praeterea ipsam constitutionem suam crasse intellegit et summatim et obscure. Nos quoque animum habere nos scimus ; quid sit animus, ubi sit, qualis sit aut unde, nescimus. Qualis ad nos[1] animi nostri sensus, quamvis naturam eius ignoremus ac sedem, talis ad omnia animalia constitutionis suae sensus est. Necesse est enim id sentiant, per quod alia quoque sentiunt, necesse est eius sensum habeant, cui parent, a quo reguntur.

13 Nemo non ex nobis intellegit esse aliquid, quod impetus suos moveat ; quid sit illud ignorat. Et conatum sibi esse scit ; quis sit aut unde sit, nescit. Sic infantibus quoque animalibusque principalis partis suae sensus est non satis dilucidus nec expressus.

14 "Dicitis," inquit, "omne animal primum constitutioni suae conciliari, hominis autem constitutionem rationalem esse et ideo conciliari hominem sibi non tamquam animali, sed tamquam rationali ? Ea enim parte sibi carus est homo, qua homo est. Quomodo ergo infans conciliari constitutioni ratio-

---

[1] After *nos* Haase del. *pervenerit.*

understand a definition which is obscure to the majority of Roman citizens!" Your objection would be true if I spoke of living creatures as understanding "a definition of constitution," and not "their actual constitution." Nature is easier to understand than to explain; hence, the child of whom we were speaking does not understand what "constitution" is, but understands *its own* constitution. He does not know what "a living creature" is, but he feels that he is an animal. Moreover, that very constitution of his own he only understands confusedly, cursorily, and darkly. We also know that we possess souls, but we do not know the essence, the place, the quality, or the source, of the soul. Such as is the consciousness of our souls which we possess, ignorant as we are of their nature and position, even so all animals possess a consciousness of their own constitutions. For they must necessarily feel this, because it is the same agency by which they feel other things also; they must necessarily have a feeling of the principle which they obey and by which they are controlled. Everyone of us understands that there is something which stirs his impulses, but he does not know what it is. He knows that he has a sense of striving, although he does not know what it is or its source. Thus even children and animals have a consciousness of their primary element, but it is not very clearly outlined or portrayed.

"You maintain, do you," says the objector, "that every living thing is at the start adapted to its constitution, but that man's constitution is a reasoning one, and hence man is adapted to himself not merely as a living, but as a reasoning, being? For man is dear to himself in respect of that wherein he is a man. How, then, can a child, being not yet

403

nali potest, cum rationalis nondum sit ? " Unicui-
15 que aetati sua constitutio est, alia infanti, alia puero,
alia seni; omnes ei constitutioni conciliantur in
qua sunt. Infans sine dentibus est : huic constitutioni suae conciliatur. Enati sunt dentes ; huic
constitutioni conciliatur. Nam et illa herba, quae
in segetem frugemque ventura est, aliam constitutionem habet tenera et vix eminens sulco, aliam,
cum convaluit et molli quidem culmo, sed quo ferat
onus suum, constitit, aliam cum flavescit et ad aream
spectat et spica eius induruit ; in quamcumque constitutionem venit, eam tuetur, in eam componitur.
16 Alia est aetas infantis, pueri, adulescentis, senis ;
ego tamen idem sum, qui et infans fui et puer et
adulescens. Sic, quamvis alia atque alia cuique constitutio sit, conciliatio constitutionis suae eadem est.
Non enim puerum mihi aut iuvenem aut senem, sed
me natura commendat. Ergo infans ei constitutioni suae conciliatur, quae tunc infanti est, non
quae futura iuveni est. Neque enim, si aliquid illi
maius in quod transeat, restat, non hoc quoque in
17 quo nascitur, secundum naturam est. Primum sibi
ipsum conciliatur animal, debet enim aliquid esse,
ad quod alia referantur. Voluptatem peto, cui ?
Mihi. Ergo mei curam ago. Dolorem refugio, pro
quo ? Pro me. Ergo mei curam ago. Si omnia
404

gifted with reason, adapt himself to a reasoning constitution?" But each age has its own constitution, different in the case of the child, the boy, and the old man; they are all adapted to the constitution wherein they find themselves. The child is toothless, and he is fitted to this condition. Then his teeth grow, and he is fitted to that condition also. Vegetation also, which will develop into grain and fruits, has a special constitution when young and scarcely peeping over the tops of the furrows, another when it is strengthened and stands upon a stalk which is soft but strong enough to bear its weight, and still another when the colour changes to yellow, prophesies threshing-time, and hardens in the ear— no matter what may be the constitution into which the plant comes, it keeps it, and conforms thereto. The periods of infancy, boyhood, youth, and old age, are different; but I, who have been infant, boy, and youth, am still the same. Thus, although each has at different times a different constitution, the adaptation of each to its constitution is the same. For nature does not consign boyhood or youth, or old age, to me; it consigns me to them. Therefore, the child is adapted to that constitution which is his at the present moment of childhood, not to that which will be his in youth. For even if there is in store for him any higher phase into which he must be changed, the state in which he is born is also according to nature. First of all, the living being is adapted to itself, for there must be a pattern to which all other things may be referred. I seek pleasure; for whom? For myself. I am therefore looking out for myself. I shrink from pain; on behalf of whom? Myself. Therefore, I am looking out for myself. Since I gauge all my actions with reference

propter curam mei facio, ante omnia est mei cura.
Haec animalibus inest cunctis nec inseritur, sed in-
nascitur.

18 Producit fetus suos natura, non abicit. Et quia
tutela certissima ex proximo est, sibi quisque com-
missus est. Itaque, ut in prioribus epistulis dixi,
tenera quoque animalia et materno utero vel ovo[1]
modo effusa, quid sit infestum, ipsa[2] protinus norunt
et mortifera devitant. Umbram quoque trans-
volantium reformidant obnoxia avibus rapto viventibus.

Nullum animal ad vitam prodit sine metu mortis.
19 "Quemadmodum," inquit, "editum animal intellectum
habere aut salutaris aut mortiferae rei potest?"
Primum quaeritur, an intellegat, non quemadmodum intellegat. Esse autem illis intellectum ex
eo apparet, quod nihil amplius, si intellexerint,
facient. Quid est, quare pavonem, quare anserem
gallina non fugiat, at tanto minorem et ne notum
quidem sibi accipitrem? Quare pulli faelem timeant,
canem non timeant? Apparet illis inesse nocituri
scientiam non experimento collectam; nam ante-
20 quam possint experisci, cavent.[3] Deinde ne hoc
casu existimes fieri, nec metuunt alia quam debent
nec umquam obliviscuntur huius tutelae et dili-

---

[1] *ovo* Bartsch; *quo* BA.
[2] *ipsa* Hense; *ipsi* or *ipsis* MSS.
[3] *experisci cavent* Buecheler; *experisciavent, experiri
cavent,* or *experis cavent* MSS.

---

[a] Seneca is both sound and modern in his account of
animal "intelligence." It is instinct, due to sensory-motor
reactions, and depending largely upon type heredity.

to my own welfare, I am looking out for myself before all else. This quality exists in all living beings—not engrafted but inborn.

Nature brings up her own offspring and does not cast them away ; and because the most assured security is that which is nearest, every man has been entrusted to his own self. Therefore, as I have remarked in the course of my previous correspondence, even young animals, on issuing from the mother's womb or from the egg, know at once of their own accord what is harmful for them, and avoid death-dealing things.[a] They even shrink when they notice the shadow of birds of prey which flit overhead.

No animal, when it enters upon life, is free from the fear of death. People may ask : " How can an animal at birth have an understanding of things wholesome or destructive ? " The first question, however, is *whether* it can have such understanding, and not *how* it can understand. And it is clear that they have such understanding from the fact that, even if you add understanding, they will act no more adequately than they did in the first place. Why should the hen show no fear of the peacock or the goose, and yet run from the hawk, which is a so much smaller animal not even familiar to the hen ? Why should young chickens fear a cat and not a dog ? These fowls clearly have a presentiment of harm—one not based on actual experiments ; for they avoid a thing before they can possibly have experience of it. Furthermore, in order that you may not suppose this to be the result of chance, they do not shrink from certain other things which you would expect them to fear, nor do they ever forget vigilance and care in this regard ;

gentiae ; aequalis est illis a pernicioso fuga. **Praeter-**
ea non fiunt timidiora vivendo.

Ex quo quidem apparet non usu illa in hoc pervenire, sed naturali amore salutis suae. Et tardum
est et varium, quod usus docet ; quicquid natura
21 tradit, et aequale omnibus est et statim. Si tamen
exigis, dicam quomodo omne animal perniciosa intellegere conatur ? Sentit se carne constare ; itaque sentit, quid sit, quo secari caro, quo uri, quo
opteri possit, quae sint animalia armata ad nocendum ; horum speciem trahit inimicam et hostilem.
Inter se ista coniuncta sunt ; simul enim conciliatur
saluti suae quidque et iuvantia[1] petit, laesura for-
midat. Naturales ad utilia impetus, naturales a
contrariis aspernationes sunt ; sine ulla cogitatione,
quae hoc dictet, sine consilio fit, quidquid natura
praecepit.

22 Non vides, quanta sit subtilitas apibus ad fin-
genda domicilia, quanta dividua laboris obeundi
undique[2] concordia ? Non vides, quam nulli mortalium imitabilis illa aranei textura, quanti operis
sit fila disponere, alia in rectum inmissa firmamenti
loco, alia in orbem currentia ex denso rara, qua
minora animalia, in quorum perniciem[3] illa ten-
23 duntur, velut retibus implicata teneantur ? Nascitur

---

[1] *iuvantia* Haase ; *iuvant illa* Bp ; *vivant illa* A.
[2] *obeundi undique* Buecheler ; *obeundi(que)* MSS.
[3] *perniciem* later MSS. ; *praetium* Bp ; *p̄rium* A.

they all possess equally the faculty of avoiding what is destructive. Besides, their fear does not grow as their lives lengthen.

Hence indeed it is evident that these animals have not reached such a condition through experience; it is because of an inborn desire for self-preservation. The teachings of experience are slow and irregular; but whatever Nature communicates belongs equally to everyone, and comes immediately. If, however, you require an explanation, shall I tell you how it is that every living thing tries to understand that which is harmful? It feels that it is constructed of flesh; and so it perceives to what an extent flesh may be cut or burned or crushed, and what animals are equipped with the power of doing this damage; it is of animals of this sort that it derives an unfavourable and hostile idea. These tendencies are closely connected; for each animal at the same time consults its own safety, seeking that which helps it, and shrinks from that which will harm it. Impulses towards useful objects, and revulsion from the opposite, are according to nature; without any reflection to prompt the idea, and without any advice, whatever Nature has prescribed, is done.

Do you not see how skillful bees are in building their cells? How completely harmonious in sharing and enduring toil? Do you not see how the spider weaves a web so subtle that man's hand cannot imitate it; and what a task it is to arrange the threads, some directed straight towards the centre, for the sake of making the web solid, and others running in circles and lessening in thickness—for the purpose of tangling and catching in a sort of net the smaller insects for whose ruin the spider spreads the web? This art is born, not taught;

409

ars ista, non discitur. Itaque nullum est animal
altero doctius. Videbis araneorum pares telas, par
in favis angulorum omnium foramen. Incertum est
et inaequabile, quidquid ars tradit; ex aequo[1]
venit, quod natura distribuit. Haec nihil magis
quam tutelam sui et eius peritiam tradidit, ideoque
24 etiam simul incipiunt et discere et vivere. Nec est
mirum cum eo nasci illa, sine quo frustra nascerentur.
Primum hoc instrumentum in illa natura contulit ad
permanendum,[2] conciliationem et caritatem sui.
Non poterant salva esse, nisi vellent. Nec[3] hoc
per se profuturum erat, sed sine hoc nulla res pro-
fuisset. In[4] nullo deprendes vilitatem sui, ne
neglegentiam quidem. Tacitis quoque et brutis,
quamquam in cetera torpeant, ad vivendum sol-
lertia est. Videbis, quae aliis inutilia sunt, sibi ipsa
non deesse. Vale.

CXXII.

Seneca Lvcilio svo salvtem

1 Detrimentum iam dies sensit. Resiluit aliquan-
tum, ita tamen ut liberale adhuc spatium sit, si
quis cum ipso, ut ita dicam, die surgat. Officiosior
meliorque, si quis illum exspectat et lucem primam
excipit[5]; turpis, qui alto sole semisomnus iacet,
cuius vigilia medio die incipit; et adhuc multis hoc

---

[1] *ex aequo* Pinc.; *ex equo* Harl.; *et quo* BA[1]p.
[2] After *permanendum* Bartsch del. *in.*
[3] After *nec* Hense del. *non.* [4] Before *in* Bartsch del. *sed.*
[5] *excipit* Gruter; *exuit* BAp.

---

[a] A theme developed by Cicero (*De fin.* iii. 16): *placet
. . . simul atque natum sit animal . . . , ipsum sibi conciliari et commendari ad se conservandum.*

and for this reason no animal is more skilled than any other. You will notice that all spider-webs are equally fine, and that the openings in all honeycomb cells are identical in shape. Whatever art communicates is uncertain and uneven; but Nature's assignments are always uniform. Nature has communicated nothing except the duty of taking care of themselves and the skill to do so; that is why living and learning begin at the same time. No wonder that living things are born with a gift whose absence would make birth useless. This is the first equipment that Nature granted them for the maintenance of their existence—the quality of adaptability and self-love. They could not survive except by desiring to do so. Nor would this desire alone have made them prosper, but without it nothing could have prospered. In no animal can you observe any low esteem, or even any carelessness, of self. Dumb beasts, sluggish in other respects, are clever at living. So you will see that creatures which are useless to others are alert for their own preservation.[a] Farewell.

CXXII. ON DARKNESS AS A VEIL FOR WICKEDNESS

The day has already begun to lessen. It has shrunk considerably, but yet will still allow a goodly space of time if one rises, so to speak, with the day itself. We are more industrious, and we are better men if we anticipate the day and welcome the dawn; but we are base churls if we lie dozing when the sun is high in the heavens, or if we wake up only when noon arrives; and even then to many it seems not yet

THE EPISTLES OF SENECA

2 antelucanum est. Sunt qui officia lucis noctisque
perverterint nec ante diducant oculos hesterna
graves crapula quam adpetere nox coepit. Qualis
illorum condicio dicitur, quos natura, ut ait Vergilius,
sedibus nostris subditos e contrario posuit,

> Nosque ubi primus equis Oriens adflavit anhelis,
> Illis sera rubens accendit lumina Vesper ;

talis horum contraria omnibus non regio, sed vita
est. Sunt quidam in eadem urbe antipodes, qui,
ut M. Cato ait, nec orientem umquam solem viderunt
3 nec occidentem. Hos tu existimas scire quemadmodum vivendum sit, qui nesciunt quando ? Et
hi mortem timent, in quam se vivi condiderunt ?
Tam infausti quam nocturnae aves sunt. Licet in
vino unguentoque tenebras suas exigant, licet epulis
et quidem in multa fericula [1] discoctis totum per-
versae vigiliae tempus educant, non convivantur,
sed iusta sibi faciunt. Mortuis certe interdiu
parentatur.

At mehercules nullus agenti dies longus est.
Extendamus vitam ; huius et officium et argumentum actus est. Circumscribatur nox, et aliquid ex
4 illa in diem transferatur. Aves, quae conviviis
conparantur, ut inmotae facile pinguescant, in
obscuro continentur ; ita sine ulla exercitatione
iacentibus tumor [2] pigrum corpus invadit, et superba
umbra iners sagina subcrescit. At istorum cor-

---

[1] *fericula* Turnebus ; *pericula* BAp.
[2] *tumor* later MSS. ; *timor* BAp.

---

[a] Vergil, *Georg.* i. 250 f.
[b] Cato, Frag. p. 110 Jordan.
[c] *i.e.*, owls, of ill omen.
[d] In connexion with the *Parentalia*, Feb. 13-21, and at
other anniversary observations, the ceremonies were held in
the daytime.

dawn. Some have reversed the functions of light and darkness; they open eyes sodden with yesterday's debauch only at the approach of night. It is just like the condition of those peoples whom, according to Vergil, Nature has hidden away and placed in an abode directly opposite to our own:

> When in our face the Dawn with panting steeds
> Breathes down, for them the ruddy evening kindles
> Her late-lit fires.[a]

It is not the country of these men, so much as it is their life, that is "directly opposite" to our own. There may be Antipodes dwelling in this same city of ours who, in Cato's words,[b] "have never seen the sun rise or set." Do you think that these men know *how* to live, if they do not know *when* to live? Do these men fear death, if they have buried themselves alive? They are as weird as the birds of night.[c] Although they pass their hours of darkness amid wine and perfumes, although they spend the whole extent of their unnatural waking hours in eating dinners—and those too cooked separately to make up many courses—they are not really banqueting; they are conducting their own funeral services. And the dead at least have their banquets by daylight.[d]

But indeed to one who is active no day is long. So let us lengthen our lives; for the duty and the proof of life consist in action. Cut short the night; use some of it for the day's business. Birds that are being prepared for the banquet, that they may be easily fattened through lack of exercise, are kept in darkness; and similarly, if men vegetate without physical activity, their idle bodies are overwhelmed with flesh, and in their self-satisfied retirement the fat of indolence grows upon them. Moreover, the bodies of those who have sworn allegiance to the hours of

413

pora, qui se tenebris dicaverunt, foeda visuntur.
Quippe suspectior illis quam morbo pallentibus color
est, languidi et evanidi albent, et in vivis caro morti-
cina est. Hoc tamen minimum in illis malorum
dixerim. Quanto plus tenebrarum in animo est!
Ille in se stupet, ille caligat, invidet caecis. Quis
umquam oculos tenebrarum causa habuit?

5 Interrogas, quomodo haec animo pravitas fiat
aversandi diem et totam vitam in noctem trans-
ferendi? Omnia vitia contra naturam pugnant,
omnia debitum ordinem deserunt. Hoc est luxuriae propositum, gaudere perversis nec tantum
discedere a recto, sed quam longissime abire, deinde
6 etiam e contrario stare. Non videntur tibi contra
naturam vivere qui ieiuni [1] bibunt, qui vinum recipiunt inanibus venis et ad cibum ebrii transeunt?
Atqui frequens hoc adulescentium vitium est, qui
vires excolunt, ut in ipso paene balinei limine inter
nudos bibant, immo potent et sudorem, quem move-
runt potionibus crebris ac ferventibus, subinde de-
stringant. Post prandium aut cenam bibere vul-
gare est; hoc patres familiae rustici faciunt et verae
voluptatis ignari. Merum illud delectat, quod non
innatat cibo, quod libere penetrat ad nervos; illa
ebrietas iuvat, quae in vacuum venit.

7 Non videntur tibi contra naturam vivere qui
commutant cum feminis vestem? Non vivunt

---

[1] *qui ieiuni* Pinc. and cod. Harl.; *ieiuni* BAp.

[a] A vice which Seneca especially abhors; *cf. Ep.* xv. 3
multum potionis altius ieiunio iturae.
[b] By wearing silk gowns of transparent material.

darkness have a loathsome appearance. Their complexions are more alarming than those of anaemic invalids; they are lackadaisical and flabby with dropsy; though still alive, they are already carrion. But this, to my thinking, would be among the least of their evils. How much more darkness there is in their souls! Such a man is internally dazed; his vision is darkened; he envies the blind. And what man ever had eyes for the purpose of seeing in the dark?

You ask me how this depravity comes upon the soul—this habit of reversing the daylight and giving over one's whole existence to the night? All vices rebel against Nature; they all abandon the appointed order. It is the motto of luxury to enjoy what is unusual, and not only to depart from that which is right, but to leave it as far behind as possible, and finally even take a stand in opposition thereto. Do you not believe that men live contrary to Nature who drink fasting,[a] who take wine into empty veins, and pass to their food in a state of intoxication? And yet this is one of youth's popular vices—to perfect their strength in order to drink on the very threshold of the bath, amid the unclad bathers; nay even to soak in wine and then immediately to rub off the sweat which they have promoted by many a hot glass of liquor! To them, a glass after lunch or one after dinner is *bourgeois*; it is what the country squires do, who are not connoisseurs in pleasure. This unmixed wine delights them just because there is no food to float in it, because it readily makes its way into their muscles; this boozing pleases them just because the stomach is empty.

Do you not believe that men live contrary to Nature who exchange the fashion of their attire with women?[b] Do not men live contrary to Nature who

contra naturam qui spectant, ut pueritia splendeat
tempore alieno ? Quid fieri crudelius vel miserius
potest ? Numquam vir erit, ut diu virum pati
possit ? Et cum illum contumeliae sexus eripuisse
8 debuerat, non ne aetas quidem eripiet ? Non
vivunt contra naturam qui hieme concupiscunt
rosam fomentoque aquarum calentium et calorum
apta mutatione bruma lilium,[1] florem vernum,
exprimunt[2] ? Non vivunt contra naturam[3] qui
pomaria in summis turribus serunt ? Quorum silvae
in tectis domuum ac fastigiis nutant,[4] inde ortis
radicibus quo inprobe cacumina egissent ? Non
vivunt contra naturam qui fundamenta thermarum in
mari iaciunt et delicate natare ipsi sibi non[5] videntur,
nisi calentia stagna fluctu ac tempestate feriantur ?
9 Cum instituerunt omnia contra naturae consuetudinem velle, novissime in totum ab illa desuescunt.
" Lucet : somni tempus est. Quies est : nunc
exerceamur, nunc gestemur, nunc prandeamus.
Iam lux propius accedit ; tempus est cenae. Non
oportet id facere, quod populus. Res sordida est
trita ac vulgari via vivere. Dies publicus relinquatur : proprium[6] nobis ac peculiare mane fiat."
10 Isti vero mihi defunctorum loco sunt. Quantulum
enim a funere absunt et quidem acerbo, qui ad faces
et cereos vivunt ? Hanc vitam agere eodem tem-

---

[1] *bruma lilium* Pinc. ; *brumalium* BAp.
[2] *exprimunt* later MSS. ; *primaint* BA ; *primunt* p.
[3] *contra naturam* later MSS. ; *conaturam* BAp.
[4] *nutant* later MSS. ; *mutant* BAp.
[5] *non* add. later MSS.
[6] *proprium* later MSS. ; *proprius* or *propius* BAp.

---

[a] Not literally translated. For the same thought see
Ep. xlvii. 7, etc.

endeavour to look fresh and boyish at an age un-
suitable for such an attempt ? What could be more
cruel or more wretched ? Cannot time and man's
estate ever carry such a person beyond an artificial
boyhood ?[a] Do not men live contrary to Nature
who crave roses in winter, or seek to raise a spring
flower like the lily by means of hot-water heaters
and artificial changes of temperature ? Do not men
live contrary to Nature who grow fruit-trees on the
top of a wall ? Or raise waving forests upon the
roofs and battlements of their houses—the roots
starting at a point to which it would be outlandish
for the tree-tops to reach ? Do not men live contrary to Nature who lay the foundations of bath-
rooms in the sea and do not imagine that they can
enjoy their swim unless the heated pool is lashed as
with the waves of a storm ?

When men have begun to desire all things in
opposition to the ways of Nature, they end by entirely
abandoning the ways of Nature. They cry : " It is
daytime : let us go to sleep ! It is the time when
men rest : now for exercise, now for our drive, now
for our lunch ! Lo, the dawn approaches : it is
dinner-time ! We should not do as mankind do. It
is low and mean to live in the usual and conventional
way. Let us abandon the ordinary sort of day. Let
us have a morning that is a special feature of ours,
peculiar to ourselves ! " Such men are, in my
opinion, as good as dead. Are they not all but
present at a funeral—and before their time too—
when they live amid torches and tapers ?[b] I remember that this sort of life was very fashionable at

---

[b] The symbols of a Roman funeral. For the same practice, purposely performed, see *Ep.* xii. 8 (and the note of
W. C. Summers).

pore multos meminimus, inter quos et Acilium
Butam, praetorium, cui post patrimonium ingens
consumptum Tiberius paupertatem confitenti " sero,"
11 inquit, " experrectus es." Recitabat Montanus
Iulius carmen, tolerabilis poeta et amicitia Tiberi
notus et frigore. Ortus et occasus libentissime in-
serebat. Itaque cum indignaretur quidam illum
toto die recitasse et negaret accedendum ad recita-
tiones eius, Natta Pinarius ait : " Numquam possum
liberalius agere : paratus sum illum audire ab ortu
12 ad occasum." Cum hos versus recitasset :

> Incipit ardentes Phoebus producere flammas,
> Spargere se[1] rubicunda dies, iam tristis hirundo
> Argutis reditura cibos inmittere[2] nidis
> Incipit et molli partitos ore ministrat,

Varus eques Romanus, M. Vinicii comes, cenarum
bonarum adsectator, quas improbitate linguae mere-
batur, exclamavit : " incipit Buta dormire." Deinde
13 cum subinde recitasset :

> Iam sua pastores stabulis armenta locarunt,
> Iam dare sopitis nox pigra silentia terris
> Incipit,

idem Varus inquit : " Quid dicis ? Iam nox est ?
Ibo et Butam salutabo." Nihil erat notius hac eius
vita in contrarium circumacta ; quam, ut dixi, multi

---

[1] *se* later MSS. ; om. BA.
[2] *inmittere* later MSS. ; *mittere* BAp.

---

[a] Called by Tacitus, *Ann.* iv. 34, a *Seiani cliens.*
[b] Baehrens, *Frag. Poet. Rom.* p. 355.
[c] *i.e.*, Procne, in the well-known nightingale myth.
[d] Son of the P. Vinicius ridiculed in *Ep.* xl. 9. He was
husband of Julia, youngest daughter of Germanicus. and
was poisoned by Messalina.

one time : among such men as Acilius Buta, a person of praetorian rank, who ran through a tremendous estate and on confessing his bankruptcy to Tiberius, received the answer : "You have waked up too late !" Julius Montanus was once reading a poem aloud ; he was a middling good poet, noted for his friendship with Tiberius, as well as his fall from favour. He always used to fill his poems with a generous sprinkling of sunrises and sunsets. Hence, when a certain person was complaining that Montanus had read all day long, and declared that no man should attend any of his readings, Natta Pinarius [a] remarked : "I couldn't make a fairer bargain than this : I am ready to listen to him from sunrise to sunset !" Montanus was reading, and had reached the words : [b]

'Gins the bright morning to spread forth his flames clear-
    burning ; the red dawn
Scatters its light ; and the sad-eyed swallow [c] returns to
    her nestlings,
Bringing the chatterers' food, and with sweet bill sharing
    and serving.

Then Varus, a Roman knight, the hanger-on of Marcus Vinicius, [d] and a sponger at elegant dinners which he earned by his degenerate wit, shouted : "Bed-time for Buta !" And later, when Montanus declaimed :

Lo, now the shepherds have folded their flocks, and the
    slow-moving darkness
'Gins to spread silence o'er lands that are drowsily lulled
    into slumber,

this same Varus remarked : "What ? Night already ? I'll go and pay my morning call on Buta !" You see, nothing was more notorious than Buta's upside-down manner of life. But this life, as I said, was

14 eodem tempore egerunt. Causa autem est ita
vivendi quibusdam, non quia aliquid existiment
noctem ipsam habere iucundius, sed quia nihil iuvat
solitum,[1] et gravis malae conscientiae lux est, et
omnia concupiscenti aut contemnenti, prout magno
aut parvo empta sunt, fastidio est lumen gratuitum.
Praeterea luxuriosi vitam suam esse in sermonibus,
dum vivunt, volunt; nam si tacetur, perdere se
putant operam. Itaque male habent,[a] quotiens
faciunt[2] quod excidat fama.

Multi bona comedunt, multi amicas habent. Ut
inter istos nomen invenias, opus est non tantum
luxuriosam rem, sed notabilem facere; in tam occupata civitate fabulas vulgaris nequitia non invenit.

15 Pedonem Albinovanum narrantem audieramus, erat
autem fabulator elegantissimus, habitasse se supra
domum S. Papini. Is erat ex hac turba lucifugarum.
"Audio," inquit, "circa horam tertiam noctis flagel-
lorum sonum. Quaero, quid faciat; dicitur rationes
accipere. Audio circa horam sextam noctis clamo-
rem concitatum; quaero, quid sit; dicitur vocem
exercere. Quaero circa horam octavam noctis, quid

16 sibi ille sonus rotarum velit; gestari dicitur. Circa
lucem discurritur, pueri vocantur, cellarii, coqui
tumultuantur. Quaero, quid sit; dicitur mulsum et
halicam poposcisse, a balneo exisse. Excedebat,"

[1] *solitum* later MSS.; *oblitum* BAp.
[2] *male habent quociens faciunt* later MSS. and cod. Harl.;
aliquotiens faciunt BAp.

---

[a] *i.e.*, is punishing his slaves for errors in the day's work.

fashionable at one time. And the reason why some men live thus is not because.they think that night in itself offers any greater attractions, but because that which is normal gives them no particular pleasure ; light being a bitter enemy of the evil conscience, and, when one craves or scorns all things in proportion as they have cost one much or little, illumination for which one does not pay is an object of contempt. Moreover, the luxurious person wishes to be an object of gossip his whole life ; if people are silent about him, he thinks that he is wasting his time. Hence he is uncomfortable whenever any of his actions escape notoriety.

Many men eat up their property, and many men keep mistresses. If you would win a reputation among such persons, you must make your programme not only one of luxury but one of notoriety ; for in such a busy community wickedness does not discover the ordinary sort of scandal. I heard Pedo Albinovanus, that most attractive story-teller, speaking of his residence above the town-house of Sextus Papinius. Papinius belonged to the tribe of those who shun the light. "About nine o'clock at night I hear the sound of whips. I ask what is going on, and they tell me that Papinius is going over his accounts.[a] About twelve there is a strenuous shouting ; I ask what the matter is, and they say he is exercising his voice. About two A.M. I ask the significance of the sound of wheels ; they tell me that he is off for a drive. And at dawn there is a tremendous flurry—calling of slaves and butlers, and pandemonium among the cooks. I ask the meaning of this also, and they tell me that he has called for his cordial and his appetizer, after leaving the bath. His dinner," said Pedo, "never went

inquit, " huius diem cena minime, valde enim frugaliter vivebat ; nihil consumebat nisi noctem. Itaque
credendo dicentibus illum quibusdam avarum et
sordidum vos," inquit, " illum et lychnobium dicetis."

17 Non debes admirari, si tantas invenis vitiorum
proprietates ; varia sunt, innumerabiles habent
facies, comprendi eorum genera non possunt. Simplex recti cura est, multiplex pravi, et quantumvis
novas declinationes capit. Idem moribus evenit ;
naturam sequentium faciles sunt, soluti sunt, exiguas
differentias habent ; his distorti plurimum et omni-

18 bus et inter se dissident. Causa tamen praecipua
mihi videtur huius morbi vitae communis fastidium.
Quomodo cultu se a ceteris distinguunt, quomodo
elegantia cenarum, munditiis vehiculorum, sic se [1]
volunt separare etiam temporum dispositione.[2]
Nolunt solita peccare,[3] quibus peccandi praemium
infamia est. Hanc petunt omnes isti, qui, ut ita
dicam, retro [4] vivunt.

19 Ideo, Lucili, tenenda nobis via est, quam natura
praescripsit, nec ab illa declinandum ; illam se-
quentibus omnia facilia, expedita sunt, contra illam
nitentibus non alia vita est quam contra aquam
remigantibus. Vale.

---

[1] *se* add. Hense.
[2] *dispositione* Muretus ; *dispositiones* MSS.
[3] *peccare* Erasmus ; *spectare* MSS.
[4] *retro* Pincianus ; *recto* MSS.

---

[a] *i.e.*, balancing the custom of the ordinary Roman, whose
dinner never continued beyond nightfall.
[b] " ' A liver by candle-light,' with a play on the word
λίχνος, ' luxurious ' " (Summers).

beyond the day,[a] for he lived very sparingly; he was lavish with nothing but the night. Accordingly, if you believe those who call him tight-fisted and mean, you will call him also a 'slave of the lamp.'"[b]

You should not be surprised at finding so many special manifestations of the vices; for vices vary, and there are countless phases of them, nor can all their various kinds be classified. The method of maintaining righteousness is simple; the method of maintaining wickedness is complicated, and has infinite opportunity to swerve. And the same holds true of character; if you follow nature, character is easy to manage, free, and with very slight shades of difference; but the sort of person I have mentioned possesses badly warped character, out of harmony with all things, including himself. The chief cause, however, of this disease seems to me to be a squeamish revolt from the normal existence. Just as such persons mark themselves off from others in their dress, or in the elaborate arrangement of their dinners, or in the elegance of their carriages; even so they desire to make themselves peculiar by their way of dividing up the hours of their day. They are unwilling to be wicked in the conventional way, because notoriety is the reward of their sort of wickedness. Notoriety is what all such men seek— men who are, so to speak, *living backwards*.

For this reason, Lucilius, let us keep to the way which Nature has mapped out for us, and let us not swerve therefrom. If we follow Nature, all is easy and unobstructed; but if we combat Nature, our life differs not a whit from that of men who row against the current. Farewell.

CXXIII.

Seneca Lvcilio svo salvtem

1 Itinere confectus incommodo magis quam longo
in Albanum meum multa nocte perveni ; nihil
habeo parati nisi me. Itaque in lectulo lassitudinem
pono, hanc coci ac pistoris moram boni consulo.
Mecum enim de hoc ipso loquor, quam nihil sit
grave, quod leviter excipias,[1] indignandum nihil
2 nisi[2] ipse indignando adstruas. Non habet panem
meus[3] pistor ; sed habet vilicus, sed habet atriensis,
sed habet colonus. " Malum panem " inquis. Ex-
specta : bonus fiet. Etiam illum tibi tenerum et
siligineum fames reddet. Ideo non est ante edendum quam illa imperat ; exspectabo ergo nec ante
edam quam aut bonum panem habere coepero aut
3 fastidire desiero. Necessarium est parvo adsue-
scere : multae difficultates locorum, multae temporum etiam locupletibus et instructis ad voluptatem[4] prohibentes[5] occurrent. Quidquid vult habere nemo potest, illud potest, nolle quod non habet,
rebus oblatis hilaris uti. Magna pars libertatis est
bene moratus venter et contumeliae patiens.
4 Aestimari non potest, quantam voluptatem capiam
ex eo, quod lassitudo mea sibi ipsa adsuescit ; non
unctores, non balineum, non ullum aliud remedium

---

[1] After *excipias, quod* del. by Buecheler.
[2] *nisi* later MSS. ; om. BA.
[3] *meus* later MSS. ; *meum* BA.
[a] *ad voluptatem* P. Thomas ; *advobus optantem* BA.
[5] *prohibentes* Pinc. ; *prohibent et* BA.

CXXIII. ON THE CONFLICT BETWEEN PLEASURE AND VIRTUE

Wearied with the discomfort rather than with the length of my journey, I have reached my Alban villa late at night, and I find nothing in readiness except myself. So I am getting rid of fatigue at my writing-table : I derive some good from this tardiness on the part of my cook and my baker. For I am communing with myself on this very topic — that nothing is heavy if one accepts it with a light heart, and that nothing need provoke one's anger if one does not add to one's pile of troubles by getting angry. My baker is out of bread ; but the overseer, or the house-steward, or one of my tenants can supply me therewith. "Bad bread!" you say. But just wait for it ; it will become good. Hunger will make even such bread delicate and of the finest flavour. For that reason I must not eat until hunger bids me ; so I shall wait and shall not eat until I can either get good bread or else cease to be squeamish about it. It is necessary that one grow accustomed to slender fare : because there are many problems of time and place which will cross the path even of the rich man and one equipped for pleasure, and bring him up with a round turn. To have whatsoever he wishes is in no man's power ; it is in his power not to wish for what he has not, but cheerfully to employ what comes to him. A great step towards independence is a good-humoured stomach, one that is willing to endure rough treatment.

You cannot imagine how much pleasure I derive from the fact that my weariness is becoming reconciled to itself ; I am asking for no slaves to rub me

425

quam temporis quaero. Nam quod labor contraxit,
quies tollit. Haec qualiscumque cena aditiali [1]
5 iucundior erit. Aliquod enim experimentum animi
sumpsi subito ; hoc enim est simplicius et verius.
Nam ubi se praeparavit et indixit sibi patientiam,
non aeque apparet, quantum habeat verae firmitatis ;
illa sunt certissima argumenta, quae ex tempore
dedit, si non tantum aequus molestias,[2] sed placidus
aspexit ; si non excanduit, non litigavit ; si quod
dari deberet ipse sibi non desiderando supplevit et
cogitavit aliquid consuetudini suae, sibi nihil deesse.
6 Multa quam supervacua essent, non intelleximus,
nisi deesse coeperunt ; utebamur enim illis, non
quia debebamus, sed quia habebamus. Quam multa
autem paramus, quia alii paraverunt, quia apud
plerosque sunt ! Inter causas malorum nostrorum
est, quod vivimus ad exempla, nec ratione conponi-
mur sed consuetudine abducimur.

Quod, si pauci facerent, nollemus imitari, cum
plures facere coeperunt, quasi honestius sit, quia
frequentius, sequimur. Et recti [3] apud nos locum
7 tenet error, ubi publicus factus est. Omnes iam sic
peregrinantur, ut illos Numidarum praecurrat equi-
tatus, ut agmen cursorum antecedat ; turpe est
nullos esse, qui occurrentis via deiciant, aut [4] qui

---

[1] *aditiali* Erasmus ; *adiali* BA.
[2] *molestias* Windhaus ; *molesta* later MSS. ; *modestia* BA.
[3] *recti* later MSS. ; *retu* BA.
[4] *deiciant aut* later MSS. ; *deiciantur ut* BA.

---

[a] *i.e.*, a dinner given by an official when he entered upon
(*adeo*) his office.

down, no bath, and no other restorative except time
For that which toil has accumulated, rest can lighten.
This repast, whatever it may be, will give me more
pleasure than an inaugural banquet.[a] For I have
made trial of my spirit on a sudden—a simpler and
a truer test. Indeed, when a man has made prepara-
tions and given himself a formal summons to be
patient, it is not equally clear just how much real
strength of mind he possesses ; the surest proofs are
those which one exhibits off-hand, viewing one's
own troubles not only fairly but calmly, not flying
into fits of temper or wordy wranglings, supplying
one's own needs by not craving something which
was really due, and reflecting that our habits may
be unsatisfied, but never our own real selves. How
many things are superfluous we fail to realize until
they begin to be wanting ; we merely used them
not because we needed them but because we had
them. And how much do we acquire simply because
our neighbours have acquired such things, or because
most men possess them ! Many of our troubles may
be explained from the fact that we live according to
a pattern, and, instead of arranging our lives according to reason, are led astray by convention.
   There are things which, if done by the few, we
should refuse to imitate ; yet when the majority
have begun to do them, we follow along—just as
if anything were more honourable because it is
more frequent ! Furthermore, wrong views, when
they have become prevalent, reach, in our eyes, the
standard of righteousness. Everyone now travels with
Numidian outriders preceding him, with a troop of
slave-runners to clear the way ; we deem it disgraceful to have no attendants who will elbow crowds
from the road, or will prove, by a great cloud of dust,

honestum hominem venire magno pulvere ostendant.
Omnes iam mulos habent, qui crustallina et murrina
et caelata magnorum artificum manu portent;
turpe est videri eas te habere sarcinas totas, quae
e tuto[1] concuti possint. Omnium paedagogia ob-
lita facie vehuntur, ne sol, ne frigus teneram cutem
laedat; turpe est neminem esse in comitatu tuo[2]
puerorum, cuius sana facies medicamentum de-
sideret.

8 Horum omnium sermo vitandus est : hi sunt, qui
vitia tradunt et alio aliunde transerunt.[3] Pessimum
genus horum hominum videbatur, qui verba gesta-
rent; sunt quidam, qui vitia gestant. Horum
sermo multum nocet; nam etiam si non statim
profecit, semina in animo relinquit sequiturque nos
etiam cum ab illis discessimus, resurrecturum postea
9 malum. Quemadmodum qui audierunt symphoniam,
ferunt secum in auribus modulationem illam ac
dulcedinem cantuum, quae cogitationes impedit nec
ad seria patitur intendi, sic adulatorum et prava
laudantium sermo diutius haeret quam auditur.
Nec facile est animo dulcem sonum excutere;
prosequitur et durat et ex intervallo recurrit. Ideo
cludendae sunt aures malis vocibus et quidem
primis ; quom initum[4] fecerunt admissaeque insunt
10 plus audent. Inde ad haec pervenitur verba:

---

[1] *tuto* later MSS.; *toto* BA; *e toto* Buecheler.
[2] *comitatu tuo* Buecheler; *comitatu(o)* BA.
[3] *transerunt* Hense; *transeunt* BA.
[4] *quom initum* Buecheler; *quam initium* A (*nam*) B.

---

[a] For the *symphonia* see *Ep.* li. 4 and note. Compare also
the *commissiones*, orchestral exhibitions, composed of many
voices, flutes, and brass instruments, *Ep.* lxxxiv. 10.

that a high dignitary is approaching! Everyone now possesses mules that are laden with crystal and myrrhine cups carved by skilled artists of great renown; it is disgraceful for all your baggage to be made up of that which can be rattled along without danger. Everyone has pages who ride along with ointment-covered faces, so that the heat or the cold will not harm their tender complexions; it is disgraceful that none of your attendant slave-boys should show a healthy cheek, not covered with cosmetics.

You should avoid conversation with all such persons: they are the sort that communicate and engraft their bad habits from one to another. We used to think that the very worst variety of these men were those who vaunted their words; but there are certain men who vaunt their wickedness. Their talk is very harmful; for even though it is not at once convincing, yet they leave the seeds of trouble in the soul, and the evil which is sure to spring into new strength follows us about even when we have parted from them. Just as those who have attended a concert *a* carry about in their heads the melodies and the charm of the songs they have heard — a proceeding which interferes with their thinking and does not allow them to concentrate upon serious subjects,—even so the speech of flatterers and enthusiasts over that which is depraved sticks in our minds long after we have heard them talk. It is not easy to rid the memory of a catching tune; it stays with us, lasts on, and comes back from time to time. Accordingly, you should close your ears against evil talk, and right at the outset, too; for when such talk has gained an entrance and the words are admitted and are in our minds, they become more shameless. And then we begin to

429

" Virtus et philosophia et iustitia verborum inanium
crepitus est. Una felicitas est bene vitae facere.
Esse, bibere, frui patrimonio, hoc est vivere, hoc
est se mortalem esse meminisse. Fluunt dies et
inreparabilis vita decurrit; dubitamus sapere? Quid
iuvat aetati [1] non semper voluptates recepturae
interim, dum potest, dum poscit, ingerere frugalitatem? Eo mortem praecurre et quidquid illa
ablatura est, iam sine tibi interire.[2] Non amicam
habes, non puerum, qui amicae moveat invidiam;
cottidie sobrius prodis; sic cenas tamquam epheme-
ridem patri adprobaturus: non est istud vivere,
11 sed alienae vitae interesse. Quanta dementia est
heredis sui res procurare et sibi negare omnia, ut
tibi ex amico inimicum magna faciat hereditas.
Plus enim gaudebit tua morte,[3] quo plus acceperit.
Istos tristes et superciliosos alienae vitae censores,
suae hostes, publicos paedagogos assis ne feceris
nec dubitaveris bonam vitam quam opinionem bonam
malle."

12 Hae voces non aliter fugiendae sunt quam illae,
quas Ulixes nisi alligatus praetervehi noluit. Idem
possunt; abducunt a patria, a parentibus, ab amicis,
a virtutibus et in turpem vitam misera nisi

---

[1] *sapere? Quid iuvat aetati* Buecheler and Hense: *quod
iuvat sapere et aetati* BA.
[2] *sine tibi interire* Hense; *sibi interere* BA.
[3] *tua morte* later MSS.; *tuamor* B¹A.

speak as follows: " Virtue, Philosophy, Justice—this is a jargon of empty words. The only way to be happy is to do yourself well. To eat, drink, and spend your money is the only real life, the only way to remind yourself that you are mortal. Our days flow on, and life—which we cannot restore—hastens away from us. Why hesitate to come to our senses? This life of ours will not always admit pleasures; meantime, while it can do so, while it clamours for them, what profit lies in imposing thereupon frugality? Therefore get ahead of death, and let anything that death will filch from you be squandered now upon yourself. You have no mistress, no favourite slave to make your mistress envious; you are sober when you make your daily appearance in public; you dine as if you had to show your account-book to ' Papa'; but *that* is not living, it is merely going shares in someone else's existence. And what madness it is to be looking out for the interests of your heir, and to deny yourself everything, with the result that you turn friends into enemies by the vast amount of the fortune you intend to leave! For the more the heir is to get from you, the more he will rejoice in your taking-off! All those sour fellows who criticize other men's lives in a spirit of priggish-ness and are real enemies to their own lives, playing schoolmaster to the world—you should not consider them as worth a farthing, nor should you hesitate to prefer good living to a good reputation."

These are voices which you ought to shun just as Ulysses did; he would not sail past them until he was lashed to the mast. They are no less potent; they lure men from country, parents, friends, and virtuous ways; and by a hope that, if not base, is ill-starred, they wreck them upon a life of baseness.

431

turpi spe illidunt.[1]   Quanto satius est rectum sequi
limitem et eo se perducere, ut ea demum sint tibi
13 iucunda, quae honesta.   Quod adsequi poterimus,
si scierimus [2] duo esse genera rerum, quae nos aut
invitent aut fugent.   Invitant ut divitiae, voluptates, forma, ambitio, cetera blanda et adridentia ;
fugat labor, mors, dolor, ignominia, victus adstrictior.
Debemus itaque exerceri, ne haec timeamus, ne illa
cupiamus.   In contrarium pugnemus et ab invi-
tantibus recedamus, adversus petentia concitemur.

14   Non vides, quam diversus sit descendentium habitus et ascendentium ?   Qui per pronum eunt, re-
supinant corpora, qui in arduum, incumbunt.   Nam
si descendas, pondus suum in priorem partem dare,
si ascendas, retro abducere cum vitio, Lucili, consentire est.   In voluptates descenditur, in aspera
et dura subeundum est ; hic inpellamus corpora,
illic refrenemus.

15   Hoc nunc me existimas dicere, eos tantum per-
niciosos esse auribus nostris, qui voluptatem laudant,
qui doloris [3] metus, per se formidabiles res, in-
cutiunt ?   Illos quoque nocere nobis existimo, qui
nos sub specie Stoicae sectae hortantur ad vitia.
Hoc enim iactant : solum sapientem et doctum esse
amatorem.   " Solus sapit [4] ad hanc artem ; aeque

----

[1] *in turpem vitam misera nisi turpis illidunt* Cod. Harl.,
turpi spe Capps ; *inter spem vitam misera nisi turpis
inludunt* BA[1].
[2] *scierimus* later MSS. ; *fecerimus* BA.
[3] *doloris* Pinc. ; *dolores* BA.
[4] *sapit* Buecheler ; *apte* BA.

----

[a] *i.e.*, to live by Stoicism rather than by Epicureanism.
[b] Meaning, in line with the Stoic paradoxes, that only
the sage knows how to be rightly in love.

How much better to follow a straight course and attain a goal where the words "pleasant" and "honourable" have the same meaning ! [a] This end will be possible for us if we understand that there are two classes of objects which either attract us or repel us. We are attracted by such things as riches, pleasures, beauty, ambition, and other such coaxing and pleasing objects ; we are repelled by toil, death, pain, disgrace, or lives of greater frugality. We ought therefore to train ourselves so that we may avoid a fear of the one or a desire for the other. Let us fight in the opposite fashion : let us retreat from the objects that allure, and rouse ourselves to meet the objects that attack.

Do you not see how different is the method of descending a mountain from that employed in climbing upwards ? Men coming down a slope bend backwards ; men ascending a steep place lean forward. For, my dear Lucilius, to allow yourself to put your body's weight ahead when coming down, or, when climbing up, to throw it backward is to comply with vice. The pleasures take one down hill, but one must work upwards toward that which is rough and hard to climb ; in the one case let us throw our bodies forward, in the others let us put the check-rein on them.

Do you believe me to be stating now that only those men bring ruin to our ears, who praise pleasure, who inspire us with fear of pain — that element which is in itself provocative of fear ? I believe that we are also injured by those who masquerade under the disguise of the Stoic school and at the same time urge us on into vice. They boast that only the wise man and the learned is a lover.[b] "He alone has wisdom in this art ; the wise man too is

THE EPISTLES OF SENECA

conbibendi et convivendi sapiens est peritissimus.
Quaeramus, ad quam usque aetatem iuvenes amandi
16 sint." Haec Graecae consuetudini data sint,[1] nos
ad illa potius aures derigamus : " Nemo est casu
bonus. Discenda virtus est. Voluptas humilis res
et pusilla est et in nullo habenda pretio, communis
cum mutis animalibus, ad quam minima et con-
temptissima advolant. Gloria vanum et volucre[2]
quiddam est auraque mobilius. Paupertas nulli
malum est nisi repugnanti. Mors malum non est ;
quid quaeris ? Sola ius aecum generis humani.
Superstitio error insanientis[3] est ; amandos timet ;
quos colit, violat. Quid enim interest, utrum deos
neges an infames ? "
17 Haec discenda, immo ediscenda sunt ; non debet[4]
excusationes vitio philosophia[4] suggerere. Nullam
habet spem salutis aeger,[5] quem ad intemperantiam
medicus hortatur. VALE.

CXXIV.

SENECA LVCILIO SVO SALVTEM

1   Possum multa tibi veterum praecepta referre,
      Ni refugis tenuisque piget cognoscere curas.

Non refugis autem nec ulla te subtilitas abigit.

---

[1] *haec . . . sint* later MSS. ; om. BA.
[2] *volucre* Schweighaeuser ; *volve* B[1]A ; *volatile* B[2] ;
volubile later MSS.
[3] *insanientis* Schweighaeuser ; *insanandus* BA ; *insanus*
later MSS.
[4] *debet* and *philosophia* Muretus ; *debes* and *philosophiae*
BA.
[5] *aeger* later MSS. ; *aeque* BA.

434

best skilled in drinking and feasting. Our study ought to be this alone : up to what age the bloom of love can endure ! " All this may be regarded as a concession to the ways of Greece ; we ourselves should preferably turn our attention to words like these : " No man is good by chance. Virtue is something which must be learned. Pleasure is low, petty, to be deemed worthless, shared even by dumb animals—the tiniest and meanest of whom fly towards pleasure. Glory is an empty and fleeting thing, lighter than air. Poverty is an evil to no man unless he kick against the goads. Death is not an evil ; why need you ask ? Death alone is the equal privilege of mankind. Superstition is the misguided idea of a lunatic ; it fears those whom it ought to love ; it is an outrage upon those whom it worships. For what difference is there between denying the gods and dishonouring them ? "

You should learn such principles as these, nay rather you should learn them by heart ; philosophy ought not to try to explain away vice. For a sick man, when his physician bids him live recklessly, is doomed beyond recall. Farewell.

CXXIV. ON THE TRUE GOOD AS ATTAINED
BY REASON

> Full many an ancient precept could I give,
> Didst thou not shrink, and feel it shame to learn
> Such lowly duties.[a]

But you do not shrink, nor are you deterred by any subtleties of study. For your cultivated mind

[a] Vergil, *Georg.* i. 176 f.

Non est elegantiae tuae tam magna sectari secure.[1]
Illud probo, quod omnia ad aliquem profectum
redigis et tunc tantum offenderis, ubi summa subtilitate nihil agitur. Quod ne nunc quidem fieri
laborabo. Quaeritur, utrum sensu conprendatur an
intellectu bonum? Huic adiunctum est in mutis
animalibus et infantibus non esse.

2 Quicumque voluptatem in summo ponunt, sensi-
bile iudicant bonum, nos contra intellegibile, qui
illud animo damus. Si de bono sensus iudicarent,
nullam voluptatem reiceremus, nulla enim non invitat, nulla non [2] delectat; et e contrario nullum
dolorem volentes subiremus, nullus enim non offendit
3 sensum. Praeterea non essent digni reprehensione,
quibus nimium voluptas placet quibusque summus est
doloris timor. Atqui inprobamus gulae ac libidini
addictos et contemnimus illos, qui nihil viriliter
ausuri sunt doloris metu. Quid autem peccant, si
sensibus, id est iudicibus boni ac mali, parent?
His enim tradidistis adpetitionis et fugae arbitrium.

4 Sed videlicet ratio isti rei praeposita est; illa [3]
quemadmodum de beata vita,[4] quemadmodum de
virtute, de honesto, sic et de bono maloque con-

---

[1] *secure.* Buecheler; *sicuti* or *sicut* MSS.
[2] *nulla non* later MSS.; *nulla* BA.
[3] *illa* Haase; *illi* BA.
[4] *de beata vita* Madvig; *debeat deb(v) ita* BA.

is not wont to investigate such important subjects in a free-and-easy manner. I approve your method in that you make everything count towards a certain degree of progress, and in that you are disgruntled only when nothing can be accomplished by the greatest degree of subtlety. And I shall take pains to show that this is the case now also. Our question is, whether the Good is grasped by the senses or by the understanding; and the corollary thereto is that it does not exist in dumb animals or little children.

Those who rate pleasure as the supreme ideal hold that the Good is a matter of the senses; but we Stoics maintain that it is a matter of the understanding, and we assign it to the mind. If the senses were to pass judgment on what is good, we should never reject any pleasure; for there is no pleasure that does not attract, no pleasure that does not please. Conversely, we should undergo no pain voluntarily; for there is no pain that does not clash with the senses. Besides, those who are too fond of pleasure and those who fear pain to the greatest degree would in that case not deserve reproof. But we condemn men who are slaves to their appetites and their lusts, and we scorn men who, through fear of pain, will dare no manly deed. But what wrong could such men be committing if they looked merely to the senses as arbiters of good and evil? For it is to the senses that you and yours have entrusted the test of things to be sought and things to be avoided!

Reason, however, is surely the governing element in such a matter as this; as reason has made the decision concerning the happy life, and concerning virtue and honour also, so she has made the decision

stituit. Nam apud istos vilissimae parti datur de
meliore sententia, ut de bono pronuntiet sensus,
obtunsa res et hebes et in homine quam in aliis
5 animalibus tardior. Quid si quis vellet non oculis,
sed tactu minuta discernere? Subtilior ad hoc acies
nulla quam oculorum et intentior daret bonum
malumque dinoscere. Vides in quanta ignorantia
veritatis versetur et quam humi sublimia ac divina
proiecerit, apud quem de summo, bono malo, iudicat
6 tactus. "Quemadmodum," inquit, "omnis scientia
atque ars aliquid debet habere manifestum sensu-
que conprehensum, ex quo oriatur et crescat, sic
beata vita fundamentum et initium a manifestis
ducit et eo, quod sub sensum cadat. Nempe vos
a manifestis beatam vitam initium sui capere dicitis."
7 Dicimus beata esse, quae secundum naturam sint.
Quid autem secundum naturam sit, palam et protinus apparet, sicut quid sit integrum. Quod
secundum naturam est, quod contigit protinus nato,
non dico bonum, sed initium boni. Tu summum
bonum, voluptatem, infantiae donas, ut inde in-
cipiat nascens, quo consummatus homo pervenit.
8 Cacumen radicis loco ponis. Si quis diceret illum
in materno utero latentem, sexus quoque incerti,[1]

---

[1] *incerti* Erasmus; *incepti* BA.

---

[a] *i.e.*, the Epicureans.
[b] *i.e.*, the advocate of the " touch " theory.

with regard to good and evil. For with them ^a the vilest part is allowed to give sentence about the better, so that the senses—dense as they are, and dull, and even more sluggish in man than in the other animals,—pass judgment on the Good. Just suppose that one should desire to distinguish tiny objects by the touch rather than by the eyesight! There is no special faculty more subtle and acute than the eye, that would enable us to distinguish between good and evil. You see, therefore, in what ignorance of truth a man spends his days and how abjectly he has overthrown lofty and divine ideals, if he thinks that the sense of touch can pass judgment upon the nature of the Supreme Good and the Supreme Evil! He ^b says: "Just as every science and every art should possess an element that is palpable and capable of being grasped by the senses (their source of origin and growth), even so the happy life derives its foundation and its beginnings from things that are palpable, and from that which falls within the scope of the senses. Surely you admit that the happy life takes its beginnings from things palpable to the senses." But we define as "happy" those things that are in accord with Nature. And that which is in accord with Nature is obvious and can be seen at once—just as easily as that which is complete. That which is according to Nature, that which is given us as a gift immediately at our birth, is, I maintain, not a Good, but the beginning of a Good. You, however, assign the Supreme Good, pleasure, to mere babies, so that the child at its birth begins at the point whither the perfected man arrives. You are placing the tree-top where the root ought to be. If anyone should say that the child, hidden in its mother's womb, of unknown sex too, delicate,

tenerum et inperfectum et informem iam in aliquo
bono esse, aperte videretur errare. Atqui quantulum interest inter eum, qui cum [1] maxime vitam
accipit, et illum, qui maternorum viscerum latens
onus est? Uterque, quantum ad intellectum boni
ac mali, aeque maturus est, et non magis infans
adhuc boni capax est quam arbor aut mutum aliquod
animal.

Quare autem bonum in arbore animalique muto
non est? Quia nec ratio. Ob hoc in infante quoque
non est, nam et huic deest; tunc ad bonum per-
9 veniet, cum ad rationem pervenerit. Est aliquod
inrationale [2] animal, est aliquod nondum rationale,
est rationale sed inperfectum; in nullo horum
bonum, ratio illud secum adfert. Quid ergo inter
ista, quae rettuli, distat? In eo, quod inrationale
est, numquam erit bonum. In eo, quod nondum
rationale est, tunc esse bonum non potest. Esse
in eo, quod rationale est [3] sed inperfectum, iam
10 potest bonum, sed non est. Ita dico, Lucili: bonum
non in quolibet corpore, non in qualibet aetate
invenitur et tantum abest ab infantia, quantum a
primo ultimum, quantum ab initio perfectum. Ergo
nec in tenero, modo coalescente corpusculo est.
Quidni non sit? Non magis quam in semine.

[1] *qui cum* Erasmus; *quicumq.* BA.
[2] *irrationale* later MSS.; *in ratione* BA. BA write *est
aliquod in ratione animal* twice.
[3] *esse in eo quod rationale est* Buecheler and Schweighaeuser; *sed in eo q. est rationale* later MSS.; om. BA.

[a] According to the Stoics (and other schools also), the
" innate notions," or groundwork of knowledge, begin to
be subject to reason after the attainment of a child's seventh
year.
[b] *i.e.*, they are limited to " practical judgment."

unformed, and shapeless—if one should say that this child is already in a state of goodness, he would clearly seem to be astray in his ideas. And yet how little difference is there between one who has just lately received the gift of life, and one who is still a hidden burden in the bowels of the mother! They are equally developed, as far as their understanding of good or evil is concerned; and a child is as yet no more capable of comprehending the Good than is a tree or any dumb beast.

But why is the Good non-existent in a tree or in a dumb beast? Because there is no reason there, either. For the same cause, then, the Good is non-existent in a child, for the child also has no reason; the child will reach the Good only when he reaches reason.[a] There are animals without reason, there are animals not yet endowed with reason, and there are animals who possess reason, but only incompletely[b]; in none of these does the Good exist, for it is reason that brings the Good in its company. What, then, is the distinction between the classes which I have mentioned? In that which does not possess reason, the Good will never exist. In that which is not yet endowed with reason, the Good cannot be existent at the time. And in that which possesses reason but only incompletely, the Good is capable of existing, but does not yet exist. This is what I mean, Lucilius: the Good cannot be discovered in any random person, or at any random age; and it is as far removed from infancy as last is from first, or as that which is complete from that which has just sprung into being. Therefore, it cannot exist in the delicate body, when the little frame has only just begun to knit together. Of course not—no more than in the seed. Granting

11 Hoc si dicas, aliquod arboris ac sati bonum novimus;
hoc non est in prima fronde, quae emissa cum
maxime solum rumpit. Est aliquod bonum tritici;
hoc nondum est in herba lactente nec cum folliculo
se exerit spica mollis, sed cum frumentum aestas
et debita maturitas coxit. Quemadmodum omnis
natura bonum suum nisi consummata non profert,
ita hominis bonum non est in homine, nisi cum illi[1]

12 ratio perfecta est. Quod autem hoc bonum?
Dicam: liber animus, erectus, alia subiciens sibi,
se nulli. Hoc bonum adeo non recipit infantia, ut
pueritia non speret, adulescentia inprobe speret;
bene agitur cum senectute, si ad illud longo studio
intentoque pervenit. Si hoc est[2] bonum, et intellegibile est.

13 " Dixisti," inquit, " aliquod bonum esse arboris,
aliquod herbae; potest ergo aliquod esse et infantis."
Verum bonum nec in arboribus nec in mutis animalibus; hoc, quod in illis bonum est, precario bonum
dicitur. " Quod est?" inquis. Hoc, quod secundum cuiusque naturam est. Bonum quidem cadere
in mutum animal nullo modo potest; felicioris
meliorisque naturae est. Nisi ubi rationi locus est,

14 bonum non est. Quattuor hae naturae sunt, arboris,
animalis, hominis, dei; haec duo, quae rationalia

---

[1] *illi* later MSS.; *illa* BA.
[2] *est* Rossbach; *et* BA.

---

[a] Just as Academic and Peripatetic philosophers sometimes defined as " goods " what the Stoics called " advan-
tages."

the truth of this, we understand that there is a certain kind of Good of a tree or in a plant; but this is not true of its first growth, when the plant has just begun to spring forth out of the ground. There is a certain Good of wheat: it is not yet existent, however, in the swelling stalk, nor when the soft ear is pushing itself out of the husk, but only when summer days and its appointed maturity have ripened the wheat. Just as Nature in general does not produce her Good until she is brought to perfection, even so man's Good does not exist in man until both reason and man are perfected. And what is this Good? I shall tell you: it is a free mind, an upright mind, subjecting other things to itself and itself to nothing. So far is infancy from admitting this Good that boyhood has no hope of it, and even young manhood cherishes the hope without justification; even our old age is very fortunate if it has reached this Good after long and concentrated study. If this, then, is the Good, the good is a matter of the understanding.

"But," comes the retort, "you admitted that there is a certain Good of trees and of grass; then surely there can be a certain Good of a child also." But the true Good is not found in trees or in dumb animals; the Good which exists in them is called "good" only by courtesy.[a] "Then what is it?" you say. Simply that which is in accord with the nature of each. The real Good cannot find a place in dumb animals—not by any means; its nature is more blest and is of a higher class. And where there is no place for reason, the Good does not exist. There are four natures which we should mention here: of the tree, animal, man, and God. The last two, having reasoning power, are of the

sunt, eandem naturam habent, illo[1] diversa sunt,
quod alterum inmortale, alterum mortale est. Ex
his ergo unius bonum natura perficit, dei scilicet,
alterius cura, hominis. Cetera tantum[2] in sua
natura perfecta sunt, non vere perfecta, a quibus
abest ratio.

Hoc enim demum perfectum est, quod secundum
universam naturam perfectum, universa autem
natura rationalis est. Cetera possunt in suo genere
15 esse perfecta. In quo non potest beata vita esse,
nec id potest, quo beata vita efficitur, beata autem
vita bonis efficitur. In muto animali non est beata
vita nec id, quo beata vita[3] efficitur, in muto animali
16 bonum non est. Mutum animal sensu conprendit
praesentia. Praeteritorum reminiscitur, cum id
incidit, quo sensus admoneretur ; tamquam equus[4]
reminiscitur viae, cum ad initium eius admotus[5]
est. In stabulo quidem nulla illi viae est quamvis
saepe calcatae memoria. Tertium vero tempus, id
est futurum, ad muta non pertinet.

17 Quomodo ergo potest eorum videri perfecta natura,
quibus usus perfecti temporis non est ? Tempus
enim tribus partibus constat, praeterito, praesente,
venturo. Animalibus tantum quod gravissimum est
intra cursum datum, praesens. Praeteriti rara memoria est nec umquam revocatur nisi praesentium
18 occursu. Non potest ergo perfectae naturae bonum

---

[1] *illo* Schweighaeuser ; *illa* BA.
[2] *tantum* cod. Harl. and Schweighaeuser ; *tam* BA.
[3] *nec . . . vita* later MSS. ; om. BA.
[4] *equus* later MSS. ; *quos* BA.
[5] *admotus* Erasmus ; *admotum* BA.

same nature, distinct only by virtue of the immortality of the one and the mortality of the other. Of one of these, then—to wit God—it is Nature that perfects the Good; of the other—to wit man—pains and study do so. All other things are perfect only in their particular nature, and not truly perfect, since they lack reason.

Indeed, to sum up, that alone is perfect which is perfect according to nature as a whole, and nature as a whole is possessed of reason. Other things can be perfect according to their kind. That which cannot contain the happy life cannot contain that which produces the happy life; and the happy life is produced by Goods alone. In dumb animals there is not a trace of the happy life, nor of the means whereby the happy life is produced; in dumb animals the Good does not exist. The dumb animal comprehends the present world about him through his senses alone. He remembers the past only by meeting with something which reminds his senses; a horse, for example, remembers the right road only when he is placed at the starting-point. In his stall, however, he has no memory of the road, no matter how often he may have stepped along it. The third state—the future—does not come within the ken of dumb beasts.

How, then, can we regard as perfect the nature of those who have no experience of time in its perfection? For time is three-fold,—past, present, and future. Animals perceive only the time which is of greatest moment to them within the limits of their coming and going—the present. Rarely do they recollect the past—and that only when they are confronted with present reminders. Therefore the Good of a perfect nature cannot exist in an im-

in inperfecta esse natura, aut si natura talis hoc
habet,[1] habent et sata. Nec illud nego, ad ea, quae
videntur secundum naturam, magnos esse mutis
animalibus impetus et concitatos, sed inordinatos
ac turbidos. Numquam autem inordinatum [2] est
bonum aut turbidum.

19 "Quid ergo ?" inquis, "muta animalia perturbate
et indisposite moventur ?" Dicerem [3] illa perturbate
et indisposite moveri, si natura illorum ordinem
caperet ; nunc moventur secundum naturam suam.
Perturbatum enim id est, quod esse aliquando et non
perturbatum potest ; sollicitum est, quod potest
esse securum. Nulli vitium est, nisi cui virtus potest
esse ; mutis animalibus talis ex natura sua motus
20 est. Sed ne te diu teneam, erit aliquod [4] bonum
in muto animali, erit aliqua virtus, erit aliquid perfectum, sed nec bonum absolute nec virtus nec
perfectum. Haec enim rationalibus solis contin-
gunt, quibus datum est scire quare, quatenus, quemadmodum. Ita bonum in nullo est, nisi in quo ratio.

21 Quo nunc pertineat ista disputatio quaeris, et
quid animo tuo profutura sit ? Dico : et exercet
illum et acuit et utique aliquid acturum occupatione
honesta tenet. Prodest autem etiam quo moratur
ad prava properantes.[5] Sed et illud [6] dico : nullo
modo prodesse possum magis, quam si tibi bonum

---

[1] si . . . habet Buecheler ; si naturalia habet. hoc habet
BA.
[2] aut before inordinatum removed by Bartsch.
[3] dicerem later MSS. ; dicere BA.
[4] aliquod Harl. ; aliquando BA.
[5] properantes Madvig ; properante(i) MSS.
[6] et illud Harl. ; illum BA.

perfect nature ; for if the latter sort of nature should possess the Good, so also would mere vegetation. I do not indeed deny that dumb animals have strong and swift impulses toward actions which seem according to nature, but such impulses are confused and disordered. The Good, however, is never confused or disordered.

"What!" you say, "do dumb animals move in disturbed and ill-ordered fashion?" I should say that they moved in disturbed and ill-ordered fashion, if their nature admitted of order ; as it is, they move in accordance with their nature. For that is said to be "disturbed" which can also at some other time be "not disturbed"; so, too, that is said to be in a state of trouble which can be in a state of peace. No man is vicious except one who has the capacity of virtue ; in the case of dumb animals their motion is such as results from their nature. But, not to weary you, a certain sort of good will be found in a dumb animal, and a certain sort of virtue, and a certain sort of perfection—but neither the Good, nor virtue, nor perfection in the absolute sense. For this is the privilege of reasoning beings alone, who are permitted to know the cause, the degree, and the means. Therefore, good can exist only in that which possesses reason.

Do you ask now whither our argument is tending, and of what benefit it will be to your mind? I will tell you : it exercises and sharpens the mind, and ensures, by occupying it honourably, that it will accomplish some sort of good. And even that is beneficial which holds men back when they are hurrying into wickedness. However, I will say this also : I can be of no greater benefit to you than by revealing the Good that is rightly yours, by

447

tuum ostendo, si te a mutis animalibus separo, si
22 cum deo pono. Quid, inquam, vires corporis alis
et exerces? Pecudibus istas maiores ferisque natura concessit. Quid excolis formam? Cum omnia
feceris, a mutis animalibus decore vinceris. Quid
capillum[1] ingenti diligentia comis? Cum illum vel
effuderis more Parthorum vel Germanorum modo
vinxeris vel, ut Scythae solent, sparseris, in quolibet
equo densior iactabitur iuba, horrebit in leonum
cervice formonsior. Cum te ad velocitatem pa-
23 raveris, par lepusculo non eris. Vis tu relictis, in
quibus vinci te necesse est, dum in aliena niteris,
ad bonum reverti tuum?

Quod est hoc? Animus scilicet emendatus ac
purus, aemulator dei, super humana se extollens,
nihil extra se sui ponens. Rationale animal es.
Quod ergo in te bonum est? Perfecta ratio. An
tu ad suum finem hanc evocas, in quantum potest
plurimum crescere? Tunc beatum esse te iudica,
24 cum tibi ex ea[2] gaudium omne nascetur, cum visis,
quae homines eripiunt, optant, custodiunt, nihil
inveneris, non dico quod malis, sed quod velis.
Brevem tibi formulam dabo, qua te metiaris, qua
perfectum esse iam sentias : tunc habebis tuum,
cum intelleges infelicissimos esse felices. VALE.

[1] *capillum* later MSS. ; *eapullum* BA.
[2] *tibi ex ea* later MSS. ; *tibi ex* BA.

---

[a] One of the most conspicuous Stoic paradoxes maintained
that " the wise man is a God."

taking you out of the class of dumb animals, and by placing you on a level with God. Why, pray, do you foster and practise your bodily strength? Nature has granted strength in greater degree to cattle and wild beasts. Why cultivate your beauty? After all your efforts, dumb animals surpass you in comeliness. Why dress your hair with such unending attention? Though you let it down in Parthian fashion, or tie it up in the German style, or, as the Scythians do, let it flow wild—yet you will see a mane of greater thickness tossing upon any horse you choose, and a mane of greater beauty bristling upon the neck of any lion. And even after training yourself for speed, you will be no match for the hare. Are you not willing to abandon all these details—wherein you must acknowledge defeat, striving as you are for something that is not your own—and come back to the Good that is really yours?

And what is this Good? It is a clear and flawless mind, which rivals that of God,[a] raised far above mortal concerns, and counting nothing of its own to be outside itself. You are a reasoning animal. What Good, then, lies within you? Perfect reason. Are you willing to develop this to its farthest limits—to its greatest degree of increase? Only consider yourself happy when all your joys are born of reason, and when—having marked all the objects which men clutch at, or pray for, or watch over—you find nothing which you will desire; mind, I do not say *prefer*. Here is a short rule by which to measure yourself, and by the test of which you may feel that you have reached perfection: " You will come to your own when you shall understand that those whom the world calls fortunate are really the most unfortunate of all." Farewell.

449

APPENDIX A

Ep. xciv. deals, on the whole, with the question whether doctrines without precepts are enough for the student and the philosopher; *Ep.* xcv. whether precepts without doctrines will suffice. Seneca concludes that they are both necessary and are complementary to one another, especially in view of the complicated life which one is called upon to live, with its many duties and choices. The terms discussed, with some of the Greek original definitions, may be summed up as follows:—

(1) The outward expressions of ἐπιστήμη (*scientia*, knowledge) and of the κοιναὶ ἔννοιαι (*notiones communes*, προλήψεις, innate ideas) are found in the form of ἀξιώματα (*pronuntiata*, incontrovertible statements), δόγματα (*placita, decreta, scita*, doctrines, tenets, dogmas, principles). Determined by ὅροι (*definitiones*, definitions), they are tested by their ἀξία (*honestum*, moral value), by the κριτήριον (*norma iudicii*, standard of judgment) or κανών (*lex, regula*, etc.), and by the ὀρθὸς λόγος (*recta ratio*, universal law, etc.). By such means the doctrines of philosophy are contrasted with δόξα (*opinio*) and with a κατάληψις (*cognitio* or *comprehensio*) which falls short of completeness and perfection. Conduct which results from a thorough understanding and performance of such doctrines is κατόρθωμα (τέλειον καθῆκον, *perfectum officium*, "absolute duty")

451

APPENDIX A

(2) The *pars praeceptiva* (παραινετική) of philosophy, which deals with "average duty" (καθῆκον, *commune* or *medium officium*), is approved, among others, by Posidonius, Cicero (see the *De Officiis*), and Seneca. It is related to active living and to the ἀδιάφορα (*media* or *indifferentia*) (see Subject Index) which play so large a rôle in the individual's daily existence. This department of "counsel," "admonition," or "advice" has many forms. For παραίνεσις (*monitio*) are needed: the λόγος προτρεπτικός (*exhortatio*), τόπος ὑποθετικός (*suasio*), ἀποτροπή (*dissuasio*), ἐπιτίμησις (*obiurgatio*), λόγος παραμυθητικός (*consolatio*), αἰτιολογία (*causarum inquisitio*), ἠθολογία (*descriptio*), and all the gamut of precepts which run from blame to praise. These are reinforced by ἀπόδειξις (*probatio, argumentum*, proof) and by such helps as χρεῖαι, ἀπομνημονεύματα (*sententiae*, proverbs, maxims).

By such stages of advancement, προκοπή (*progressio*), and relying upon παραδείγματα (*exempla*), one rises, through practical precepts and the observance of duties, to an appreciation of the virtues, the contemplative mastery of the Universe, and to the Supreme Good, conformity with Nature (ὁμολογουμένως τῇ φύσει ζῆν (*vivere convenienter naturae*).

APPENDIX B

THE following publications may profitably be consulted by one who wishes to investigate Seneca's prose further:

E. ALBERTINI. *La Composition dans les ouvrages philosophiques de Sénèque.* Paris, 1923 (with full bibliography of recent works).

A. BOURGERY. *Sénèque prosateur, études littéraires et grammaticales sur la prose de Sénèque le philosophe.* Paris, 1922.

With special reference to *Ep.* xc. and other passages, one may consult :—

I. HEINEMANN. *Poseidonios' metaphysische Schriften.* Breslau, 1921.

K. REINHARDT. *Poseidonios.* Munich, 1921.

INDEX OF PROPER NAMES

455

INDEX OF PROPER NAMES

456

INDEX OF PROPER NAMES

457

SUBJECT INDEX

(to the three volumes of Seneca's *Epistulae Morales*)

459

SUBJECT INDEX

461

SUBJECT INDEX

note, lxxii. 6 ff., lxxv. 8 ff.; *proficiens*, cix. 15

pseudomenos, xlv. 10 and note

REAPSE, cviii. 32

Reason (*ratio*), as curb of passions, xxxvii. 4; defined, lxvi. 12 ff. and note; the source of perfection and the good, cxxiv. 23 f.

Retirement, as contrasted with participation in affairs, viii. 1 ff., x. 1 f., xiv. 3 ff., xix. *passim*, xxii. *passim*, xxxvi. *passim*, lvi. 1 ff.; mistaken idea of, lv. 4 ff., xciv. 69 ff.; in Seneca's own case, lvi. 9 ff., lxxiii. *passim*

SAGE, dual make-up of the, lxxi. 27 and note

sapere, as distinguished from *sapientia*, cxvii. 1 ff.

Scientific observation, on Etna, li. 1; Etna and Sicily, lxxix. 1 ff.; xc. 10 ff.

Self-sufficiency, ix. 13 ff., etc.

Senses, inadequacy of the, lxvi. 35

sepse, cviii. 32

Sin, and reform, xxv. 1-3, cxi. *passim*; its removal through knowledge, xxviii. 9 f., xxix. 4 ff., xlii. 1 ff., 1. 4 ff.; one's own, lxviii. 8 ff.; reasons for, xciv. 13 f., 21; and conscience, xcvii. 12 ff.

Slavery, xlvii. *passim*

Soul, defined, cxiii. 14 and note; divinity of the, xli. 5 ff.; its contemplative function, lxv. 16 ff.; source and destination, lxxxviii. 34; sustainer of life, xcii. 1 ff. and note; parts of the, xcii. 8 ff. and note; unity of the, cxiii. 14 and note; ruler of the body, cxiv. 23 ff.; indicator of character, cxiv. 1 ff.

Soul after Death, various possibilities, lxxi. 16 and note; its release, lxv. 16 ff., lxxix. 12, xcii. 30 ff.; method of departure, lvii. 6 ff., lxxvi. 33; eternity of the, cii. 21 ff., cxx. 17 ff.; transmigration, cviii. 17 ff.; reunion of friends in another world, lxxviii. 28

species, in relation to *genus*, lviii. 8 ff.

Style, eccentric in case of Maecenas xix. 9 f., cxiv. 4 ff.; rapid, xl. 2 ff.; national characteristics of, xl. 11 f.; of Lucilius, xlvi. 2, lix. 4 ff.; simplicity and sincerity of, lxxxv. 3 ff.; of Fabianus, c. 1 ff.

Suicide, xxiv. 25, xxx. 15, lviii. 32 ff., lxx. 4 ff. and note, lxxvii. 5 ff.

supervacua, xlii. 6 ff., cx. 12 ff.

Supreme Good, defined, lxvi. 6 ff.; according to Epicurus *ib.*, 45 ff., lxxi. *passim*, lxxii. 5, lxxiv. 16, 26; another definition, lxxxv. 20; source of, lxxxvii. 21; xcii. 5 ff.; independence of the, ix. 15, cix. 1 ff.

Syllogisms, futility of, xlv. 8 ff.; as *interrogationes*, *quaestiunculae*, "posers," logical fallacies, xlviii. 4 ff., xlix. 8 f., lxxxiii. 8 ff., 21 ff., lxxxiii. 8 ff., lxxxv. *passim*; on the Good, riches, poverty, etc., lxxxvii. *passim*; vanity of, xlix. 20 ff.; *cavillationes*, *sophismata*, cxi. *passim*, cxiii. 26, cxvii. 25 ff.

TABELLARIAE (*naves*), packet-ships from Alexandria, lxxvii. 1 f.

Theatre, hollowness of the profession, lxxx. 7 f.

Time, saving of, i. *passim*, xxxii. 3 f., xlix. 2 ff.; discussed, lxxxviii. 33 f. and note

translationes (metaphors), proper use of, lix. 6

Transplanting, of olive-trees and vines, lxxxvi. 14 ff.

Travel, and peace of mind, xxviii. 1-8; hardships of sea-voyaging, liii. 1 ff.; by land, lvii. 1 ff.; vanity of, lxix. 1 ff., civ. 13 ff.

VIRTUE (*passim*), acquisition of, l. 7 ff.; power of, lxiv. 6 ff., lxvi. 2 ff.; uniformity of, lxxi. 8 ff., lxxix. 10 ff.; identical with truth, lxxi. 16; twofold aspect of, xciv. 45 f.; a vision of, cxv. 3 ff.; divided into its parts, cxx. 11 f.

Virtues (prudence, justice, bravery, temperance), discussed, lxvii. 3 ff., lxxxv. *passim*, lxxxviii. 29 ff.;

462

SUBJECT INDEX

prudence, bravery, justice, etc., xcv. 55 ff.; whether they possess life, cxiii. *passim*

Voice, training of the, xv. 7 ff.

WEALTH, as handicap to philosophy, xvii. *passim*; as a source of evil, lxxxvii. 22 ff.; to be avoided, civ. 84; scorn of, cviii. 11 f.; emptiness of, cx. 14 ff.; the curse of, cxv. 9 ff.; the true variety, cxix. 5 ff.

Wisdom (*sapientia*, σοφία), defined, xx. 5, lxxxviii. 32 f.; as an art, xxix. 3; the heritage of, lxiv. 7 f.; defined by Socrates, lxxi. 7, lxxxiv. 12 f.; distinguished from philosophy, lxxxix. 4 ff.; her accomplishments, xc. 26 ff.; mutual benefits of, cix. 1 ff.